Albuquerque Museum History Collection

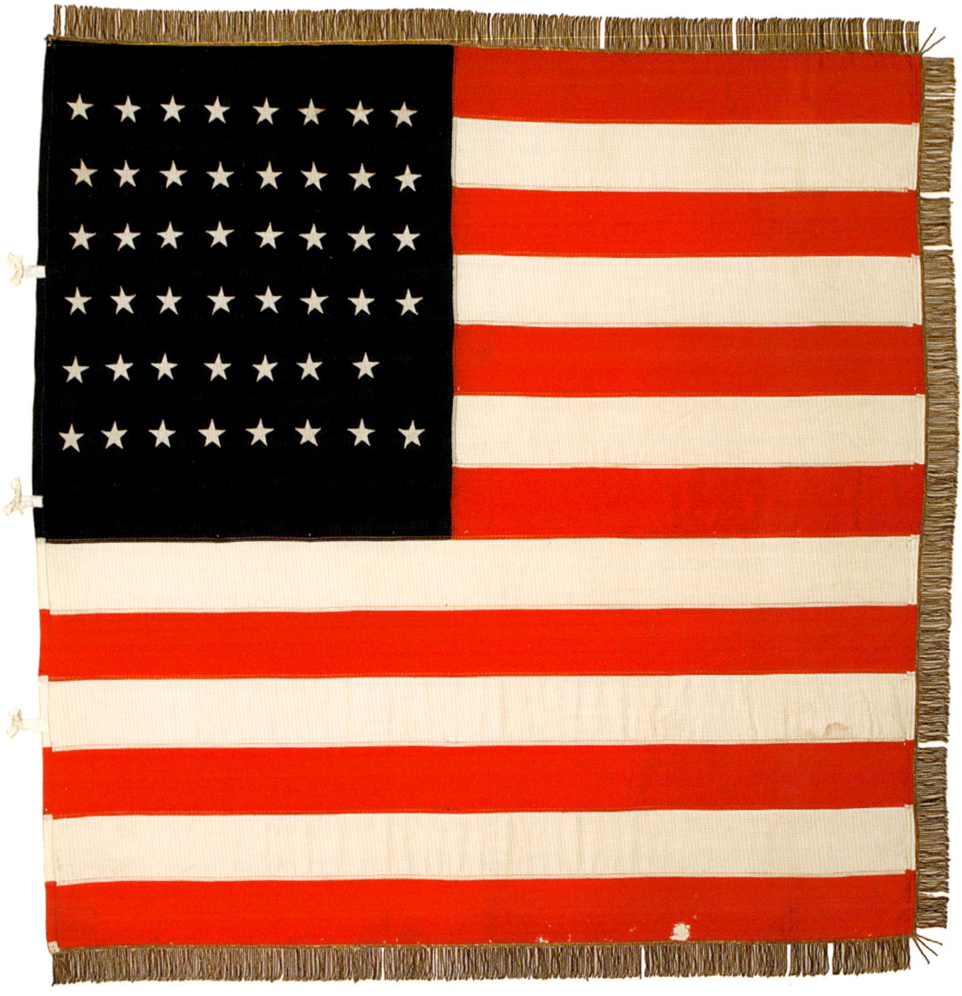

Albuquerque Museum History Collection

Only in Albuquerque

Deborah C. Slaney

ALBUQUERQUE MUSEUM COLLECTION SERIES

MUSEUM OF NEW MEXICO PRESS
SANTA FE

 The Museum of New Mexico Press is a division of the New Mexico Department of Cultural Affairs.

Director: Anna Gallegos
Editorial director: Lisa Pacheco
Art and production director: David Skolkin
Designed by Michael Motley
Composition: Set in Minion and Gill Sans Nova
Manufactured in China
10 9 8 7 6 5 4 3 2 1

Library of Congress Cataloging-in-Publication Data available from the publisher upon request.

ISBN 978-0-89013-632-4

Museum of New Mexico Press
PO Box 2087
Santa Fe, New Mexico 87504
mnmpress.org

Front cover: Cueva family *repostero*, 1620–40 (plate 12); *back cover*: Route 66 highway sign, 1940–50 (plate 186); *frontispiece:* Forty-seven-star flag, 1912 (plate 166).

Contents

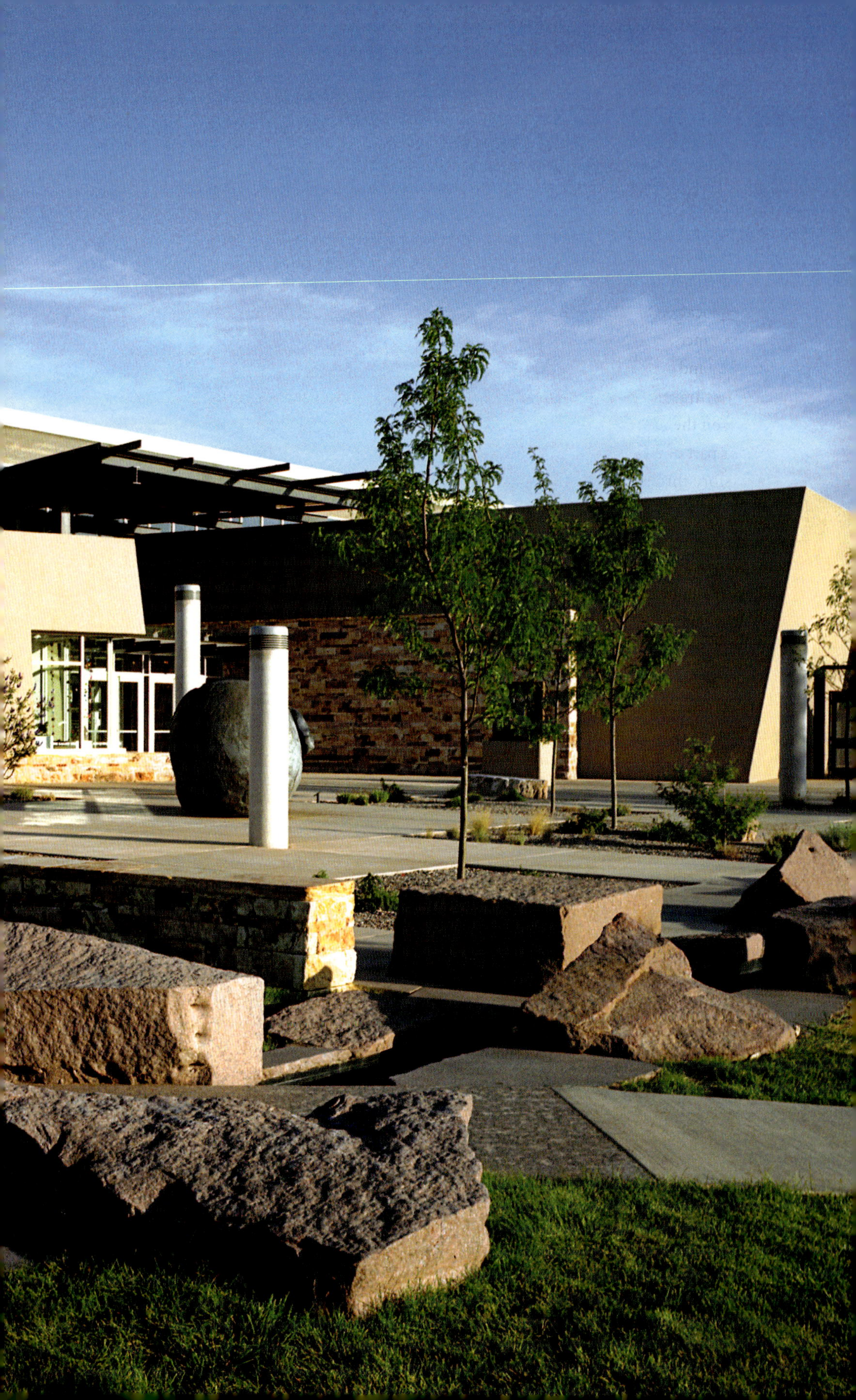

Foreword

Cathy L. Wright

In 2017 the Albuquerque Museum celebrated its fiftieth anniversary. From its beginnings in Old Town, to its residence in the old Sunport air terminal, to its present Old Town location, the institution has grown along with the City of Albuquerque and its importance as the largest city in New Mexico. The Museum collects and displays the history and art of the region, reflecting the interests of the many people who have lived or traveled here. It was built on a firm foundation established by decades of work on the part of dedicated staff and volunteers.

As part of the anniversary celebration, the Museum staff has chosen to document our story through the publication of a series of collection guides highlighting the photo archives, history, and art collections of the Museum. Published by the Museum of New Mexico Press, with the assistance of the Albuquerque Museum Foundation, the guides were released over the course of a year starting in the summer of 2017. The Museum is about art, history, and people. The guides reflect this focus, and the collections help us fulfill our mission to engage the community and to share stories of our rich heritage and many cultures.

We are very excited to have launched the history collection guide as the third of the series. One of the unique qualities of the Albuquerque Museum is its holdings of both art and historical artifacts, which help to tell a rich story of the central Rio Grande valley. Our art and history curators frequently combine both collections to embroider engaging narratives that invite visitors to reflect on their own part of the story. Artifacts can tap into our memories, reminding us of the past and helping us to anticipate the future. We are fortunate that so many people have contributed to building and recording Albuquerque's history, and that we have many visible signs of our history still intact. The Albuquerque Museum goes beyond the usual city museum, interpreting the story of the greater central Rio Grande valley and the many people who have traveled the crossroads of New Mexico. By commemorating our history through exhibits, publications, and collections, the Museum holds the history of Albuquerque in its hands for the city and its citizens, bringing Albuquerque to the world.

This guide's narrative is authored by Deborah Slaney. As curator of history since 2001, Deb has produced books chronicling Albuquerque's history, including *Wonders of the Weavers/Maravillas de los tejedores: Nineteenth-Century Río Grande Weavings from the Collection of the Albuquerque Museum*, *Jewel of the Railroad Era: Albuquerque's Alvarado Hotel*, and numerous exhibitions, such as *Route 66: Radiance, Rust, and Revival on the Mother Road.*

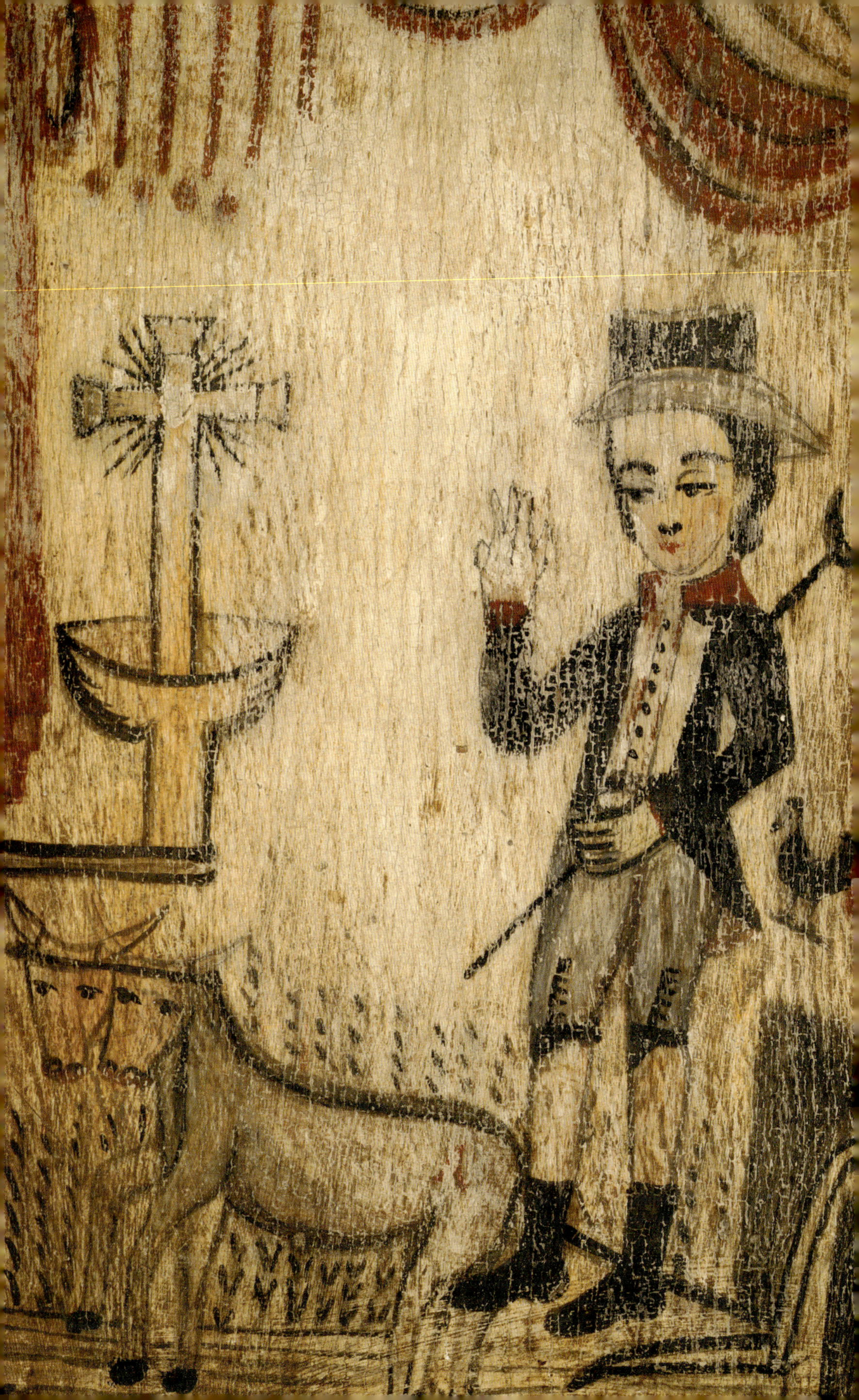

Acknowledgments

The Albuquerque Museum is grateful to those who have helped make this publication possible. We thank the City of Albuquerque Cultural Services Department, Albuquerque Museum Board of Trustees, Albuquerque Museum Foundation Board of Trustees, and the Museum Docents for their strong support of the Museum's history exhibitions and programs. To the many individuals and organizations who have contributed objects to the History Collection, thank you for your generosity.

This guide could not have been completed without the prolonged efforts of the Museum staff, especially Alyssa Ashbacher, Amy Baskette, Elizabeth Becker, Christopher Bratton, Andrew Connors, Jessica Coyle, Denise Crouse, Glenn Fye, Cynthia García, Patti Gonzales, Keith Lee, Titus O'Brien, Steven Pettit, Robin McClannahan, Emily Stovel, Michael Stuart, and Alondra Toca-Díaz, as well as Rita Butler, Elaine Richardson, and Maureen Ryan of the Museum Foundation, whose assistance with collections, photography, technology, programming, marketing, and donor development made this project a reality.

In addition, the efforts of the administrative, maintenance, and security staff are appreciated, for they create a work environment that allows the History program to succeed. Special thanks are due to director Cathy Wright and director emeritus James Moore, whose visions for the Albuquerque Museum have helped build the History Collection, and to director Emily Blaugrund Fox and the late Debra Romero of the Foundation for cheering this publication forward.

The Museum's History Advisory Committee members, including Louise Campbell-Tolber, chair Ann Carson, chair emeritus Mary Davis, Jerome Goss, Harvey Grasty, Tom Keleher, Rita Longino, Terri Salazar, and Judith Suiter, as well as ex-officio members, have played a huge role in judiciously approving acquisitions for the History Collection.

We also thank Anna Gallegos, director; Lisa Pacheco, editorial director; and David Skolkin, art director; at the Museum of New Mexico Press and Michael Motley, book designer, for their thoughtful production of this book. Collection photographers include Damian Andrus, David Nufer, and Dick Ruddy. Museum editor Dawn Hall's expert suggestions make anything we write so much better.

I remain grateful for the knowledge of my colleagues Tom Antreasian, Ed Boles, Robin Gavin, John Grassham, Rick Hendricks, Kathy Howard, Paul A. Hutton, Mo Palmer, Diana Pardue, David Phillips, Marian Rodee, Joe Sabatini, Matthew Schmader, Marilee Schmit Nason, Robert Tórrez, Robert Woltman, and Holly Young.

Finally, I acknowledge my family, and especially my husband, Jim Iwerks, for their support.

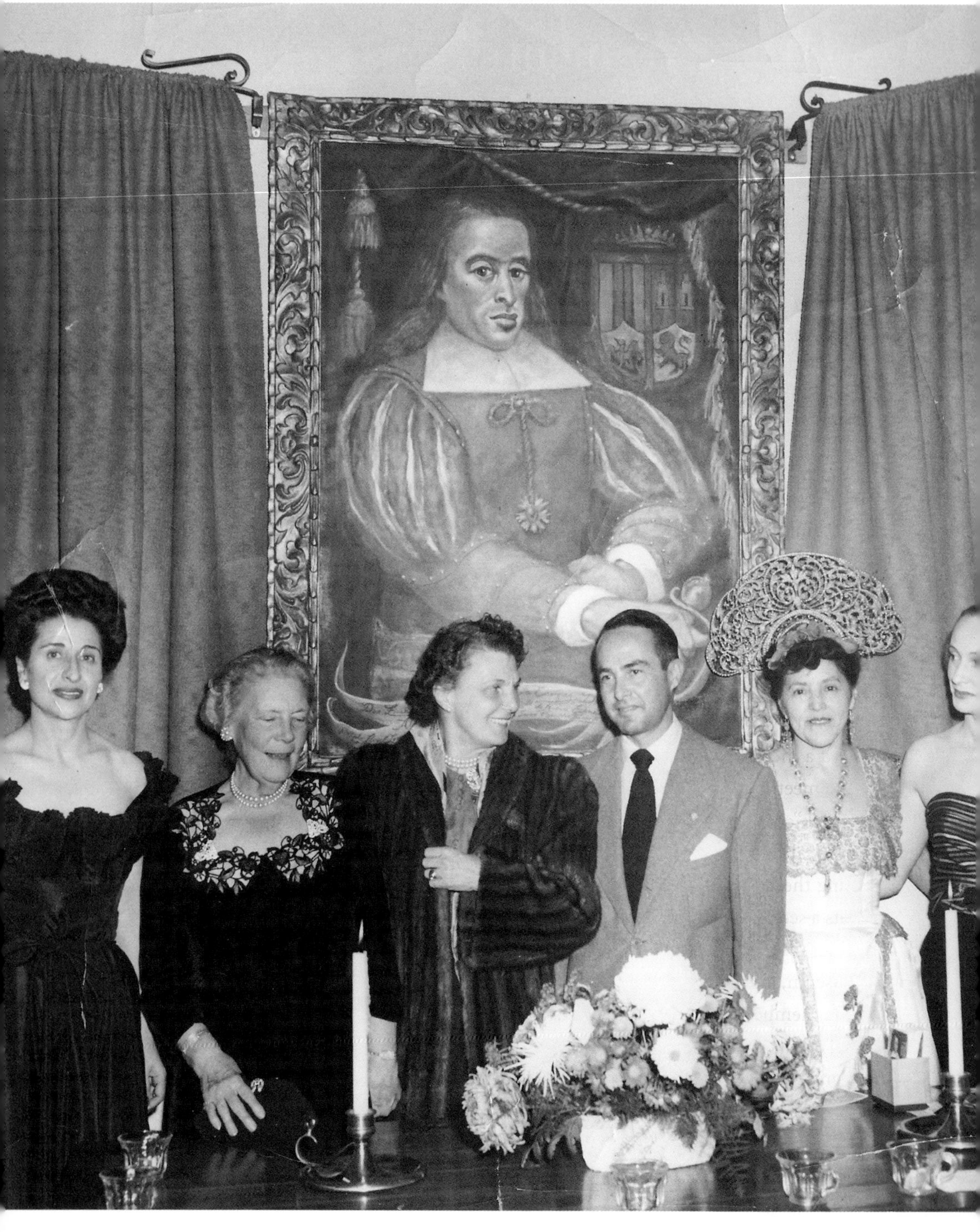

Introduction

"We think the time is right to start a museum," stated Albuquerque Historical Society president Richard Worthen to a journalist in 1962.[1] That was the year the AHS opened a small museum in Old Town Plaza—the first ever to feature exhibits of local Albuquerque history. Donating its collection to the City of Albuquerque in 1967, the Society sparked a chain of events that, in only fifty years, resulted in a major regional museum for international art and local history.

Twenty years earlier, on a cold winter's day in 1947, Dr. and Mrs. Leroy Jones hosted a meeting for nineteen guests in their Old Albuquerque home. By the end of the meeting an eager Elizabeth Bennett and her husband, local businessman J. R. "Dick" Bennett, had fulfilled their dream of establishing the Old Albuquerque Historical Society (fig. 1). Cofounder Carmen Espinosa credited Elizabeth with getting the ball rolling. "For every enterprise of note, there is an individual who plants a seed. . . . Her village charmed her; its history, its people, and their culture," Espinosa noted in 1984.[2] The Society vowed to preserve local landmarks, establish a museum, and restore Old Town Plaza to its former glory. By the end of the year its 142 members were busy funding plaza improvements, organizing meetings and social events, and collecting artifacts connected to Albuquerque history. "We always had great parties at La Placita Restaurant," recalled society member Carlotta Fischer.[3]

Figure 1: *Left to right:* Concha Ortiz y Pino de Kleven, two unidentified women, artist Lloyd Goff, Carmen Espinosa, and Elizabeth Bennett with Goff's portrait of Francisco Cuervo y Valdés, 1956. Gift of Kathryn Bennett. PA2007.18.1.

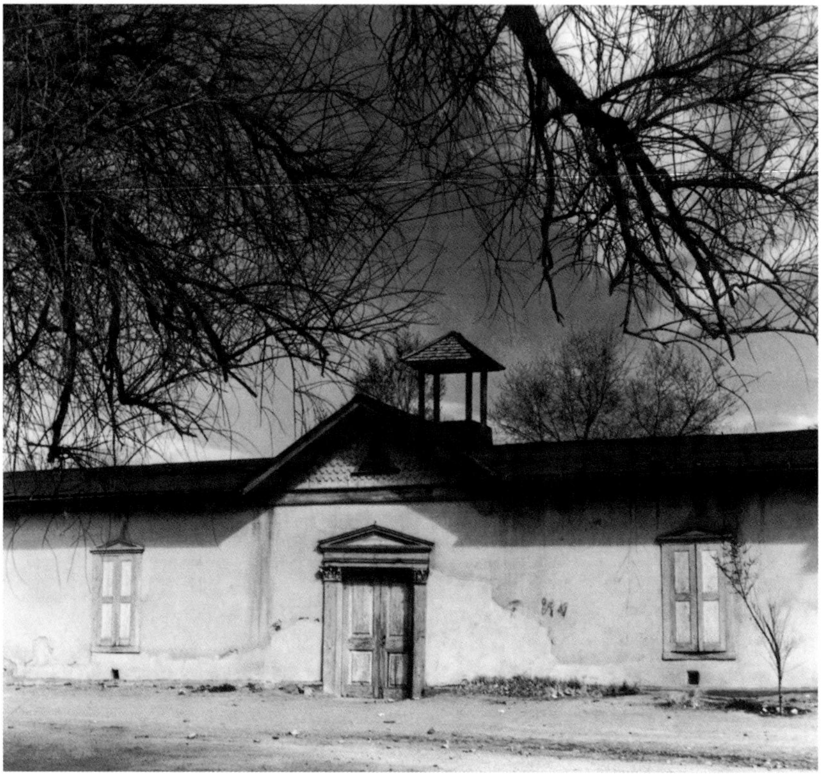

THE ALBUQUERQUE HISTORICAL SOCIETY MUSEUM

In 1961–62 the organization re-formed as the Albuquerque Historical Society and opened a small museum in Old Town's Our Lady of the Angels School at 320 Romero Street (fig. 2). Richard Worthen, president of the Society, was cited as instrumental in the Museum's founding.[4] Artist and Old Town merchant Robert Hooton served as the fledgling Museum's first director. Society members volunteered to staff the Museum, care for its growing collection, create exhibits, and solicit donations. "I used to collect the quarters and take them to the bank," recalled former secretary Margaret "Peggy" Dike.[5]

The Albuquerque Historical Society Museum's first exhibits were developed from artifacts in its collection and loans from Society members. Early exhibits focused on Old Town and pioneer families. Newspaper articles describe exhibits of local citizens'

Figure 2: *Our Lady of the Angels School, Old Town,* 1943. Photograph by John Collier Jr. Museum purchase, Library of Congress. PA1972.154.1.

collections, historic photographs, agricultural tools, trading post souvenirs, and mechanical gadgets.[6] Dr. Sarah Louise Cook, a descendant of Albuquerque resident Captain Zenas H. Bliss, who served at the head of Company K, 28th US Colored Troops, during the Civil War, donated her family collection to the Society during that first year.

> *Although Albuquerque was seventy years old when the Declaration of Independence was signed, the city has no museum to preserve its history and art. A combined historical, art, and scientific museum would fill a community need.*
> —Dorothea Fricke Whitcraft, 1963

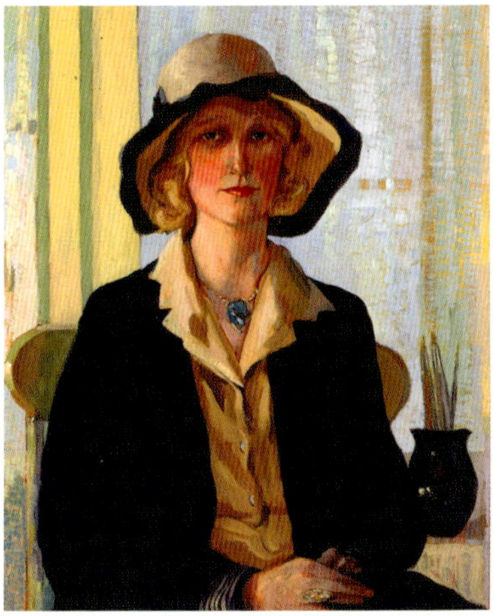

As early as 1935, various individuals and groups began to generate interest in establishing a city museum to preserve the art, history, and science of the Rio Grande valley. A small museum called the Albuquerque Modern Museum appeared (date unknown) at 3800 Rio Grande Boulevard, but it never had a permanent home. A survey was conducted to determine public interest in a city museum, and in 1961 a small group of citizens formed the Albuquerque Museum Association. Leading the pack was artist and Historical Society member Dorothea Fricke Whitcraft (fig. 3), who was also a founding member of the New Mexico Art League, and Albuquerque Historical Society president Gene Caulkins, who spearheaded efforts for a larger museum.

In September 1959, the Albuquerque branch of the Civic Affairs Committee, American Association of University Women, published a survey to determine community interest in developing a museum in Albuquerque. The results indicated that most wanted to see a combination history/science museum, history museum, or art center, and that ideal locations could be the Civic Auditorium, State Fairgrounds, Winrock Center, the University of New Mexico, or any site near Route 66.[7]

Figure 3: Nils Hogner, *Portrait of Dorothea Whitcraft*, 1930. Oil, canvas, 29 3/16 × 25 3/8 in. Gift of Mrs. Mary Fricke, Fern Dahlberg Johnson, and Mrs. E. Howard Pepper. PC1972.25.1.

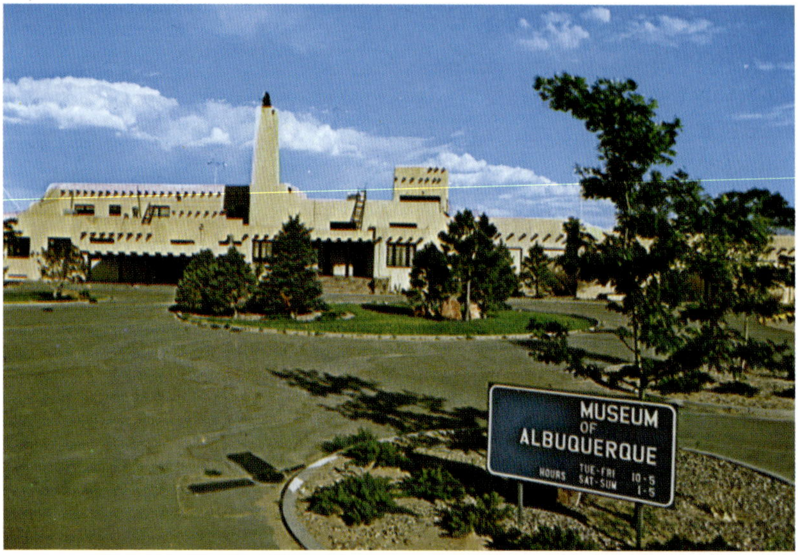

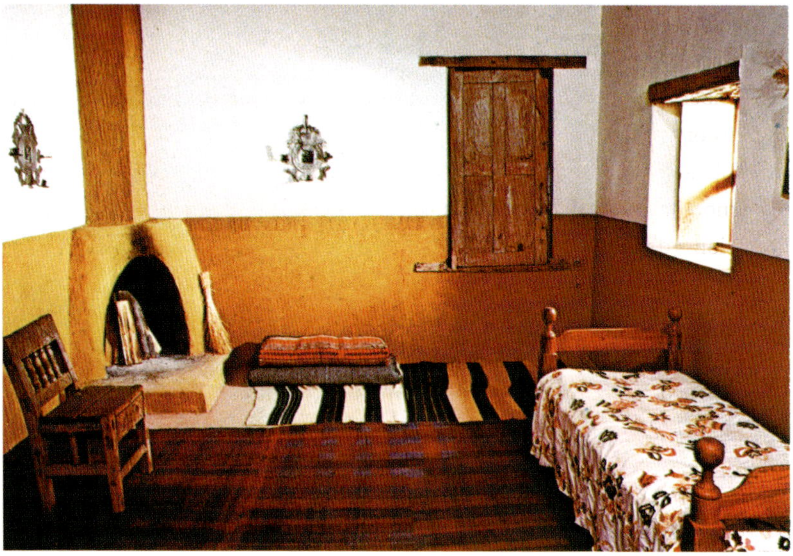

Figure 4: Postcard, *Museum of Albuquerque*, at the William P. Cutter Memorial Building, 1971. Museum of Albuquerque Association. Photograph by G. F. Crabtree. PA2002.15/AP540.

Figure 5: Postcard, Ward Alan Minge's *Una Casa* exhibit at the Museum of Albuquerque, ca. 1972. Museum of Albuquerque Association.

THE MUSEUM OF ALBUQUERQUE

Support from a number of special interest groups grew through the years, and in 1967 the City Commission established the Museum of Albuquerque and appointed a board of trustees. The decision on where to establish the city's first museum was narrowed down to the Albuquerque Airport—later known as the William P. Cutter Memorial Building—Albuquerque's former Spanish-Pueblo Revival airport on Yale Boulevard, designed by Ernest H. Blumenthal in 1939. A picturesque airport but less functional for a museum, the facility often leaked, and the storage area was occasionally taken over for use by Customs. "It was (and still is) an impressive structure, with polished flagstone floors and carved vigas," former curator of exhibits Robert "Bob" Woltman recalls. "I was hired as the Museum's graphic designer, and my office space was in the basement, an area shared with the photo archive darkroom. Clanking hot water pipes snaked across the low ceiling. They made it comfortably warm in the coldest winter months, but most of the time it was stifling and stuffy. The room's only window was at the bottom of a well, and when open, what seemed like an acre of dust from the west mesa blew in." Bob and the fledgling staff also had a habit of "catching the rays" out on top of the roof of the control tower.[8]

The Museum of Albuquerque celebrated its grand opening in the Cutter Building on September 7, 1967, with inaugural exhibits of regional art, aviation history, and natural history (fig. 4).[9] The grand premiere and dinners, hosted by the families of board chair Richard Bice and foundation member Nicholas Dazzo, were attended by Governor David Cargo, Senator Clinton P. Anderson, and members of the City Commission, Albuquerque Museum Association, New Mexico Arts Commission, Albuquerque Historical Society, and American Association of University Women.[10] Admittance to the opening was free with a donation of art and artifacts connected to the Rio Grande valley. In a monumental gesture, the Albuquerque Historical Society donated its entire collection—over nine hundred artifacts, works of art, books, photographs, and documents—to the Museum, along with funding for future exhibitions.[11]

Under directors Frank Crabtree and later Richard Conn and Suzanne de Borhegyi, much of the work to preserve the collection was initially accomplished by Museum and Historical Society volunteers. Docent emeritus Renate Manz remembers, "When we first started working for the Museum of Albuquerque, we did anything they asked of us. We led tours, helped with programs, organized and cleaned the collections, and even put together an exhibit from things in our own collections. Later, we split off from the volunteers and became the Museum's docents. There were only ten of us, and Julia Seligman was one of the first."[12]

Staff and programs grew rapidly, and by the late 1970s, the Museum was averaging ten exhibitions per year with operating expenses of less than two dollars per visitor. The History Collection had grown to over ten thousand items thanks to additional donations from the Albuquerque High School, the family of local aviator Frank Speakman, and others. One major exhibition developed for the Museum was the private collection of Corrales historian Ward Alan Minge, who helped install *Una Casa de Nuevo Mexico*, a period eighteenth- to nineteenth-century interior featuring a parlor, kitchen, and portal (fig. 5).[13] His work with the Museum eventually led, in the mid-1980s and 1990s, to discussions about the future of his collection and historic adobe rancho (ranch house), Casa San Ysidro.

> *I think Albuquerque has reached a point in its development where it's ready for a sort of cultural renaissance. . . . Albuquerque has a particularly rich melding of cultures, a colorful history.*
> —Suzanne de Borhegyi, 1974

THE ALBUQUERQUE MUSEUM OF ART, HISTORY, AND SCIENCE

Every museum eventually endures a little drama, and by the mid-1970s the Museum of Albuquerque found itself in the midst of controversy over its future location. The board and director were advocating for a new museum space, citing a lack of room to stage and prepare for exhibitions and inadequate storage space for the growing collection. Many believed that the new museum should be located near Old Town Plaza. Others looked closely at the Ilfeld Building, the old American Furniture Company building, and the Civic Auditorium as potential new locations.

Finally, on July 7, 1975, the Albuquerque City Council passed a resolution designating the Navajo Freight property in Old Town as the Museum's permanent home. The 1975 general obligation bond proposal for the new museum failed, but it passed in 1977. Former director James Moore remembers that the project could not have proceeded without support at the highest levels of city government. "Harry Kinney should be given a lot of credit because without his support in the bond issues, nothing would have happened. Harry was very smart and saw the importance of the architectural program," Moore recalls.[14]

> *The Museum has done a miraculous job from the beginning. . . . In the last eighteen months, it has produced the highest quality shows with the fewest dollars.*
> —V. B. Price, 1981

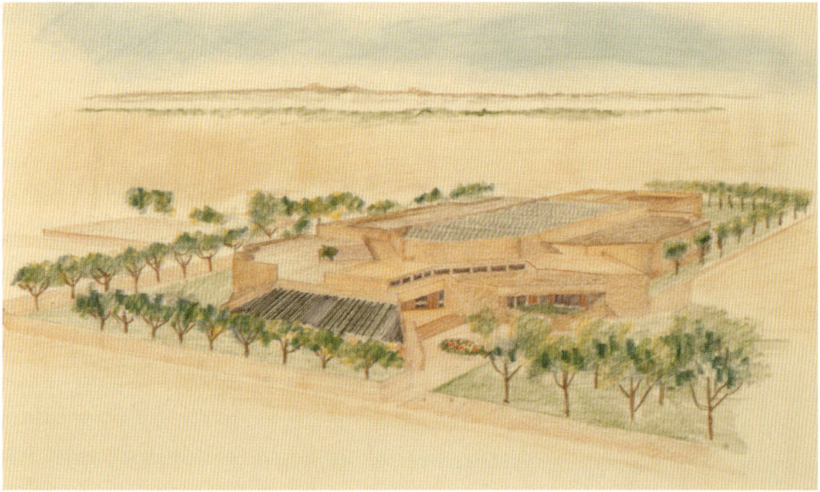

The new Albuquerque Museum of Art, History, and Science, designed by noted modernist architect Antoine Predock, opened on August 5, 1979 (fig. 6). The solar panels installed on the roof and south facade helped heat the building's cantankerous hot water system, making the facility what is believed to be the first solar-assisted museum in the world. The Museum's inaugural exhibitions featured cultural arts, automotive history, and wind energy. Mayors David Rusk and Harry Kinney both attended the ribbon-cutting ceremony. Joan Mondale, wife of Vice President Walter Mondale, attended as guest of honor and pronounced the new museum "a people place," adding, "You have built a museum that will be loved by absolutely everyone."[15] Albuquerque author and Museum board member V. B. Price and his father, film legend and art historian Vincent Price, served as media front men for the marketing campaign.

FOUR CENTURIES: A HISTORY OF ALBUQUERQUE

By the 1980s the Museum had established a balanced program of exhibits and programs promoted by the Albuquerque Museum Foundation and area radio and television stations. Vincent Price, always the showman, cheerfully plugged the Museum in the local newspapers, staging himself between shelves of artifacts in storage to attract attention. The Museum established a docent program to help interpret the exhibitions for museum visitors.

Figure 6: Antoine Predock, rendering of the design for the Albuquerque Museum, 1978. Colored pencil, paper, 20 1/4 × 33 3/8 in. Albuquerque Museum.

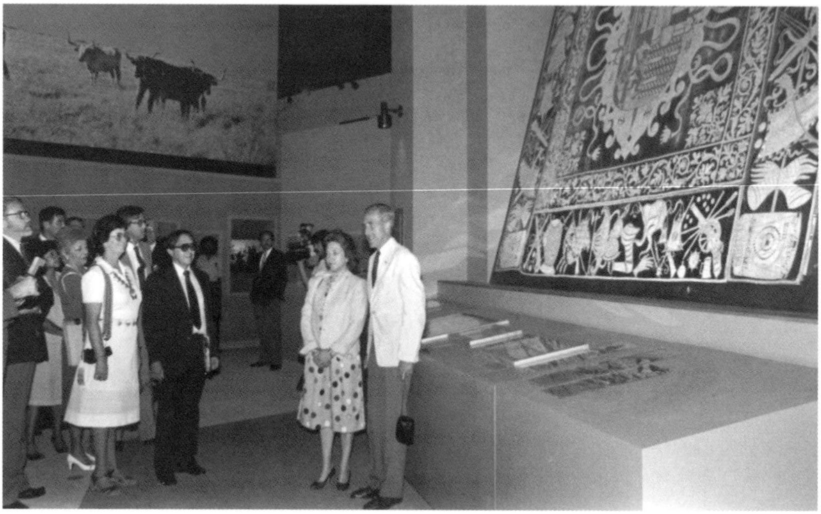

The next order of business was to create a long-term exhibition presenting Albuquerque's history. Featuring one of the country's top collections of Spanish Colonial armor and New Mexican ironwork, *Four Centuries* opened to great reviews in 1983 (figs. 7–9). Former curator of history Byron Johnson remembers, "When we began planning the *Four Centuries* exhibit, we surveyed the historical community and public to ask what they thought was important. . . . Many interviewees favored building a collection of arms and armor—what was brought to New Mexico by the conquistadors—and a cartographic collection showing the changing perceptions of New Mexico. We began by going to Oñate y Salazar. . . . We were able to match the equipment and supplies described in the inventories to the artifacts, utilizing sources such as the catalog of the Royal Armoury of Madrid and the Estruch Armoury in Barcelona."[16] James Moore recalls that he advised the Museum board that the project

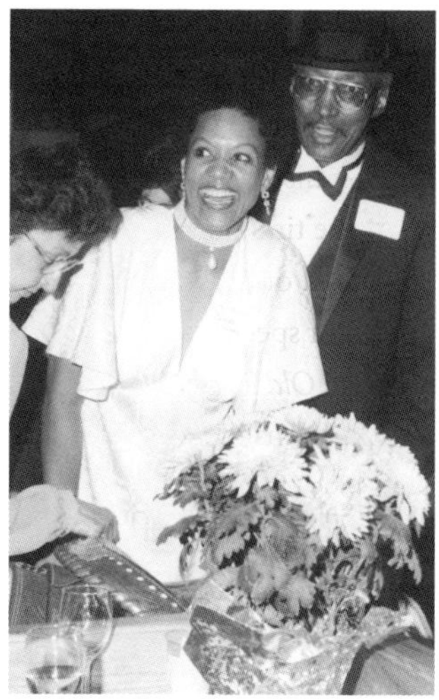

Figure 7: Don Beltrán Osorio y Díez de Rivera, 18th Duke of Alburquerque, Spain, and the Duchess at the opening of *Four Centuries: A History of Albuquerque*, 1983. PA1993.31.

Figure 8: Albuquerque Museum Foundation members Bill and Pamela Gooden at the *Four Centuries* opening reception, 1983. PA1993.31.

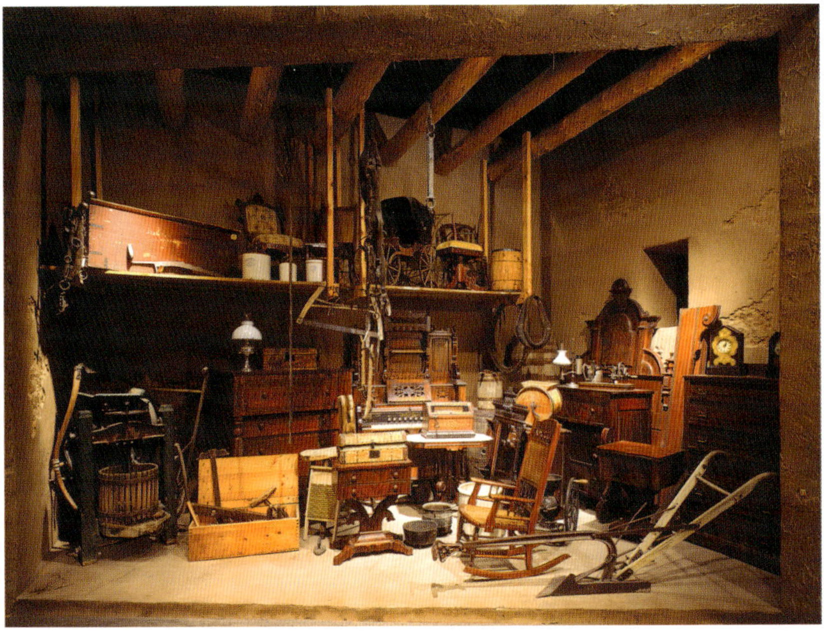

just couldn't be completed without bond funds for building a collection. "Passing that first bond issue was critical. I suspect that we spent almost all of the first bond issue on history collections."[17]

At the time, there was no series of publications on local history, so the Museum developed one. Johnson recalls, "It focused on aspects of Albuquerque history too narrow or specialized for presses such as the University of New Mexico."[18] Major titles included *Old Town, Albuquerque, New Mexico: A Guide to Its History and Architecture* (Byron Johnson, 1970) and *Works and Days: A History of San Felipe Neri Church, 1868–1895* (J. Thomas Steele, 1983). The series continues to the present day.

CASA SAN YSIDRO: THE GUTIÉRREZ/MINGE HOUSE

By the mid-1990s the Albuquerque Museum handed its role in science education over to other local museums but continued to focus on art and history exhibitions. In 1997, historian Ward Alan Minge and his wife, Shirley, donated their historic Corrales property, Casa San Ysidro: The Gutiérrez/Minge House, to the City of Albuquerque (fig. 10). A city bond fund helped the Museum acquire the Minges' outstanding collection of eighteenth- and nineteenth-century Hispano furnishings

Figure 9: Santa Fe Trade Warehouse in *Four Centuries: A History of Albuquerque*, ca. 1998.

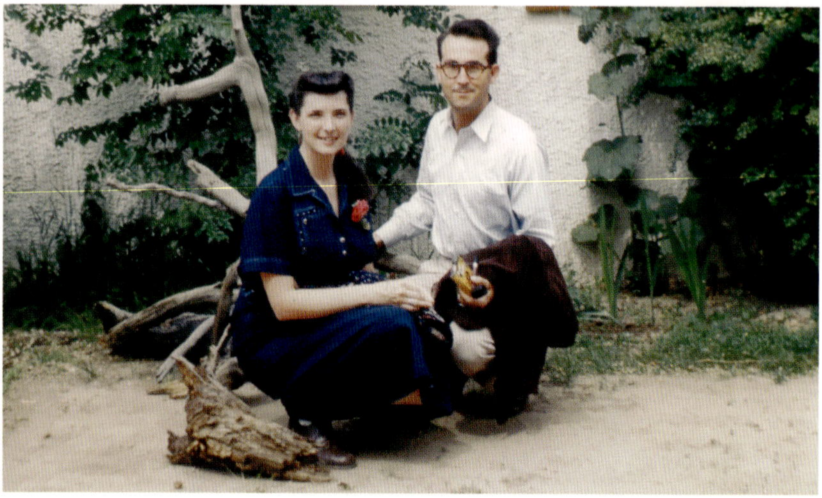

and artifacts. Casa San Ysidro—listed on the State Register of Cultural Properties and managed through a partnership between the City of Albuquerque, the Village of Corrales, Sandoval County, and the State of New Mexico—opened to the public as a wing of the Museum's History Department in 1998 (fig. 11). Since that time, visitation has more than doubled, and the site has become an official point on the National Park Service's Camino Real de la Tierra Adentro Interpretive Trail. Plans are now under way to re-envision the long-term use and sustainability of Casa San Ysidro, which is nearing its twentieth anniversary as a historic house museum.

> *The Casa San Ysidro project will help us to preserve the architectural integrity and collections of this historic site, and provide a full complement of educational programs to our visitors. There are many ways that you can participate in the exciting future of the Albuquerque Museum. We hope that you will join us!*
> —Cathy Wright, Museum Director, 2007

ALBUQUERQUE MUSEUM OF ART AND HISTORY

The twenty-first century has brought exciting changes to the Albuquerque Museum. In April 2005, the Museum completed its Phase I expansion, which has enriched visitors' on-site experiences. Improvements included an additional changing-exhibition gallery and lecture spaces, a café, a special events area, an amphitheater, gift shop,

Figure 10: Ward Alan and Shirley Minge, Albuquerque, 1951–52. Courtesy of Ward Alan Minge.
Figure 11: Gran sala (great hall) at Casa San Ysidro, 1984.

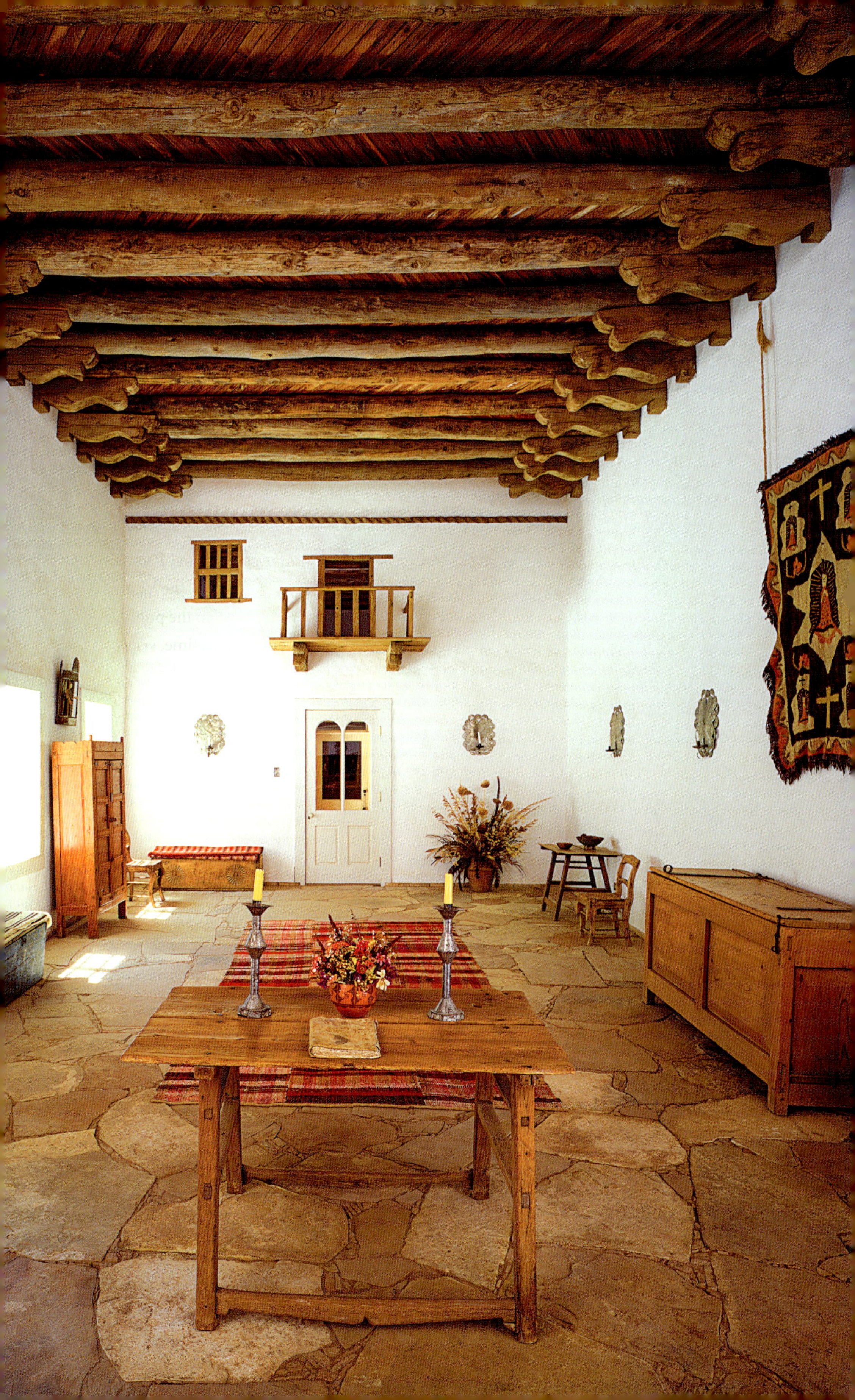

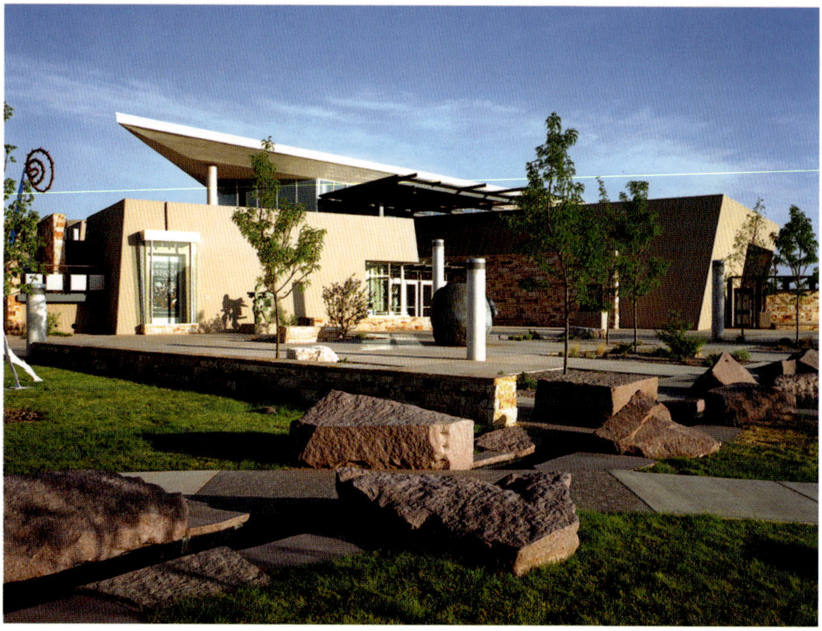

and an improved collections staging area (fig. 12). Designed by the firm of Rohde May Keller McNamara, the building is expansive, inspiring, and admired by all. The Albuquerque Museum Foundation raised an impressive $1.8 million toward the project.

> *Everyone has been focused on delivering a top-quality project, a newly revitalized museum that will bring greater recognition to the city and serve our visitors with wonderful programs in the years to come.*
> —James Moore, 2004

ONLY IN ALBUQUERQUE

The Phase II renovation, completed in 2013 and supported by an additional $1.3 million capital campaign, allowed the Museum to improve existing exhibition spaces, expand its educational programs, and improve access to the collections through renovated and expanded storage facilities. Two years later the Museum completed a new long-term history exhibit, *Only in Albuquerque* (fig. 13). This highly interative exhibition presents a broadened and inclusive history of Albuquerque, focusing on a theme that

Figure 12: Albuquerque Museum of Art and History, ca. 2005.

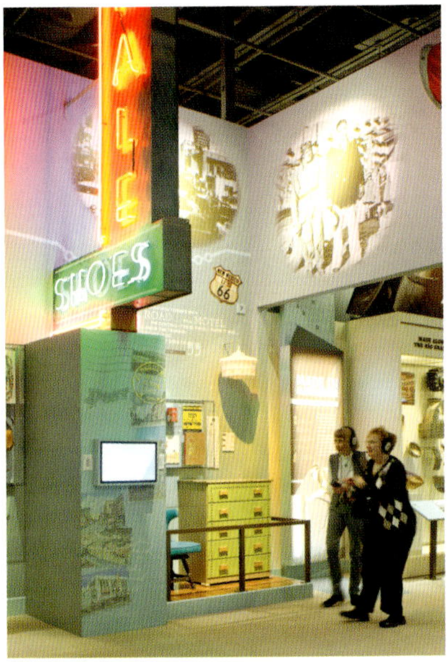

reinforces how the city and surrounding neighborhoods are unique and different from other Sunbelt cities and how the city's uniqueness ties into the natural world around us. The exhibition, as well as this collections guide, is organized into four subthemes that emphasize characteristics of the people of Albuquerque: *Spirited*, *Courageous*, *Resourceful*, and *Innovative*.

Across from the entrance to *Only in Albuquerque*, the newly opened William A. and Loretta Barrett Keleher Gallery presents short-term, community-based exhibitions, giving citizen groups the opportunity to tell their own history and to present thematic exhibits exploring contemporary issues. Already, these projects have brought more diverse visitation and increased membership.

> *On September 7, 2017, the Museum hit the "Big 5-0," and there are no signs of a slowdown. The Albuquerque Museum of Art and History, created in 1967 from grassroots organizations, has become a major regional museum that reflects our multicultural heritage.*
>
> —Deb Slaney, 2017

THE ALBUQUERQUE MUSEUM HISTORY COLLECTION

The Museum's History Collection comprises about thirty-five thousand artifacts, cultural arts, maps, photographs, and archives that interpret the history of the central Rio Grande valley from 12,000 years ago to the present. The collection also includes two historic properties: Casa San Ysidro: The Gutiérrez/Minge House in Corrales, which houses the Ward Alan and Shirley Jolly Minge Collection, and the Little House Diner, which currently houses the Albuquerque Police Department's Monte Vista Triangle substation.

The 1967 gift of the Albuquerque Historical Society's core collection, approximately nine hundred objects, helped to define the History Department's scope of collecting.

Figure 13: Visitors using interactives in *Only in Albuquerque*, 2015.

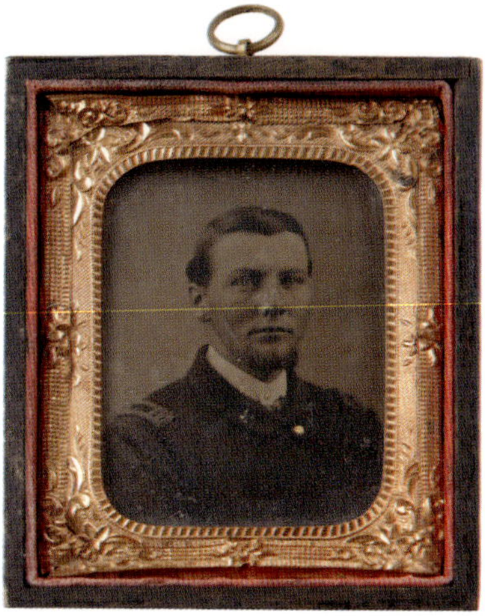

It includes objects that interpret the history of the central Rio Grande valley and, for Territorial period to twentieth-century collections, the greater Albuquerque area. The Society's core collection is strong in Albuquerque's founding families, including the Armijo and Segura families of Old Town, the Ilfelds of New Town, and Civil War veteran Zenas H. Bliss (fig. 14). Consisting mainly of domestic artifacts that would have been used from the mid-nineteenth to the early twentieth centuries, the gift helped the Museum focus on targeted acquisitions.

Reflecting the interests of the board and curators and their affiliations with the Albuquerque Archaeological Society, the Museum was briefly involved in archaeological resource management and city-sponsored archaeological excavations in the 1970s. These activities resulted in several archaeological project collections accessioned into the Museum collection, including Ancestral Pueblo and Spanish Colonial period artifacts excavated at Prieta Vista Pueblo and Tonque Pueblo.

As Museum staff began developing plans for the 1983 installation of *Four Centuries: A History of Albuquerque*, municipal bond funds approved by Albuquerque citizens helped to build the permanent collection. For years, the Albuquerque Museum was the only museum in the country to pass general obligation bonds for collections development, allowing staff to leverage private funds and foundation support for major acquisitions that support the Museum's mission.[19]

Museum staff worked with collector William Scollard and others to build a Colonial period collection that would help interpret the Spanish and Mexican periods of Albuquerque history (fig. 15). Former curator of history Byron Johnson remembers, "Bill Scollard was an aerospace engineer who had worked on projects such as the B-1 bomber. He is a gentleman with extensive connections in Spain, Portugal, and Britain among collectors and old families."[20]

As a result, the Museum's armor and armaments collection, most of which was formerly in the inventories of the Tower of London and other major armories, is considered to be one of the top ten in the country. The Museum also developed a

Figure 14: Captain Zenas H. Bliss, ca. 1864. Tintype, metal, brass, glass, paper, 3 × 2 1/4 in. Gift of the Albuquerque Historical Society via Dr. Sarah Louise Cook. PC1967.1.11C.

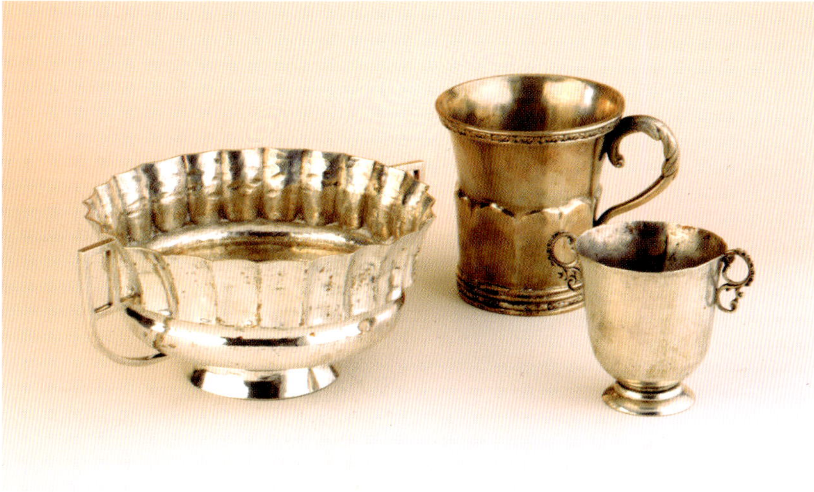

map collection. "The cartography collection was begun so that visitors would understand how the concept of New Mexico evolved. The goal was to begin with a fifteenth-century Ptolemaic map and then acquire key maps that would show sixteenth- and seventeenth-century explorations," Johnson notes.[21] Since that time, the Museum has added notable examples ranging from eighteenth-century maps depicting California as an island to mid-twentieth-century Route 66 road maps published by service stations along the highway.

In the 1970s the Museum also purchased traveling exhibitions, artists' portfolios, and even entire museum collections. An example is the Nordhaus Collection, acquired from Albuquerque attorney and ski enthusiast Robert Nordhaus, who helped found the Sandia Peak Ski Area and the Sandia Peak Tramway. Nordhaus was an avid collector of New Mexico artifacts; he exhibited them in a small transportation museum at Sandia Peak in the 1960s.

By the 1980s, the Museum in its new facility had developed the resources to manage a history collection, photograph archives, and art collection. The descendants of Ambrosio Armijo, including historian John B. Colligan and his family, have continued to make major gifts of family heirlooms to the Museum, including original furnishings from Casa Armijo and paintings and cabinet cards of Armijo descendants.

Figure 15: Mexican or Hispanic New Mexican. Bowl, mug, and two-handled cup, 1790–1870. Silver, 3 1/4 × 8 in., 3 × 2 5/8 in., and 4 × 3 3/4 in. Museum purchases, 1979 General Obligation Bonds and purchase in honor of Jane Napolitano. PC1981.134.1, 1981.71.1, and 1981.193.1.

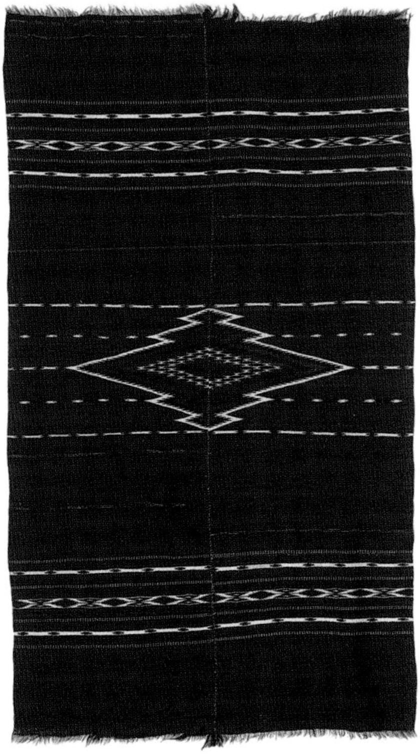

The Museum has also developed a small transportation collection including an original fire engine, a horsecar, a Ford Model T Speedster, a mail cart, wagons, and buggies. In 1983, the staff discovered an original 1911–14 Curtiss-style pusher biplane in Texas. Byron Johnson recalls, "A chance phone call uncovered it, and we arrived just as the owner was attempting to sell it. Hence, Albuquerque acquired a generic example of the earliest aircraft to fly in New Mexico and one of the oldest, largely unrestored aircraft in the world."[22]

Through city bond funds and gifts from the Albuquerque Museum Foundation, the Museum was able to purchase in the early 1980s a selection of Rio Grande weavings from art historian Larry Frank (fig. 16). Representing almost every major style and period from 1840 to 1910, the collection is used regularly by museum researchers and independent scholars. The collection was dramatically improved with the 1997 acquisition of Rio Grande weavings from Ward Alan and Shirley Jolly Minge, who also donated Casa San Ysidro. Their collection adds immeasurably to our knowledge of New Mexico weaving, making the Museum's textile collection one of the top three in the state.

The Minge Collection, comprising about 1,800 objects, also greatly improved the Museum's holdings of nineteenth-century furniture, ironwork, Pueblo and Hispano pottery, silver and copper work, agricultural and domestic implements, and filigree jewelry (fig. 17). Minge notes that the ironwork is the most systematic collection of hand-forged New Mexican tools and metalwork in the country. The Minge Collection also includes major architectural elements built into Casa San Ysidro that are significant in their own right, such as an early nineteenth-century *zaguán* (entryway) from the George Horace Long House in Ranchos de Taos and *alacenas* (cupboards with pintle hinges) made in the Pueblos of Acoma

Figure 16: Hispanic New Mexican. Frazada/blanket with ikat fibers, 1840–50. Wool, indigo, 88 × 50 in. Museum purchase, 1983 General Obligation Bonds. PC1984.25.15.

and Isleta.[23] Then-curator of history John Grassham spent much of 1997–98 at the adobe rancho overseeing renovations there, with the late Andrea Gillespie serving as Casa's first full-time curator.

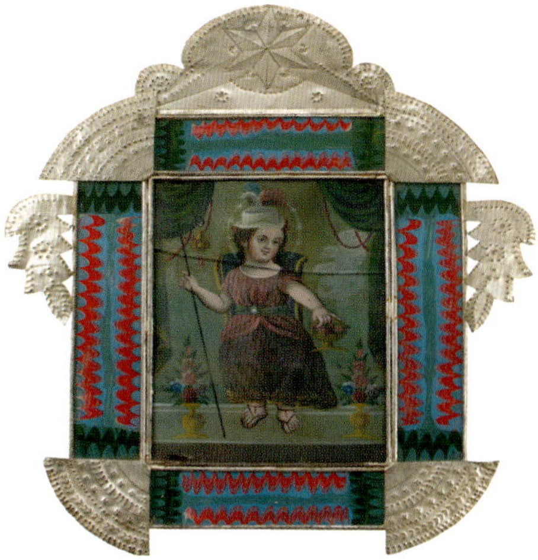

THE HISTORY COLLECTION TODAY

The new century continues to favor the Albuquerque Museum History Collection. With a corps of generous donors and multiple galleries in which to present major historical themes, the Museum has been able to build focused twentieth- and twenty-first-century collections covering such topics as the Alvarado Hotel, Route 66, and the film and television industries in Albuquerque. Collectors such as Ray and Judy Dewey, Bob and Cynthia Gallegos, Norman Sandfield, and Nancy Tucker, among many others, have contributed objects in the areas they research and collect, and they give generously to other institutions as well.

During this new century, the Museum has built its collections in ways that help interpret the diversity of the region. Adding collections from immigrant families such as the Bluehers and Matteuccis has improved the Museum's ability to tell compelling stories about nineteenth-century immigrants and their experiences.

Much effort is expended, when possible, in building collections similar to those lost in the past due to shortages of funding or space. Through a 2008 donation by Drs. Betty K. and John R. Graham, the Museum acquired a large collection of historic Pueblo and Navajo pottery, ten pieces of which were collected at the Alvarado Hotel Indian Building (fig. 18). Acquisitions like these help tell the story of the Alvarado Hotel and Fred Harvey Indian Department, once located in downtown Albuquerque near the original depot—a major story in the development of railroad-era tourism and Indian art in the Southwest.

Old Town artist Eason Eige's 2005 donation of over three hundred major examples of historic Navajo and Pueblo jewelry, complemented by an equally strong group of contemporary jewelry pieces by known makers donated to the Art Collection, established for the Museum a core collection of Navajo and Pueblo silver and lapidary work (fig. 19). And through recent gifts of historic Zuni carvings and

Figure 17: Higinio V. Gonzales. Tin frame with Mexican tin painting of Santo Niño de Atocha, ca. 1900. Tin, glass, paint, 27 1/2 × 22 1/2 in. Gift of Ward Alan and Shirley Jolly Minge. PC1997.51.47.

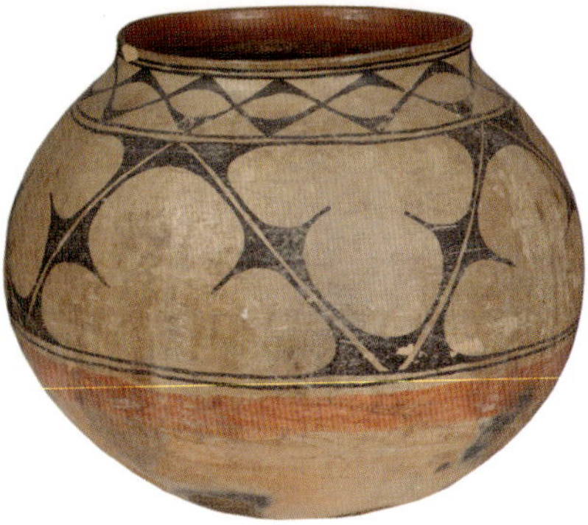

silverwork from the family of noted trader C. G. Wallace, first owner of the De Anza Motor Lodge on Central Avenue, we can better tell the story of this noted Albuquerque resident's influence on the development of Route 66–era tourism.

Much of the History Department's success is also due to having the gallery space to develop specific exhibition topics and adding carefully selected donations and purchases to fill gaps in the historical record. Ever conscious of precious space, Museum curators are cautious these days not to duplicate or over-add to the collections. Even after fifty years, a long wish list still exists; it is growing smaller, but the needed collections are rare and costly and funds are at a premium. Future acquisitions, carefully vetted by the Museum's eight-member History Advisory Committee, will build on existing strengths and help the Museum play a larger role in telling Albuquerque's twenty-first-century story.

While the focus of collecting activities has changed through time, the general scope of the Museum's permanent collections—that of the central Rio Grande valley and the greater Albuquerque area—has never changed and remains a sensible path for the Albuquerque Museum's History Collection. Visitation is stronger than ever; exhibitions and programs are of the highest quality. We at the Museum foster great relationships with staff of our fellow museums; the Museum enjoys a regional reputation as an enthusiastic lender and collaborator; and it has built a national reputation as a prime venue for major art and history traveling exhibitions. *Only in Albuquerque* can you find the Albuquerque Museum!

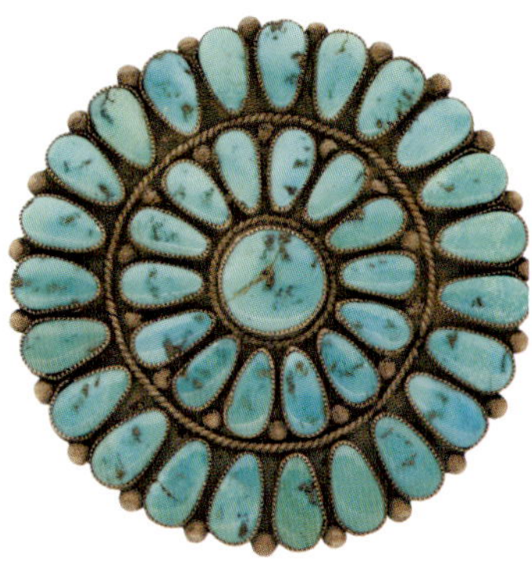

Figure 18: Cochiti Polychrome storage jar, 1860s. Natural clay, slip, and paint, 17 × 16 in. Gift of Drs. Bette K. and John R. Graham in memory of Dr. Bette Kaufman Graham. PC2008.21.19. The Grahams purchased pottery from the Fred Harvey Indian Department in 1967, just one year before its inventory was liquidated and the collection moved out of the Indian Building.

Figure 19: Zuni. Brooch, 1950s. Silver, Villa Grove turquoise, $3\,{}^{3}/_{4} \times {}^{1}/_{4}$ in. Gift of Eason Eige. PC2010.5.132.

NOTES

1. Albuquerque Museum Foundation scrapbooks, n.d., Albuquerque Museum Photo Archives, PA1993.31.
2. Carmen Espinosa on Elizabeth Bennett, Albuquerque Historical Society, 1984, Albuquerque Museum History Research files. For additional news clippings on the early history of the Museum and vintage copies of the Albuquerque Museum Foundation's publication, *Las Noticias*, see the Albuquerque Museum Photo Archives, accession PA1993.31.
3. Carlotta Fischer, personal communication, ca. 2006.
4. "6 Named to Museum Panel," unidentified newspaper clipping, September 29, 1966; Albuquerque Museum History Research Files, "Albuquerque Museum."
5. Peggy Dike, personal communication, 2003.
6. "Albuquerque History Reviewed in Exhibit Opening in Old Town," *Albuquerque Journal*, October 18, 1964.
7. King Lindell Gustafson, "The Museum Movement in Albuquerque," unpublished manuscript, May 25, 1964. Albuquerque Museum History Research Files.
8. Robert Woltman, personal communication, 2017.
9. "Dream Coming True in Museum Opening," *Albuquerque Journal*, September 3, 1967.
10. "Festivities Open Museum," *Albuquerque Tribune*, September 5, 1967.
11. "City Museum Given First Major Historical Present," *Albuquerque Journal*, October 1967.
12. Renate Manz, personal communication, 2007, 2016.
13. "Museum of Albuquerque Displays Cultural, Historical Artifacts," Albuquerque News Service clipping, October 1, 1972. Albuquerque Museum Archives, PA1993.31.
14. James Moore, personal communication, 2017.
15. Albuquerque Museum Foundation scrapbooks, n.d., Albuquerque Museum Photo Archives, PA1993.31.
16. Byron Johnson, personal communication, 2016.
17. James Moore, personal communication, 2017.
18. Johnson, personal communication, 2016.
19. James Moore, personal communication, "Quotes/Comments," Museum archives, PA1993.31.
20. Johnson, personal communication, 2016.
21. Ibid.
22. Ibid.
23. See Ward Alan Minge, *Casa San Ysidro: The Gutiérrez/Minge House in Corrales, New Mexico* (Santa Fe: Museum of New Mexico Press, 2017).

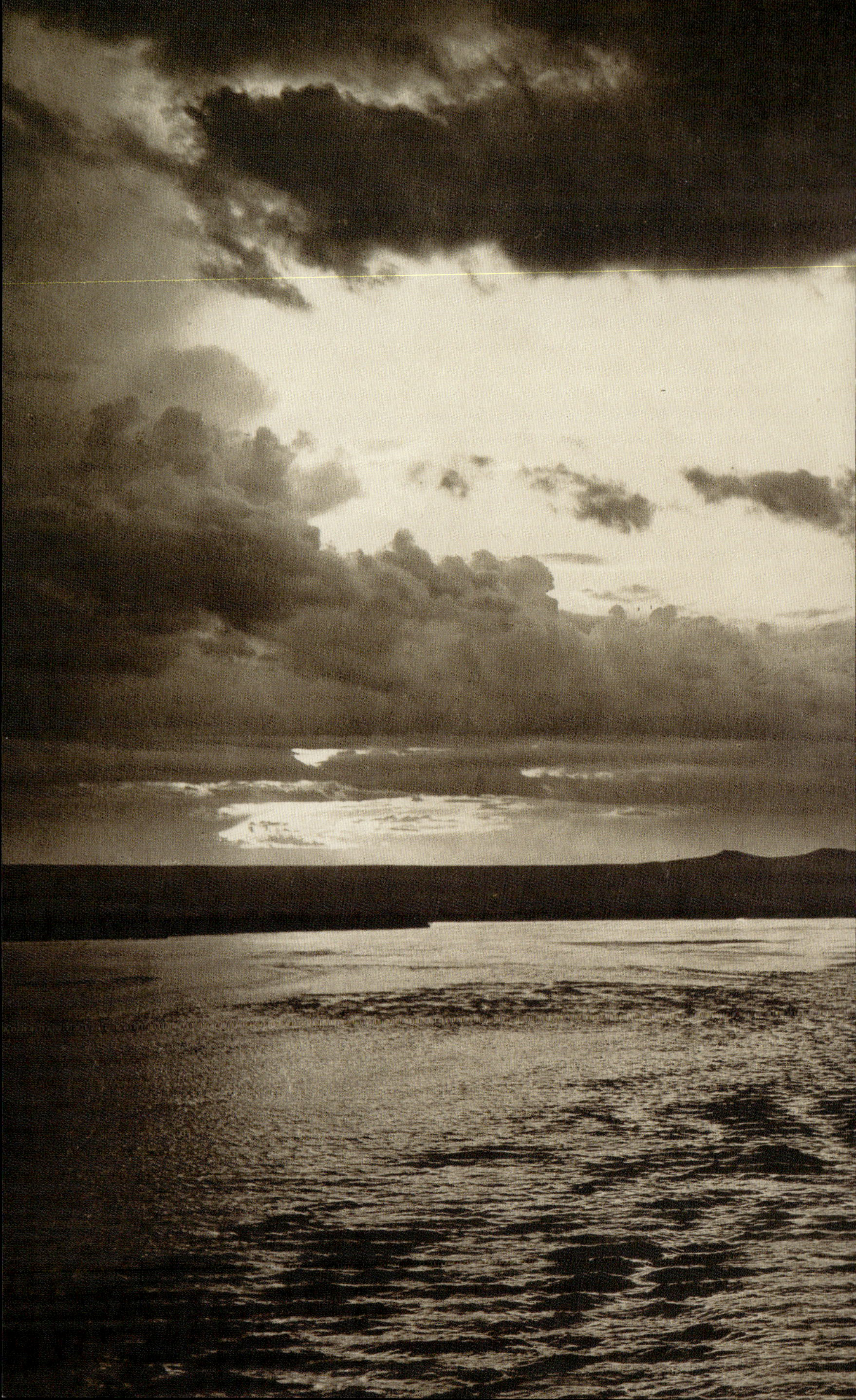

Our Land

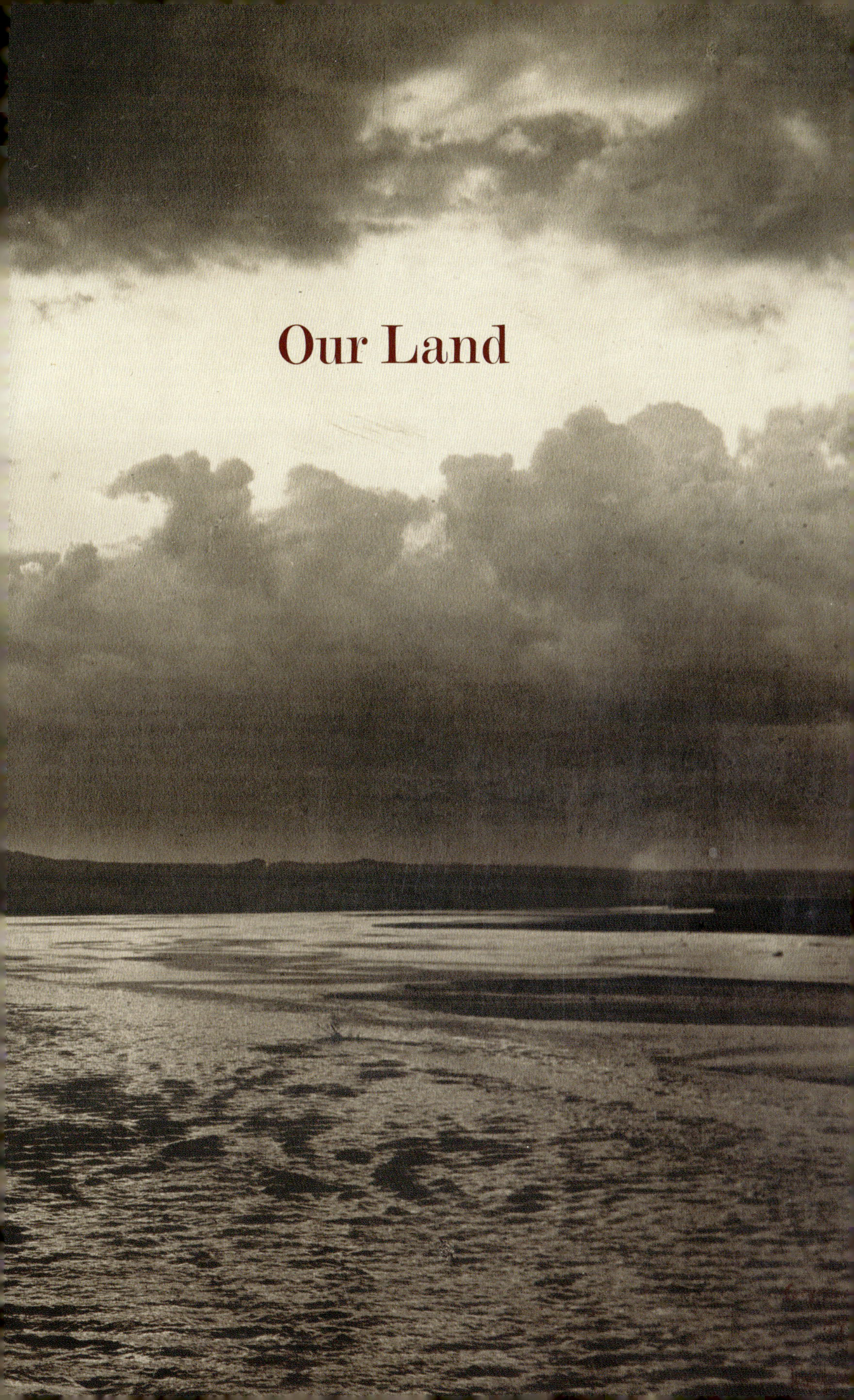

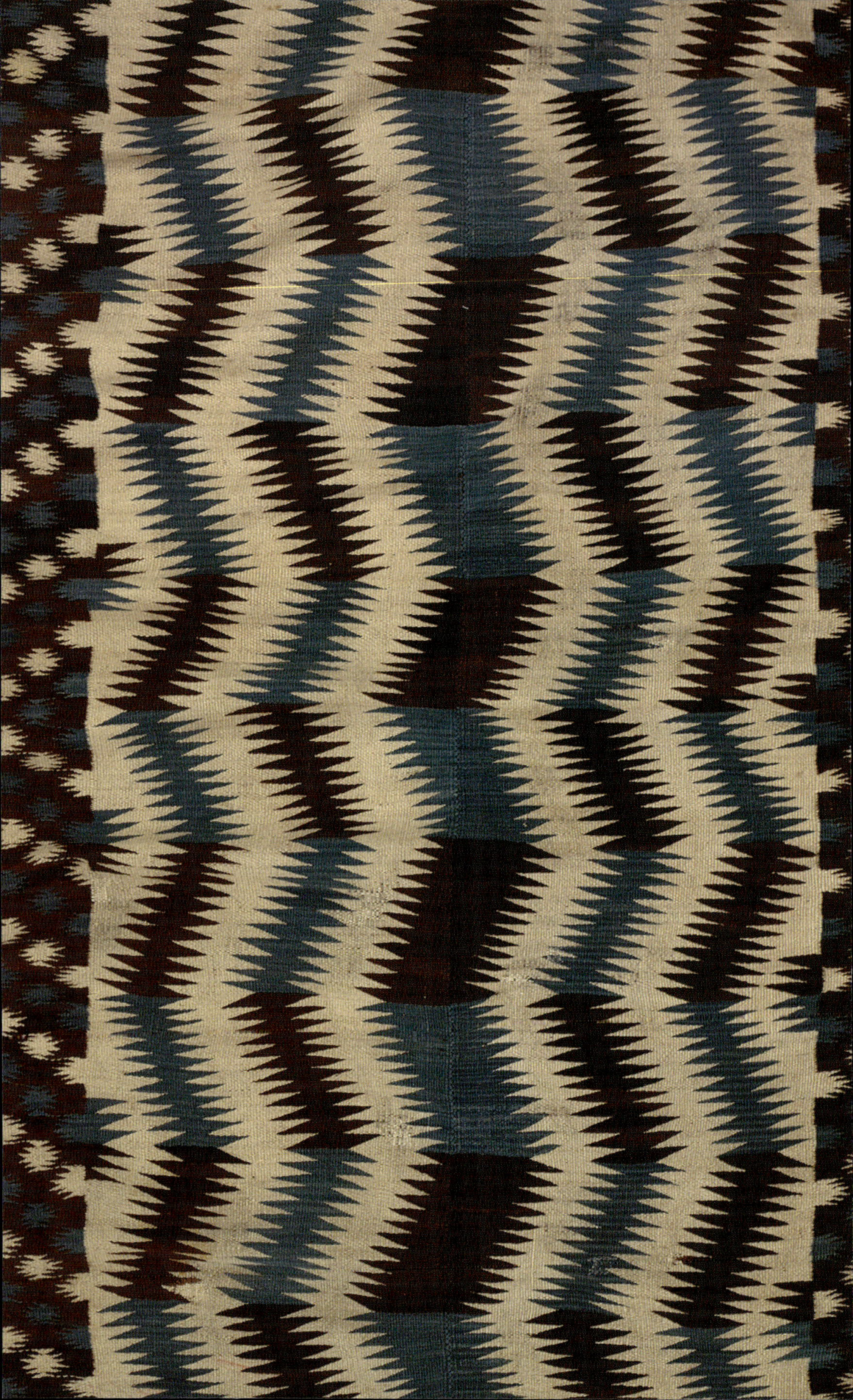

We are a culturally diverse people living along a big river in a great desert.

We see ourselves, and those who came before us, as spirited, courageous, resourceful, and innovative. Our connection to the land and to each other has produced a way of life that could happen *Only in Albuquerque.*

We live in a place of contrasts, a desert rich in natural resources, with unforgiving weather. Our land is timeless and ever changing, sprawling and hemmed in. Our land is a place of opportunity and limitations.

We live in New Mexico's central Rio Grande valley, where people first arrived around 10,000 BCE. The Rio Grande valley, a deep rift in the earth formed millions of years ago, grips our imagination even as it provides for our needs. The Sandias tower to the east; volcanoes rise from mesas to the west. Through the center runs a river, giving life to our land. We are entranced and captivated, humbled and awed.

Our four seasons are beautiful and sometimes scary. Windstorms obscure Sandia views, bury curbs, and erase paint from pickup trucks. Summer fires threaten our cottonwood bosque (forest) and mountains. Flooding and droughts re-route the Rio Grande, dictating where we build and how we farm. Natural cycles shape our land and test our resolve, connecting us to past generations of valley residents and to one another.

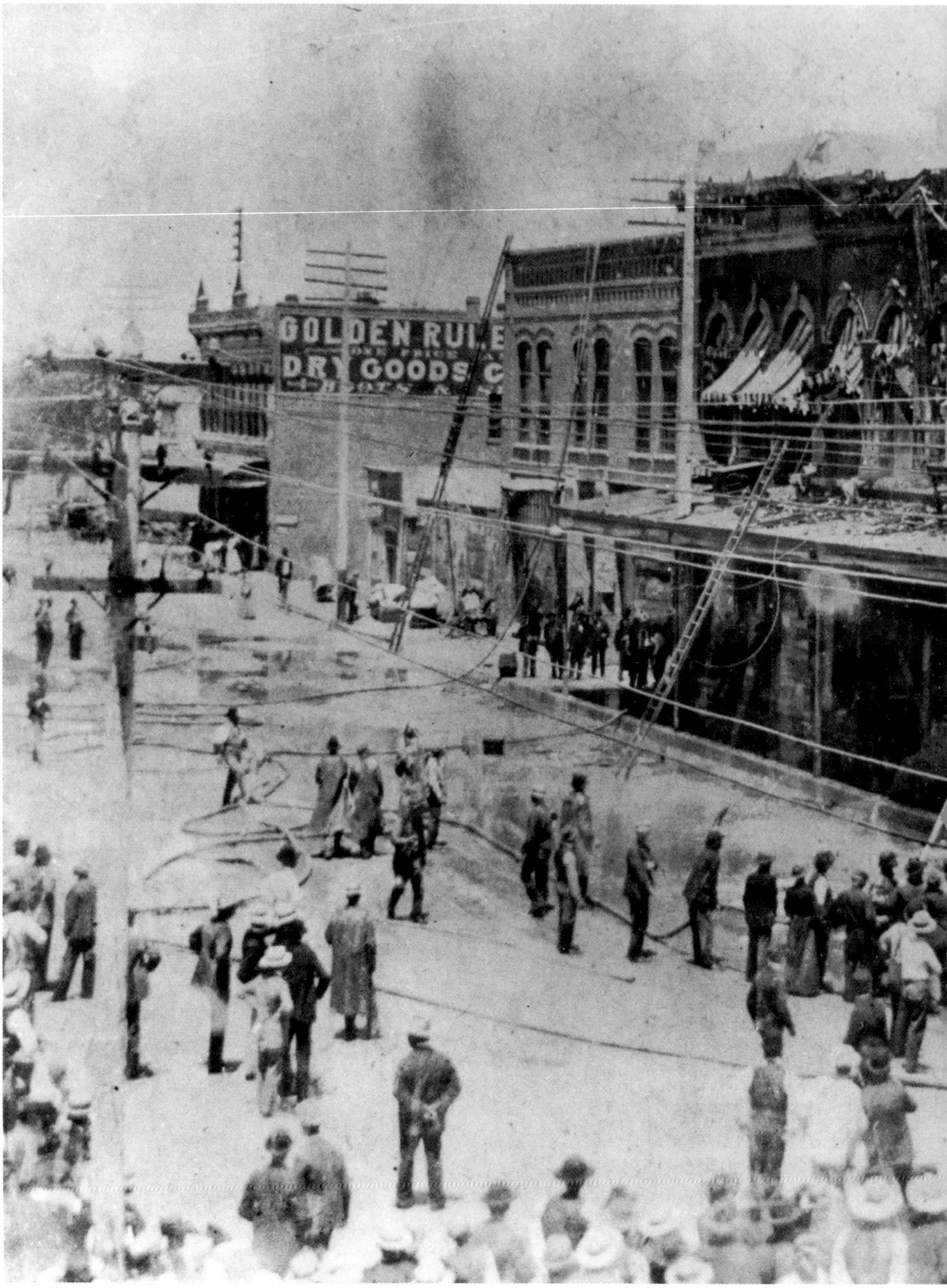
GOLDEN RULE
DRY GOODS C

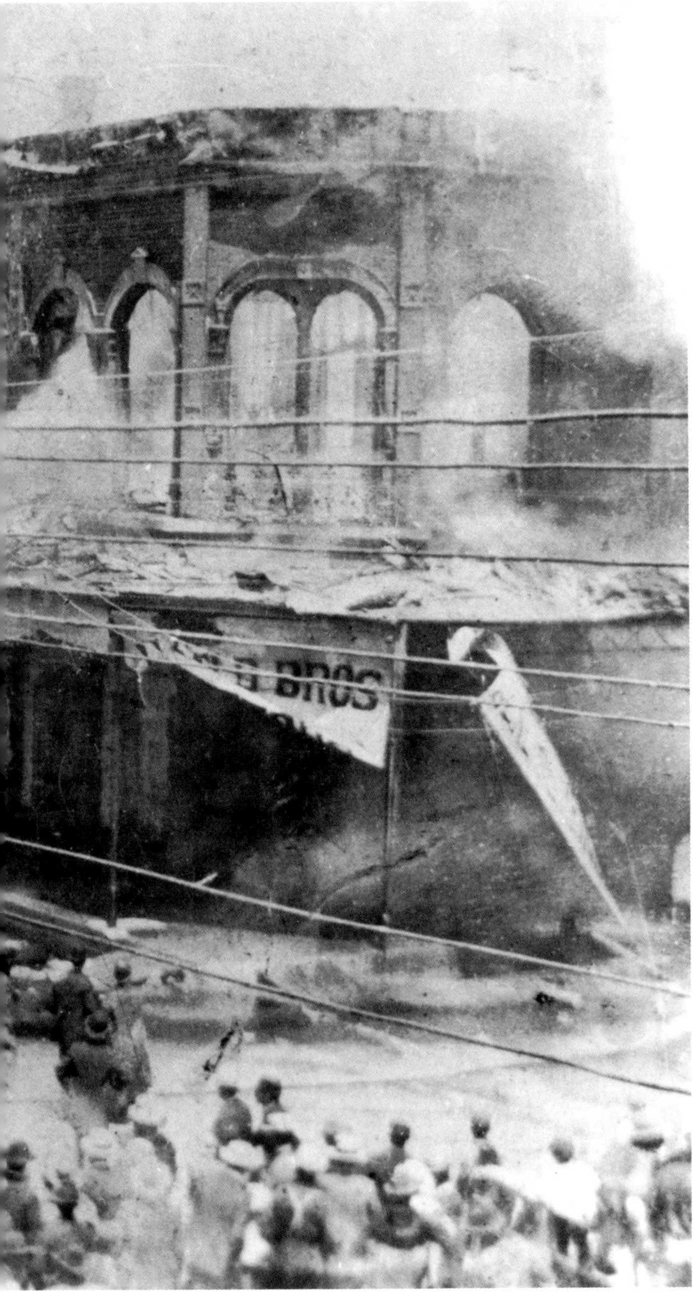

PLATE 1
Grant Building on fire, 1898
Photographer: Cobb Studio
University Libraries, University of New Mexico, Center for Southwest Research
PA1978.50.85

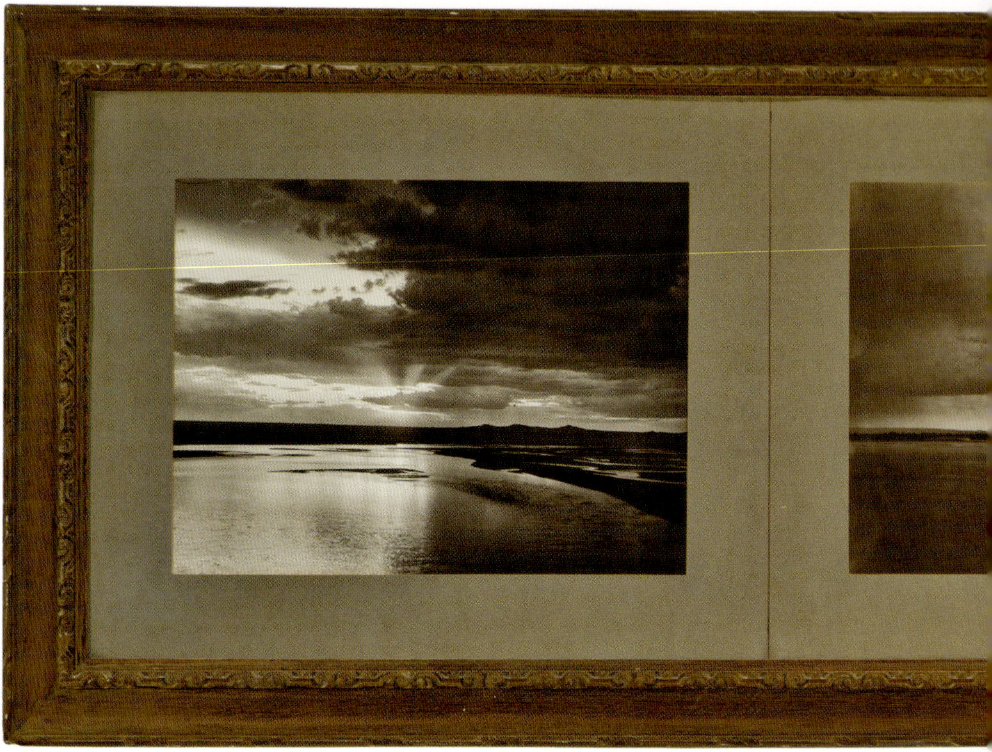

PLATE 2
William Walton
Nile of the West, 1908
Orotone prints
30 × 84 × 6 1/2 in. (overall)
Gift of the Albuquerque Historical Society
PC2007.74.1

PLATE 3 ▶
Wilson Hurley
Late Afternoon at La Cueva, 1983
Oil on canvas
72 1/2 × 108 1/2 in. (frame)
Museum purchase, 1981
General Obligation Bonds
PC1983.69.1

William Walton's three views of the Rio Grande show the river at a high-water stage, probably the result of recent flooding.

Isletans have called the river P'ay'ath. The earliest Spanish names for the Rio Grande included Río de Nuestra Señora, Guadalquivir, and Río Grande del Norte (shortened to Río del Norte).

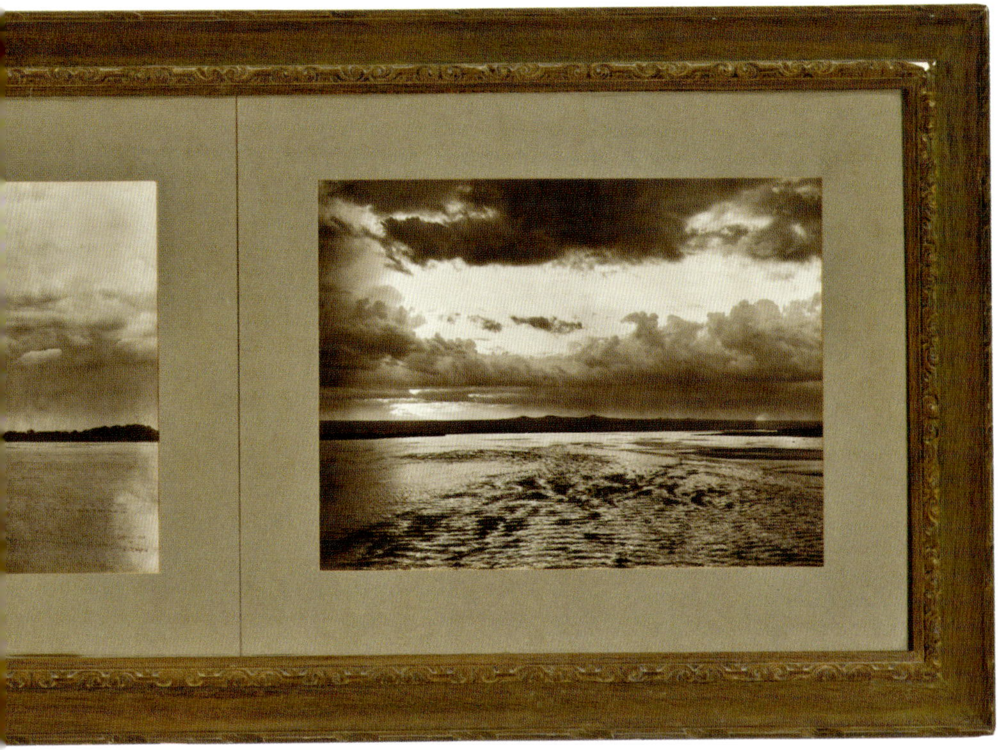

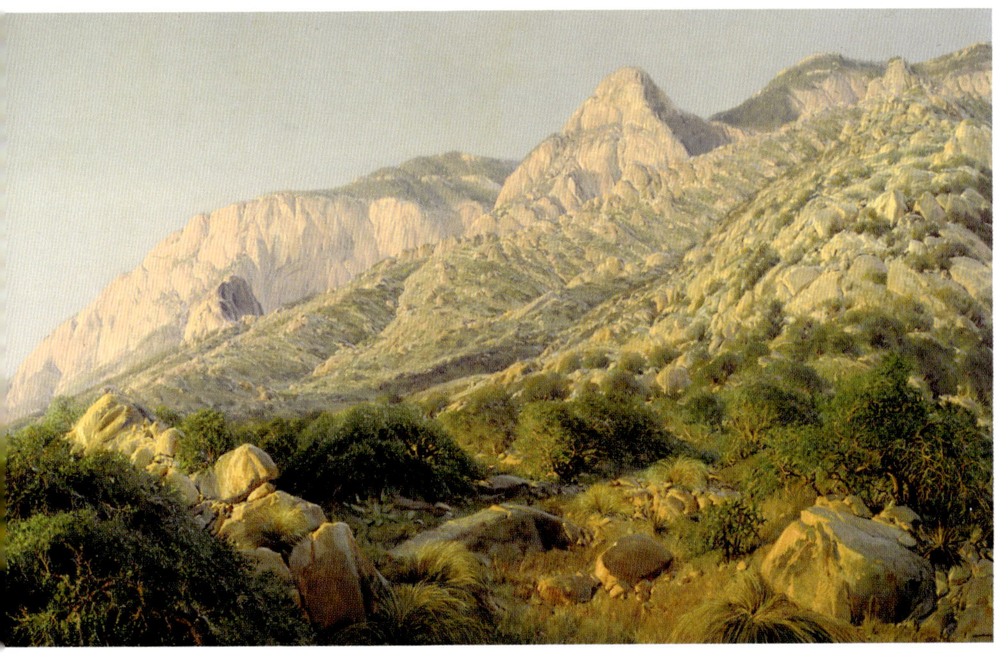

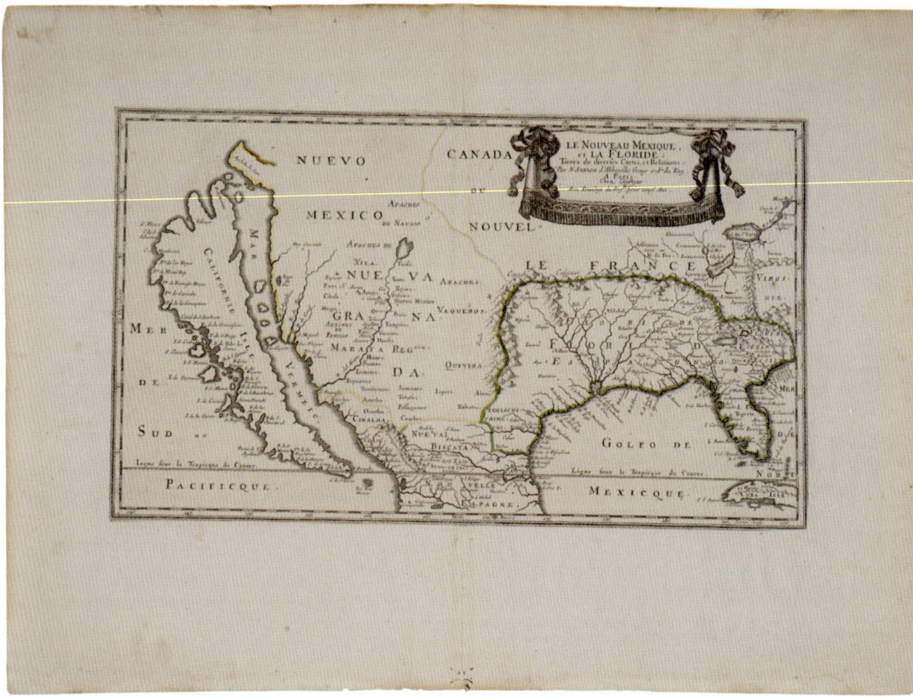

This is one of the finest charts of the Southwest. French cartographer Nicolas Sanson established a family dynasty, producing maps coveted by explorers wishing to learn more about Spanish-controlled coastlines and the potential for trade within Spanish dominions. This map was printed from an engraved copper plate in 1656 and reprinted several times. When the Sansons relocated their shop, they hammered out portions of the cartouche and re-engraved their address. Traces of their prior addresses are visible.

Engraved between the founding of Santa Fe in 1610 and the Pueblo Revolt in 1680, important features include Santa Fe, the Californie Isle, the supposed "Vermillion Sea" between California and the mainland, and the mythical lake north of Taos (Taosii) from which the Río del Norte drains, as first reported in 1583 by explorer Antonio Espejo. The prominent placement of the Navajo and various Apache bands reflects Spain's experience with Indian raids. Several Pueblos, including Zuni, Acoma, and Tiguex (Southern Tiwa), are also present.

◀ PLATE 4
Nicolas Sanson, French
Map, *Le Nouveau Mexique et La Floride*, ca. 1656–75
Copper engraving, hand illuminated, ink on paper
20 5/8 × 28 in. (overall)
Museum purchase, 1979 General Obligation Bonds
PC1981.155.8

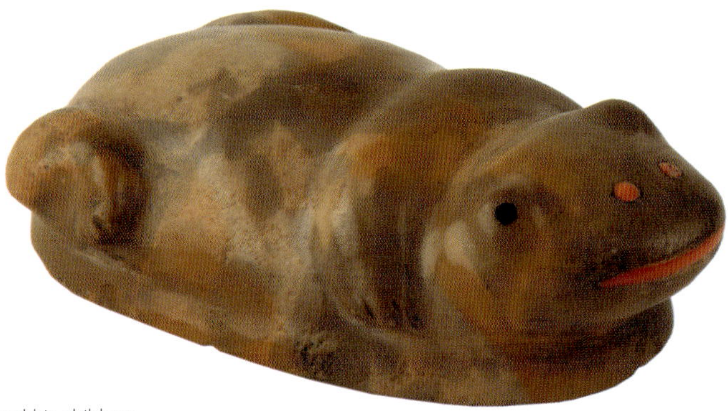

PLATE 5
Leekya, Zuni
Frog or toad carving, 1939
Zuni stone (travertine)
3 1/2 × 2 1/2 × 1 1/2 in.
Gift of Kenneth Alan Wallace and his children,
Andrew, Aaron, Susanna, Megan, and Glen
PC2010.34.4

Spadefoot toads burrow deep into the desert soil, only to emerge croaking after a heavy monsoon rain. They have a few days to mate. Their eggs quickly hatch in puddles and ponds, leaving tadpoles that grow rapidly as the puddles dry up.

Zuni master carver Leekya (1889–1966) made this frog or toad for Ken Wallace. As a child, Ken liked to play in mud puddles near the C. G. Wallace Trading Post in Zuni after thunderstorms.

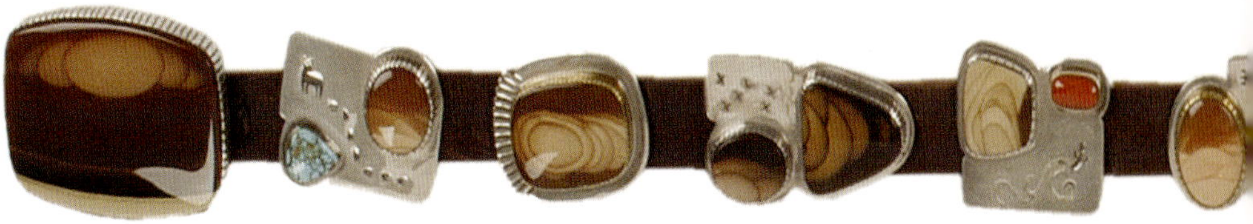

PLATES 6–7

Yazzie Johnson, Navajo, and Gail Bird, Laguna/Santo Domingo
Belt, *Bruneau Mountain Belt*, 1981
Sterling silver, Bruneau Mountain jasper, turquoise, lapis, coral, 18K gold and/or brass, and silver underlay on leather
38 × 2 × 1 in.
Museum purchase, Drs. Bette K. and John R. Graham Fund in memory of Dr. Bette Kaufman Graham
PC2012.19.1

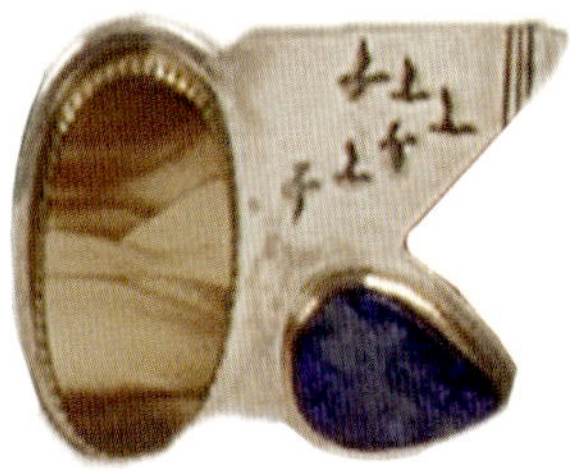

Early belts made by Yazzie Johnson and Gail Bird feature the sandhill crane, a river bird unique to the Southwest. These beautiful birds circle in flocks over the Rio Grande and feed in adjoining fields (plate 7).

For a long time, the owner of this belt was unknown. However, it appeared a number of years ago at a New Mexico auction and was subsequently sold to the Museum for exhibition in *Only in Albuquerque.*

PLATE 8 ►

Hispanic New Mexican
Frazada/Blanket Rio Grande weaving, 1850–60
Churro wool, Germantown yarn, indigo, cotton thread
81 × 51 in.
Museum purchase, 1983 General Obligation Bonds
PC1984.25.19

Lightning is a source of inspiration for weavers looking to build movement into their weavings. This weaving style was popular in the mid-1800s, and many examples may have been made in workshops directed by a master weaver.

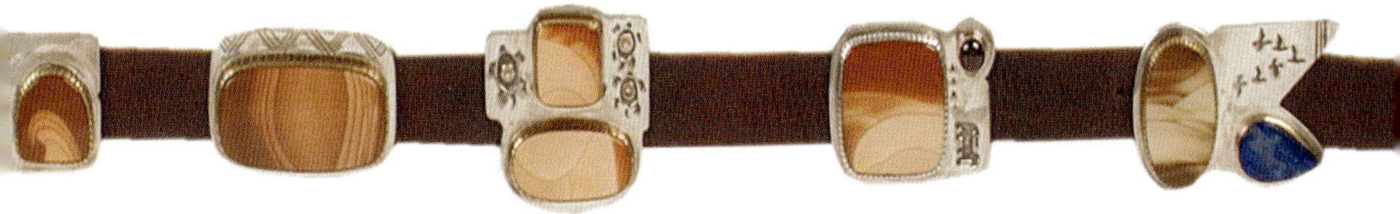

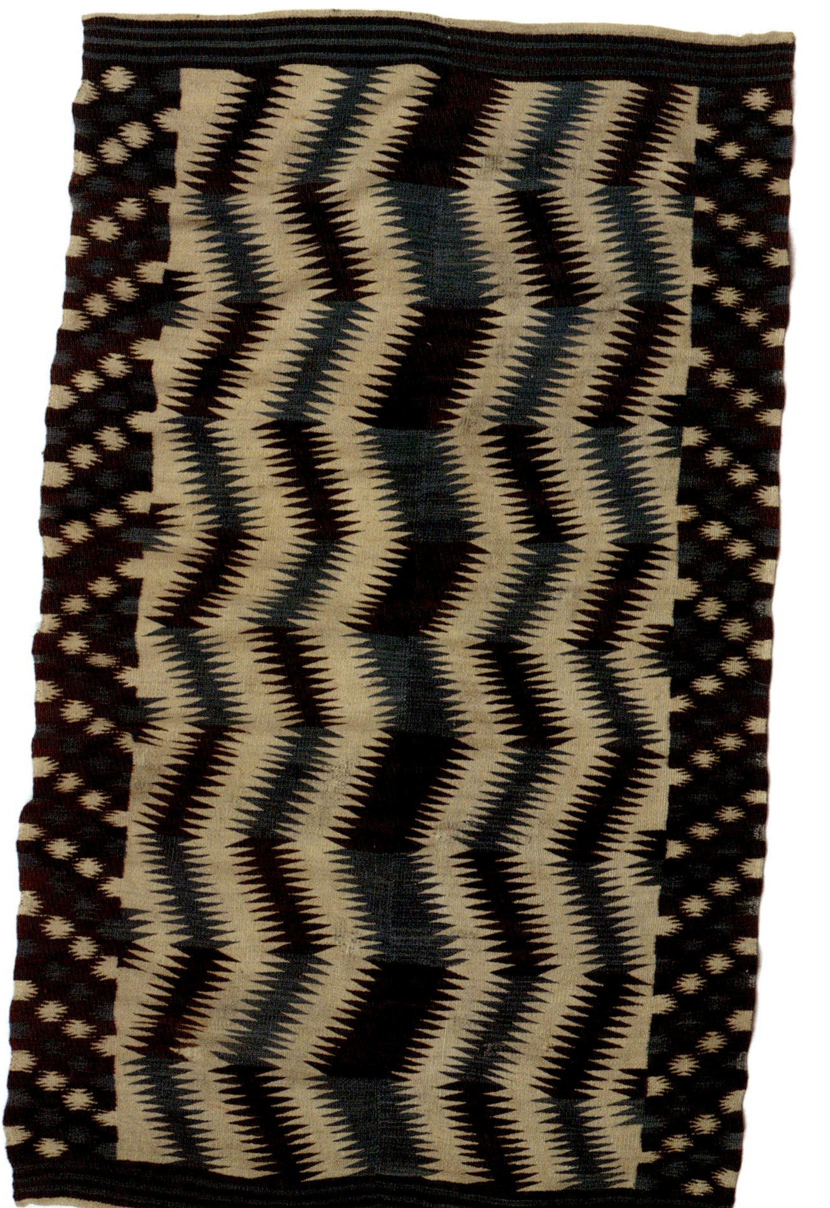

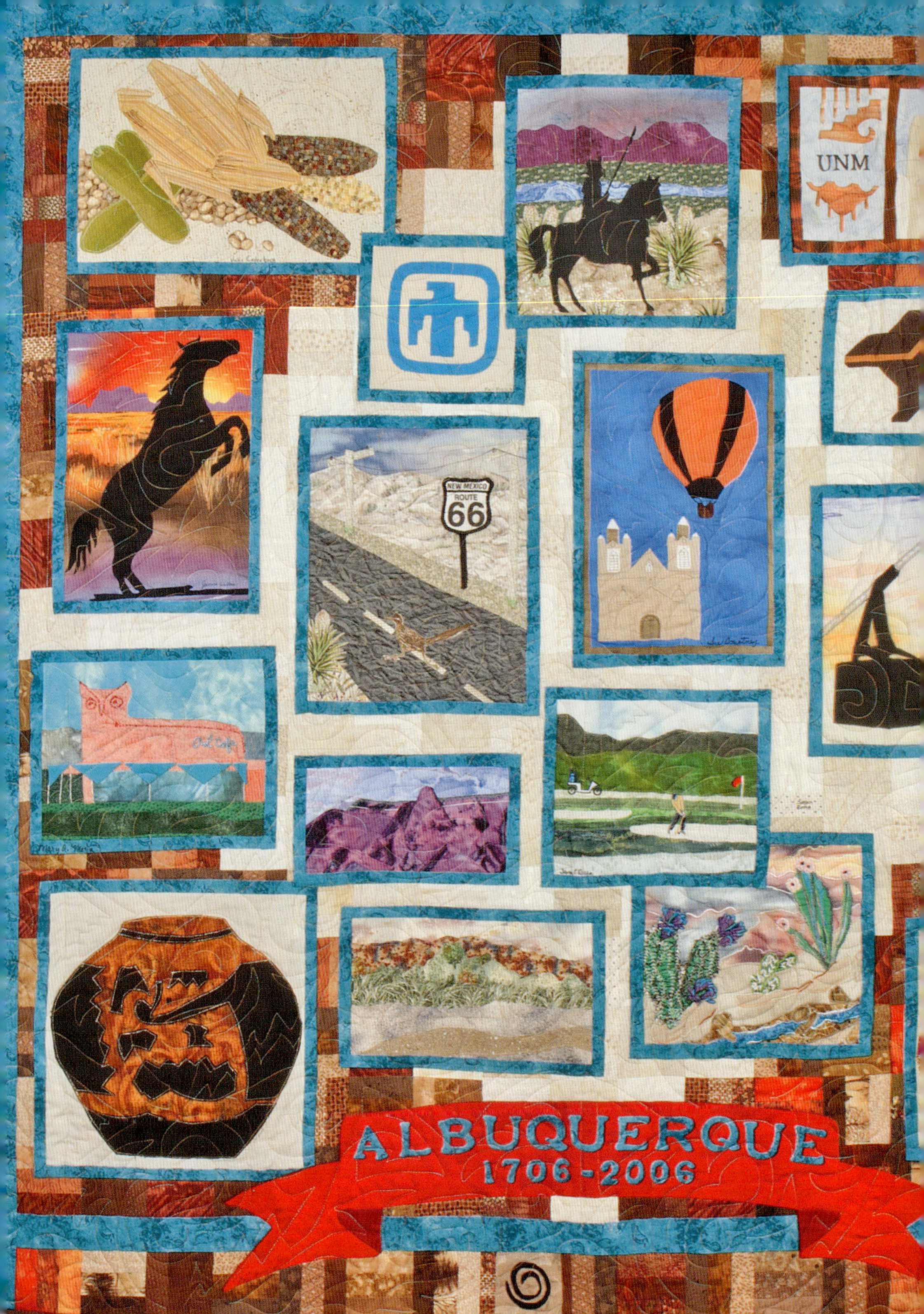
UNM
NEW MEXICO
ROUTE
66
ALBUQUERQUE
1706-2006

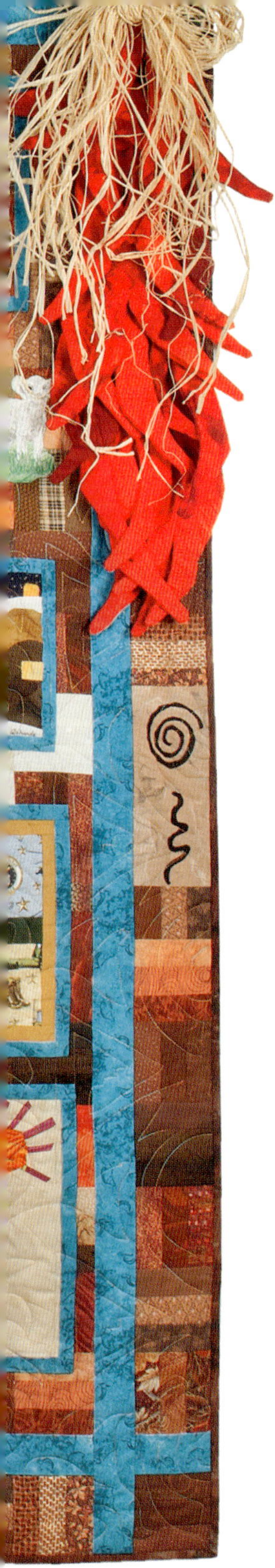

We Are Spirited

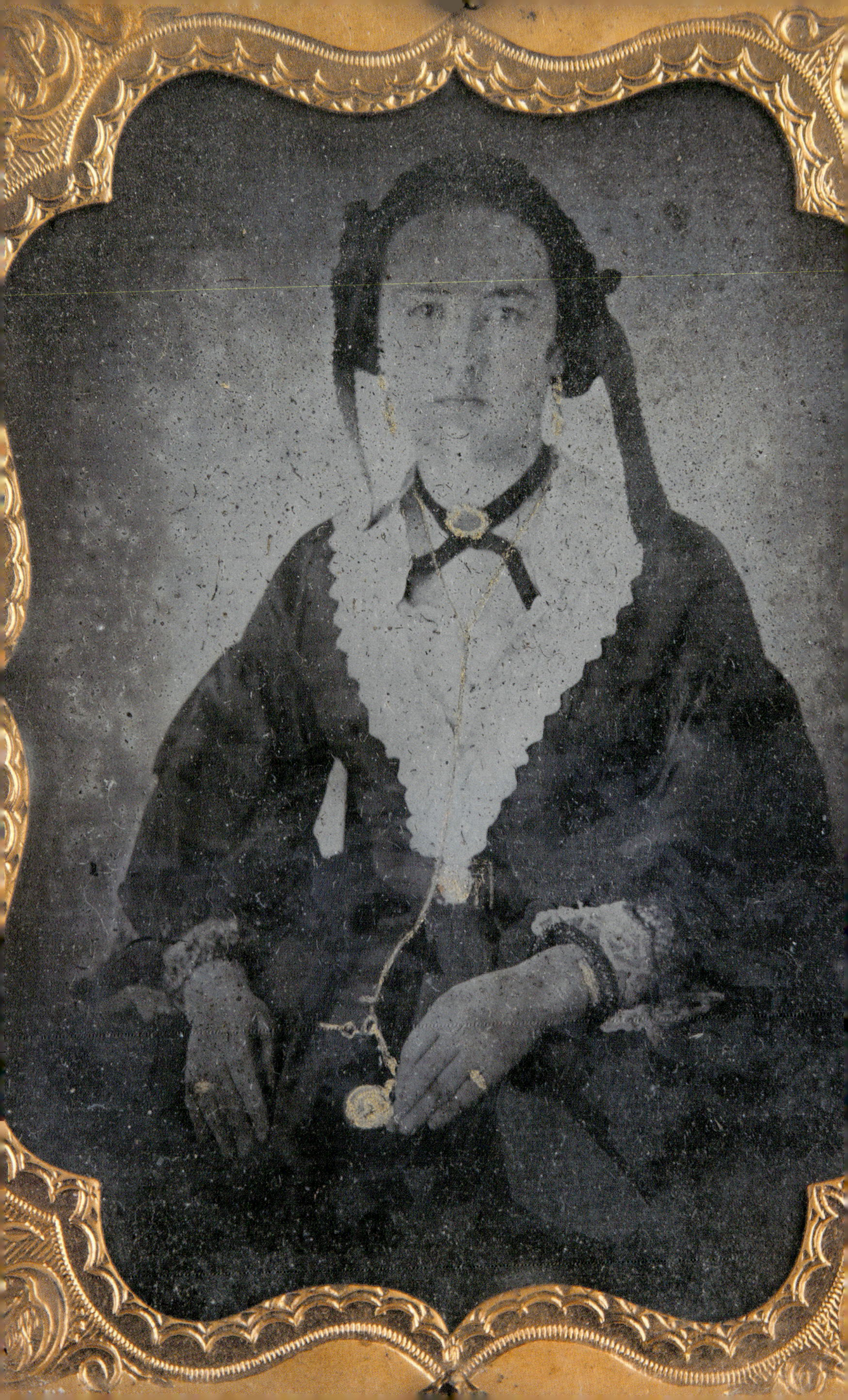

The people of Albuquerque have always been spirited.

We take pride in our city's founding in 1706, having established the only Spanish *villa* (administrative center) in the central Rio Grande valley, its location greatly influenced by our geography. Our traditions blend cultures that inform and enhance one another.

Through the many stories we share—stories of our founding families, neighborhood celebrations, food traditions, and spirituality—we discover how closely we are intertwined.

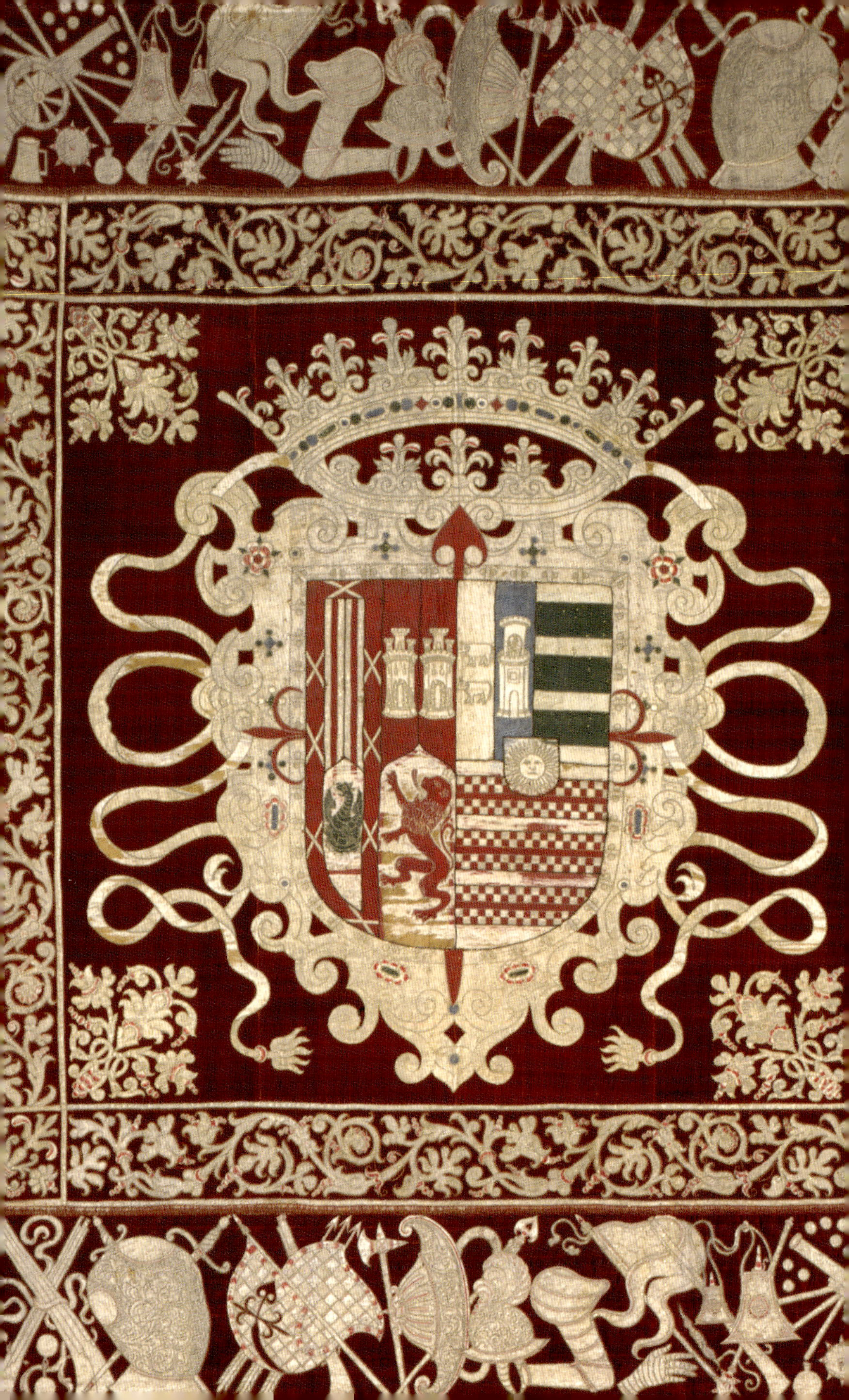

Our Founders

The story of Albuquerque's founding fills us with pride. Past accounts wobbled between fact and fiction, myth and history. But we now know more. We know our founders as brave and brazen men and women from many cultural backgrounds. We know that they created a villa, held a ceremony, raised families, and founded new communities. And we know their descendants, who still live among us.

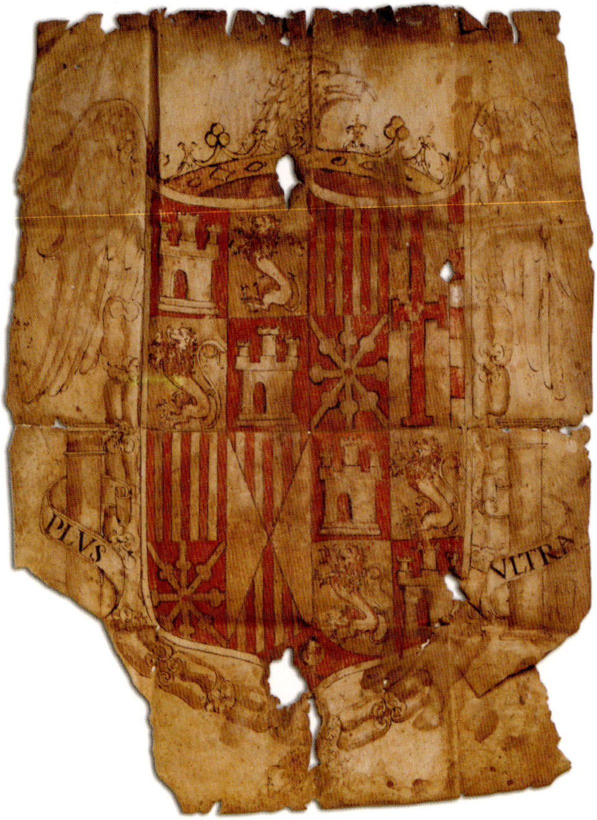

PLATE 9
Spanish
Document cover, ca. 1550
Parchment, ink
25 × 18 in.
Museum purchase, 1979
General Obligation Bonds
PC1982.16.1

Altered during the reign of Carlos I, the royal coat of arms illustrated Spanish dominion in both the Old and New Worlds. Every element of the border and shield has a specific symbolic meaning.

Symbols of the edge of the known world, the Pillars of Hercules—visible on each side of the cover—were associated in Roman times with the Strait of Gibraltar. Prior to the European discovery of lands in the Western Hemisphere, they carried the motto *Ne Plus Ultra* (No More Beyond), a reference to the new discoveries. Carlos I had the word "ne" removed to indicate his ambition to expand the Spanish Empire beyond its European possessions.

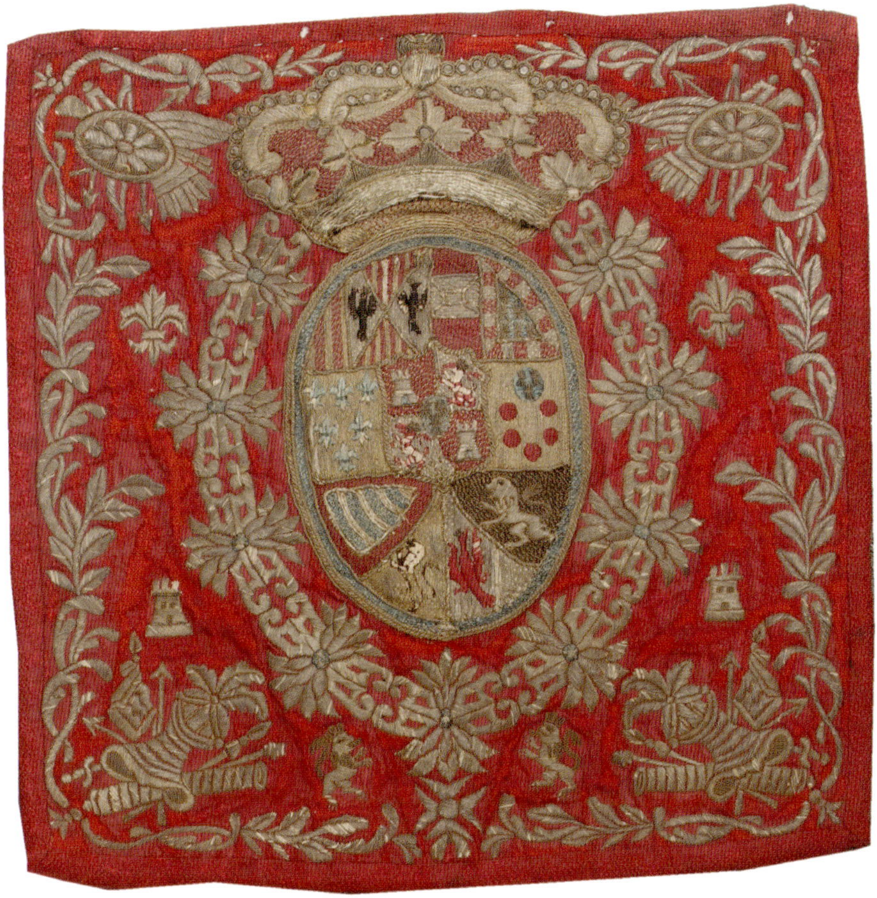

PLATE 10
Spanish
Royal standard, ca. 1759–1800
Velvet, gold and silver wire, silk
13 3/4 × 15 in.
Museum purchase, 1979 General Obligation Bonds
PC1982.29.1

Hung from a lance, this embroidered standard presents the Spanish Bourbon coat of arms. The symbols represent countries governed by Spain during the first century of Albuquerque's founding. Like the repostero, its border is decorated with trophies of war.

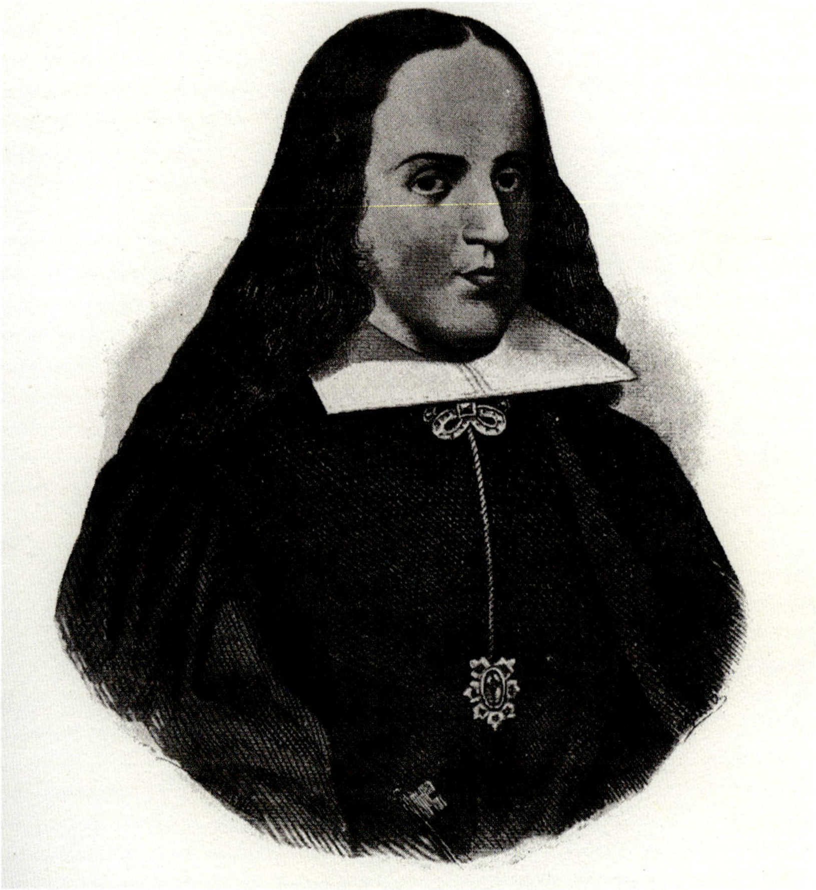

PLATE 11
Francisco Fernández de la Cueva Enríquez, eighteenth century
Horn and Wallace Publishers

In April 1706, interim governor Francisco Cuervo y Valdés wrote the 10th Duke of Alburquerque, Spain, and the viceroy of New Spain, Francisco Fernández de la Cueva Enríquez, announcing that he had named our town La Villa de Alburquerque. Fernández de la Cueva Enríquez agreed to recognize the villa but advised him to change the villa's patron saint from San Francisco Xavier to San Felipe Neri in honor of Felipe V, King of Spain.

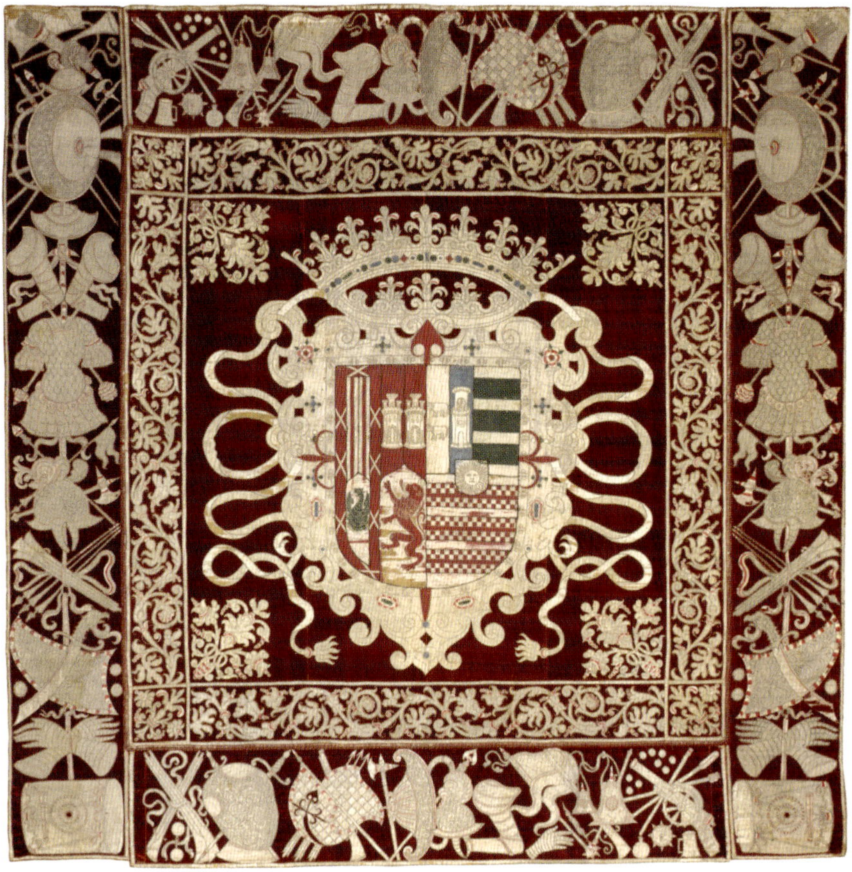

PLATE 12
Messina, Sicily
Repostero, 1620–40
Silk, linen, metallic threads
142 × 142 in.
Gift of the 18th Duke (Don Beltrán Osorio y Díez de Rivera) and Duchess of Alburquerque, Spain, via the City of Albuquerque Public Art Program
PC1973.33.1

The Cueva family *repostero* (heraldic tapestry) was originally commissioned by Francisco Fernández de la Cueva, 8th Duke of Alburquerque, Spain. Its borders feature trophies of war including helmets, swords, and battle axes. The central coat of arms includes emblems representing the duke's ancestral family names. The dragon represents the Cueva family line and is based on a family legend of an ancestor who slew a dragon in a cave. The 18th Duke of Alburquerque, Spain, presented the repostero to the people of Albuquerque during the 1956 Enchantorama celebrating our city's 250th anniversary.

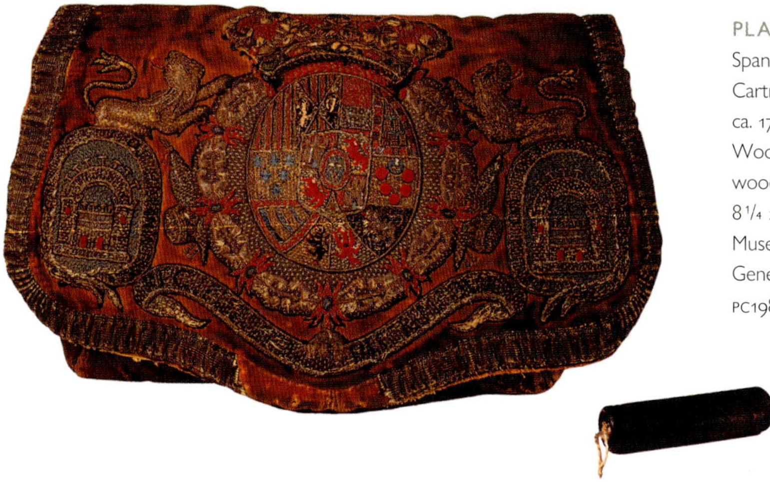

PLATE 13
Spanish
Cartridge pouch and cartridge, ca. 1700
Wool, leather, velvet, silk, wood, silver and gold thread
8 1/4 × 12 13/16 in.
Museum purchase, 1979 General Obligation Bonds
PC1982.30.1

Created very near to the year of Albuquerque's founding, this rectangular belt pouch has hand-stitched seams and a flap decorated with the Spanish royal coat of arms representing the House of Bourbon.

PLATE 14 ►
Mexican
Painting, *Nuestra Señora de Guadalupe/Our Lady of Guadalupe*, eighteenth century
Oil, canvas
37 × 28 1/2 in.
Museum purchase, 1995 General Obligation Bonds
PC1998.17.29

Nuestra Señora de Guadalupe, a vision of the Virgin Mary, is said to have appeared to Juan Diego, a peasant residing on the outskirts of Mexico City, in 1531. She promised to help the people if the bishop would build a church dedicated to her. The bishop at first refused, but after a miracle in which the image of the Virgin appeared on Juan Diego's tilma (poncho), the shrine was built and dedicated. One of New Mexico's most popular saints, Our Lady of Guadalupe is the patron of Indian and Hispanic people and is regarded as a protectress against illness, evil, and war.

In 1709, three years after La Villa de Alburquerque was founded, the 10th Duke of Alburquerque, Spain, dedicated a new shrine at Tepeyac. The shrine is depicted in a cartouche at the center of the lower edge of this oil painting. Today the basilica is the most visited Catholic pilgrimage site in the world and the world's third most-visited sacred site.

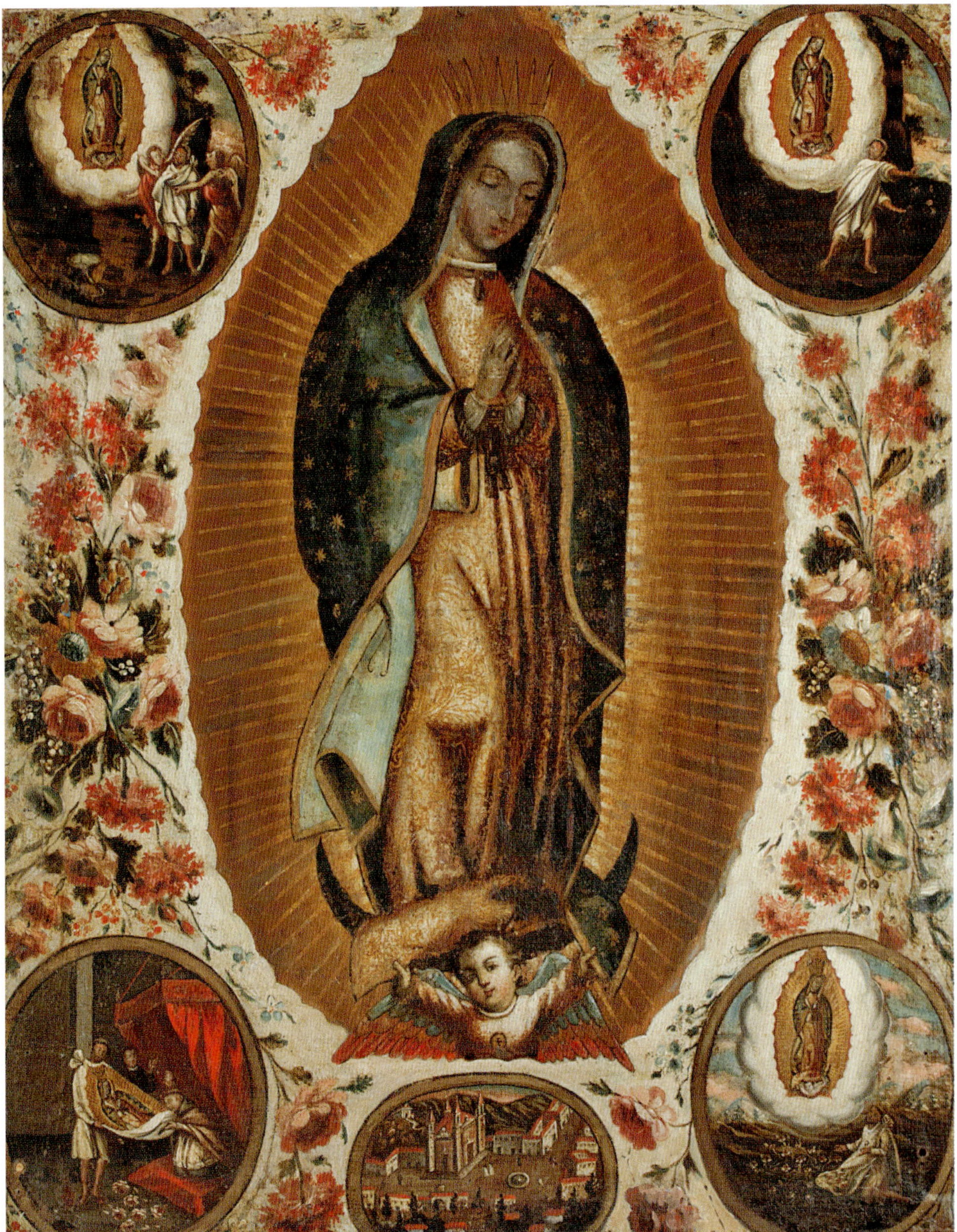

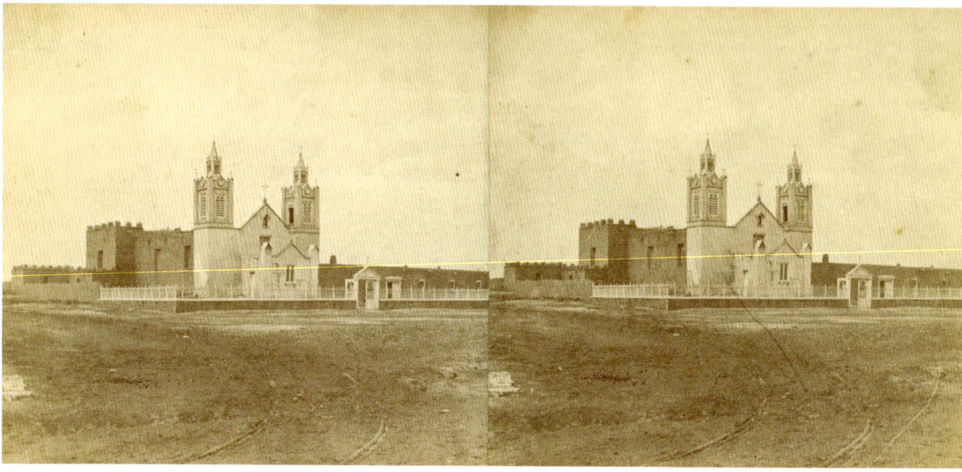

PLATE 15
Stereo card, *Valley of the Rio Grande, Church of Albuquerque*, 1871–74
Photographer: H. T. Heister
Museum purchase, Museum Photo Archives Special Revenue Fund in memory of Willie McWilliams and her family
PA2006.11.1

Alburquerque's first church was built in 1706 on the west side of the plaza, facing east. After it fell into ruin in the early 1790s, this church was built in 1793 on the north side of the plaza, facing south. San Felipe de Neri Church has served its parishioners for more than three hundred years.

▶

Old Town resident Cleto Durán's job was to clean San Felipe de Neri Church, but Durán is best known for starting the tradition of lighting *farolitos* (little lanterns) there in 1932. A priest at the church gave Cleto this bulto (religious sculpture) around that time. Created in Mexico or Spain, it had been overpainted through the years, but in the wear and flaking of the surface one can see in the intricate *estofado* (scratched patterns representing richly designed textiles) underneath.

Postdating Fray Francisco Atanasio Domínguez's 1776 inventory of the contents of San Felipe de Neri Church but predating known photographs of bultos in the altar, this bulto provides an important link between early Albuquerque devotional art and the present-day *santero* (artisan that makes santos or saints) tradition. It also corroborates Fr. Domínguez's 1776 proclamation that the church would honor her original patron saint San Felipe Neri rather than San Francisco Xavier.

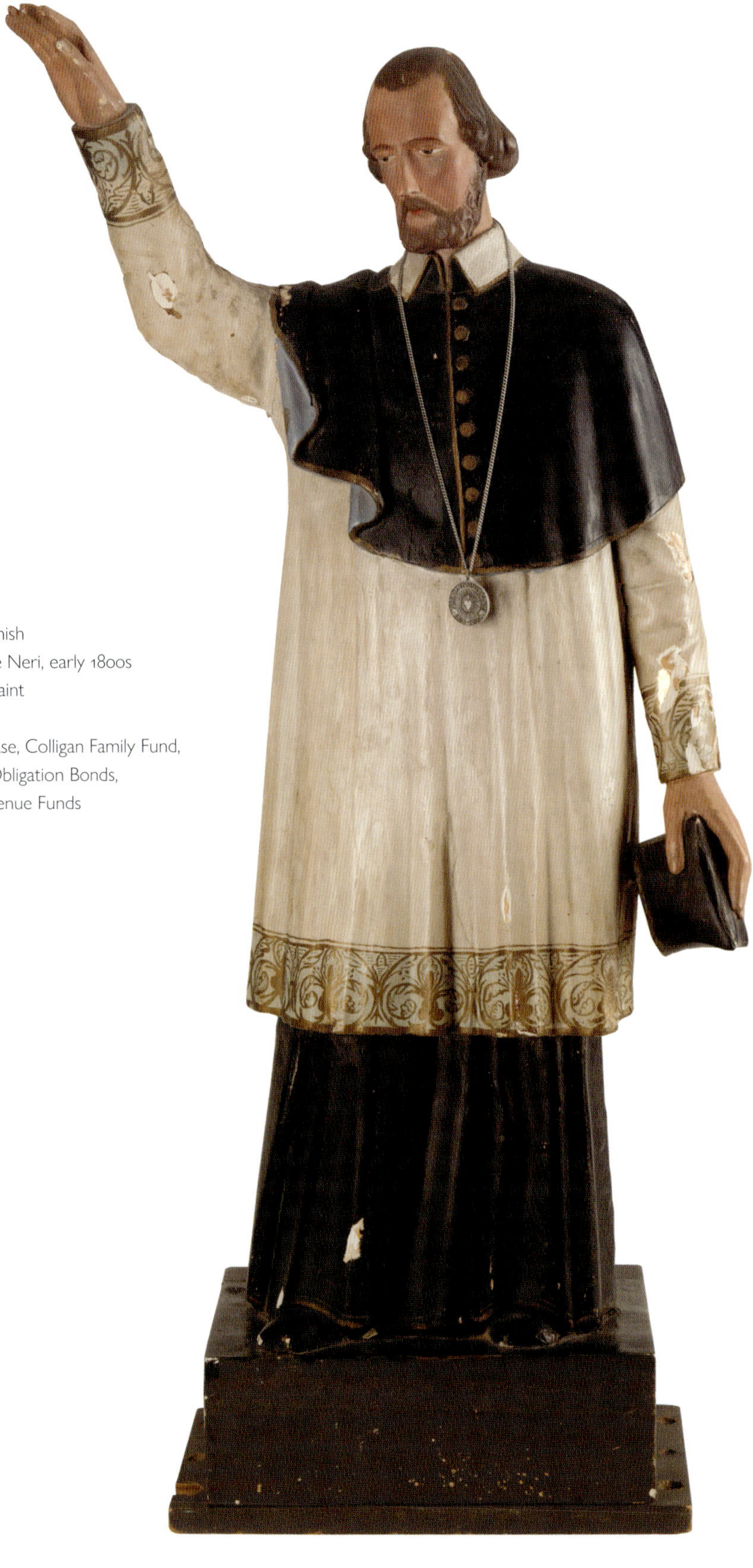

PLATE 16
Mexican or Spanish
Bulto, San Felipe Neri, early 1800s
Wood, gesso, paint
42 × 21 × 11 in.
Museum purchase, Colligan Family Fund, 2009 General Obligation Bonds, and Special Revenue Funds
PC2015.42.1

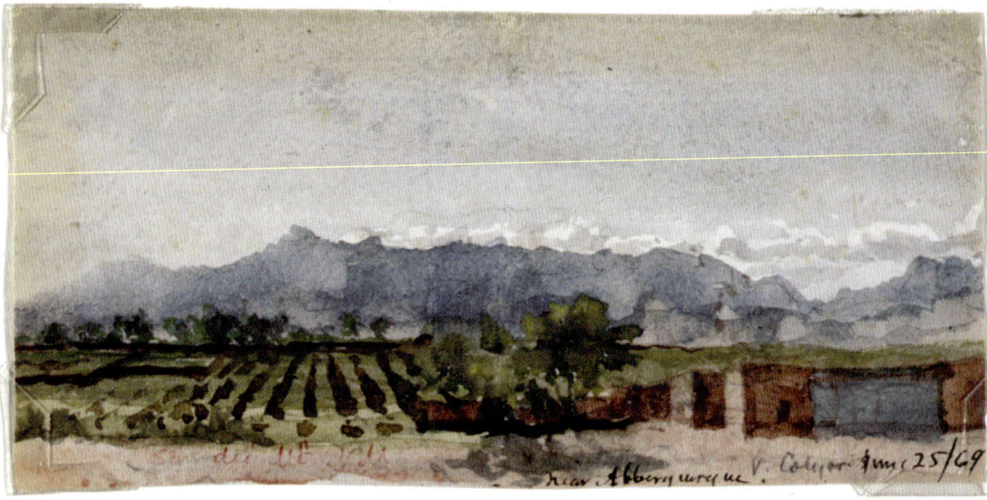

PLATE 17
Vincent Colyer, 1825–1888
San Dei Mountains near Alberquerque, 1869
Watercolor painting on paper
2 1/2 × 5 in.
Museum purchase, 1983 General Obligation Bonds
PC1985.30.12

Colyer painted this scene from a vantage point near Old Town where the Albuquerque Museum stands today, probably while he was serving as secretary to the Board of US Indian Commissioners and stationed in the Southwest. Colyer also painted scenes of Camp Craig, Santa Fe, and Pigeon's Ranch. Even into the 1860s, visitors occasionally referred to Albuquerque with two "r"s.

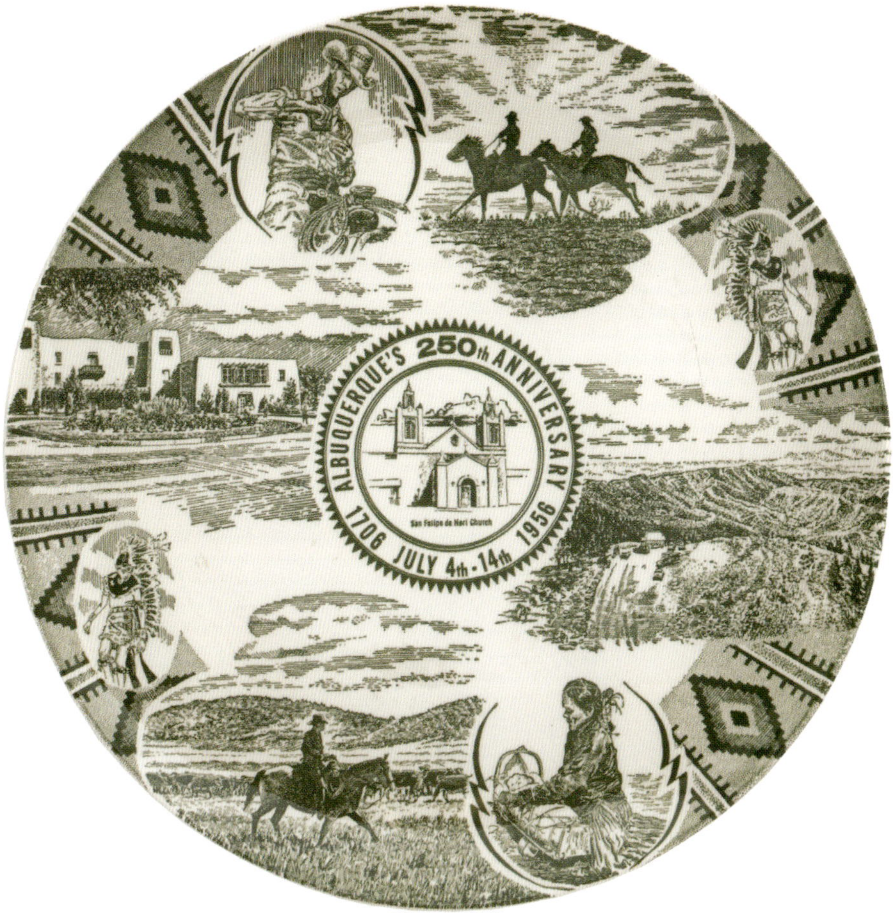

PLATE 18
Plate, 1956
Kettlesprings Kilns, Alliance, Ohio
Transfer printed earthenware
9 7/8 × 1 in.
Gift of Mrs. Harriet Saulter
PC1975.7.1

The 1956 Enchantorama featured parades, a play, and guest appearances by the 18th Duke and Duchess of Alburquerque, Spain. Men grew beards but found out later that men were clean-shaven in 1706. Women were encouraged to dispense with cosmetics during the Enchantorama, although women really did use them in the 1700s! Male participants were given official certificates naming them honorary Dukes of Alburquerque. Citizens were encouraged to fund and promote the Enchantorama by purchasing souvenirs, like this commemorative plate featuring San Felipe de Neri Church.

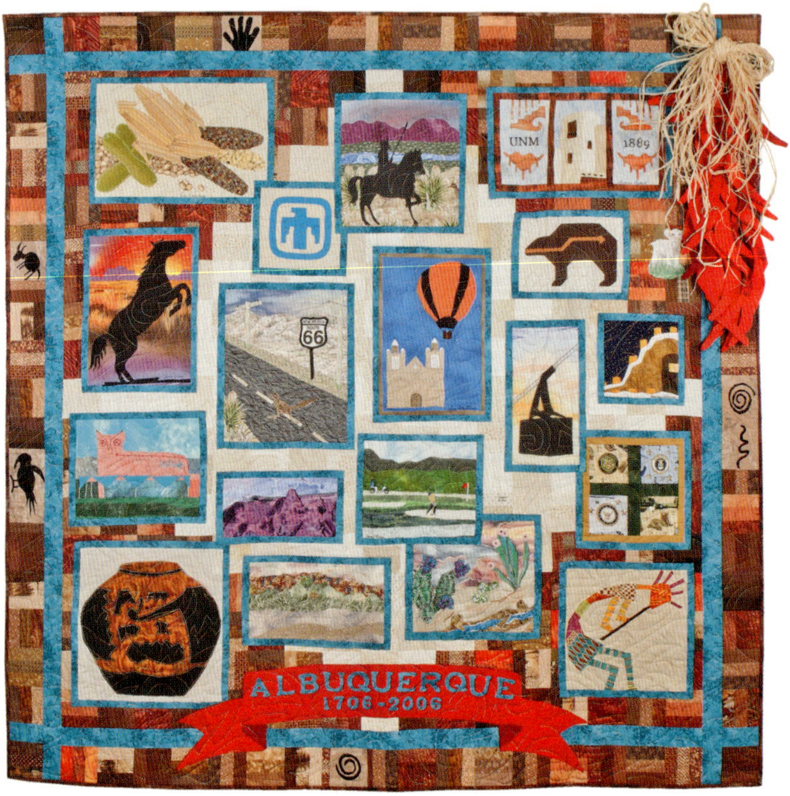

PLATE 19
New Mexico Quilters Association
Tricentennial quilt, 2006
Cotton fabric, cotton-polyester blend batting, raffia
62 × 62 × 2 in.
Gift of the New Mexico Quilters Association
PC2006.7.1

Karen Armstrong, Trisha Breslin, Vicki Cederberg, Linda Cotton, Sue Courtney, Madeline Edgar, Barbara Garey, Linda Gassaway, Adelyn Grudier, Kathy Heger, Kelly Helvie, Shirley Jewell, Lee Jordan, Ami Krenzell, Susan Linville, Louise Lucero, Laurie Marnell, Mary Moya, Lana Muraskin, Irene Perea, Fran Plisga, Lucinda Puckett, Jennifer Randock, Barbara Richards, Pat Riggin, Kathleen Rogers, Barbara Rollins, Terri Scott, Carole Shores, Dee Snider, Karen Springstead, Betty Standiferd, Connie Tecklenberg, Janice Wallace, Diane Yanney, and Susan Yates all collaborated to produce a quilt honoring the Tricentennial—Albuquerque's three hundredth birthday—in 2006. Emblems appliquéd to the quilt represent centuries of Albuquerque's history, including Pueblo pottery designs, a Spanish soldier, a red chile ristra, a Sandia Laboratories logo, ballooning, the University of New Mexico, and Route 66.

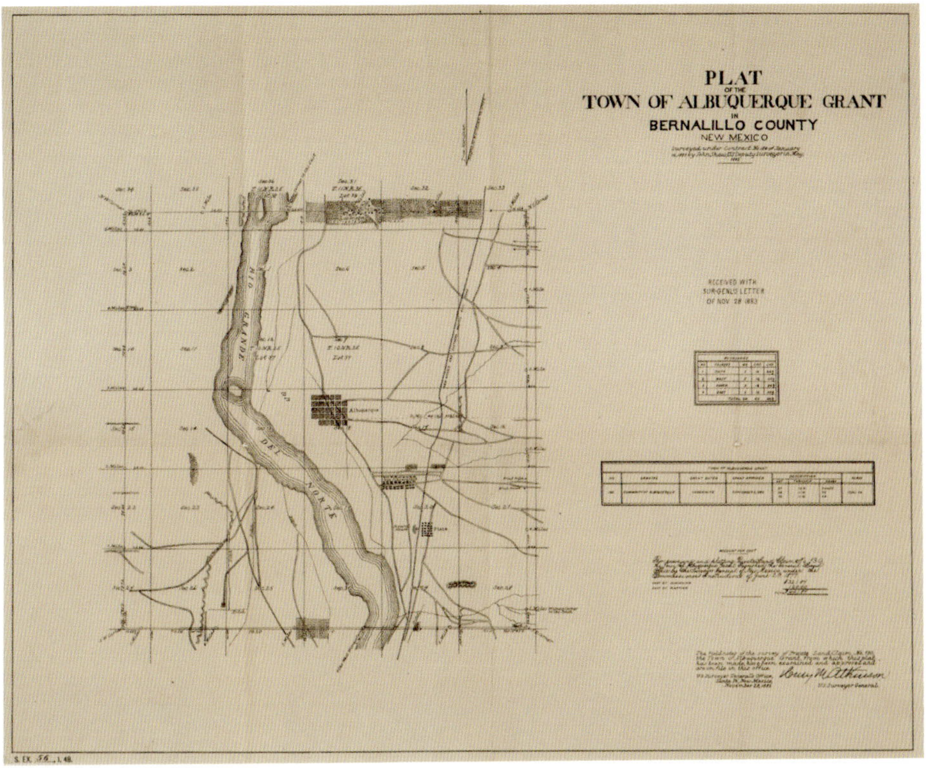

PLATE 20
Map, Town of Albuquerque Grant, 1883
US Government Printing Office
Ink, paper
17 × 21 1/2 in.
PC1984.86.1

Spain authorized the founding of Alburquerque (as it was spelled at the time) in 1706. A central plaza was carefully placed at a bend in the river away from swampy land on relatively high, fertile ground between Sandia and Isleta Pueblos. Founders established land grant boundaries and built acequias (ditches) and an *iglesia* (church). They made walls with *terrones* (sod blocks) and adobes (clay bricks). They supported roofs with hand-cut vigas (beams) and *latillas* (branches) covered with dirt.

This plat map shows the relationship of Albuquerque's Old and New Towns relative to the Rio Grande. Today, the size of Albuquerque is more than 188 square miles.

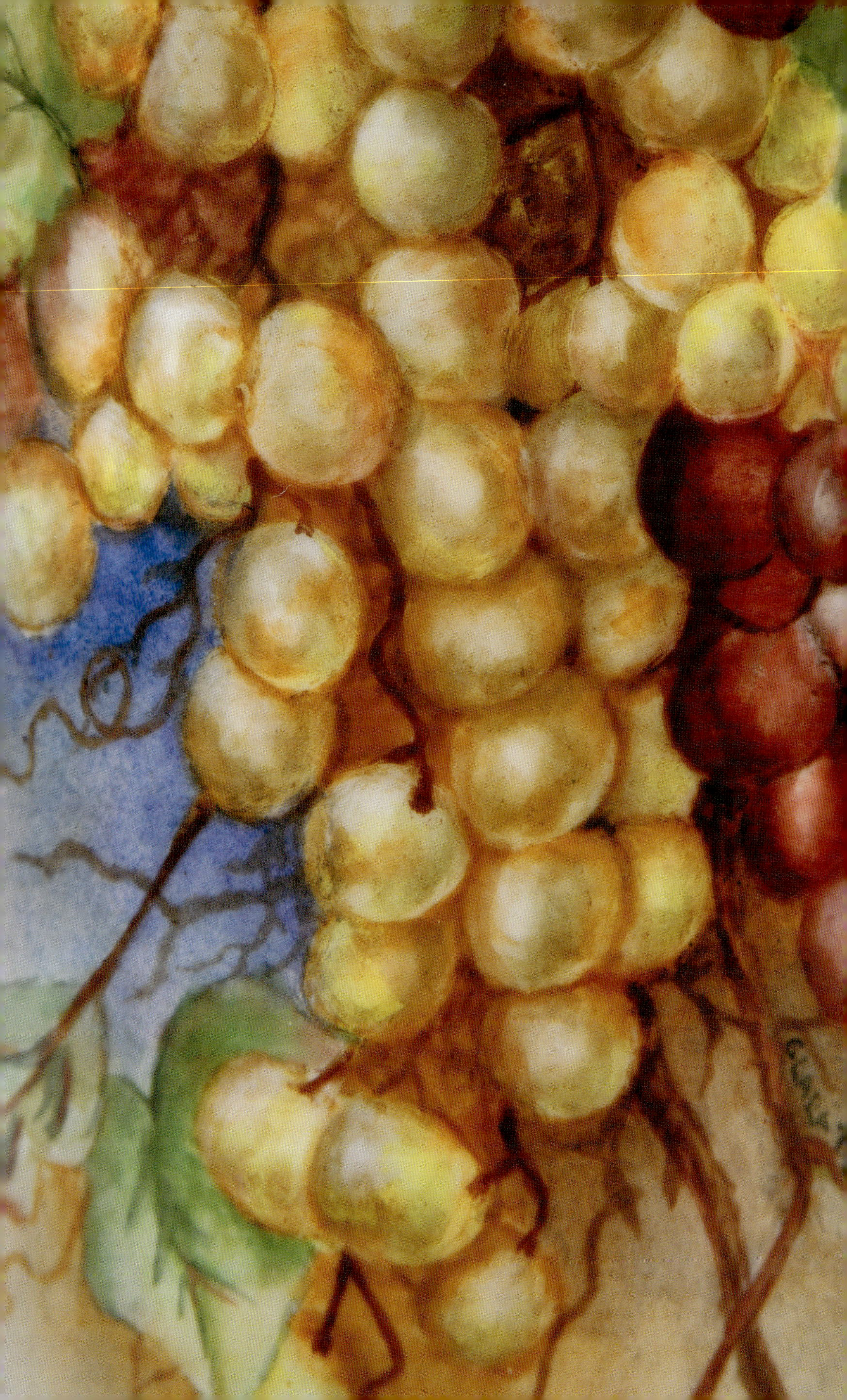

Albuquerque Communities

Our neighborhoods reflect the history and spirit of our city. As we grew from small town to major metropolis, residents formed neighborhoods marked by distinct geographical, cultural, and social differences. Three events, in particular, have shaped where we live: our founding in 1706, the arrival of the railroad in 1880, and population growth after World War II. Each brought new families, greatly increasing our diversity.

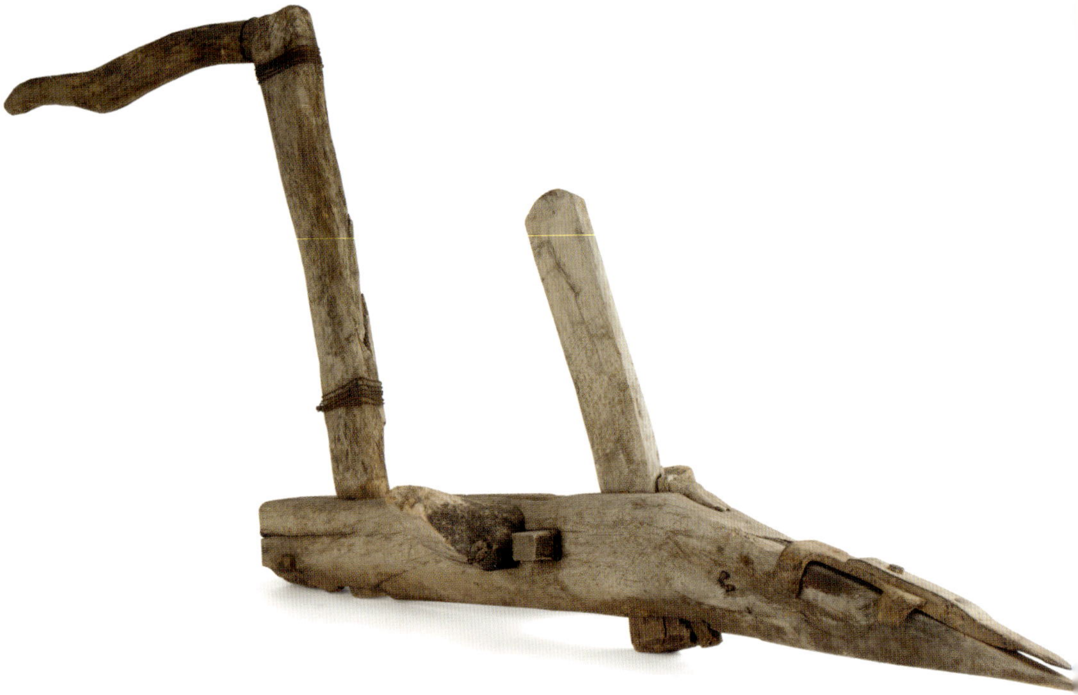

PLATE 21
Hispanic New Mexican or Mexican
Arado/Scratch plow, ca. 1850
Wood, iron
30 × 64 × 19 1/2 in.
Museum purchase
PC1981.64.11

The richest agricultural land in New Mexico lies in the central Rio Grande valley. As early as 1630, small ranchos (farms) were established alongside the Rio Grande to take advantage of the dependable water supply and fertile bottomland. One of these farms was El Paraje de las Huertas, Place of the Orchards, founded about 1632 by Diego de Trujillo southeast of what became Old Town Plaza.

Except for ox-drawn wooden plows (*arados*), all the farming implements in use were hand tools, requiring farmers to spend long hours in the fields. Many early plows did not even have iron plowshares attached.

PLATE 22
Hispanic New Mexican, possibly Mexican
Yunque/Anvil, ca. 1850
Iron
16 × 5 1/4 × 5 1/4 in.
Museum purchase, 1979 General Obligation Bonds
PC1982.192.1

Fewer than ten examples of early New Mexican anvils are known to exist. Unlike today's anvils, they were square, with a sharp point that could be driven into the flat top of a wooden stump.

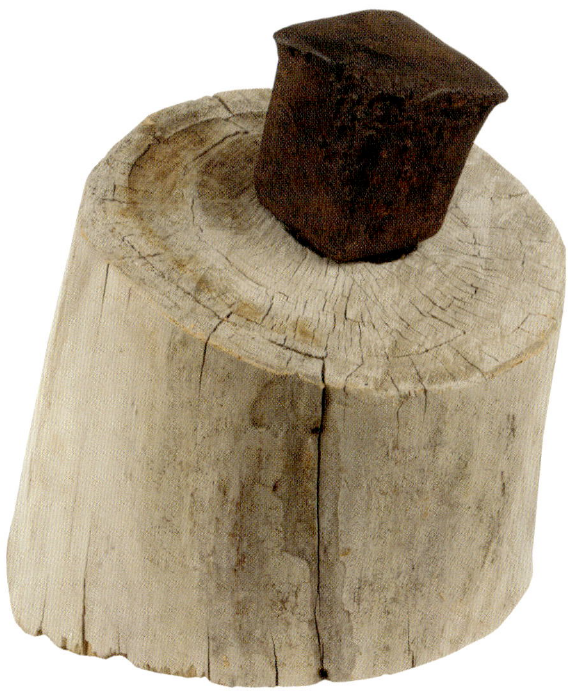

PLATE 23
Hispanic New Mexican
Frazada de boda/Wedding blanket, 1840–60
Churro wool, indigo
90 × 48 in.
Museum purchase, 1983 General Obligation Bonds
PC1984.25.26

Wedding blankets were special gifts woven by the groom's family. They are recognizable by their predominantly white backgrounds and simplified striping. The stripes at each end may have been woven to signify the families of the betrothed or the number of children they hoped to have. The warps on each end are carefully knotted, and the warp ends are tucked into the nearby wefts to make them invisible, unlike most fringed blankets.

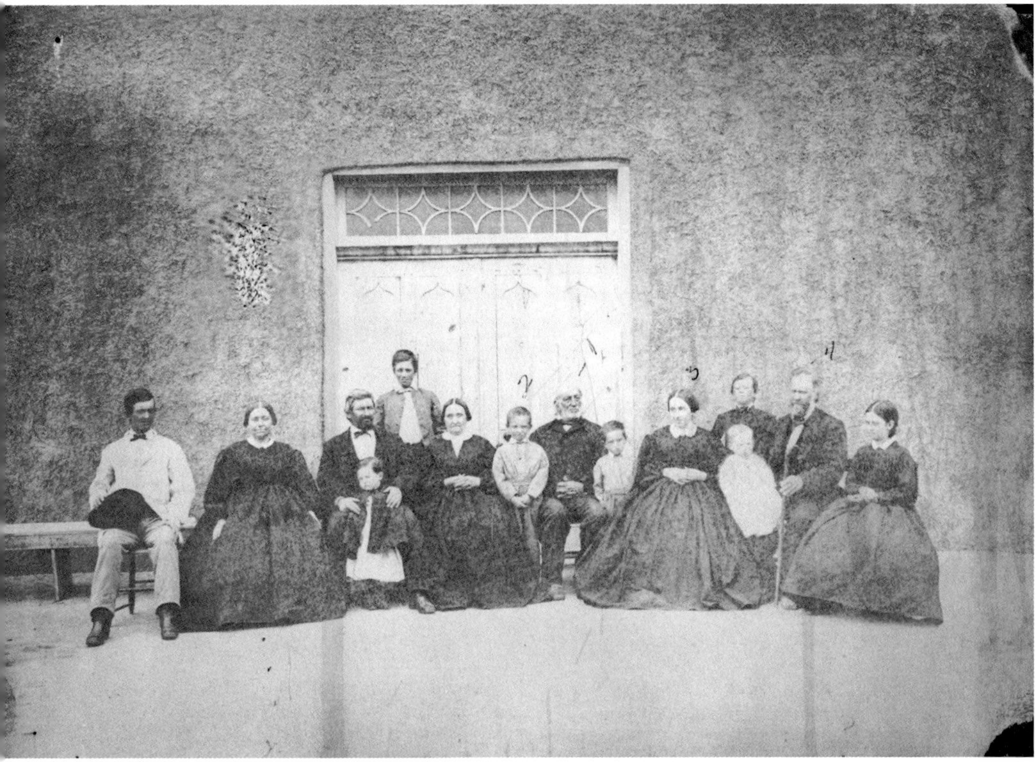

PLATE 24
The Gutiérrez and Hubbell families, ca. 1870
Gift of Cliff Erdel
PA1999.68.68

The Gutiérrez and Hubbell families were individually strong and became even stronger through strategic marriages. The families owned land and vast herds of sheep. James S. and Julianita Hubbell's son, John Lorenzo Hubbell, ran the Hubbell Trading Post in Ganado, Arizona.

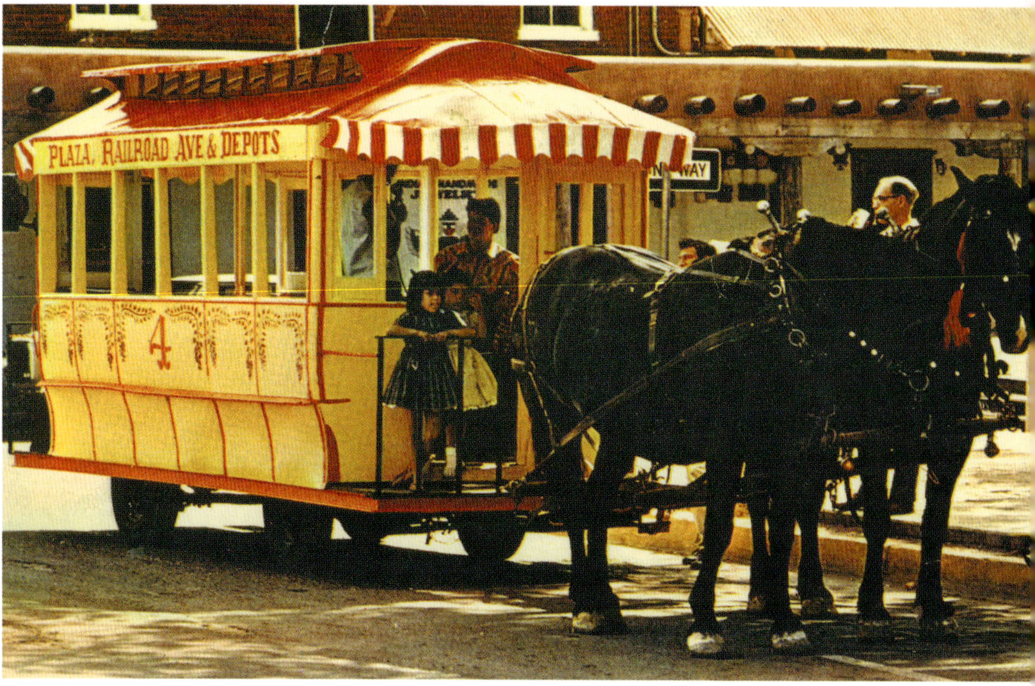

PLATE 25
John Stephenson and Co., Ltd., postcard
Horsecar, 1879
Oak, steel, paint
120 × 252 × 86 in.
Gift of Dr. Edwin H. Robison and Mr. H. B. Wood, Museum purchase
PC1977.135.1

The horsecar served as an important link between Old and New Albuquerque. Two separate routes carried commuters from their homes around Old Town Plaza east along Railroad Avenue (now Central) to First Street and then south on Front Street (now First) to the railroad yards. The Albuquerque Street Railroad Company put three horsecars into service in Albuquerque in 1879; the company ran up to six of them from May 14, 1880, until about 1903 with a fare of ten cents.

This horsecar, discovered being used as a chicken coop in a Corrales backyard in the 1950s, was rescued by the Museum and restored by a team of volunteers using blueprints and photographs.

For years after its restoration, the horsecar made periodic runs around Old Town and the New Mexico State Fair. This Southwest Post Card Company postcard from the 1980s depicts the horsecar ferrying visitors through Old Town Plaza.

PLATE 26
Mail delivery wagon, ca. 1900
Wood, iron, paint
84 × 108 × 72 in.
Museum purchase
PC1975.65.162

By the turn of the century, wagons delivered mail to both Old and New Albuquerque. The wagon was pulled by one horse and probably had a coal-fired foot warmer on the floor and a mail-sorting desk up front. Carriers delivered rural mail to just about any container left out for them, but by 1902, residents had to install mailboxes.

The cart was purchased from Albuquerque attorney and ski enthusiast Robert Nordhaus, who helped found the Sandia Peak Ski Area and the Sandia Peak Tramway. Nordhaus was an avid collector of New Mexico artifacts. The mail cart may have been exhibited in a small transportation museum operated at Sandia Peak in the 1960s.

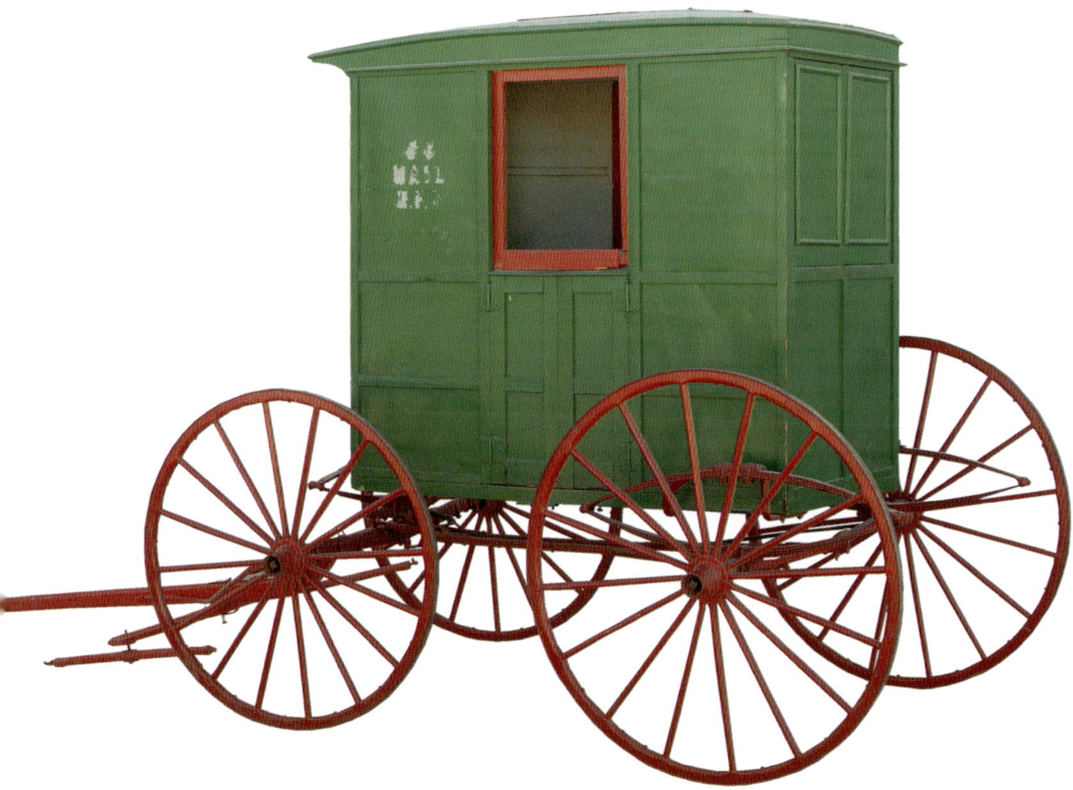

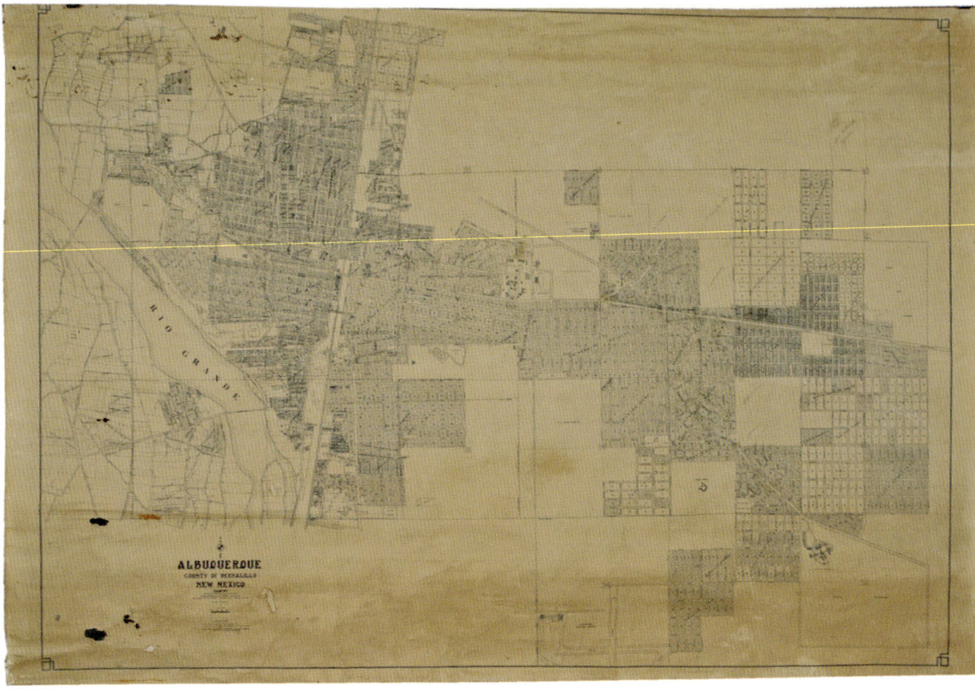

PLATE 27
Map of Albuquerque, 1889
Heliotype Printing Co.
Ink, paper
$46 \times 43\frac{5}{16}$ in. (overall)
Gift of Peter Gallagher
PC1975.44.1

By 1890 both Old Town and New Town had grown substantially. New Albuquerque developed on both sides of the railroad line, about a mile and a half east of the Plaza. Many of New Town's earliest wood frame buildings are now gone, but major portions remain in Huning Highland and other neighborhoods along Central Avenue.

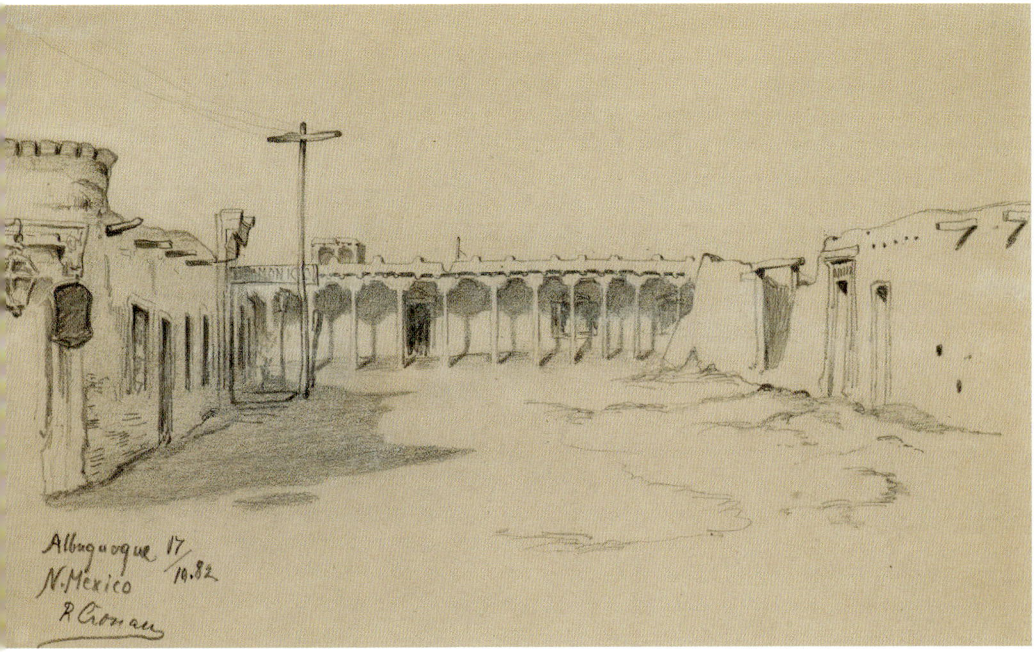

PLATE 28
Rudolf Cronau, German
Sketch, *A Street in Old Albuquerque*, 1882
Graphite, paper
8 × 11 1/2 in.
Museum purchase, 1993 General Obligation Bonds
PC1994.40.1

Artist Rudolf Cronau (1855–1939) sketched a quiet scene at the west end of James Street (now South Plaza) in Old Town that focused on eroding entryways, carinated roof parapets, a gas lamp, and a newly installed telegraph pole. In European prints created from the sketch one year later, the telegraph pole is curiously depicted as the crucified Christ, and the scene is filled with resting workers and laden burros.

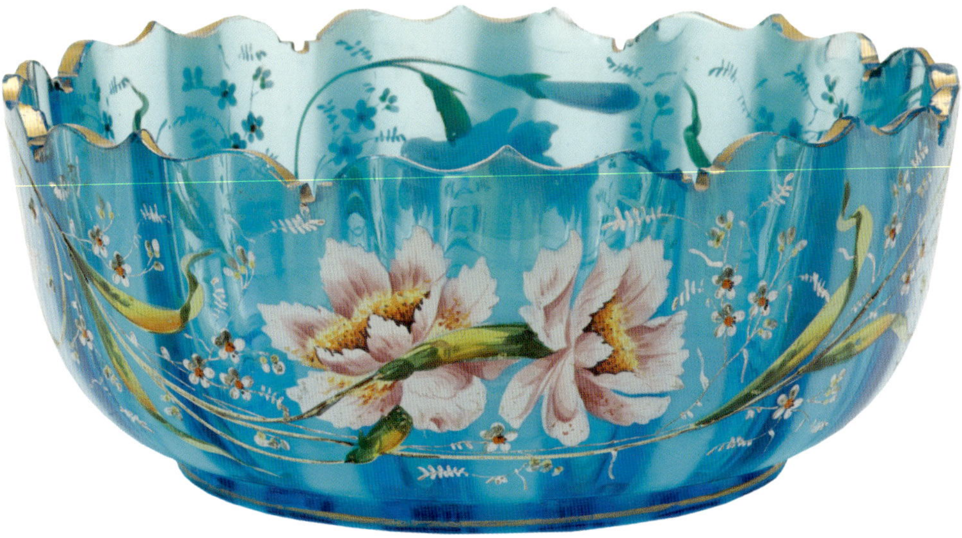

PLATE 29
Bowl, nineteenth century
Glass, paint
3 13/16 × 9 3/8 in.
Gift of the Don Ambrosio Armijo Family
via the Albuquerque Historical Society
PC1967.2.41

Ambrosio Armijo (1817–1882) and Candelaria Griego de Armijo (1832–1907) lived in Casa Armijo (now known as Patio Market) at the southeast corner of Old Town Plaza. By the late nineteenth century, most well-to-do Old Town families preferred to decorate their homes with Victorian-era furnishings from the midwestern or eastern United States or Europe.

The Armijos were one of several families who made a living shipping goods on the Chihuahua and Santa Fe Trails but made the transition from overland to railroad shipping in the 1880s. Their lives in Albuquerque bridged the Colonial, Mexican, and US territorial periods. Their property was deeded to the Albuquerque Museum Foundation in the 2000s.

PLATE 30

Candelaria Griego de Armijo, 1854–60

Ambrotype

6 3/4 × 9 1/4 × 3/4 in.

Gift of the John B. Colligan Family

PA2005.29.25

Candelaria Griego de Armijo is believed to be the earliest known image of an Old Town resident. Ambrosio and Candelaria Griego Armijo are buried in Albuquerque's Mount Cavalry Cemetery.

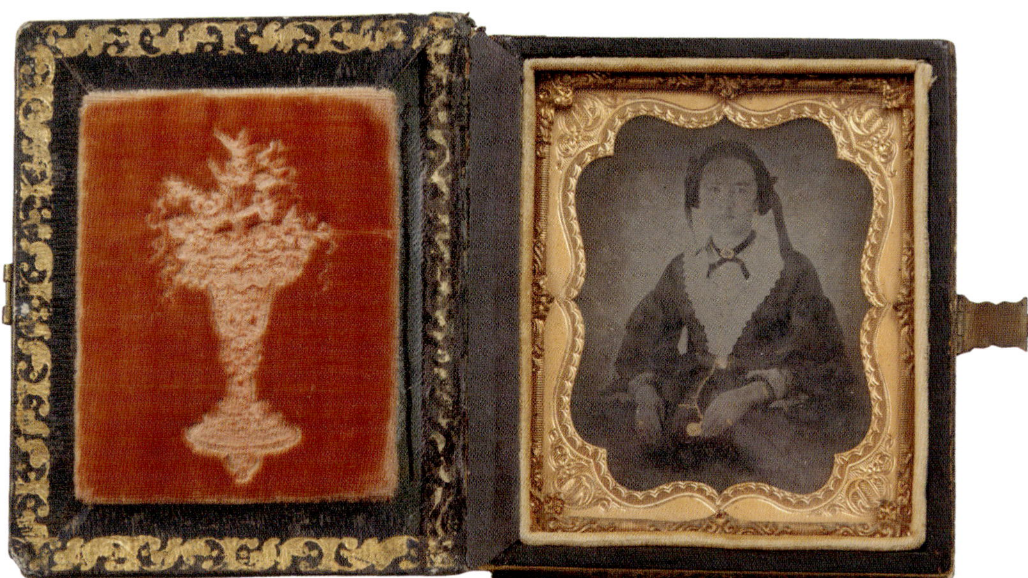

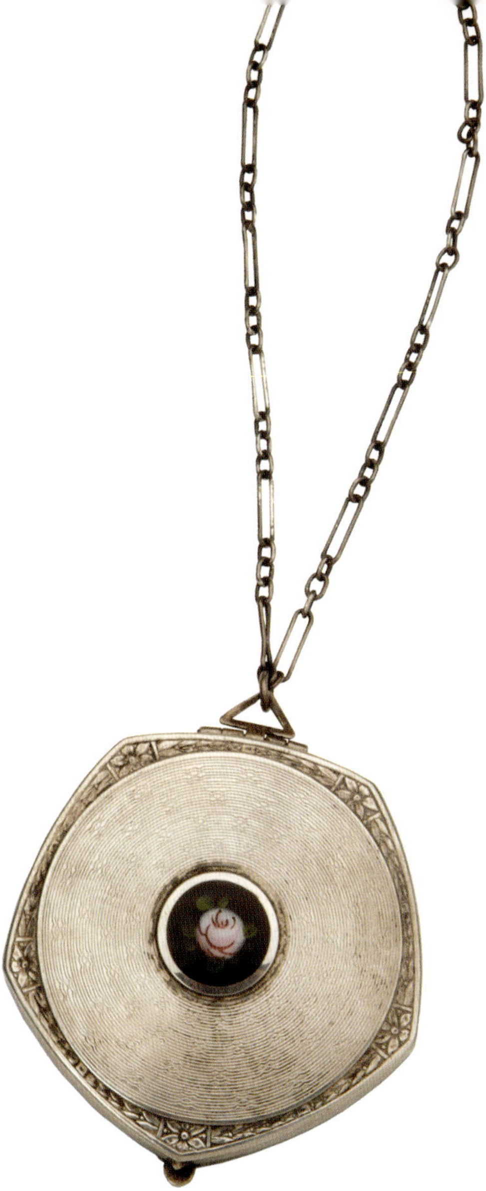

PLATE 31

Compact, ca. 1917

Sterling silver, enamel

$7\,^{1}/_{4} \times 2\,^{1}/_{8} \times {}^{3}/_{8}$ in. (closed)

Gift of Grace Borradaile Buchanan, Don Ambrosio Armijo Family, via the Albuquerque Historical Society

PC1967.2.9

Ambrosio and Candelaria Griego de Armijo's granddaughter, Rebecca Borradaile Colligan, owned this beautiful compact with a small pink rose on a blue enameled background, on a small double chain.

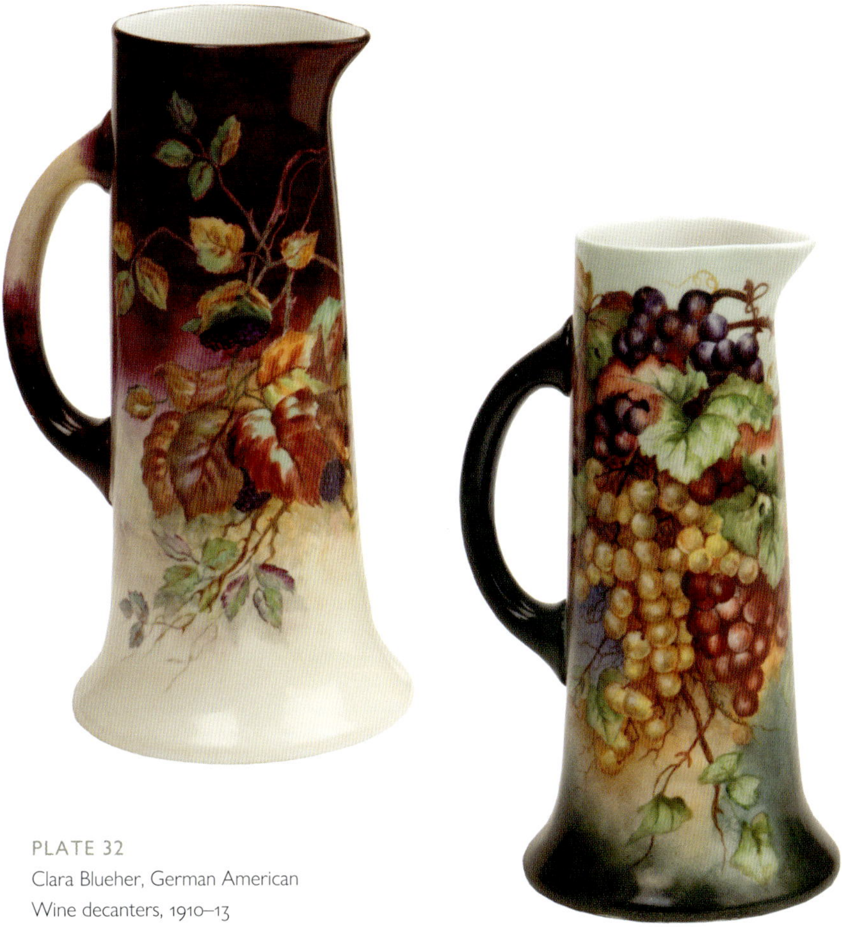

PLATE 32
Clara Blueher, German American
Wine decanters, 1910–13
French earthenware, glaze, paint
11 × 6 1/4 × 5 1/2 in. and 11 × 6 1/4 × 5 1/2 in.
Gift of Jerry L. Gates in memory of Clara Blueher
PC2013.33.1&2

Old Town resident Clara Blueher painted these wine decanters for her father, Herman Blueher, a farmer who raised tobacco on the land where the Museum and Tiguex Park are located today. The Blueher home is located on the northeast edge of Old Town Plaza. Clara Blueher became friendly with Clyde Tingley's wife, Carrie, who also painted pottery and glass.

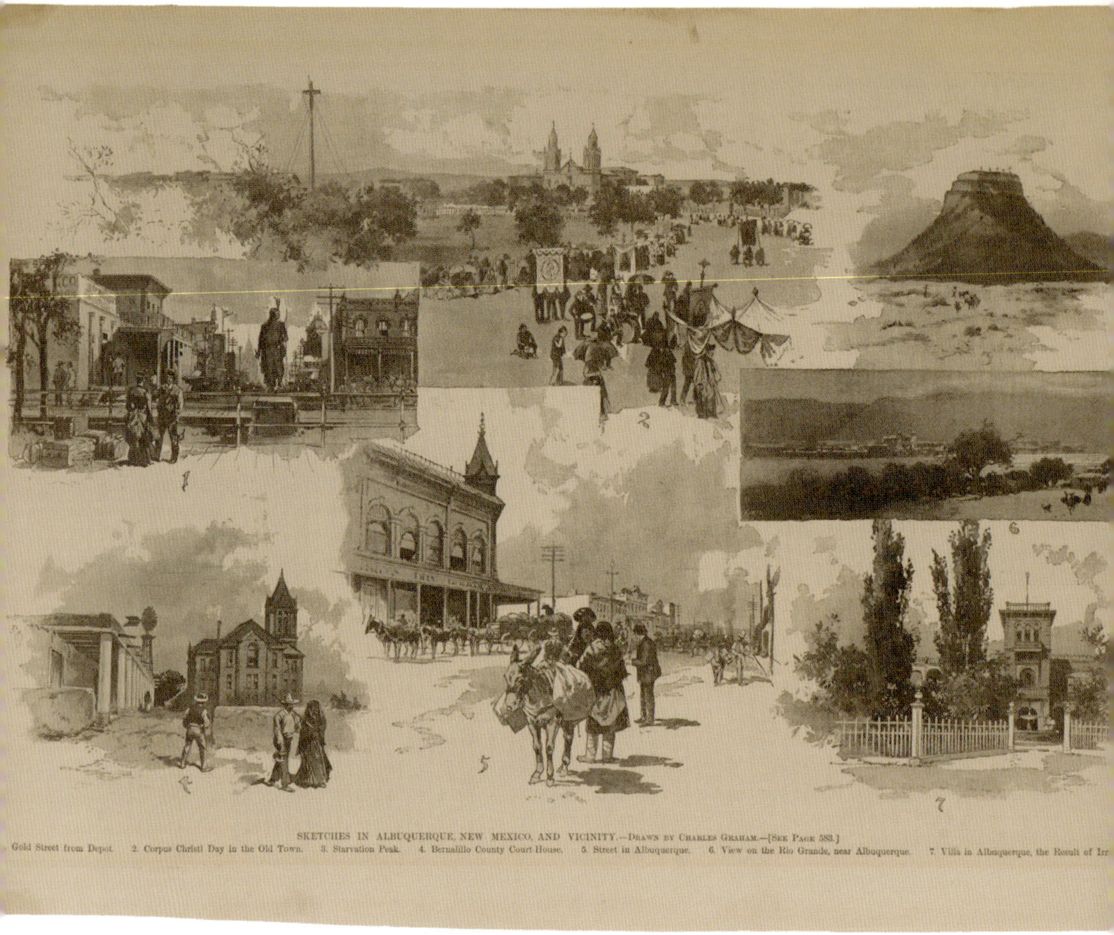

PLATE 33
Charles Graham for *Harper's Magazine*
Sketches in Albuquerque, New Mexico, 1891
Engraving; ink, paper
11 × 16 in.
Gift of Mrs. Jayne P. Lund
PC1980.141.1

By the 1890s, many of New Albuquerque's earliest wood frame buildings were being destroyed by fire. City founders enacted an ordinance requiring that new construction be made of fireproof materials. They took action to clean up the town, enacting legislation to keep the streets and ditches clear and to eliminate gambling and prostitution.

PLATE 34

Pauly Jail Company, Missouri
Bernalillo County Jail cells, 1885
Iron, paint
144 × 144 × 144 in.
Gift of the Albuquerque Police Department
PC1975.35.1

After the railroad arrived, Albuquerque became New Mexico's largest town. Lawlessness ruled; even the first sheriff, Milt Yarberry, was hanged for murder.

The Bernalillo County Jail sat on the southeast corner of Railroad (Central) and Main (Rio Grande Boulevard). Its jail cells probably arrived here via the railroad. According to one story, Mexican General José Inés Salazar called it his temporary home until sprung by his lawyer, Elfego Baca, right under the noses of Sheriff Jesus Romero and Undersheriff Salvador Armijo.

The jail served as temporary home for drunkards, murderers, and rascals until 1925. For at least forty years it sat, painted in three colors, in a city lot near the jail site until donated to the Museum in 1975.

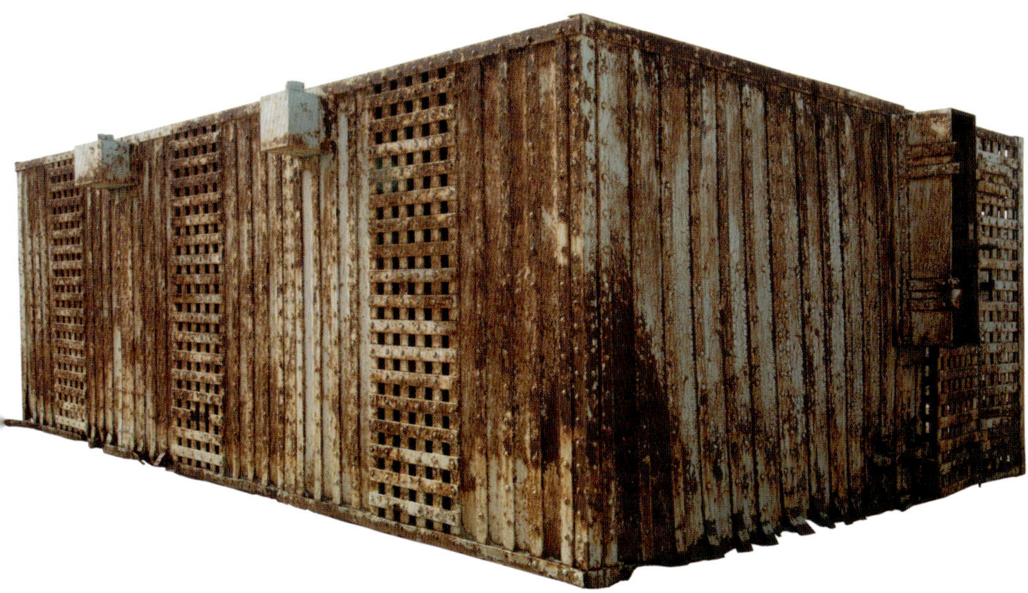

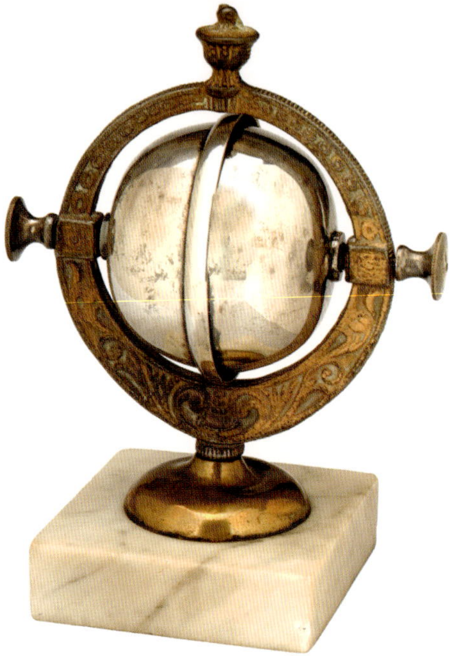

PLATE 35
Alvarado Hotel desk bell, 1890
Marble, silver plate, brass
6 3/4 × 5 × 2 in.
Museum purchase, 1979 General Obligation Bonds
PC1981.91.1

This bell sat on the registration desk in the lobby of Albuquerque's much loved Alvarado Hotel, which opened in 1902. A huge variety of travelers rang this bell: tourists, film and theater celebrities, servicemen, and tubercular patients.

Almost ten years old when the Alvarado was built, the bell may have been brought over from the old Harvey Eating House or the Santa Fe depot; both were demolished to make way for the two-and-a-half-block-long, Mission-style hotel.

PLATE 36 ▶
Medallion from the Economist Building, ca. 1905
Concrete block
63 1/4 × 49 1/16 × 4 1/2 in.
Gift of Keleher Realty Inc.
PC2016.34.1–10

This ten-piece, pressed concrete block medallion (described as terra cotta tile in the National Register Nomination form) graced the facade of the Grant Building, a double-brick, two-story structure in the El Amigo block. It was built around 1905 for the Economist Department Store, operated by David Weinman and his brother-in-law, Seymour J. Lewinson. The company was one of only a few Jewish-owned businesses that survived the transition of commerce from Old Town to New Town. Almost every building in the El Amigo block was demolished by 1985, but Keleher Realty and the Albuquerque Conservation Association sponsored a two-block excavation of the site on the south side of Central Avenue SW, between Second and Third Streets.

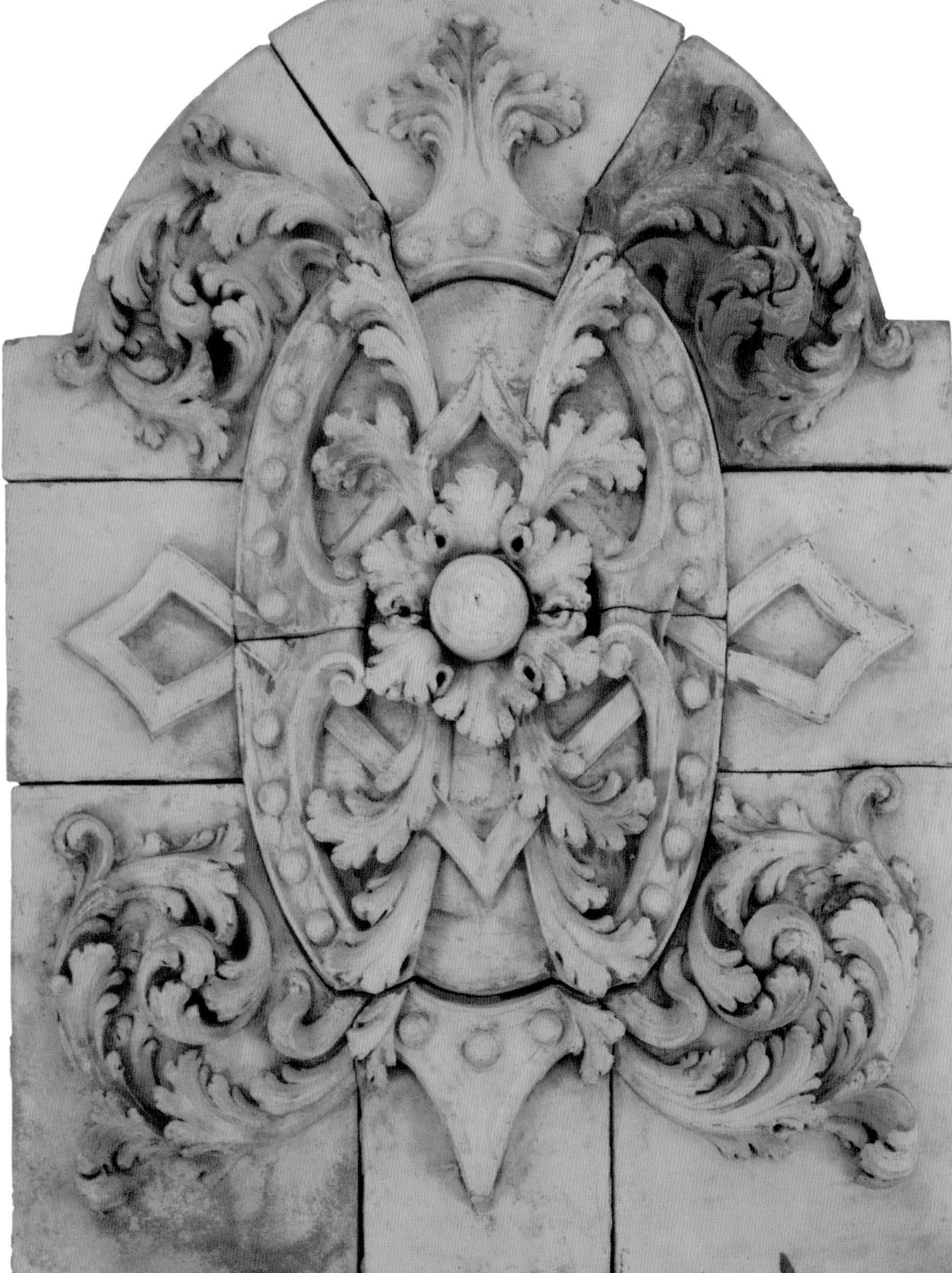

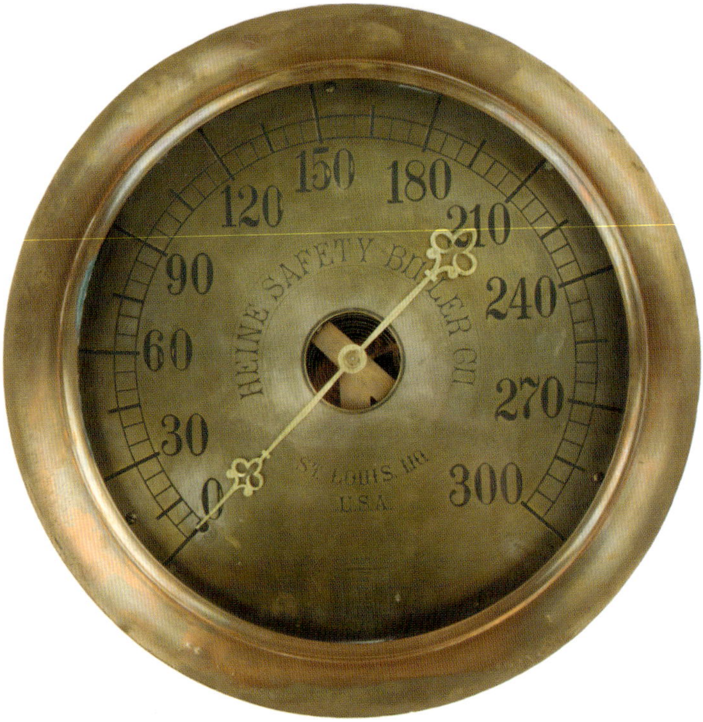

PLATE 37
Steam boiler pressure gauge, 1915
Heine Co., Saint Louis, Missouri
Brass, iron, paint
3 1/4 × 14 3/4 in.
Gift of PNM Forerunners
PC2012.36.3

Residents of New Albuquerque quickly grew impatient with the lack of services in town. By the mid-1880s they demanded electricity, mail service, telephones, and fire protection.

When water boils, it creates steam, heat, and pressure. This gauge was installed on a boiler at Prager Station, an early Albuquerque electrical generating station operated by the Albuquerque Gas and Electric Company, to measure the amount of pressure generated by the boiler. The station was named for Arthur Prager, who became president of the company in 1940.

PLATE 38

Albuquerque High School basketball scoreboard, 1950–71
Painted steel, plastic, copper wires
42 × 59 × 6 1/2 in.
Gift of Bob Myers
PC2012.37.1

Albuquerque International Rattlesnake Museum director Bob Myers found this scoreboard from the Albuquerque High School gymnasium at a local garage sale. The high school was closed for many years, then renovated and converted to loft apartments in the early 2000s.

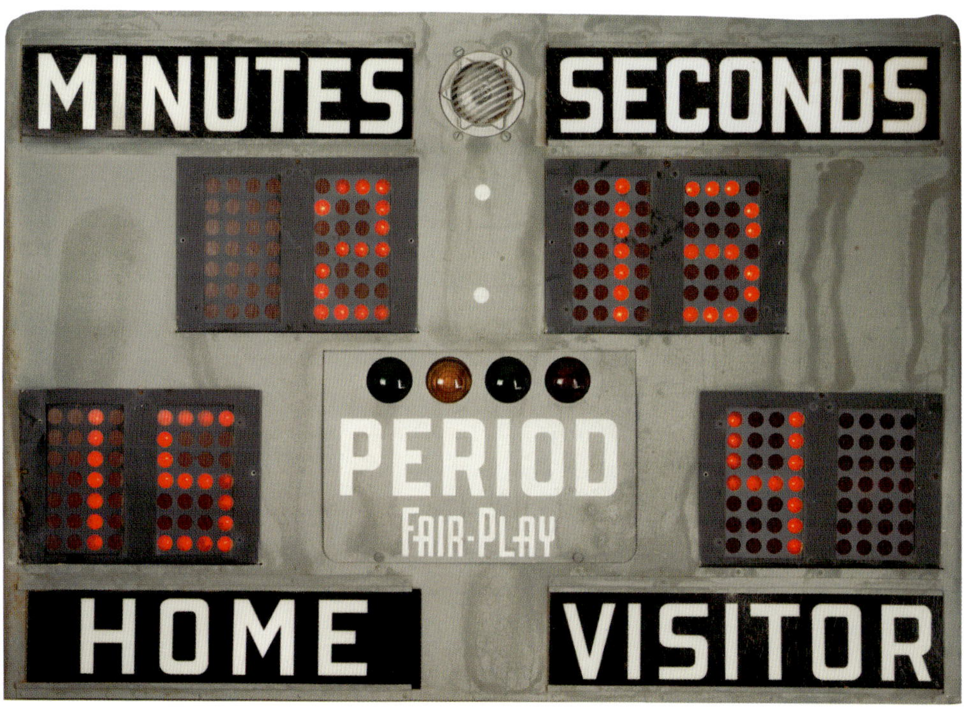

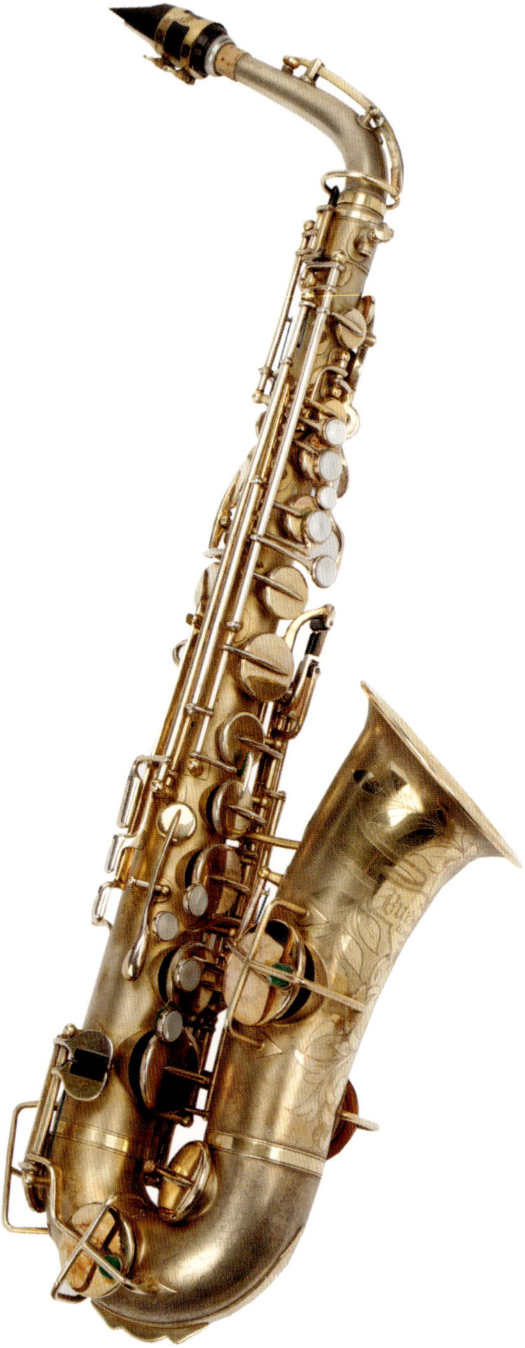

PLATE 39
Bernie May's "Golden Sax," 1926
Buescher Manufacturing Co.
Gold-plated brass
30 1/2 × 8 1/2 × 4 3/4 in.
Gift of Bernie May
PC1990.74.1.a

Bernie May's big band ensemble, The Collegians, played at the University of New Mexico. On weekends they frequented the KiMo and Sunshine Theaters, often accompanying singers Vivian Vance and Ethel Merman. Bernie May also taught music and owned May's Music at 514 Central Avenue SW, where he sold sheet music, instruments, and music lessons. One year, influential drummer Gene Krupa signed autographs there.

The Buescher Manufacturing Company was noted mainly for its saxophones, including limited edition and custom models. They adapted their sound concept to the bigger, bolder style sought out by musicians of the Big Band era.

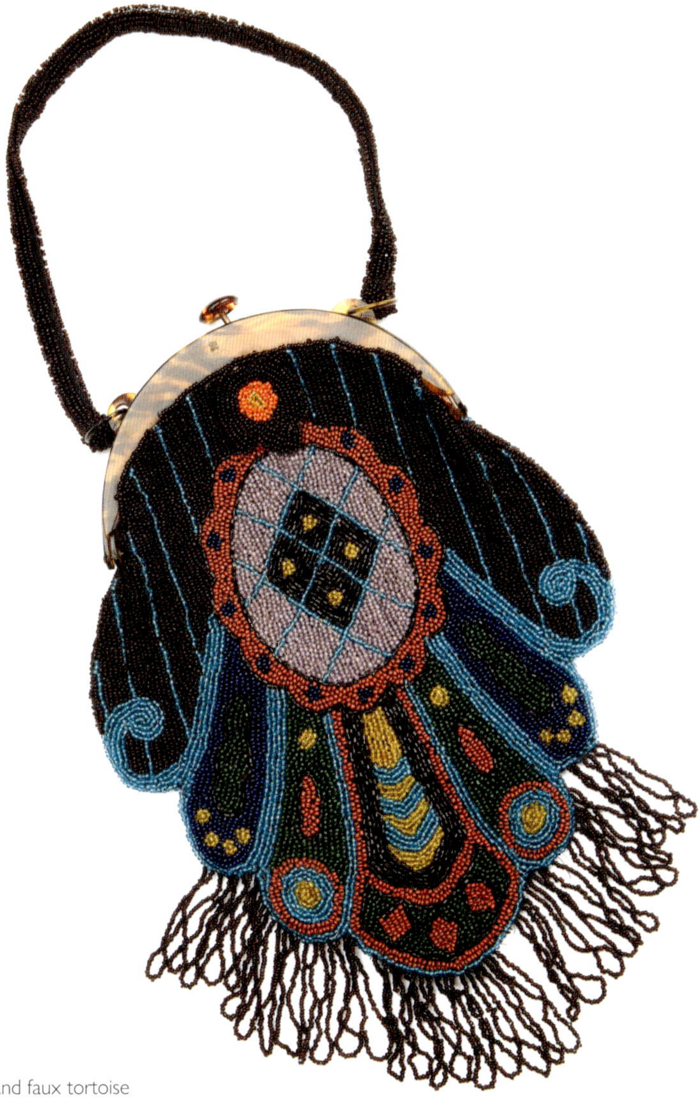

PLATE 40
French
Handbag, 1910–30
Glass beads, silk, brass, and faux tortoise
17 1/2 × 7 1/2 × 1/2 in.
Gift of Sytha Motto
PC1975.41.3

Sytha Motto was a longtime Albuquerque resident, member of the Albuquerque Historical Society, and antique collector. Her beaded French handbag was probably made at the height of the art deco period.

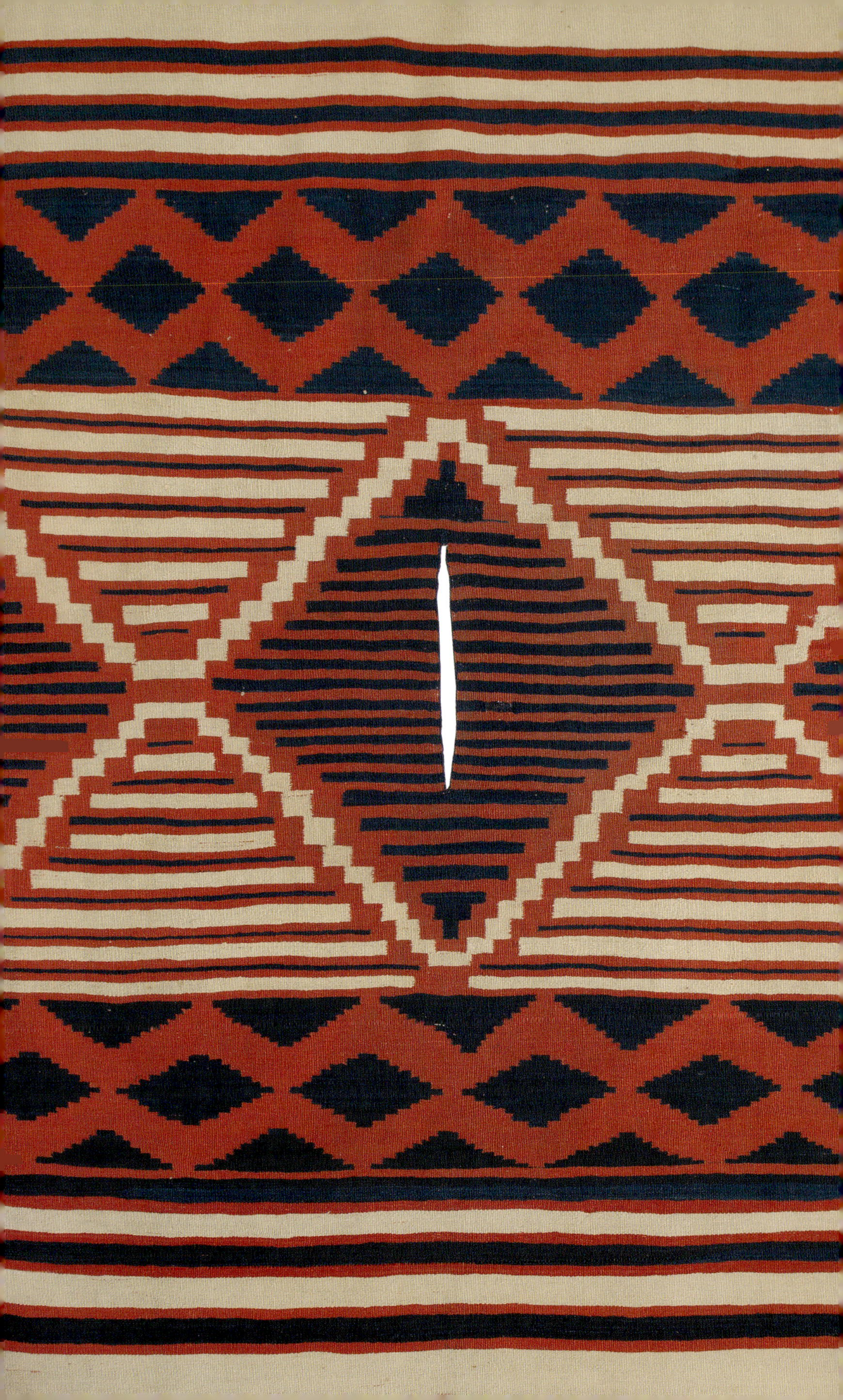

Blending Cultures

What do blue corn and green chile have in common? They reflect our blended cultures. Why are we proud of a cuisine pointedly described as "New Mexican," made up of ingredients mostly found everywhere? Because what we do with the ingredients makes them special.

We exercise our freedom to worship, publicly and privately, with equal conviction. Religion sustains us during rough times. Our spirituality infuses our art and everyday lives, tying us together no matter our religion.

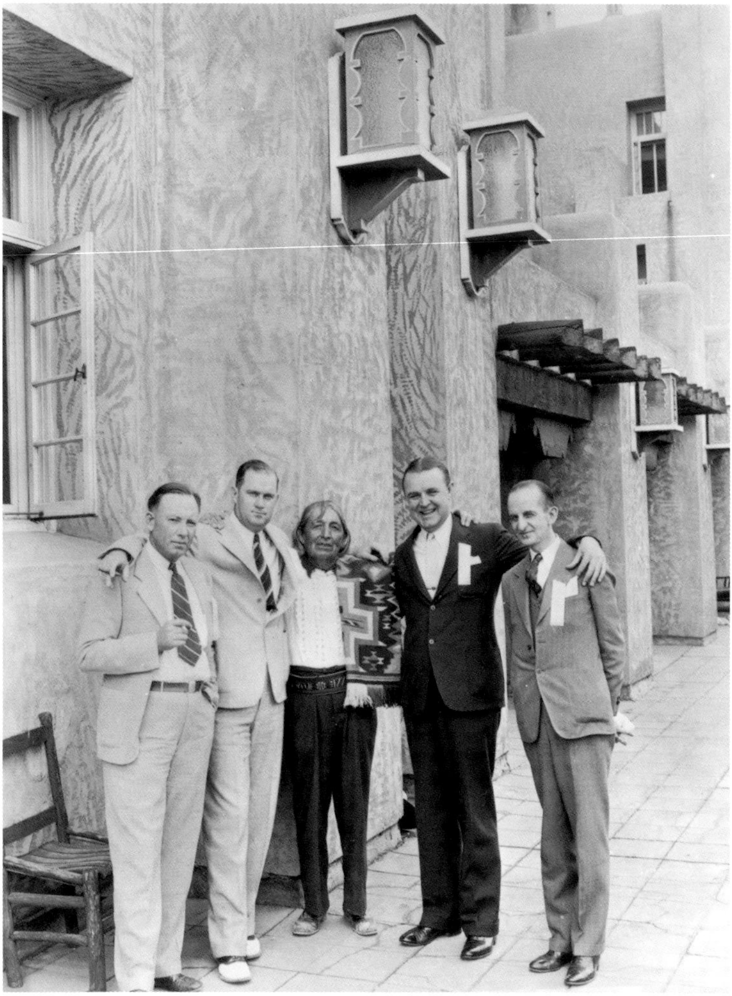

PLATE 41
Pablo Abeita *(center)*, Isleta and colleagues outside the Franciscan Hotel, ca. 1934
The Brooks Collection
Gift of Channell Graham
PA1978.151.821

▶
The shapes of the pendant beads in this necklace resemble squash blossoms. The spherical beads, made from two button halves soldered together, are of the style originally used as decorative elements on Spanish Colonial clothing. The central *naja* of Moorish origin, designed to ward off evil or protect horses in battle, was a Spanish-derived ornament used on Hispano-, Plains-, and Navajo-made bridles in the 1800s.
A similar necklace appeared in the early 2000s on TV's *Antiques Roadshow*. Their respective sizes suggest they were made at a time when gigantic necklaces were winning award ribbons at the Gallup Inter-Tribal Indian Ceremonial.

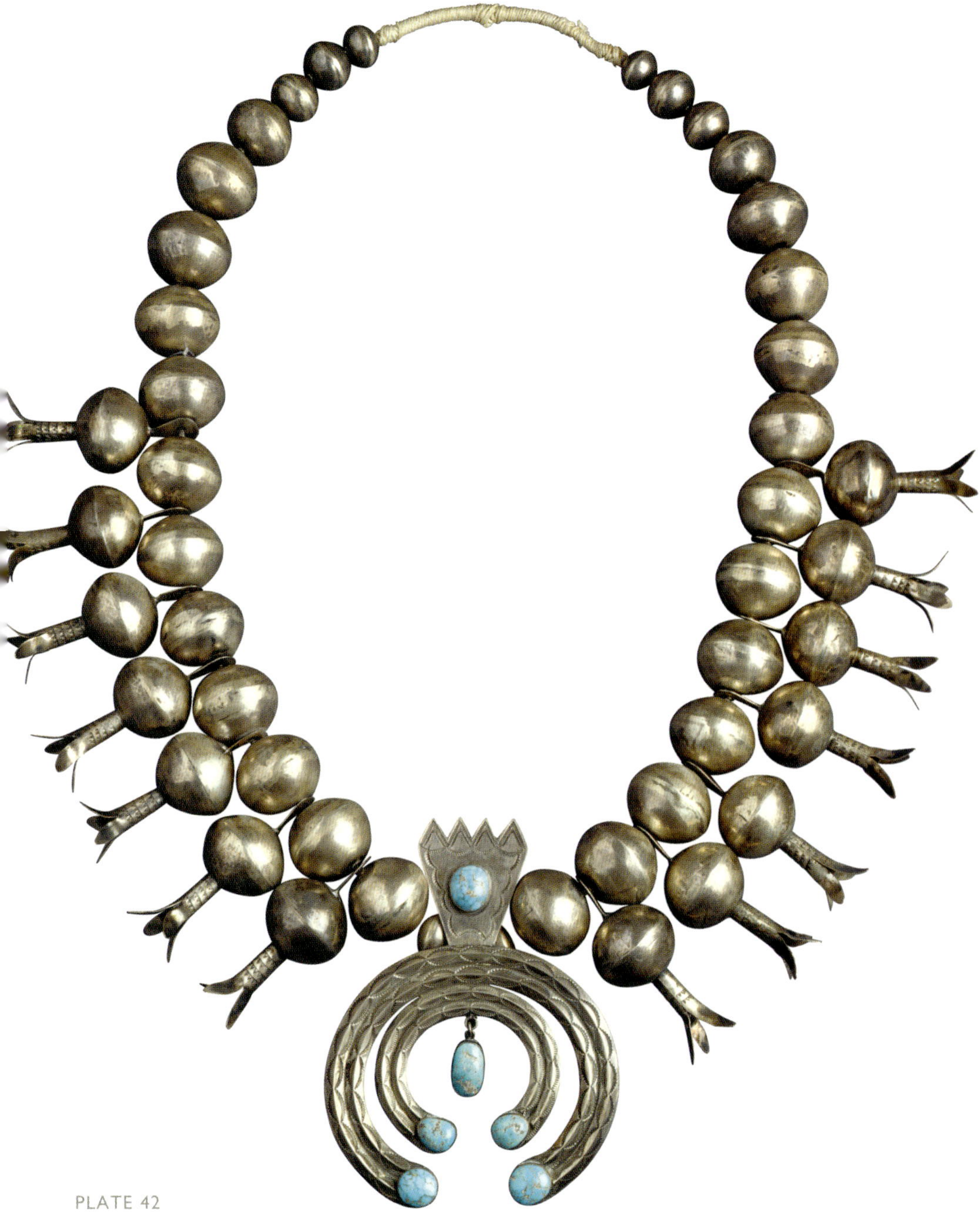

PLATE 42
Navajo
Necklace,
mid-twentieth century
Silver, turquoise
27 × 15 × 1 in.
Gift of D. T. Beals
PC1969.9.1

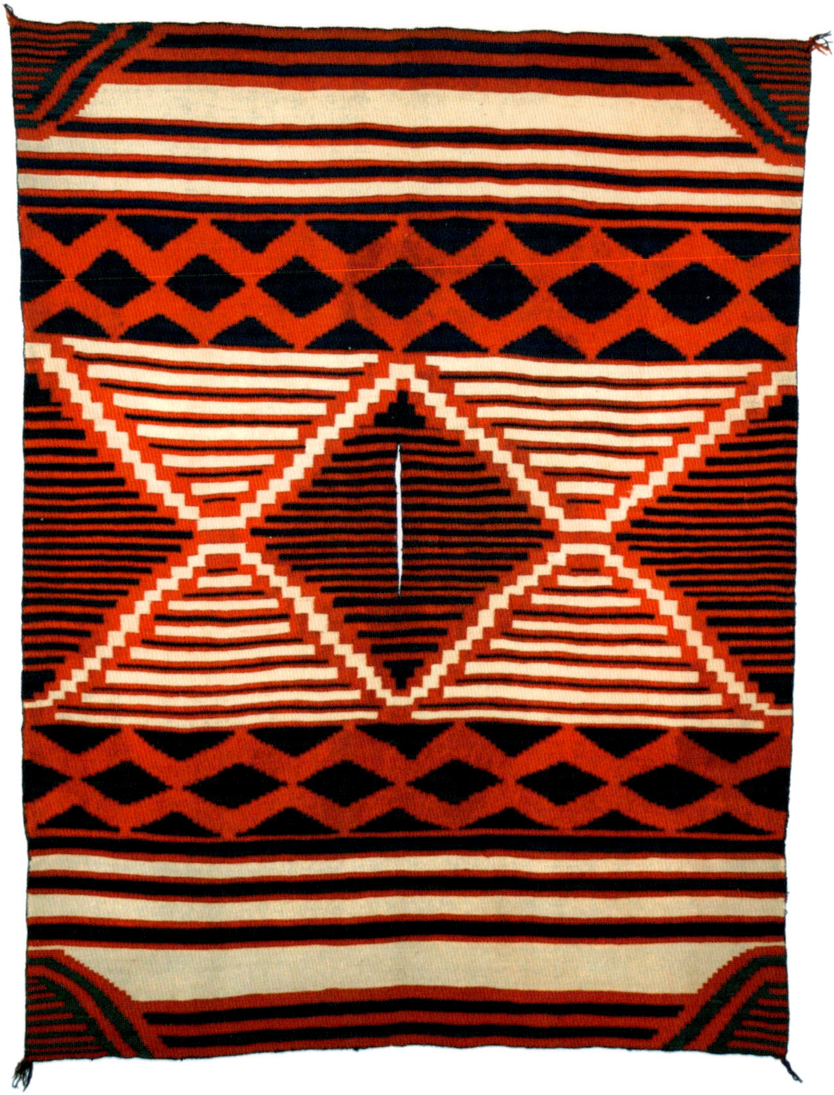

Architectural historian Bainbridge Bunting found this weaving in an abandoned New York City building; today it is considered among the rarest of classic period Navajo blankets. Unlike most, it features a center slit for the head so that the blanket can be worn as a poncho. The design is influenced by serapes made by Tlaxcalan Indians in the region of Saltillo, Mexico, in the early to mid 1800s.

The weaver used commercial cloth dyed with cochineal or lac to create the red designs. She cut the cloth into strips and unraveled the yarns into loose threads. Some weavers believe that sources for the cloth included red and blue officers' clothing. Thin red lines inserted into the beige stripes may be the weaver's hallmark, or they may have been woven in to protect the weaver or wearer.

◀ PLATE 43
Navajo
Poncho-style Navajo serape, ca. 1850
Handspun wool, indigo, raveled
wool cloth, cochineal and/or lac
67 3/8 × 54 in.
Gift of Dr. Bainbridge Bunting
PC1974.111.1

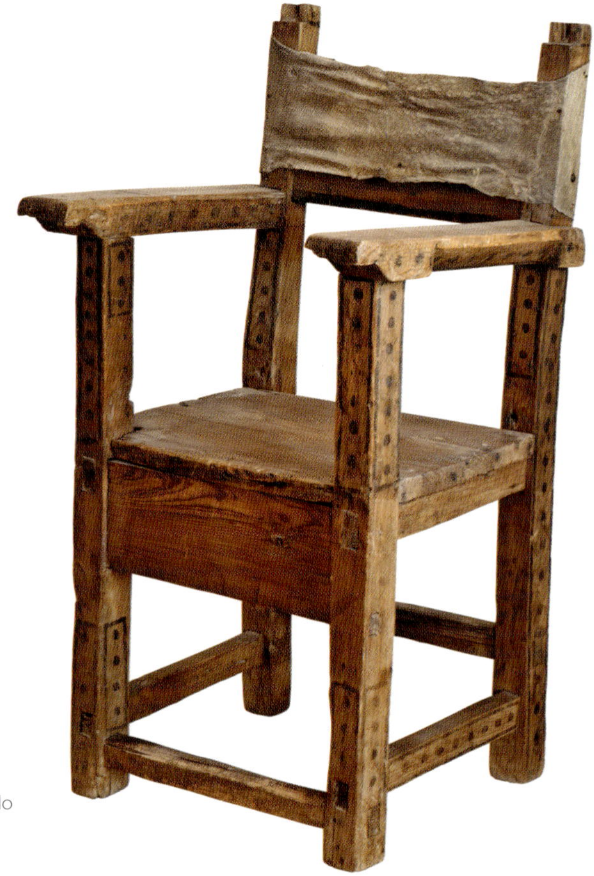

PLATE 44
Hispanic New Mexican or Pecos Pueblo
Silla/Priest's chair, ca. 1740
Wood, leather, paint, iron, bison hide
40 3/4 × 23 1/2 × 21 1/4 in.
Ward Alan and Shirley Jolly Minge Collection
Museum purchase, 1995
General Obligation Bonds
PC1998.20.22

While living at Casa San Ysidro, Dr. Ward Alan Minge acquired this eighteenth-century Hispano priest's chair, rare because it had arms in a period when most chairs did not. Minge believes the chair to have been used in the destroyed mission at the Pueblo of Taos but that it might have been made at Pecos Pueblo. It is a copy of a Spanish chair, with leather backs attached by bronze ornamental nails. The finials, which originally rose high above the arms, are missing.

The dotted motif on the chair's posts can be found on Pecos and other Pueblo pottery and are also similar to dots on carved wooden beams from the convent at Acoma Pueblo's San Estevan Mission (see plate 69).

PLATE 45

Hispanic New Mexican
Banco/Bench, early nineteenth century
Wood, probably pine
27 1/2 x 40 1/2 x 16 1/2 in.
Ward Alan and Shirley Jolly Minge Collection
Museum purchase, 1995 General Obligation Bonds
PC1998.18.17

Collected in Las Trampas in the early 1800s, this early bench is hand adzed, sawed, and planed. The diamond-shaped designs on the front apron and back rail are formed from cut patterns on each plank that, when placed in opposing directions, create a terraced cloud design. The design is similar to one often seen along the edges of a Navajo woman's dress or basket.

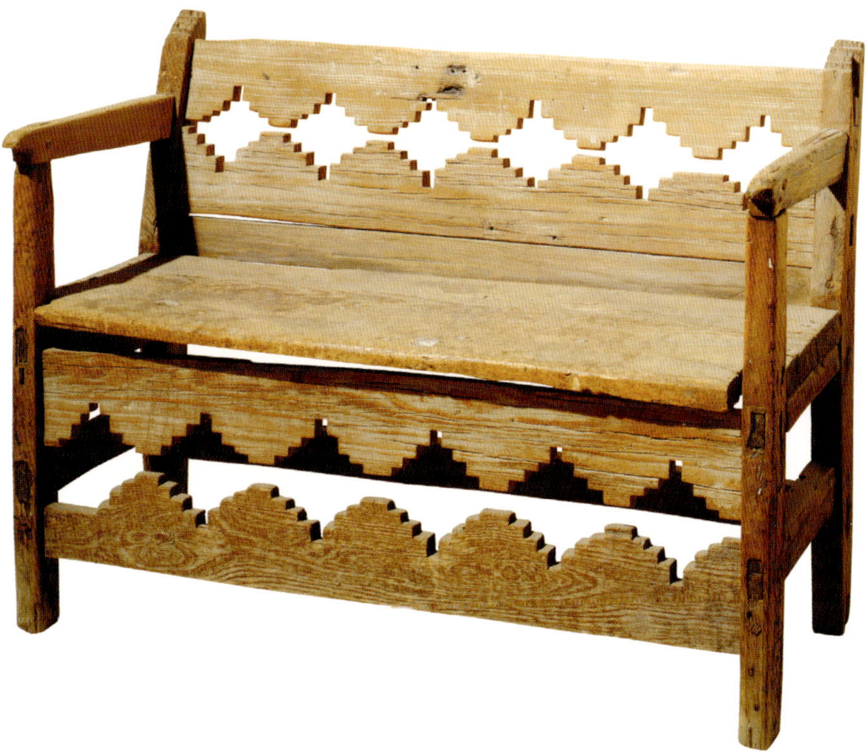

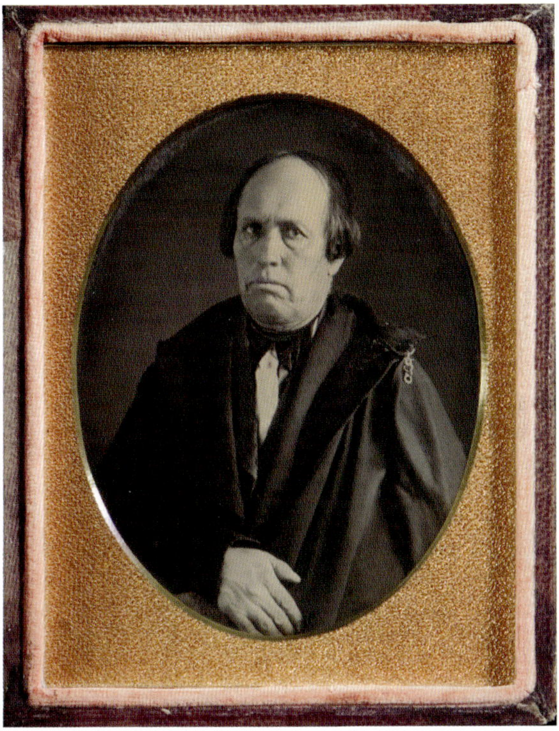

PLATE 46
Padre Antonio José Martínez, ca. 1847
Daguerreotype
Silver/copper, brass, glass, wood, leather, paper, velveteen
4 3/4 × 3 3/4 × 3/4 in.
Ward Alan and Shirley Jolly Minge Collection
Museum purchase, 1995 General Obligation Bonds
PC1998.27.29

Many New Mexicans favored annexation by the United States over becoming part of Texas, which had acted aggressively toward the region since 1841. They included Padre Antonio José Martínez (1793–1867) of Taos, also known for his contentious relationship with Archbishop Jean-Baptiste Lamy, who attempted to suppress religious brotherhood societies and the santero tradition. Dated circa 1847, this daguerreotype of Padre Martínez is believed to be the earliest known photograph of a New Mexican.

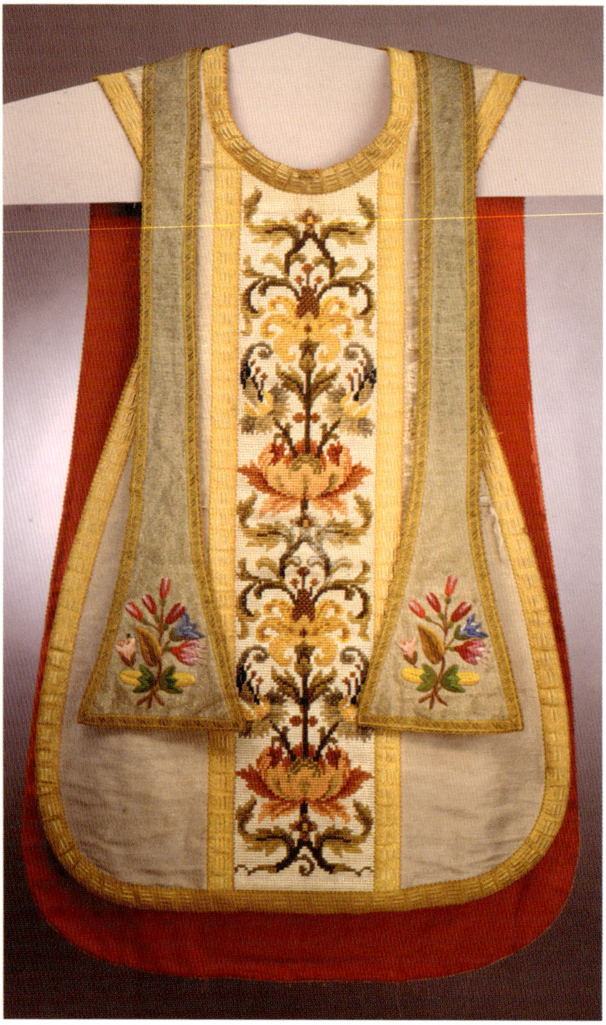

PLATE 47
Mexican
Maniple, 1850
Fabric, metallic thread
31 1/2 x 7 1/2 in.
Museum purchase, 1979
General Obligation Bonds
PC1982.79.1C

Maniples were originally intended to wipe perspiration and to dry the hands so that the Catholic priests' vestments would not be soiled. The mystical meaning of the maniple is to remind the priest of the labor, trials, and troubles of life and the rewards of bearing them in a Christian manner.

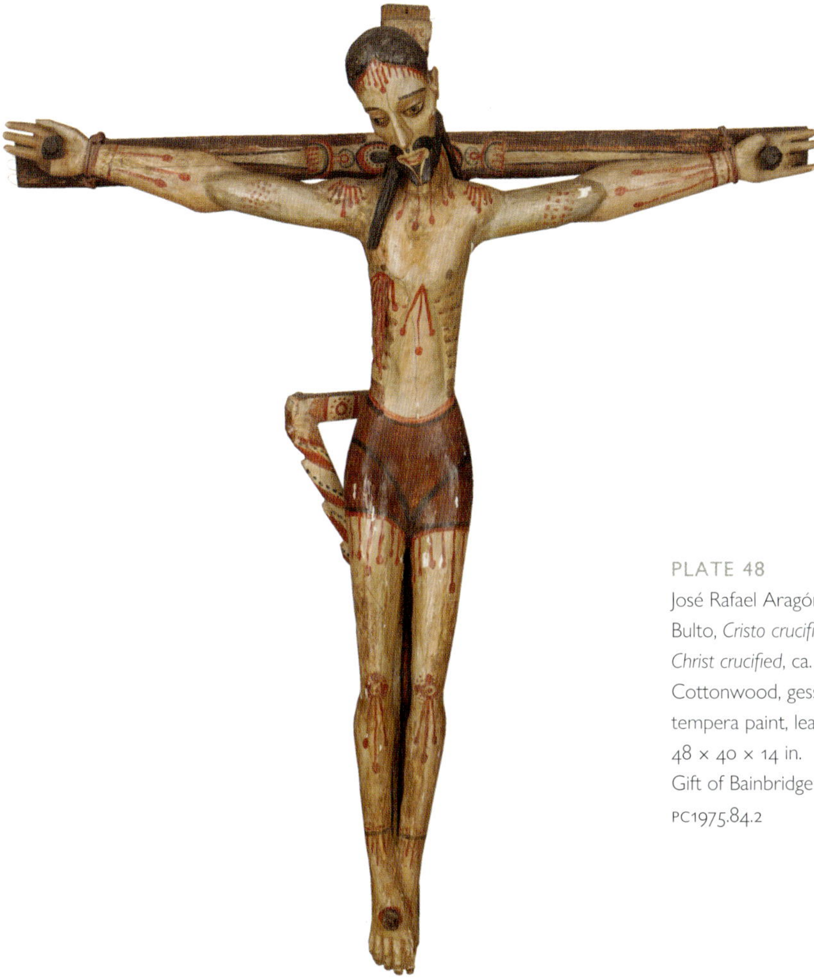

PLATE 48
José Rafael Aragón
Bulto, *Cristo crucificado/ Christ crucified*, ca. 1850
Cottonwood, gesso, tempera paint, leather
48 × 40 × 14 in.
Gift of Bainbridge Bunting
PC1975.84.2

Seventeenth-century Franciscan priests were the first to produce Christian images in New Mexico, painting on animal hides as substitutes for canvas. By the 1770s, santeros were carving and painting the Holy Trinity, Christ, the Madonna, angels, and saints. Santero art thrived until Bishop Lamy assumed religious leadership in 1851, when he sought an end to the tradition. However, many survived in the moradas (Penitente chapter houses) and private chapels.

José Rafael Aragón (b. 1783–90; d. 1862) was a prolific santero active between 1820 and 1862. He lived in the woodworker's district of Santa Fe, near Saint Francis Cathedral. Aragón completed work in many northern New Mexico churches; Bainbridge Bunting collected this very large Christ on the Cross in Rodarte, New Mexico, near Peñasco.

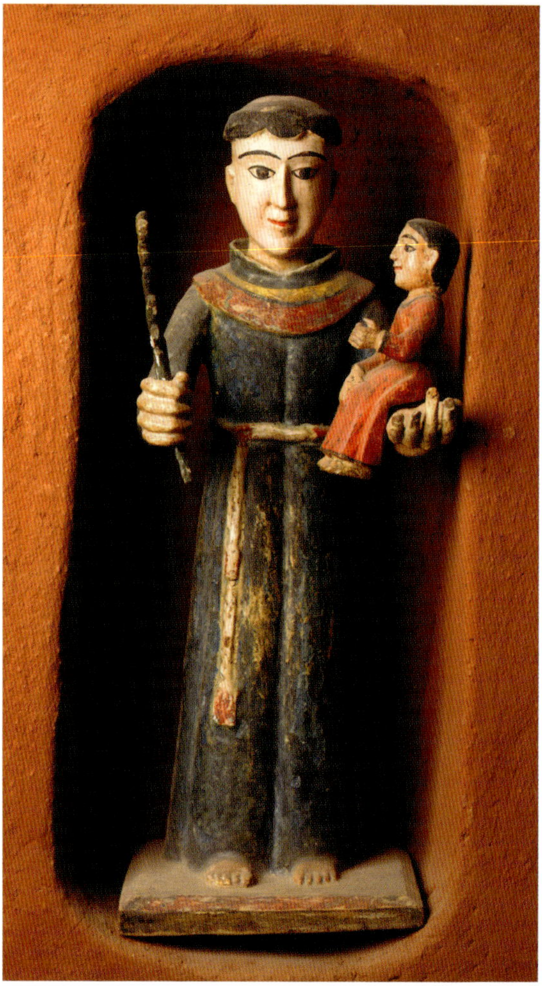

PLATE 49
José Manuel Benavides
(Santo Niño Santero)
Bulto, *San Antonio de Padua/ Saint Anthony of Padua*, ca. 1840
Wood, gesso, paint
21 1/8 × 8 × 5 7/8 in.
Museum purchase, 1979
General Obligation Bonds
PC1981.174.1

Saint Anthony of Padua is one of the most common saints found in New Mexico religious art. Saint Anthony (1195–1232) was born in Lisbon, Portugal, becoming a Franciscan after instruction by Saint Francis. San Antonio is venerated as a finder of lost articles, a patron of animals, and a patron of the home.

One of the finest santeros in New Mexico, the Santo Niño Santero (active 1830–60) is now identified as José Manuel Benavides, a sculptor who worked closely with José Rafael Aragón. Both lived in Santa Cruz de la Cañada near Santa Fe. His attributes include long slender noses, thin lips, slightly protruding almond-shaped eyes, and carefully carved hands and fingers.

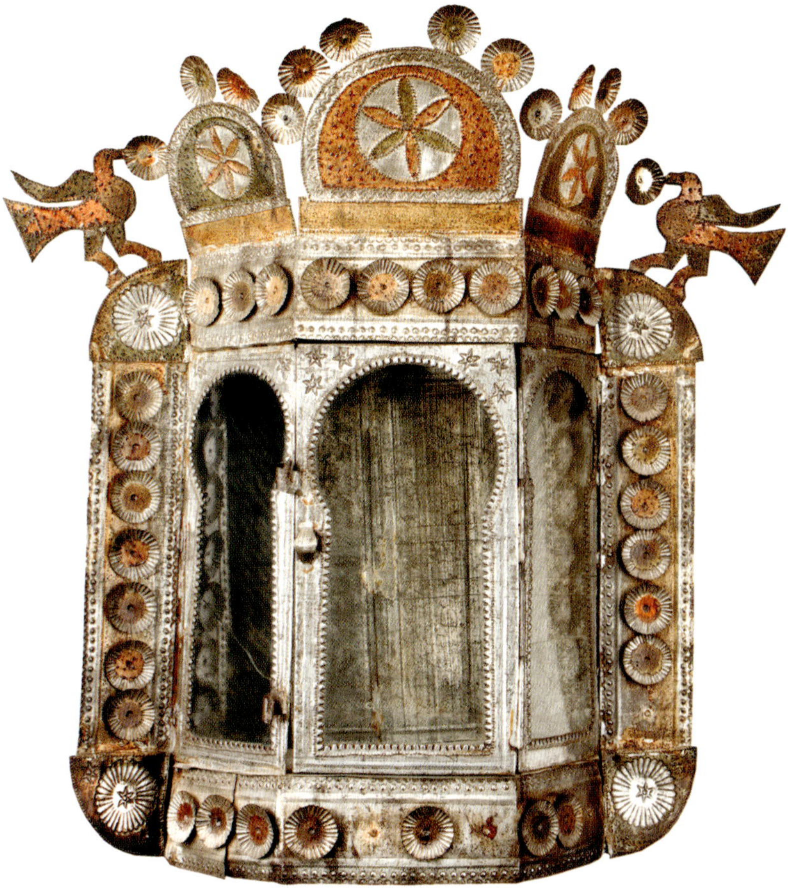

PLATE 50
Higinio V. Gonzales
Nicho/Niche, ca. 1885
Tin, glass, solder, varnish
32 11/16 × 31 7/8 × 13 5/8 in.
Gift of Ward Alan and Shirley Jolly Minge
PC1997.51.10

A tin *nicho* by Higinio V. Gonzales of Santa Fe (1842–1921) is the only corner nicho known to have been made by this prolific tinsmith, poet, author, and educator. It is also the largest known work by the master tin worker. Three-foot panels hold early glass with Moorish-style framing to enclose a bulto of San José, and two decorative Zia-style birds appear as if eating cactus fruit at the upper corners.

Collector Ward Alan Minge acquired the nicho from Tony Garcia, who collected it in Chávez, New Mexico, south of Albuquerque.

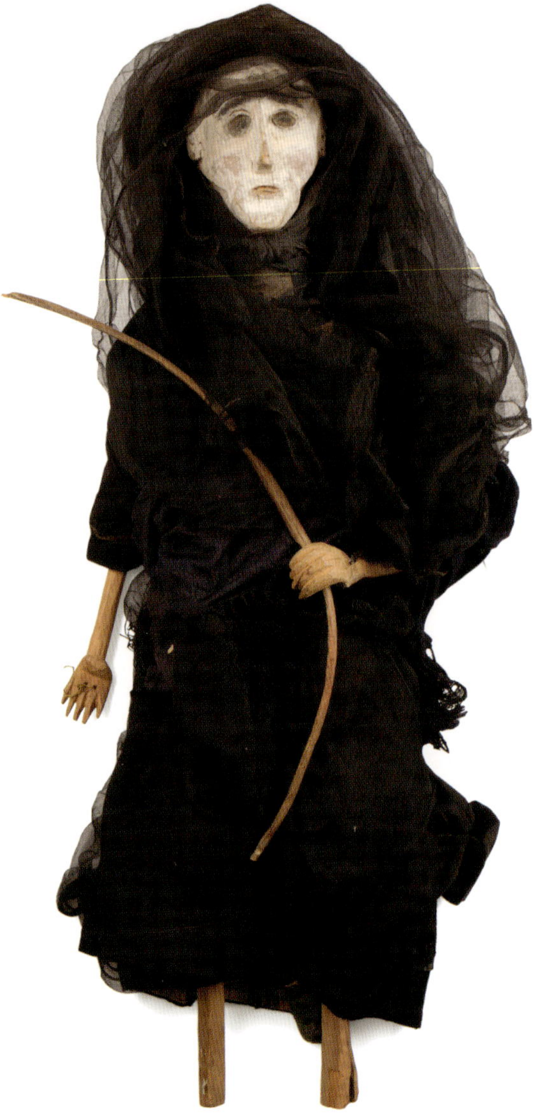

PLATE 51
Hispanic New Mexican
Doña Sebastiana (Santa Muerte), ca. 1850
Cottonwood, gypsum, paint, cotton, netting, lace
43 × 12 × 7 in.
Gift of Bainbridge Bunting
PC1975.84.5

During the nineteenth century in the mountain towns of New Mexico and southern Colorado, Hispano Catholics personified death as a female figure known as Doña Sebastiana. Penitente processions included death carts with life-size effigies, symbolizing not only the agony and death suffered by Jesus Christ on the cross but also the importance of a holy death. Doña Sebastiana is most often depicted as a skeleton with white hair, holding a bow and arrow.

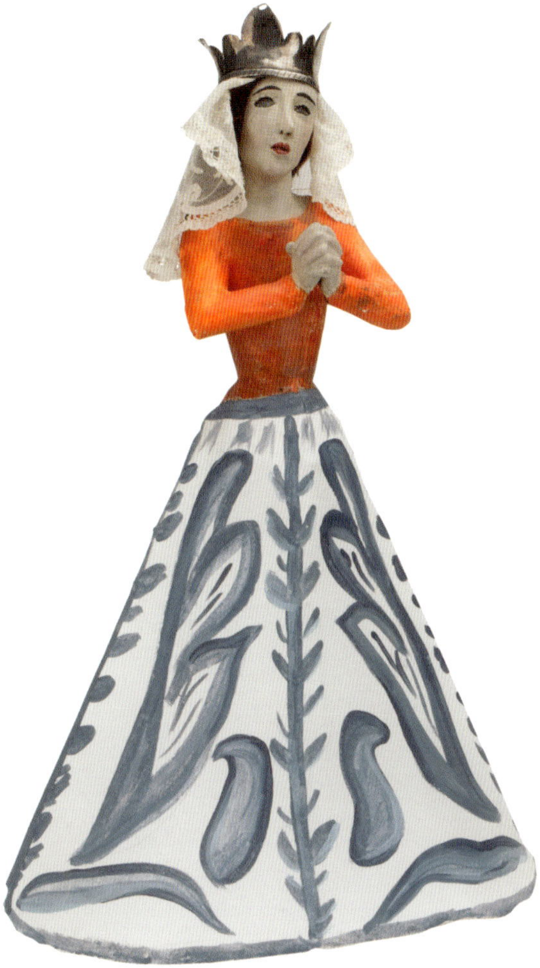

PLATE 52
Attributed to Antonio Molleno,
the School of Antonio Molleno,
or the Truchas Master
Bulto, *Nuestra Señora de los Dolores/*
Our Lady of Sorrows, 1800–45
Wood, gesso, canvas, natural pigments
22 × 14 1/2 × 8 in.
Gift of John Borradaile Colligan
PC1998.54.3.1

Doña Candelaria Griego de Armijo, wife of Don Ambrosio Armijo, received this bulto in 1868 in exchange for a contribution to San Felipe de Neri Church. In preparation for its annual journey from Albuquerque north to Alameda, the bulto would be touched up and newly clothed. The most recent restoration was done in 1989 by Guadalupe Tafoya of Ranchos de Taos, using the manners and materials of the original skirt, which was burned from decades of display near devotional candles.

Nuestra Señora de los Dolores remained for many years in the Armijo residence in Old Town. Upon her death, Mrs. Armijo bequeathed the bulto to Doña Blasa Banks of Albuquerque. In the 1930s, Banks's daughter returned *Nuestra Señora* to the Armijos' daughter, Dolores (Lola) Armijo de Borradaile. She in return gave it to John B. Colligan, who donated it to the Museum.

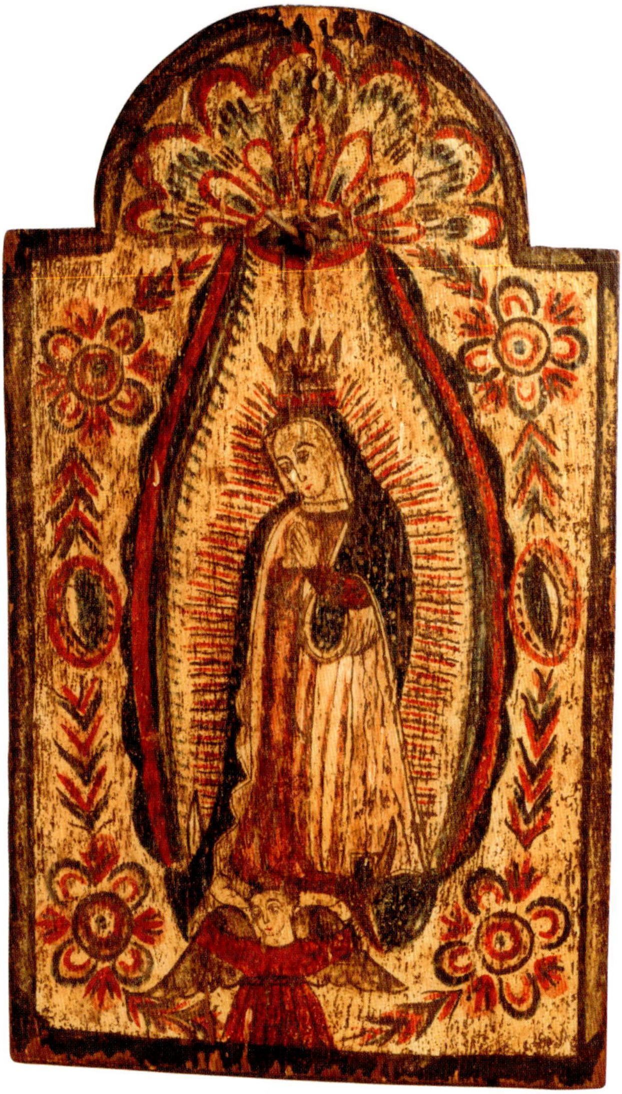

PLATE 53
Arroyo Hondo Santero
Retablo, *Nuestra Señora de Guadalupe, Our Lady of Guadalupe*, ca. 1840
Wood panel, gesso, pigment, leather
18 1/2 × 10 1/2 × 1/2 in.
Museum purchase, 1979
General Obligation Bonds
PC1982.89.1

The village of Arroyo Hondo, north of Taos, flourished in the early 1800s and became an important agricultural community. The Arroyo Hondo Santero (active 1825–40) appears to have been a regional artist who created a major commission for the village's church, Nuestra Señora de los Dolores de Arroyo Hondo.

His santos are usually half-length portraits with decorative lunettes, a linear border, and a palette of blue, white, red, and black. They have elongated bodies, angular faces with pointed chins, heavy-lidded eyes that resemble crescent moons, and long narrow noses that are wide at the base and pointed at the tip. His retablos are hand carved, indicating that he was working in the period just before milled lumber began to appear in 1846.

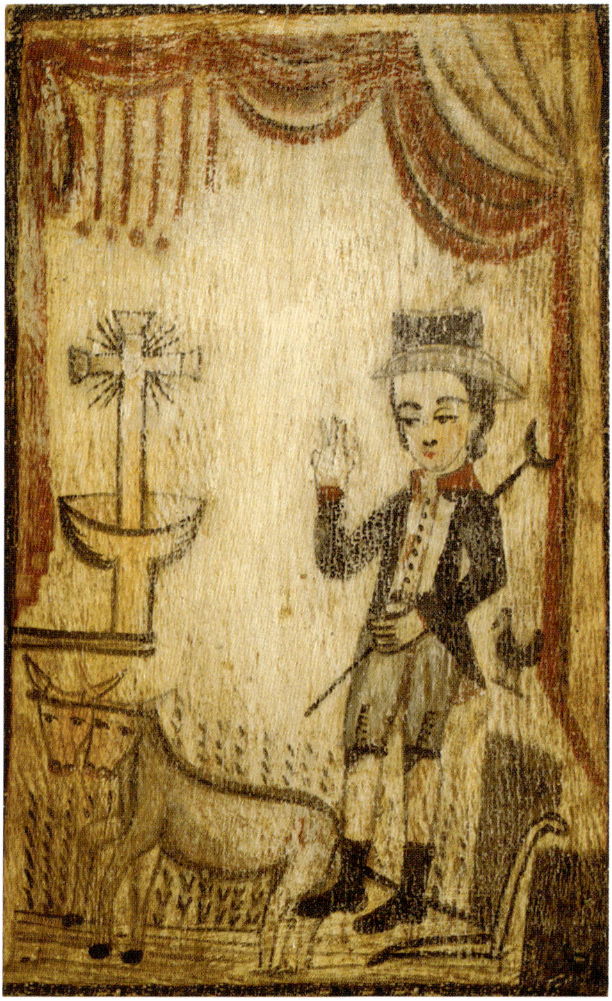

PLATE 54
José Rafael Aragón
Retablo, *San Ysidro Labrador*,
1820–62
Wood, gesso, paint
17 3/4 × 12 1/4 × 1 in.
Ward Alan and Shirley Jolly
Minge Collection
Museum purchase, 1995
General Obligation Bonds

Santero José Rafael Aragón depicts the patron saint of farmers accompanied by a scratch plow pulled by two oxen. San Ysidro Labrador is shown in farmer's clothes and a broad-brimmed hat, carrying a staff. He is often petitioned for rain and is the patron saint of Corrales, a farming community just north of Albuquerque on the west side of the Rio Grande. San Ysidro Labrador is also the patron saint of Casa San Ysidro in Corrales, built by José María Gutiérrez and renovated by Ward Alan and Shirley Jolly Minge.

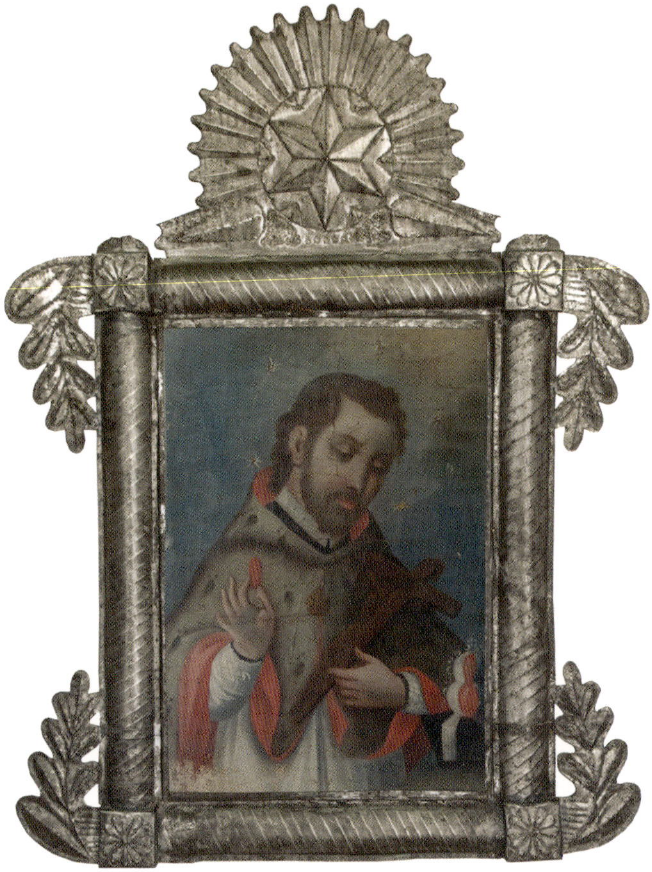

PLATE 55
Higinio V. Gonzales; Mexican
Marco con pintura/Tin frame with painting of San Juan Nepomuceno, 1865–1900 and ca. 1830
Tinplate, solder, oil, canvas
28 1/4 × 21 3/4 in. (overall)
Gift of Ward Alan and Shirley Jolly Minge
PC1997.51.18

Formerly known as the Valencia Red and Green Tinsmith, Higinio V. Gonzales was a soldier, a tinsmith, a musician, an educator, and a poet. Born a citizen of Mexico, Gonzales served in the US Army during the Civil War. By the 1860s he was creating fanciful frames out of tin cans, often adding lunettes, scallops, and bird- or leaf-shaped appendages for added decorative effect.

Many of Gonzales's tin frames held devotional images, such as this Mexican oil-on-canvas painting of San Juan Nepomuceno (ca. 1830). In New Mexico, San Juan Nepomuceno is the patron of secrecy, silence, and the Penitente Brotherhood. He protects against gossip and slander and blesses the irrigation ditches.

PLATE 56
Higinio V. Gonzales
Marco con pintura del santo/Frame with painting of San Ramon Nonato, 1865–1900
Tinplate, solder, watercolor, ink, ruled paper, glass
9 × 7 1/2 × 3/8 in.
Ward Alan and Shirley Jolly Minge Collection
Museum purchase, 1995 General Obligation Bonds
PC1998.19.16

Higinio V. Gonzales painted and titled this image of San Ramón Nonato in his own hand, helping scholar Maurice Dixon attribute works in this style to the talented tinsmith. San Ramon Nonato is the patron saint of midwives; he is petitioned for help in childbirth.

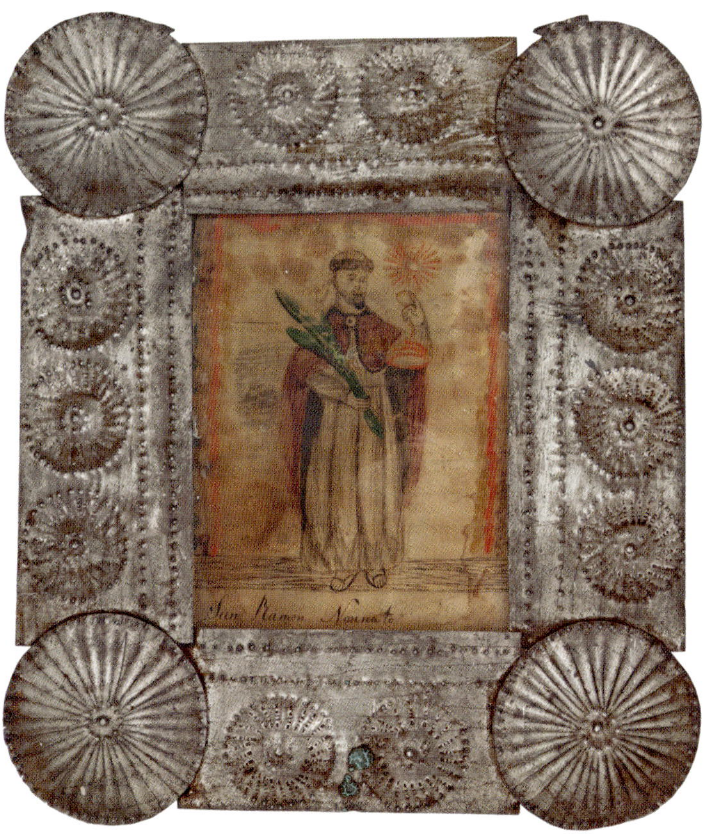

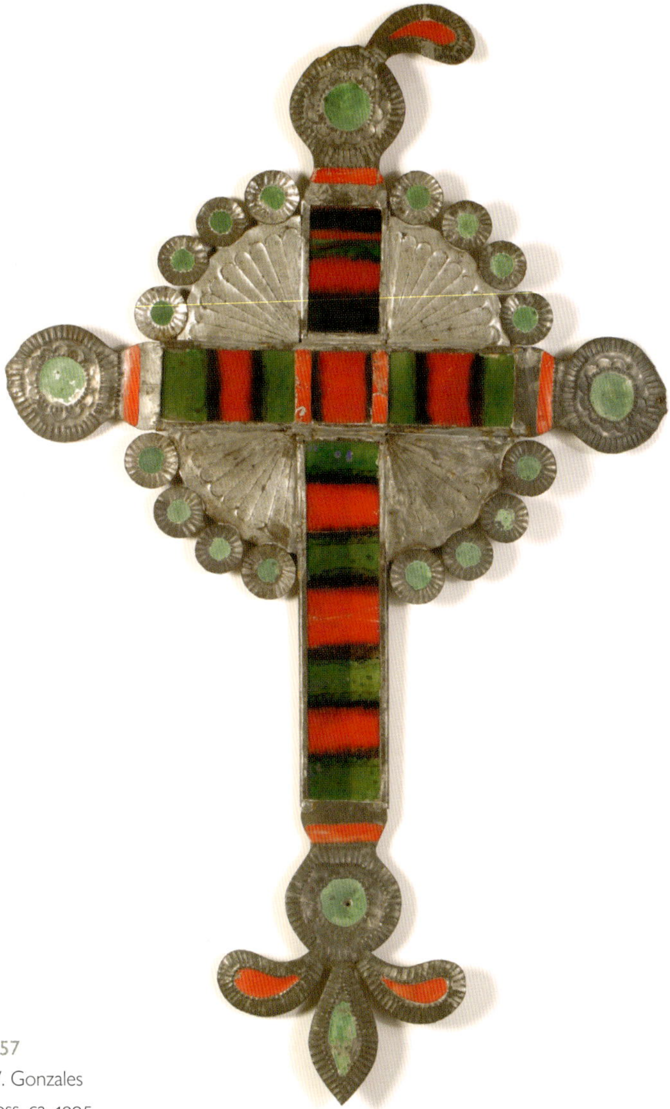

PLATE 57
Higinio V. Gonzales
Cruz/Cross, ca. 1905
Tinplate, solder, paint, glass
30 × 18 1/2 in.
Gift from the Estate of Margarita Baca Córdova
PC2008.50.1

Rafael and Juana García Baca of Belén may have acquired this cross directly from Higinio V. Gonzales around the turn of the century. After their death, the cross passed to their in-law Margarita Baca Córdova, whose son David Cruz Baca owned G&G Fuel in Barelas. His company cut, sold, and bartered firewood in the area of Isleta Pueblo.

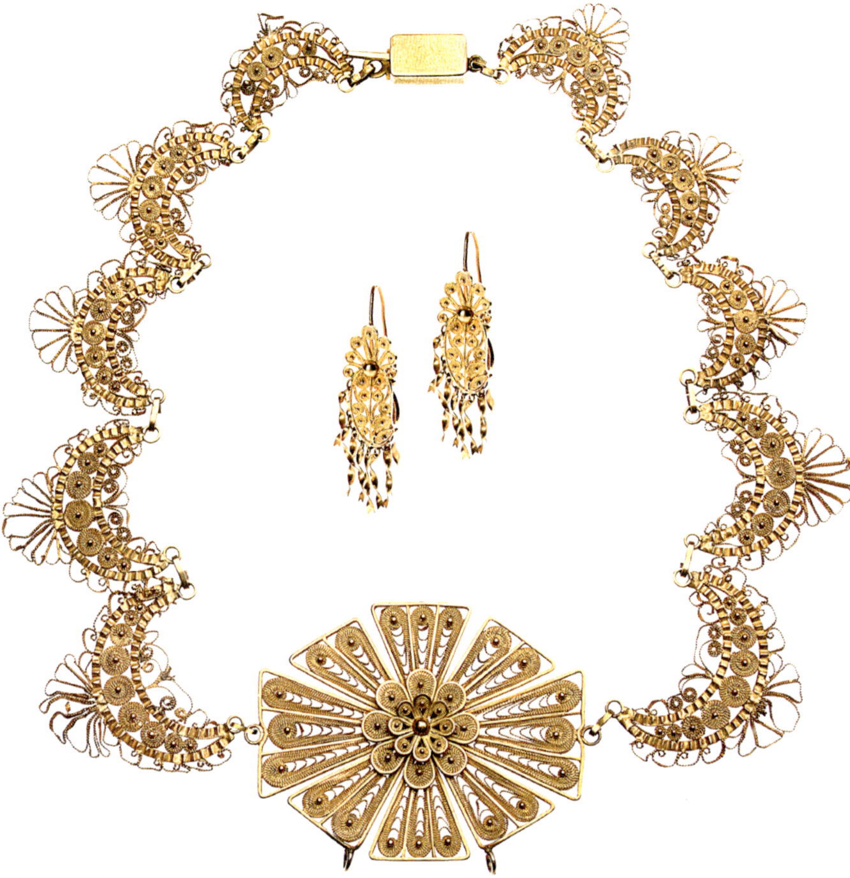

PLATE 58
Antonio Abeitia
Necklace and earrings, 1880s
Filigree, gold wire
3/4 × 2 in. and 15 × 1 3/4 × 1/2 in.
Ward Alan and Shirley Jolly Minge Collection
Museum purchase, 1995 General Obligation Bonds
PC1998.27.50 & 44

Filigree jewelry was first imported into the New World from China and the Philippines by the Spanish-funded Manila galleon trade. Eventually, the art form migrated to Mexico, and from there it became a favored product offered by New Mexican *plateros*—itinerant craftsmen working in silver or gold—who produced the valuable baubles for ladies' dowries. Filigree often appears in eighteenth- and nineteenth-century wills, indicating that the delicate jewelry was passed down through the family. These examples were made by Antonio Abeitia of Abeitia's Jewelers in Socorro.

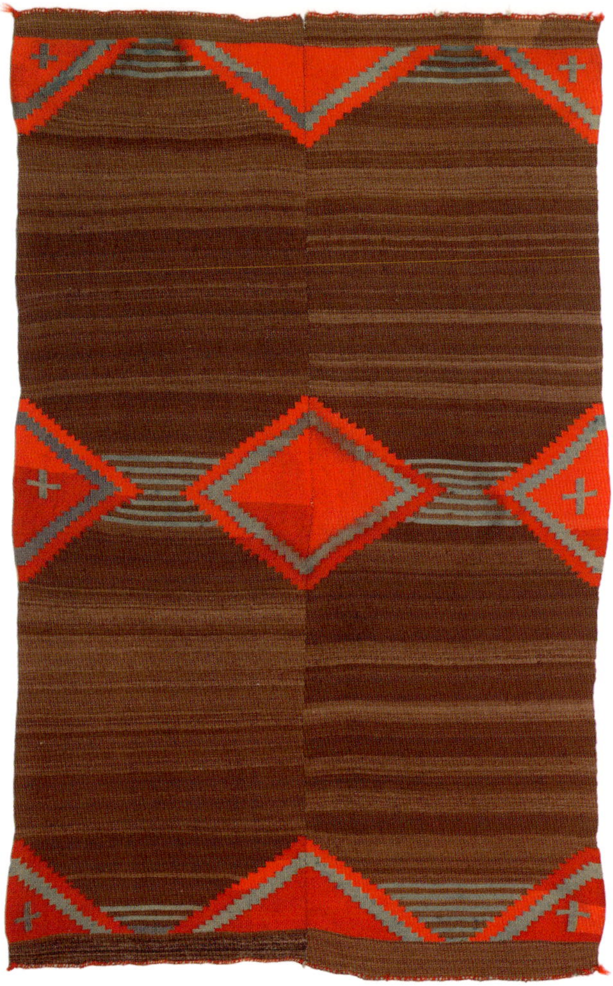

PLATE 59
Hispanic New Mexican
Frazada/Blanket, ca. 1880
Wool, cotton, synthetic dyes
86 1/2 × 48 1/4 in.
Museum purchase, 1983 General Obligation Bonds
PC1984.25.14

The weaver used synthetic dyes to add color and drama to this otherwise humble utility blanket. The pattern is a reproduction of Navajo Third Phase chief blanket design consisting of stepped diamonds and half diamonds arranged in three bands but woven into a field of mixed brown and beige yarns. The presence of a center seam confirms that the blanket was woven on a horizontal Spanish treadle loom. The warp ends were bound with red yarn at a later date.

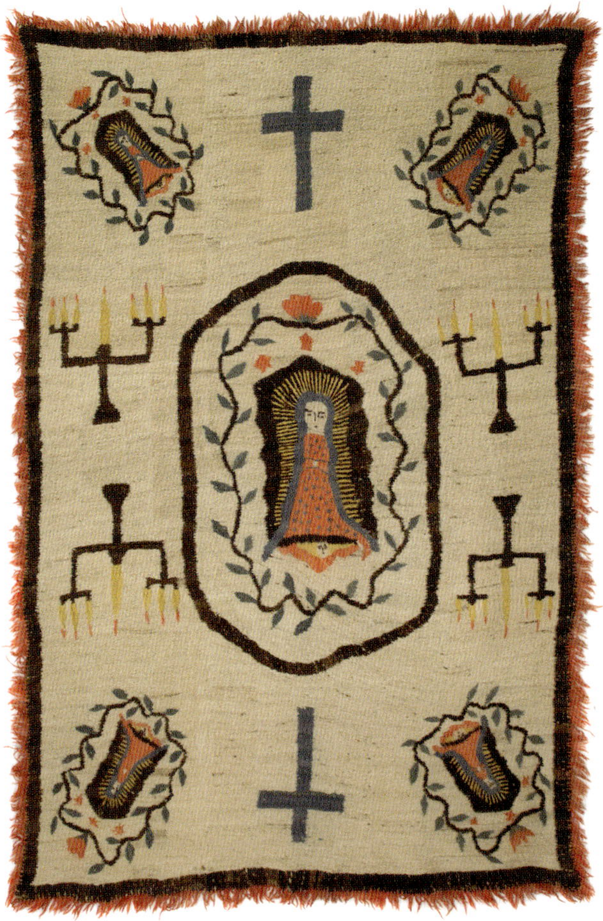

PLATE 60
Frances Graves
Carson colcha, *Our Lady of Guadalupe*, 1930s
Wool, synthetic dyes
42 1/2 × 39 in.
Gift of Mr. Kenner F. Hertford
PC1975.1.12

During the 1930s, a Mormon trader named Elmer Shupe started a business trading blankets in Carson, New Mexico. There, his sister-in-law Frances Graves learned to repair and create embroidered colchas (bedspreads). Using fragments of worn Navajo and Rio Grande weavings and unraveling them for their yarns, Graves created blanket designs that diverged from the geometric and floral motifs of Colonial Spanish and Hispano embroiderers, focusing instead on Indians, animals, wagons, saints, and Penitente processions. In this Carson colcha, Graves features images of the Virgin of Guadalupe flanked by candelabras and crosses.

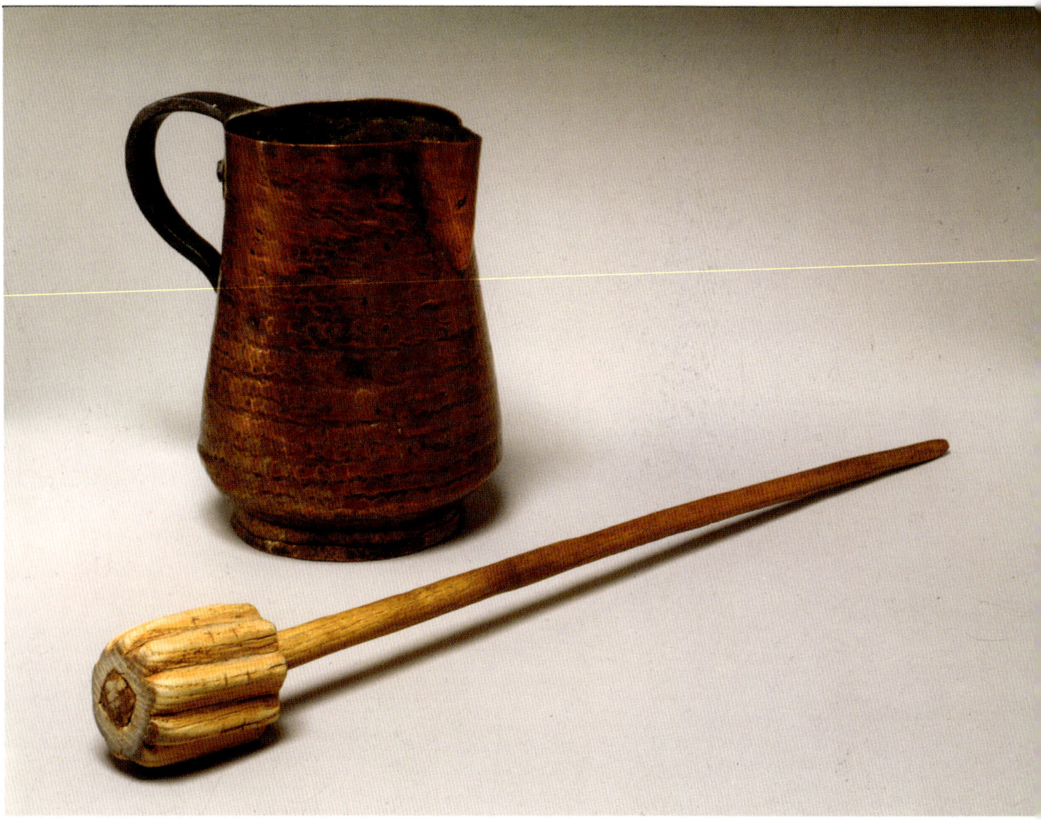

PLATE 61
Mexican or Hispanic New Mexican
Chocolatera y molinillo/Chocolate pot and muddler, eighteenth–nineteenth century
Copper, wood
6 1/2 x 6 1/4 x 4 in. and 17 9/16 x 1 9/16 in.
Gift of Ward Alan and Shirley Jolly Minge
PC1997.51.6 and PC2005.45.12

Chocolate was consumed by the Ancestral Pueblo inhabitants of Chaco Canyon, northwest of the Rio Grande valley, and by indigenous Mesoamerican cultures who traded the beans north through our region. The powdered cocoa was mixed with water and sometimes chile or corn meal, liquefied with a *molinillo* (muddler), and served cold.

Until the late nineteenth century, most items made of copper found in our region originated in Mexico near the mining districts of Michoacán. Products produced by the Tarascan copper workers included copper *cazos* (large cauldrons) and *chocolateras*, which were then traded north on the Camino Real into the central Rio Grande valley. This chocolate pot includes a hand-carved muddler used for stirring the chocolate.

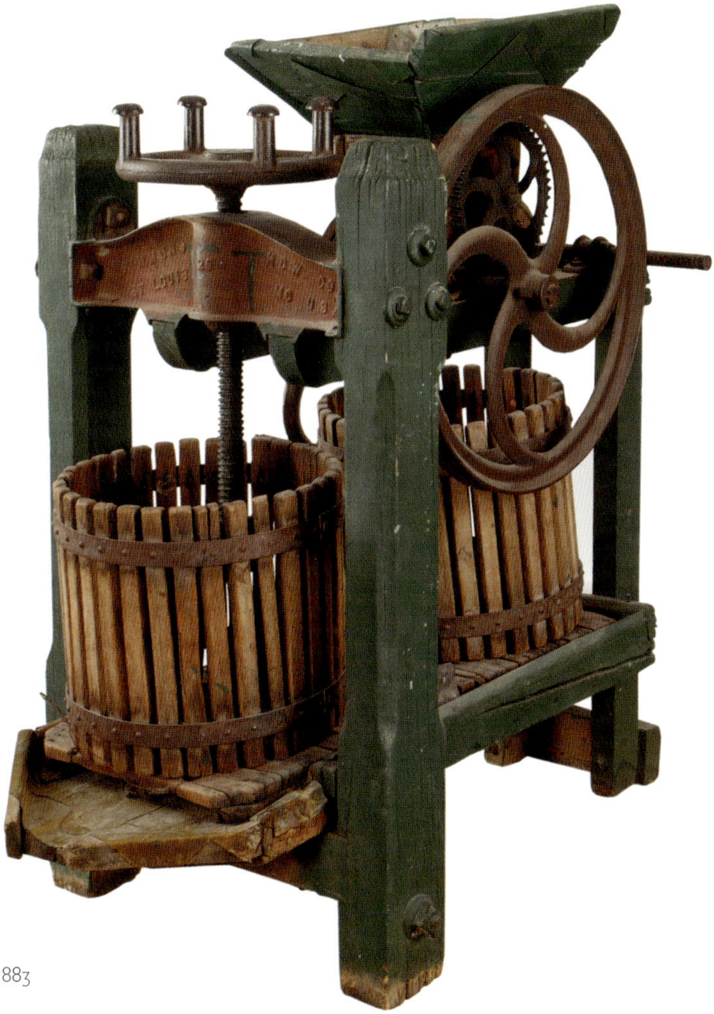

PLATE 62
Grape and cider press, ca. 1883
Eastern United States
Oak, metal
47 × 48 × 28 1/2 in.
Gift of Mrs. Joseph Tondre
PC1972.2.1.a

This press belonged to the Joseph Tondre family of Los Lunas. The Tondres immigrated to the United States from the region of Alsace-Lorraine in France in the 1840s. They arrived in the territory in 1864 and established a trading post on the east side of Isleta Pueblo. The family purchased land in Los Lentes, north of Los Lunas, and began making wine. The land where the vineyards once grew is now the site of the Katherine Gallegos Elementary School in Los Lunas.

In a good year, the Tondres could produce 87,000 gallons of wine from their famously flavorful grapes. The Jesuit priests in Albuquerque purchased grapes from the Tondre vineyards when the crop in Old Town failed or was insufficient.

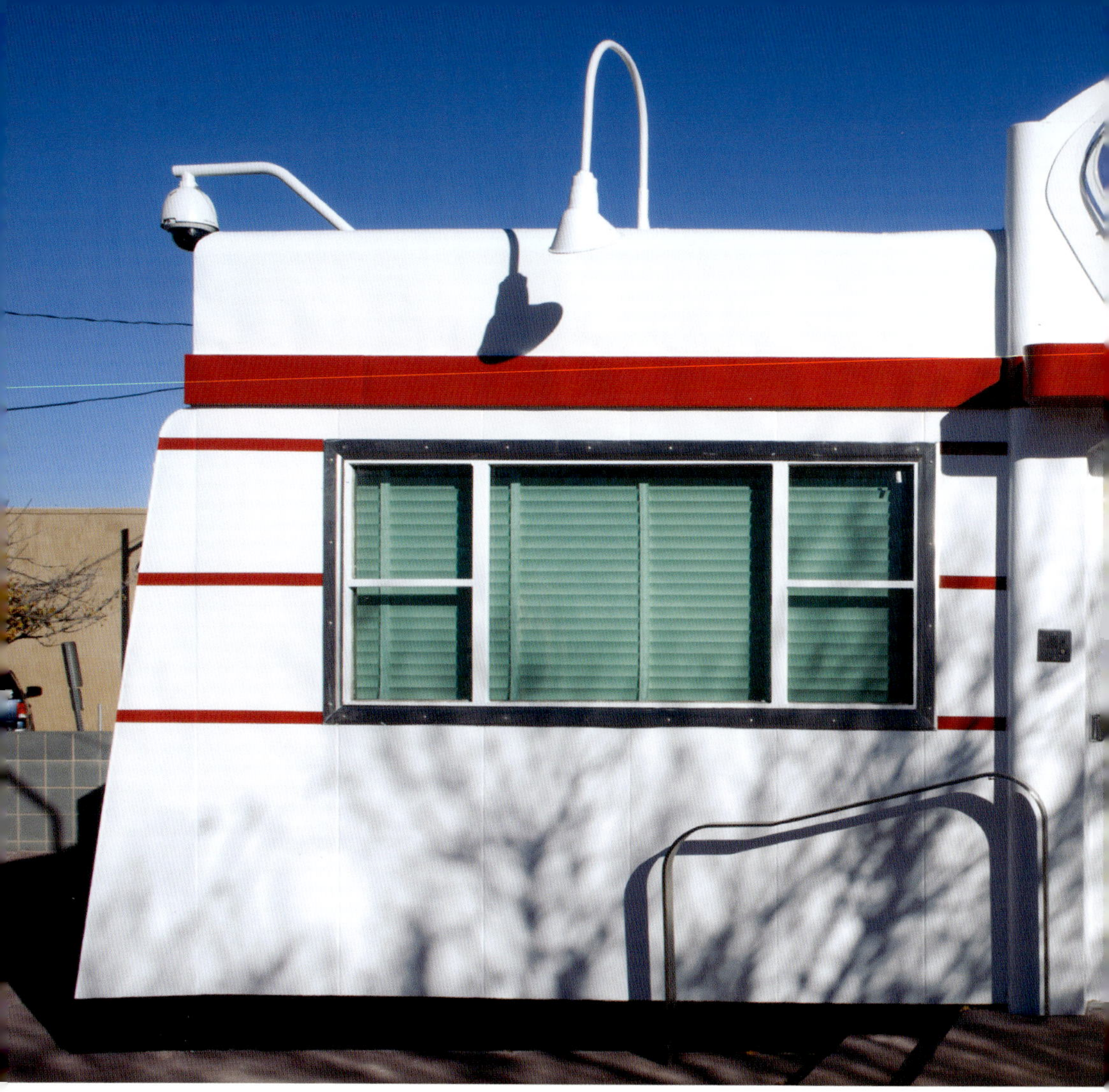

Joe and Della Hernandez opened the Little House Café on Eighth Street in 1949. The country's only Valentine Diner specializing in New Mexican food during the golden age of diners (1940s–60s), the Little House was known for its tamales, quesadillas, enchiladas, and green chile stew. Valentine Diners could be easily moved into place, could be run by two people, and were fully operational almost immediately. This diner is one of only two in New Mexico, both located in Albuquerque.

Della called her favorite customers "Dear" and posted signs reading, "I have an open mind . . . everything passes through it," "The Surgeon General has determined that hugging is good for your health," and "Se Habla Ingles." Photographs of the Pope and President Kennedy were also displayed at the counter. Today, the diner—relocated to the Monte Vista Triangle at Central Avenue—serves as an Albuquerque Police Department substation.

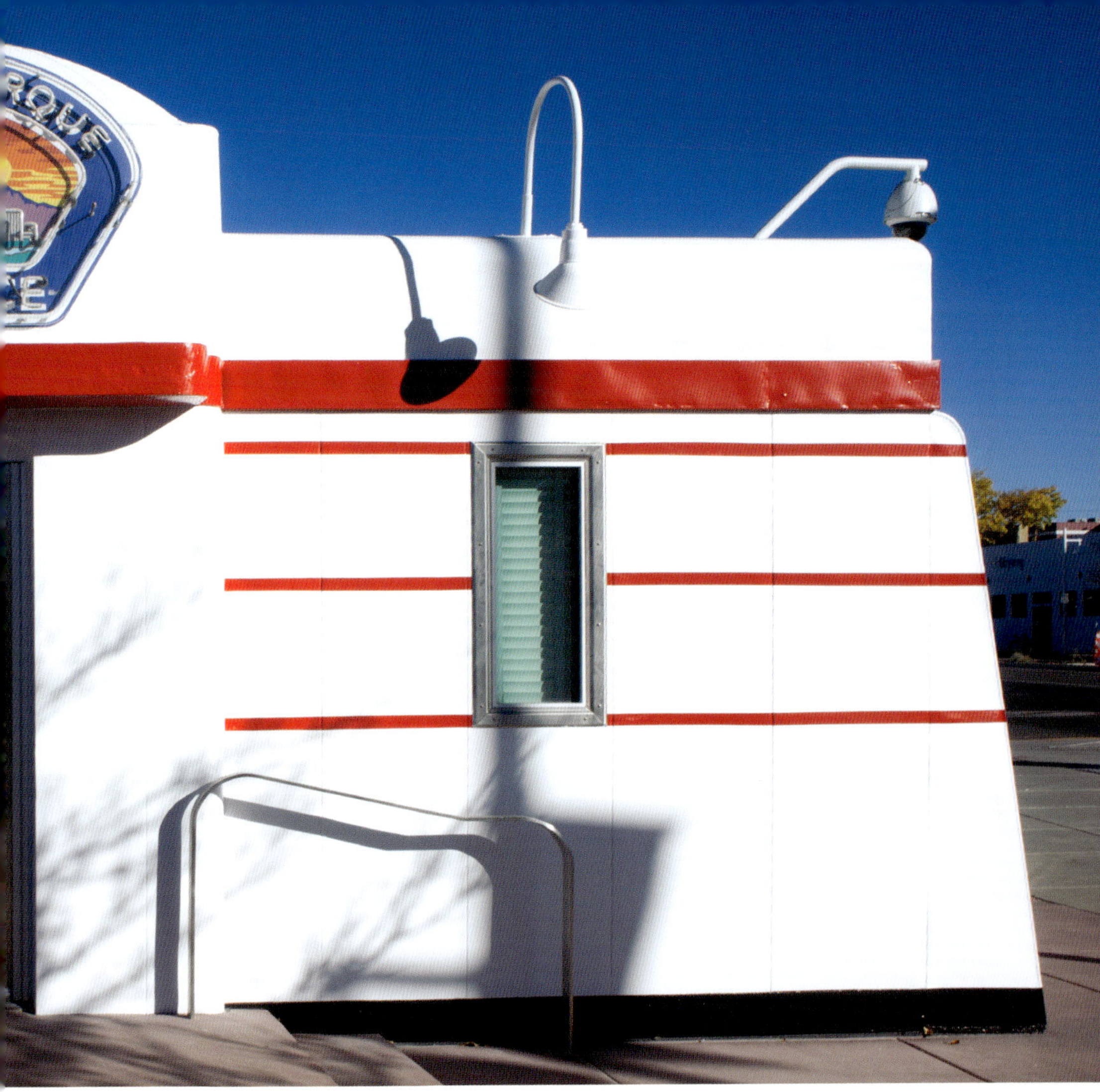

PLATE 63
Little House Café
Valentine Diner, ca. 1947
Sheet metal, chrome, glass, wood
324 × 144 × 144 in.
Gift of C. V. "Joe" Hernandez
and Della S. Hernandez
PC1993.23.492

PLATE 64 ►
Della Hernandez, 1970s
Gift of C. V. "Joe" Hernandez
and Della S. Hernandez

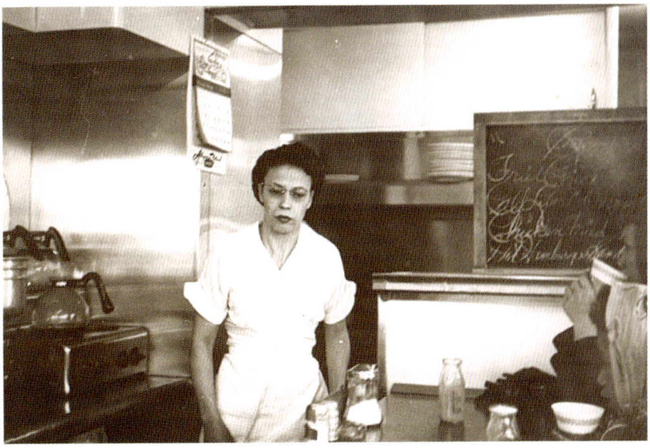

PLATE 65
Fred Harvey
Coffee can, 1940s–50s
Lithographed tin
4 1/2 x 3 1/2 in.
Museum purchase, Trust and Agency Fund
PC2007.71.1

The Fred Harvey Company packaged its own coffee for use on its Atchison, Topeka and Santa Fe Railway service and the Harvey Houses along the railroad line, including Albuquerque's Alvarado Hotel. The can's design features a Harvey Girl, one of the famous well-trained waitresses hired by the company to serve railroad passengers along the route.

Fred Harvey eating houses were known for the quality of their food and especially for their coffee. Musician Bernie May recalled, "The Alvarado guaranteed that the coffee was not more than one hour old, and they would change and dump out all the coffee of the previous hour."

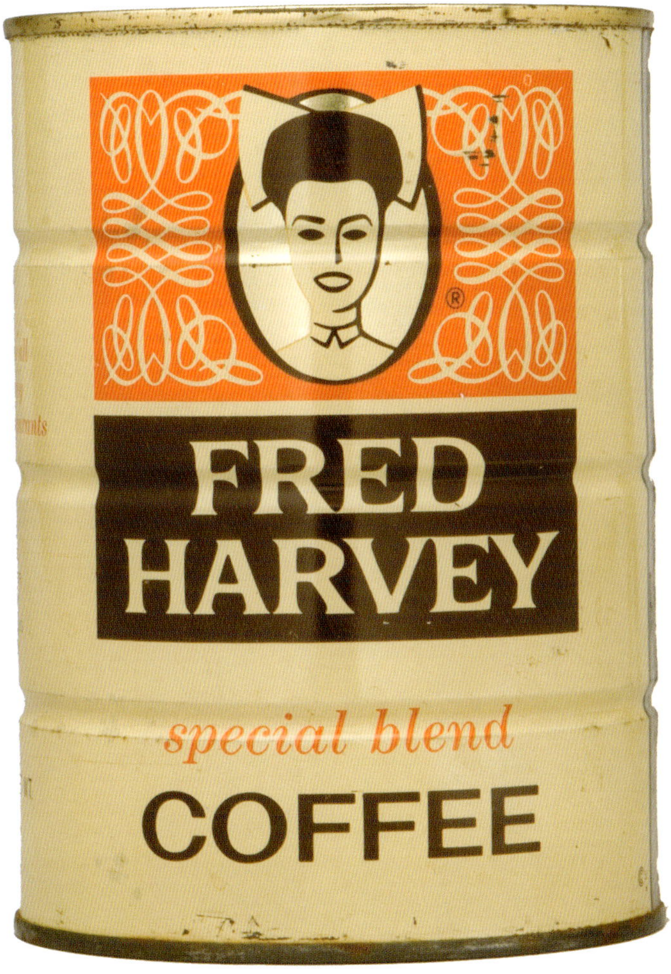
FRED
HARVEY
special blend
COFFEE

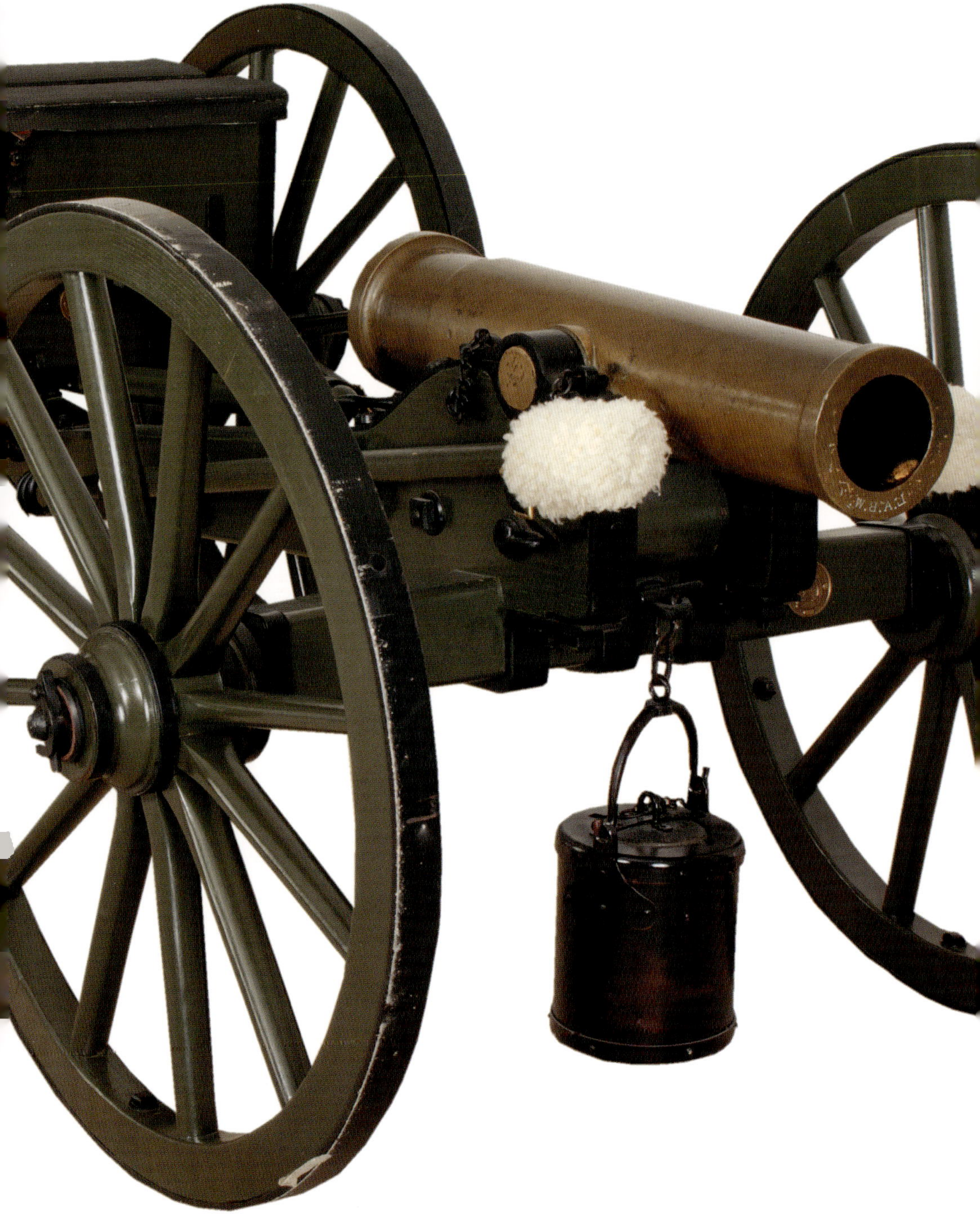

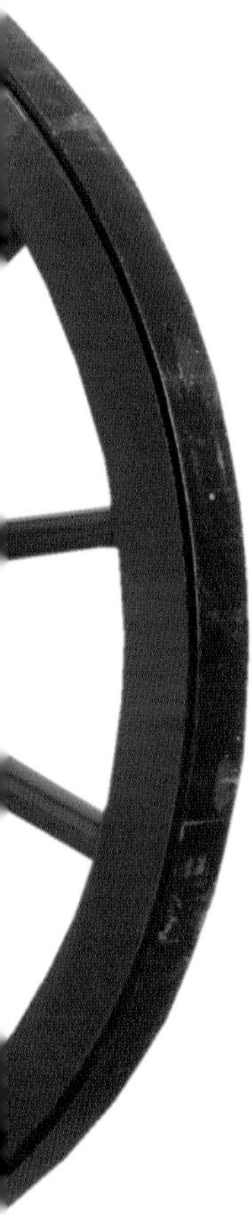

We Are Courageous

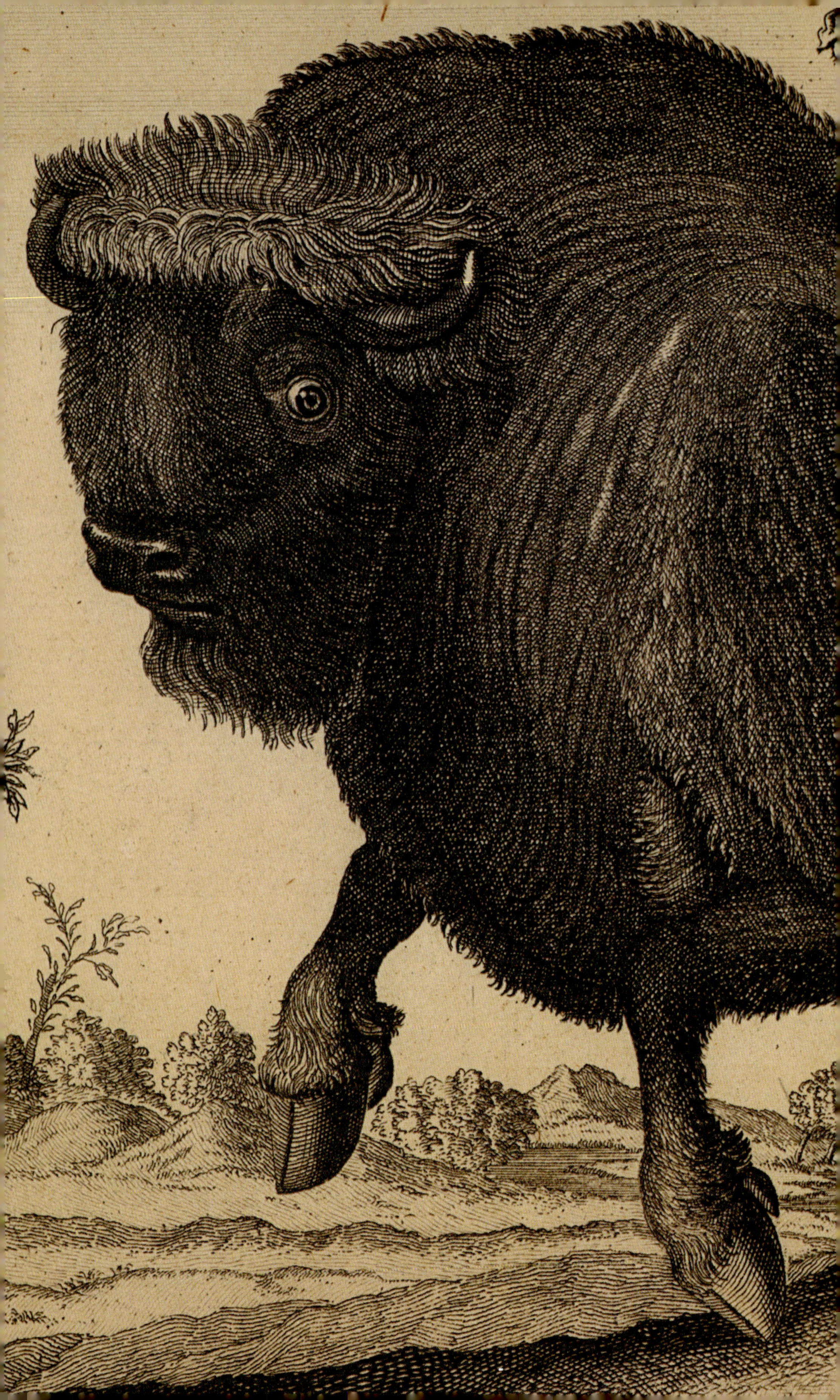

The people of Albuquerque have always been courageous.

We've faced enormous challenges over the centuries, finding creative solutions in tough situations. We fight oppression by summoning the courage to act. We suffer the conditions of conflict and war yet persevere. Those suffering economic hardships find ways to endure.

We value the stories of residents who have experienced tough times, and we look for meaning in them that helps us to improve our lives today.

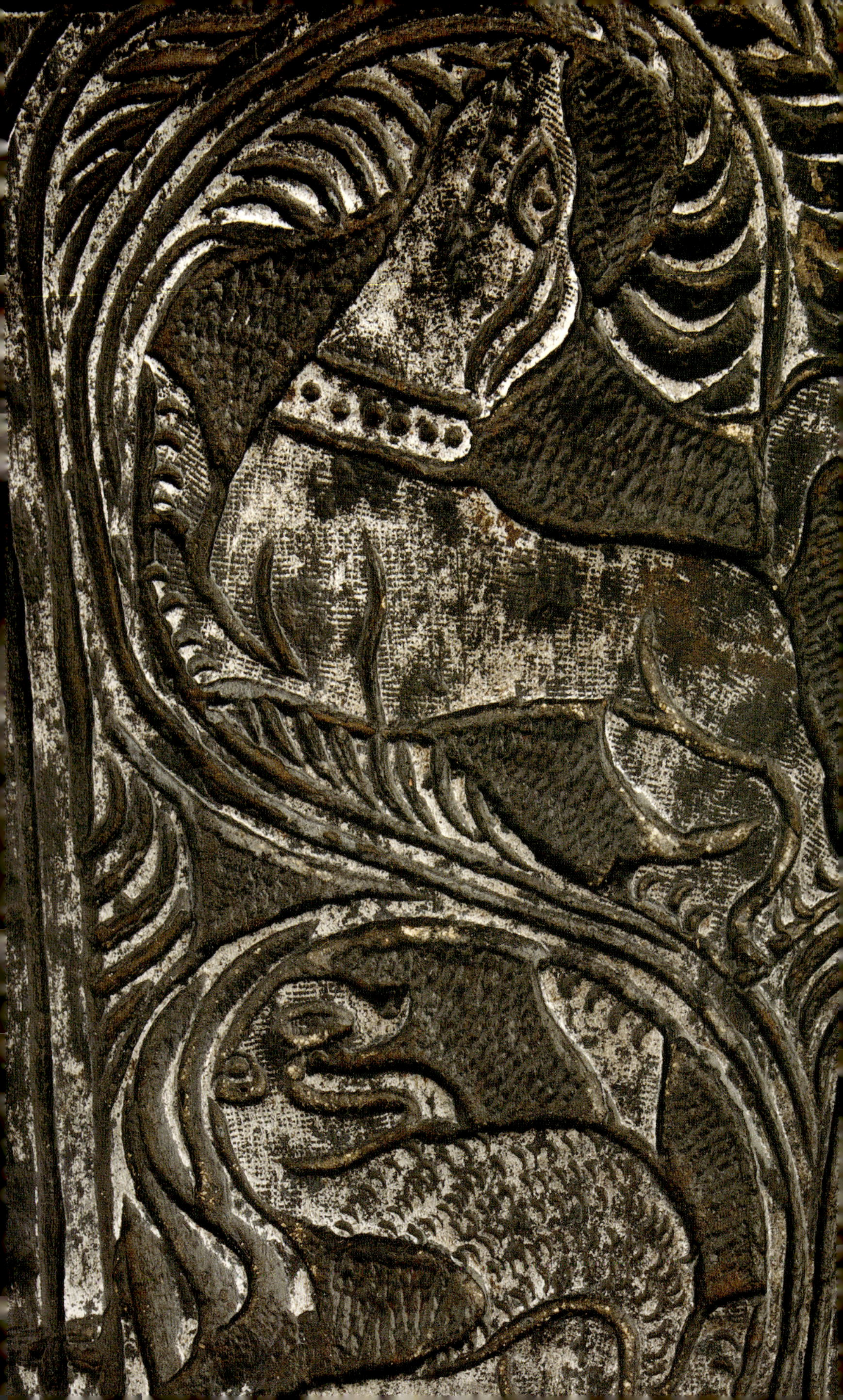

Overcoming Oppression

Indian and Hispano communities endured numerous forms of oppression, including encomienda (tribute of goods), repartimiento (forced labor), and religious persecution into the 1880s and beyond. Captives from all cultural backgrounds became forced labor for Indian and European slaveholders.

Community ties and federal laws have proven to be stronger than oppressive acts. Although discrimination persists, Albuquerque is more open-minded. Communities strive for peaceful coexistence, with greater respect for all.

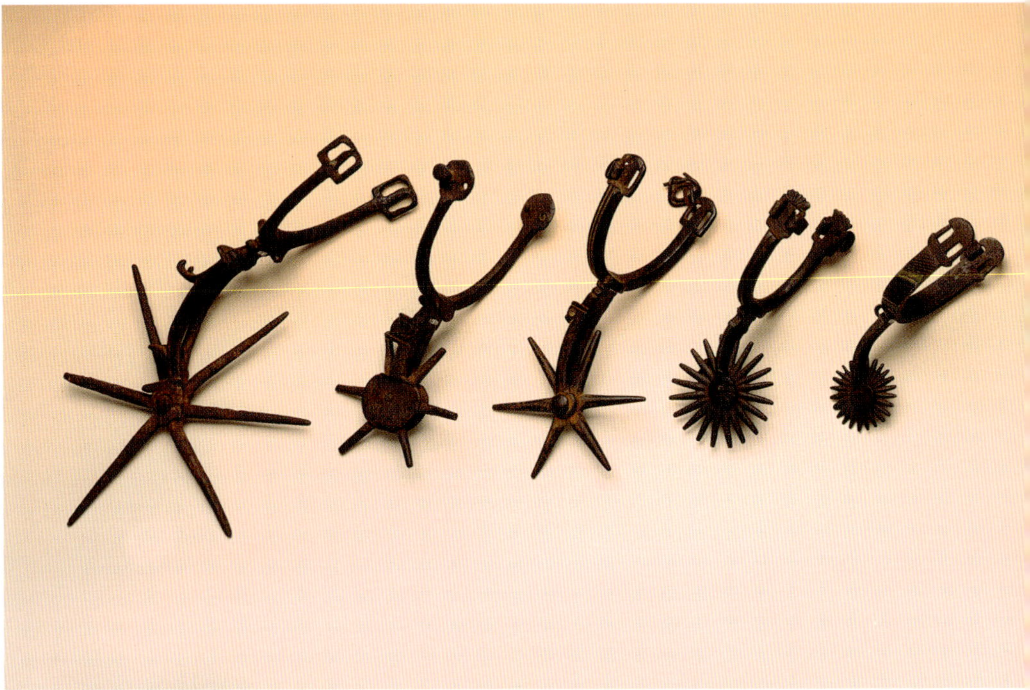

PLATE 66
Spanish or Mexican
Espuelas/Spurs, 1550–1800
Iron, leather
11 × 3 1/4 in., 8 × 4 1/4 in., 8 1/4 × 3 1/2 in., 6 3/4 × 4 in., and 6 × 4 1/4 in.
Museum purchase, 1979 General Obligation Bonds
PC1981.116.1.a and PC1981.95.2.a–d

Horses and the artifacts of the *caballero,* or Spanish horseman, are icons of the Colonial period. With the horse, caballeros could travel great distances, using height and speed to avoid flying arrows and rocks and to launch their own weapons.

Horsemens' accoutrements, such as the long-roweled *espuela grande* (far left) made in the mid-sixteenth century, were intended primarily for show because their actual use would have created serious injury to their mounts. The spurs were made in Spain, or in what is now Mexico, by indigenous Indian slaves.

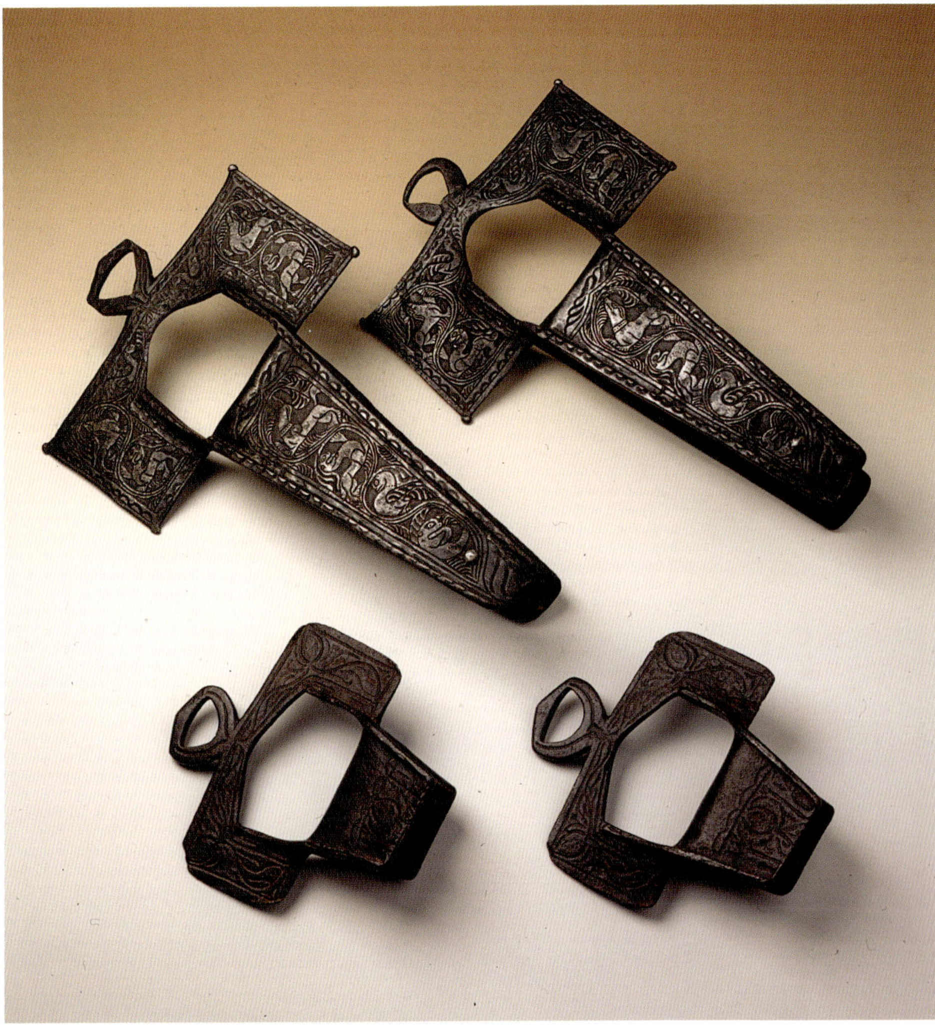

PLATE 67
Northern Mexican or Hispanic New Mexican
Estribos de cruz/Cruciform stirrups, 1700 and 1770
Iron
18 5/16 × 10 5/8 × 3 5/8 in. and 9 × 8 × 2 1/8 in.
Museum purchase, 1979 General Obligation Bonds
PC1983.25.1.a&b and PC1981.164.1.a&b

Like spurs, stirrups were commonly made by slaves near the mines of northern Mexico. Their cross shape refers to the Latin cross, and their surfaces are heavily engraved with fanciful decorations. One pair of stirrups was shortened to within three inches of the foot tread after the Royal Presidio Regulations of 1772 forbade the use of elongated stirrup shapes.

PLATE 68
Acoma
Beam, 1629–41
Wood, probably pine
122 × 5 1/4 × 4 1/4 in.
Gift of Judy and Ray Dewey
in memory of Rick Dillingham
PC2001.63.1

PLATE 69 ▶
San Estevan Mission and convent,
Acoma Pueblo, 1953
Photographers: Barnes and Caplin
Albuquerque Progress Collection
Gift of Albuquerque National Bank
PA1980.187.312

Franciscan friars taught Acoma craftsmen the art of woodworking; in fact, it is believed that a carpentry shop may have existed on the roof of San Estevan del Rey Mission's convent. Acoma laborers were forced to cut tree trunks for the mission and convent and transport them from the area of Mount Taylor—never allowing the beam to touch the ground. Now completely missing its original paint surface, this beam represents one of the earliest known examples of Colonial-period wood carving in our region.

San Estevan del Rey Mission, founded in 1629 under the direction of Fray Juan Ramirez, was completed by 1641. The mission has undergone numerous renovations, and through time its beams have been replaced and recycled into homes in and around Acoma. Members of the Lewis family received a number of them, four of which were acquired by Santa Fe ceramicist Rick Dillingham.

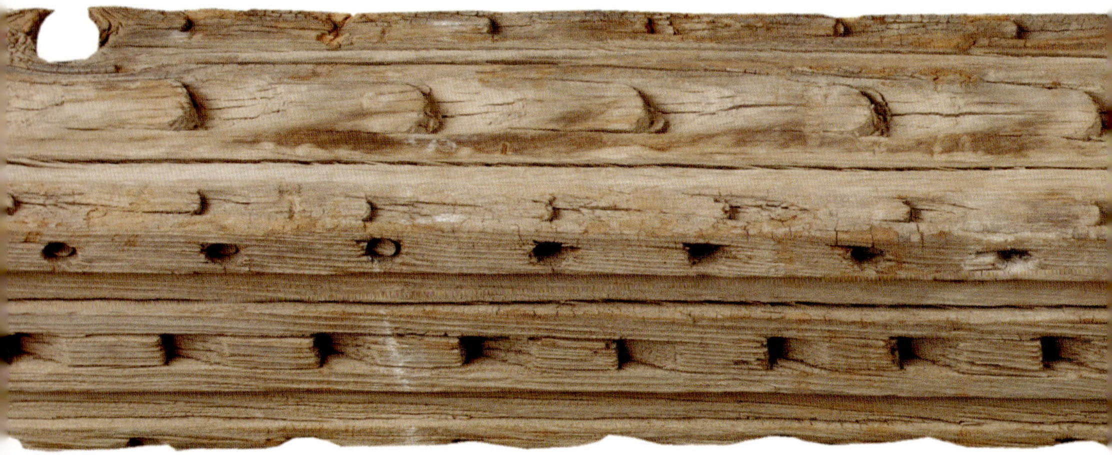

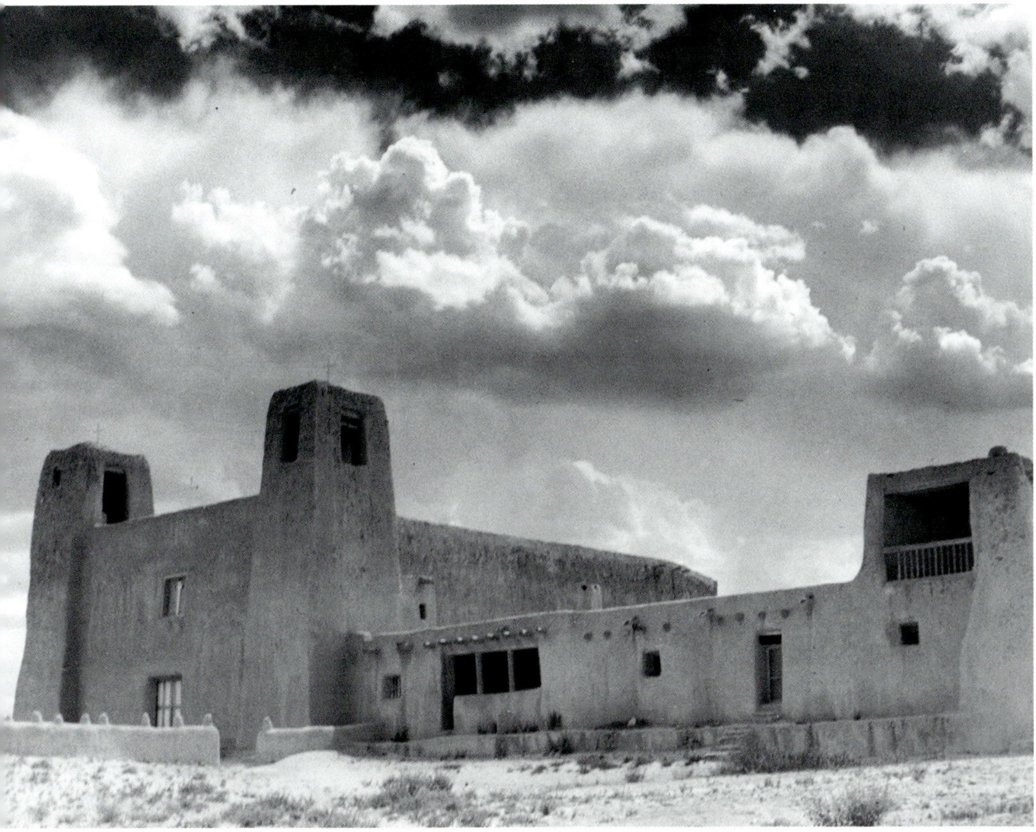

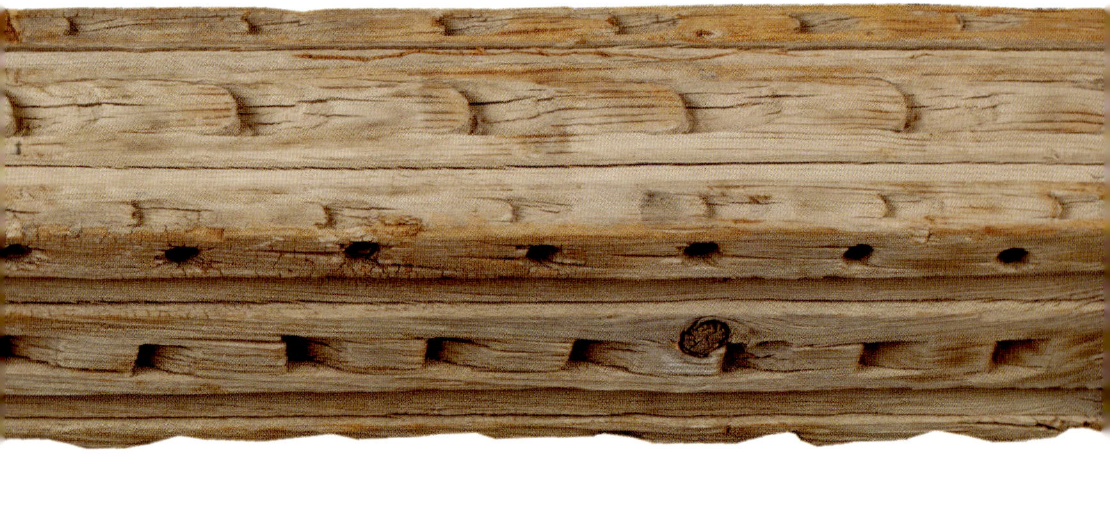

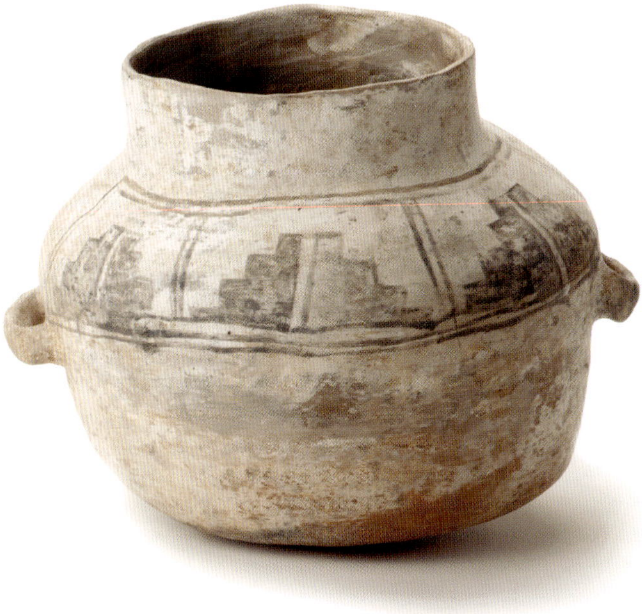

PLATE 70
Jemez
Jar, Jemez Black-on-white, sixteenth–seventeenth century
Clay, paint
9 1/2 × 11 1/2 in.
Gift of Ron Deyhle
PC2005.52.1

Jemez Black-on-white pottery spans several important events, including the 1680 Pueblo Revolt and the 1692 arrival of Don Diego de Vargas Zapata y Luján Ponce de León y Contreras to the province. Jemez lands were entered by Coronado in 1541 and later by Antonio de Espejo (1583) and Juan de Oñate (1598). Twice the Jemez conspired against the Spanish. The uprisings were suppressed until the Pueblo Revolt.

In 1694, General Diego de Vargas Zapata y Luján Ponce de León y Contreras stormed the pueblo, killing inhabitants and carrying off prisoners. The village was destroyed, reducing the tribe to the single pueblo of San Diego. In 1696 they again revolted, moving west and returning later to build the current pueblo. As a result of these brutal experiences, Jemez pottery nearly disappeared. Today, Jemez pottery is undergoing a revival through the efforts of Jemez leader and potter Joshua Madalena and others.

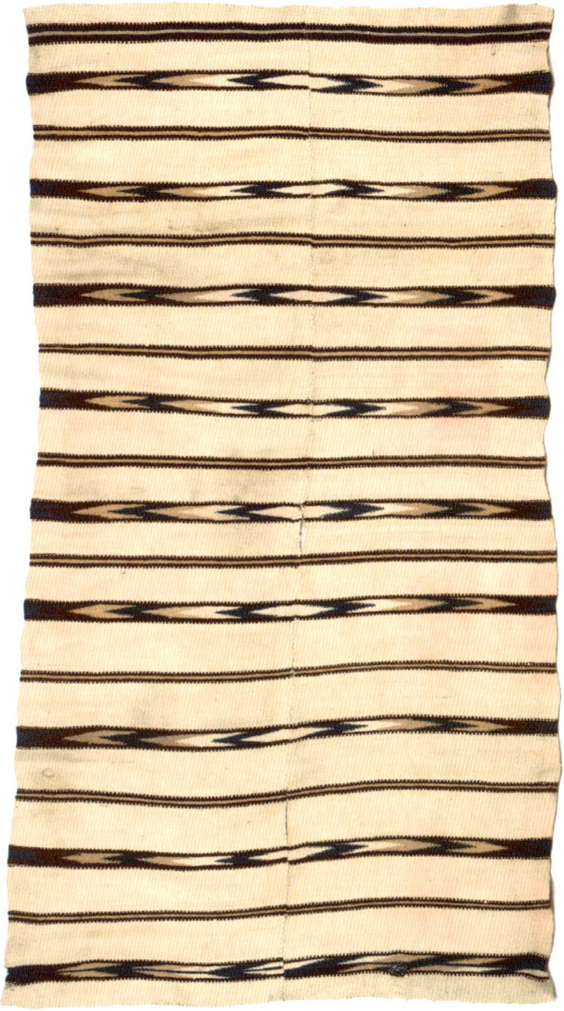

PLATE 71
Hispanic New Mexican
and/or Navajo
Frazada/Blanket, 1850–60
Wool; indigo and cota, marigold,
chamisa, or brazilwood dyes
91 × 47 1/2 in.
Museum purchase, 1983
General Obligation Bonds
PC1984.25.25
Ex-collection Larry Frank

Rio Grande blankets were sometimes woven by servants and sometimes exhibit curious weaving techniques. The extra stitches in the weft yarns of this blanket suggest that the weaver may have known how to weave in the Navajo style, using an unusual method of tapestry join that required hand stitches. It is possible that the blanket was made by a Navajo servant in a Hispano home. The weaver understood the techniques for weft-faced weaving, creating simple stripes and even *paladar* (ticking), and worked hard to create the visual effects in the chevrons.

This blanket is unusual, as there are dyed reddish gold chevrons within the overall striped pattern. The lightness of the reddish gold color suggests that the dye is vegetal, available in areas where there was no access to brazilwood dyes. The green is created from yellow vegetal dye overdyed with indigo blue. The fringe has been carefully knotted and re-sewn into the wefts.

PLATE 72
Isleta
Cross necklace, ca. 1929
Silver, padre or Hubbell beads, rawhide
20 1/2 × 3 1/2 × 3/4 in.
Gift of Eason Eige
PC2010.5.176

Pueblo artisans found creative ways to rebel against religious suppression. In addition to their association with the Christian cross, the single and double bar crosses in this silver necklace refer to the dragonfly, an insect special to Pueblo people due to its association with water. This example was acquired by the donor from the Minneapolis School of Fashion via Morningstar Traders.

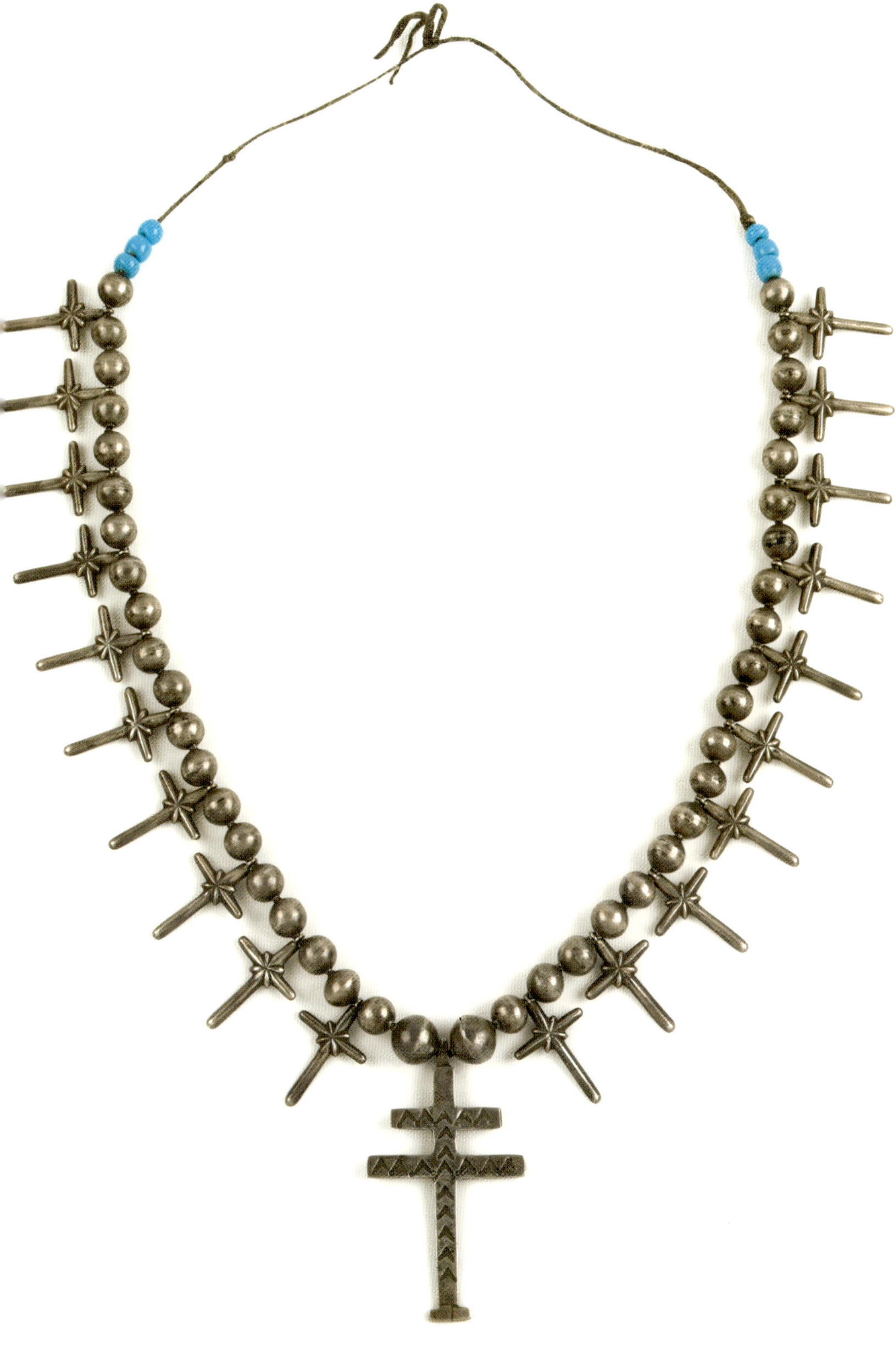

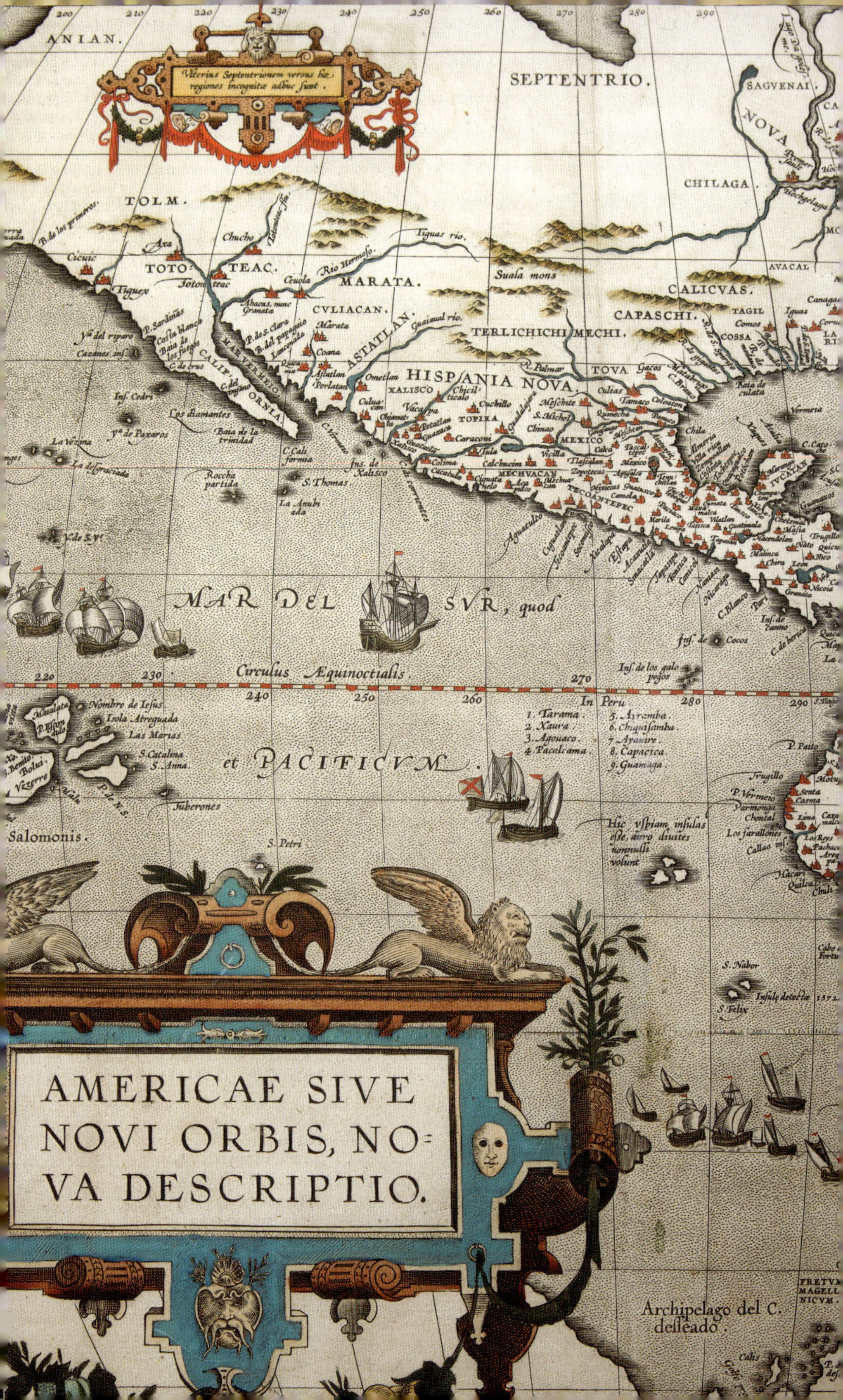
Vlterius Septentrionem versus hæ regiones incognitæ adhuc sunt.
ANIAN.
SEPTENTRIO.
SAGVENAI
NOVA
CHILAGA.
Hochelaga
TOLM.
TOTO
TEAC.
Chucho
MARATA.
CVLIACAN.
Suala mons
AVACAL
CALICVAS.
CAPASCHI.
TAGIL
Comos
COSSA
TERLICHICHI MECHI.
ASTATLAN.
Tiguas rio.
Rio Hermoso.
Guaiaual rio.
TOVA
HISPANIA NOVA.
XALISCO
CALIFORNIA
MAR VERMEIO
Los diamantes
Baia de la trinidad
C. California
S. Thomas.
Roccha partida
La Anublada
La Vezina
La desgraciada
Ins. Cedri
CVCHILLO
TOPIRA
MEXICO
MECHVACAN
TECVANTEPEC
IVCATAN
MAR DEL SVR, quod
et PACIFICVM.
Circulus Æquinoctialis.
In Peru
1. Tarama
2. Xaura
3. Agouaco
4. Pacalcama
5. Ayramba
6. Chiquisamba
7. Ayauire
8. Capacica
9. Guamaga
Ins. de Cocos
Ins. de los galopegos
Nombre de Iesus
Isola Atreguada
Las Marias
S. Catalina
S. Anna
Salomonis.
Tuberones
S. Petri
Hic vsbiam insulas esse, auro diuites nonnulli volunt
S. Nabor
S. Felix
Insule detecta 1572
Archipelago del C. desseado
FRETVM MAGELLANICVM
AMERICAE SIVE NOVI ORBIS, NOVA DESCRIPTIO.

Conflict

The people of Albuquerque have been invaded by neighboring states and ruled by different nations. They have lost their land and regained it. They have been resourceful in protecting themselves and courageous in holding their families together in times of war.

The history of Albuquerque's shifting borders reveals countless stories of bravery and of people's ability to endure life-changing events.

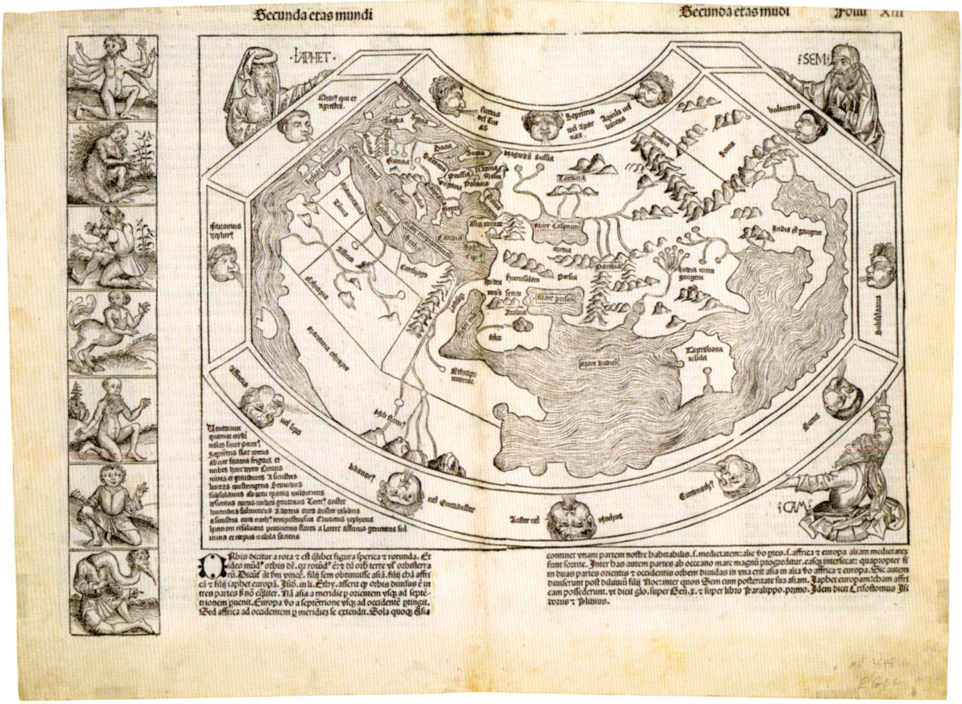

PLATE 73
Hartmann Schedel, German
Map, *Secunda Eras Mundi/Second State of the World*, July 1493
Woodblock print; ink, paper
14 1/4 x 20 3/4 in.
Museum purchase, 1979 General Obligation Bonds
PC1991.79.1

This map shows the geography of the medieval world just before Columbus's voyage in 1492 (although the map was printed in 1493, his discoveries are not included). The map was published in the *Nuremberg Chronicle*, the first to feature illustrations of many cities and countries. Hartmann Schedel, who drew the original map, was one of the first cartographers to use the printing press. Hans Pleydenwurff and Michael Wolgemut likely designed the woodcuts.

In keeping with medieval tradition, Jerusalem is at the center of the world, surrounded by the Old Testament figures of Ham, Shem, and Japheth, the sons of Noah. The twelve figures indicate the prevailing directions of the winds, and the figures on the left are mythical beings from the farthest regions of the earth, including six-armed and four-eyed men and a centaur.

PLATE 74
Tonque Pueblo
Bowl, Puaray or Kotyiti Glaze Polychrome, 1515–60
Clay, glaze paint, slip
5 1/4 × 12 7/8 in.
Gift of Richard Bice via the Albuquerque Archaeological Society
PC1974.33.11

The owner of this bowl lived at Tonque Pueblo near San Felipe Pueblo. The site was visited numerous times by Spanish explorers, beginning as early as 1540. The potter painted diagonal dashes that may represent a field of Spanish lances.

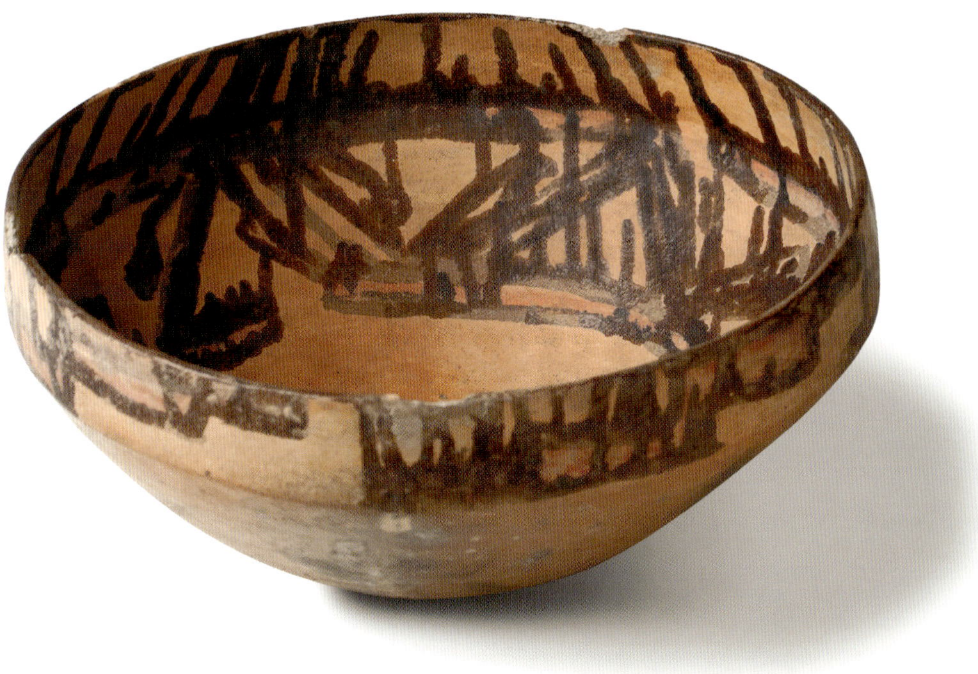

PLATE 75
Nuremberg, Germany
Morión/Helmet, ca. 1570
Iron or steel
10 1/2 × 12 3/4 in.
Museum purchase, 1979 General Obligation Bonds
PC1981.230.1

Popular by the mid-sixteenth century, the *morión* became the helmet of choice by the time conquistadors such as Juan de Oñate colonized New Spain. Examples such as this one were made in Germany for the Spanish market. The morión's curved brim provided some protection from the sun and rain. It is hand forged from one piece of metal, with a hollow comb for strength and a rope-edged brim. The entire surface is etched with designs including Spanish cavalry, a drum, a soldier with a flag, Abraham and Isaac (an allusion to the soldier's obedience to God and King), and the double-headed imperial eagle.

This morión was acquired from William Scollard for the Museum's 1983 long-term history exhibition, *Four Centuries: A History of Albuquerque*.

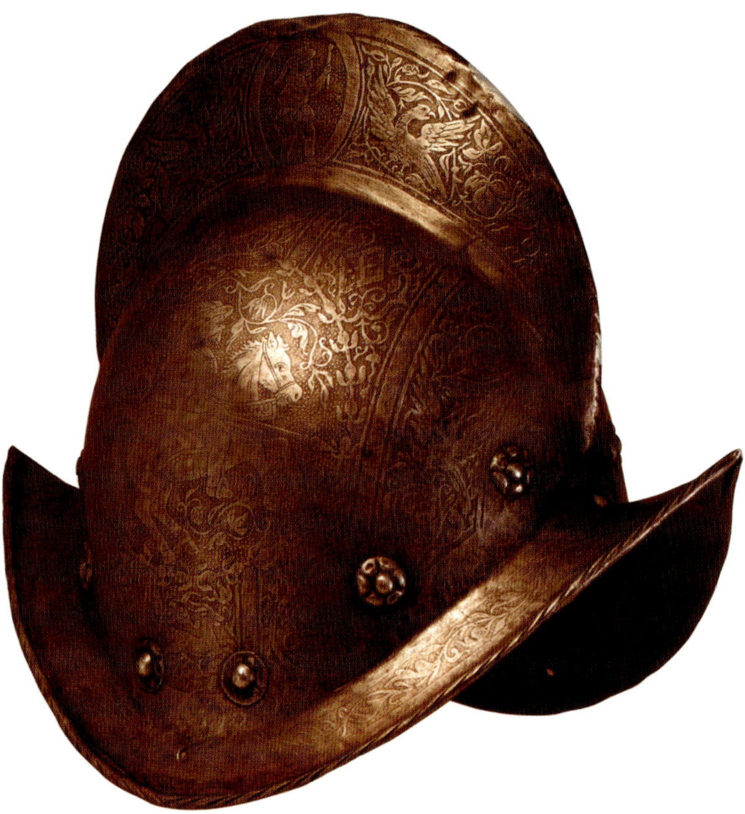

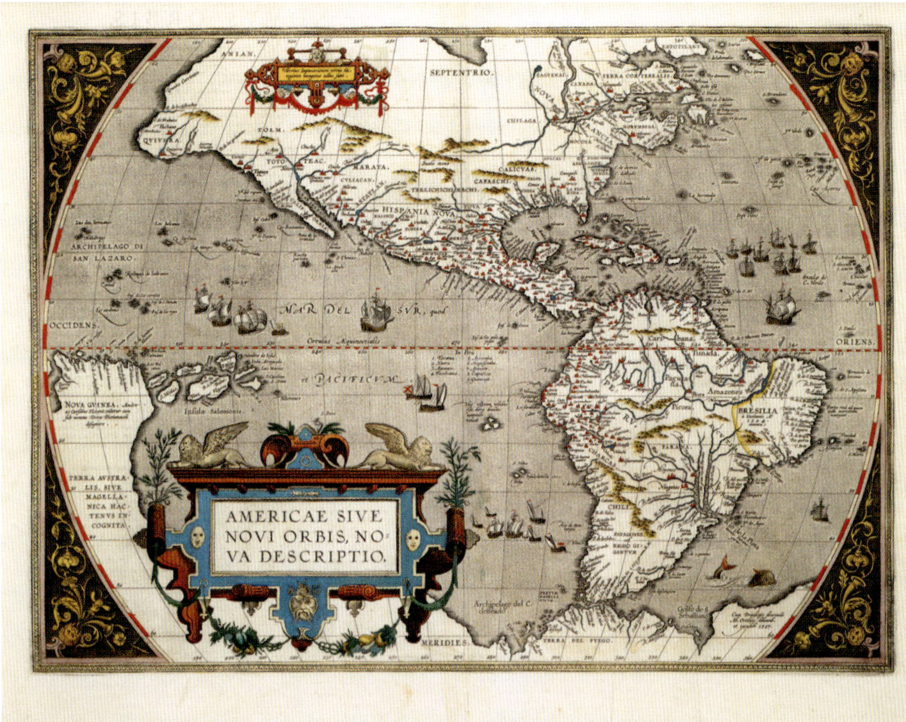

PLATE 76
Abraham Ortelius, Dutch, Belgian
Map, *Americae Sive Novi Orbis, Nova Descriptio/America or the New World, New Description*, ca. 1589
Copperplate engraving; ink, paper
18 9/16 × 23 in.
Museum purchase, 1979 General Obligation Bonds
PC1982.213.1

Originally published in Latin, this map of the Western Hemisphere appeared in the most widely read atlas of the sixteenth and seventeenth centuries, considered the most spectacular atlas ever published. Thirty-three editions were published between 1570 and 1612.

The nature of sixteenth-century navigation led to many errors. Instruments like astrolabes determined latitude (distance north to south), but no device accurately measured longitude (east to west). A roster of explorers used as sources appears on the reverse. Tiguex, Coronado's name for the region of the southern Tiwa pueblos near modern Albuquerque, is placed west of the Baja Peninsula. Quivira, the legendary golden city sought by Coronado in present-day Kansas, is located on the Pacific coast.

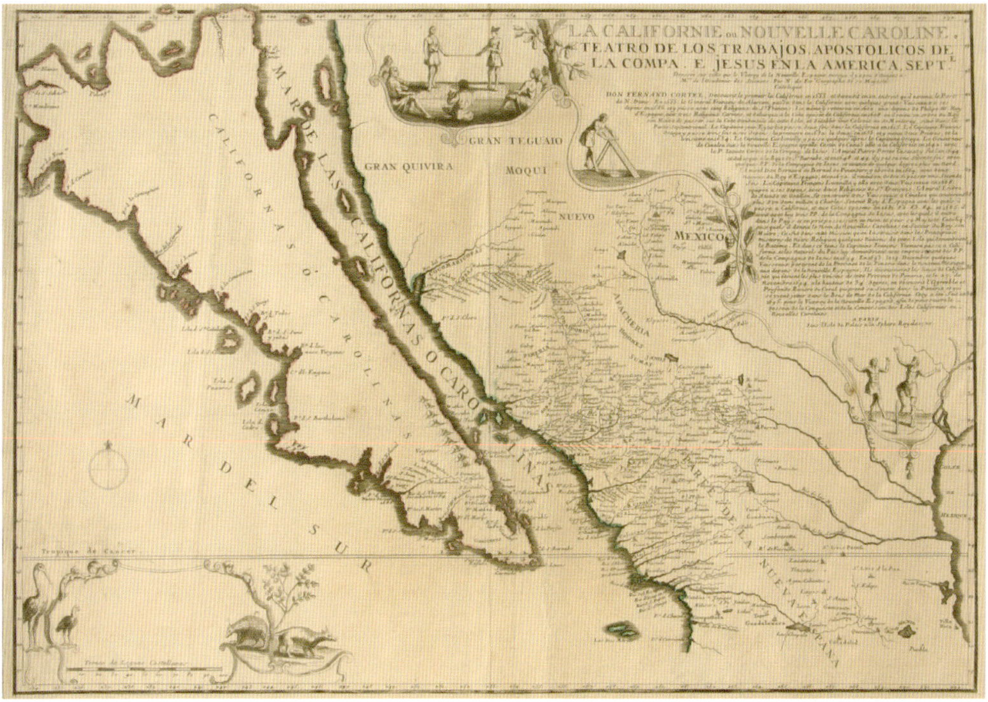

PLATE 77

Nicolas de Fer, French

La Californie ou novelle Caroline. Teatro de los Trabajos, apostolicos de la compa. E Jesus en la America, 1720

Hand-colored copper engraving; ink, paper

19 × 27 in. (image)

Museum purchase in honor of Dr. James C. Moore, Four Centuries Bond Fund

PC2005.57.1

Nicolas de Fer served as the official geographer to the Spanish throne. He drew this map based on information gathered by Padre Eusebio Francisco Kino, who traveled through Sonora, Mexico, into what is now Arizona in the 1690s. Albuquerque, founded in 1706, is therefore still absent. Many Pueblo towns are depicted along the banks of the Río del Norte (Rio Grande). California is depicted as a huge island. In 1721, just one year after Nicolas de Fer produced the map, Padre Kino discovered that California was actually attached to the continent.

To promote the abundance of the Americas for the Spanish crown, Nicolas de Fer depicted industrious Indian people and exotic animals including water birds, an armadillo, and a capybara.

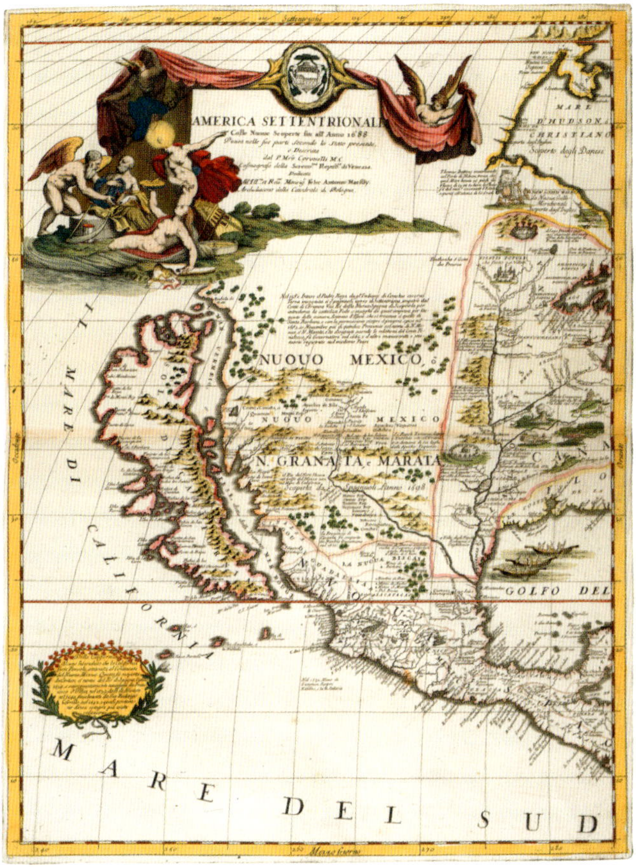

PLATE 78
F. Vicenzo Maria Coronelli, Italian
Map, *America Settentrionale*, 1688
Copperplate engraving; paper, ink, watercolor
24 7/8 × 19 1/4 in. (overall)
Museum purchase, 1979
General Obligation Bonds
PC1982.238.1.a

America Settentrionale, by the Franciscan monk Vicenzo Maria Coronelli, is one of the most accurate sixteenth-century maps of New Mexico. Coronelli's maps included new detail on New Spain and are said to have omitted nothing that would be of interest to cartographers, navigators, and explorers of the day.

Information for the New Mexico portion of the map came from a former governor of the province, Diego Peñalosa, who was exiled from the region in 1668 and settled in Paris. After removal from office and an investigation by the Inquisition in Mexico City for alleged crimes, Peñalosa prepared maps and proposals for England and France in order to entice them to invade the colony.

Coronelli's map corrected the mistaken belief that the great river—now called the Rio Grande—flowed into the Gulf of California; he firmly stated, "The Rio del Nort flows to the Gulf of Mexico, not the Sea of California." The map adopts Peñalosa's division of the Rio Grande into two parts, the Rio del Norte in the north and Rio Bravo in the south. However, it continued to perpetuate the myth of California as a great island separated from the mainland by the Vermillion Sea.

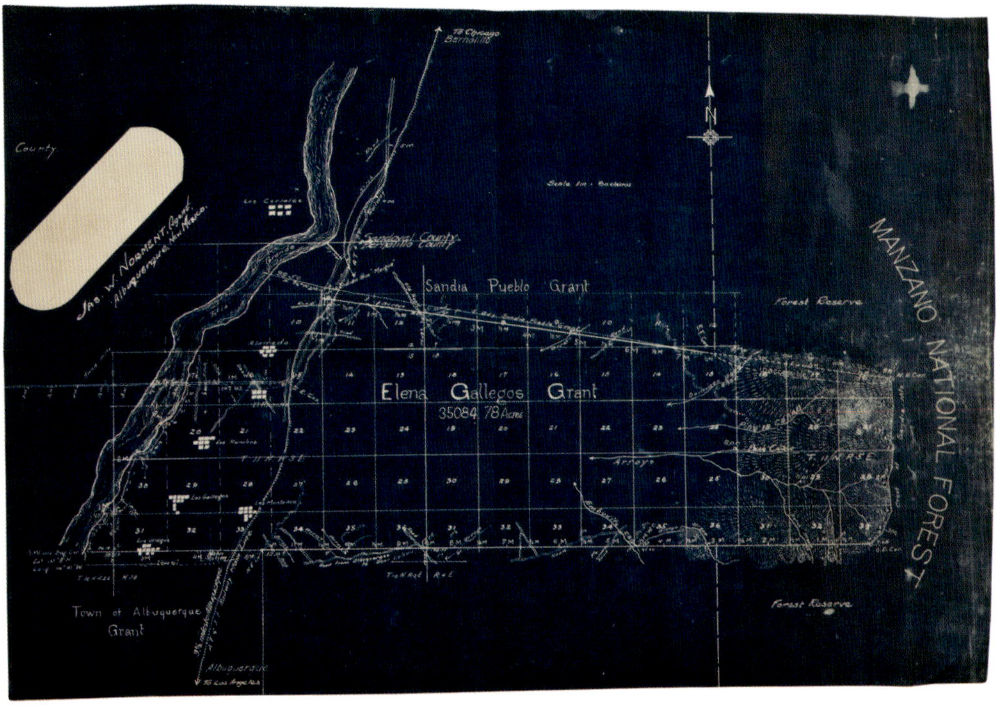

PLATE 79

James W. Norment

Blueprint map, Albuquerque area land grants, 1920s

Paper

12 1/2 × 18 in.

Gift of Sheli Armstrong

PC2013.20.10

James W. Norment's map features the gigantic Elena Gallegos Land Grant along with boundaries for Sandia Pueblo and the Town of Albuquerque grant. The Elena Gallegos land grant—stretching from the Rio Grande to the crest of the Sandia Mountains—was awarded in 1694 to Diego Montoya, although settlers may have occupied the land before the 1680 Pueblo Revolt. In 1712 the grant was reissued to Elena Gallegos. Much of northeast Albuquerque lies on this former land grant.

William Leverett Sr. and Jr., who surveyed Monte Vista and other northeast neighborhoods in the twentieth century, collected this and many other local maps during their careers as surveyors.

PLATE 80
Spanish
Cajafuerte/Strongbox, ca. 1775
Iron, leather
34 1/2 × 43 7/8 × 24 9/16 in.
Museum purchase, 1991 General Obligation Bonds
PC1993.49.2.a

This *cajafuerte* is a superb example of an actual "treasure chest." Made in Europe of heavy iron as early as the seventeenth century, this type of chest was sold to the sailing nations, including Spain, to use for transportation of gold, silver, documents, and other valuables. Once loaded, it would be extremely difficult to steal.

The cajafuerte was owned by poet and rancher Maria Chabot, a friend and an associate of Georgia O'Keeffe. Her paternal grandfather was the English ambassador to Mexico during the Mexican Revolution in 1910. Her family fled Mexico City, traveling by wagon, and settled in San Antonio, where Maria later received the chest from her mother, who had acquired it from a local Hispano family that had used it for generations. Chabot studied Spanish and archaeology in Mexico City and moved to New Mexico in 1931, where she helped found the Santa Fe Indian Market.

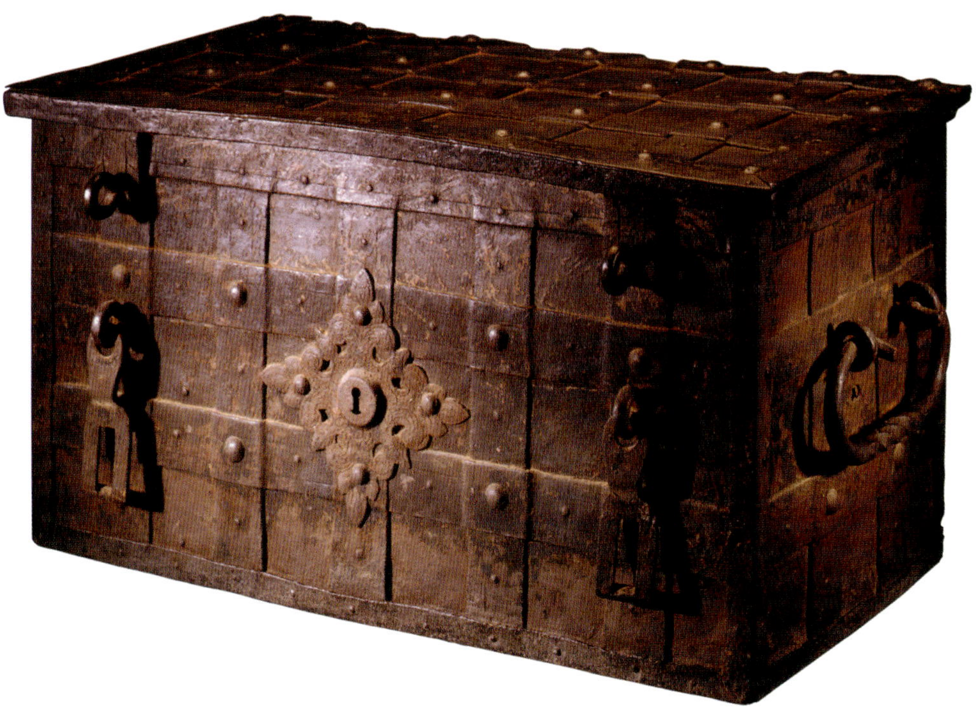

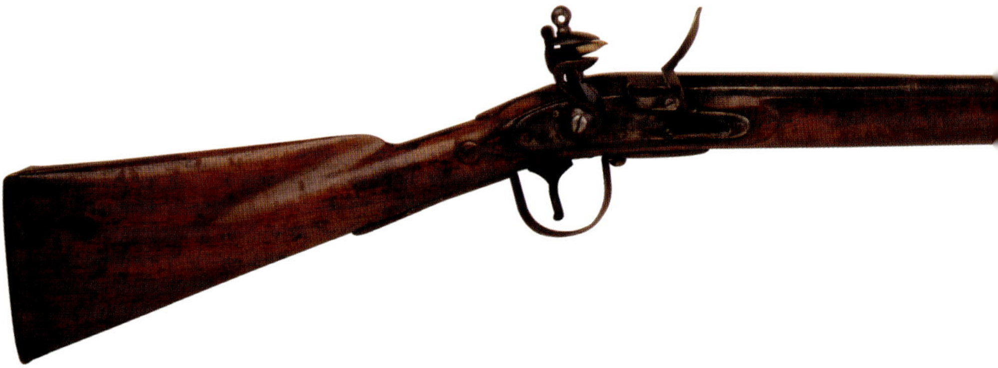

PLATE 81
Spanish
Fusil/Light musket, 1779
Walnut, steel, brass
54 1/2 × 2 × 7 1/4 in.
Museum purchase, 1979 General Obligation Bonds
PC1982.99.1

Manufactured the year of Governor Juan Bautista de Anza's victory over the Comanches, who were decimating Spanish and Pueblo settlements in the Rio Grande valley, this light musket has all the characteristics set by the regulations of 1752. Two makers' symbols are located on the barrel. Few of these weapons survived on the frontier because of the harsh conditions; only three were known to exist in the United States at its time of acquisition in 1982. The musket, acquired from William Scollard, was made in Spain and probably used in New Spain.

PLATE 82 ▶
Spanish
Pistola/Cavalry pistol and holster, 1791–1800 and ca. 1790
Iron, steel, walnut, brass, leather
16 1/4 × 6 1/4 × 2 1/2 in. and 29 3/4 × 6 1/2 × 2 1/2 in.
Museum purchase, 1979 General Obligation Bonds
PC1981.216.1 and PC1982.39.1

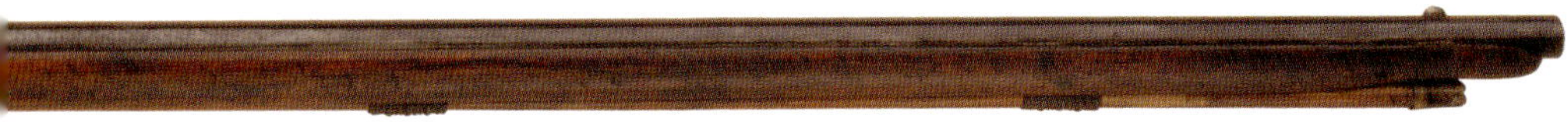

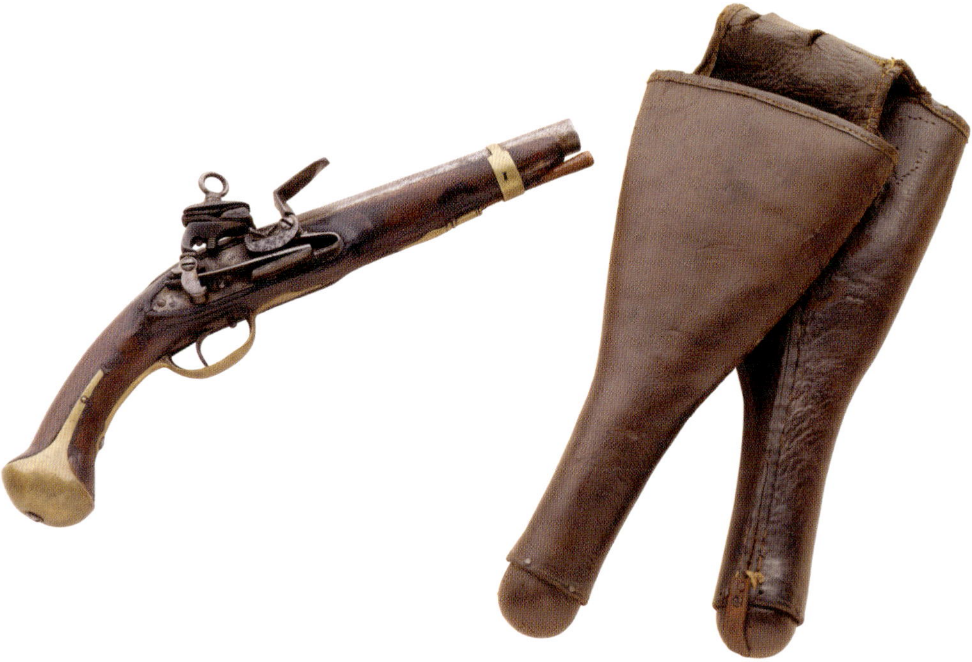

Cavalry pistols were issued in pairs to the regular army with saddle holsters but were sold to the militia and Indian scouts. This example conforms to the regulations of 1791; it has a Miguelet flintlock and is .69 caliber. It was desirable to have *pistolas*, *fusiles*, and *escopetas* of the same caliber so that ammunition would be interchangeable. The two large holsters are attached by a black leather saddle strap.

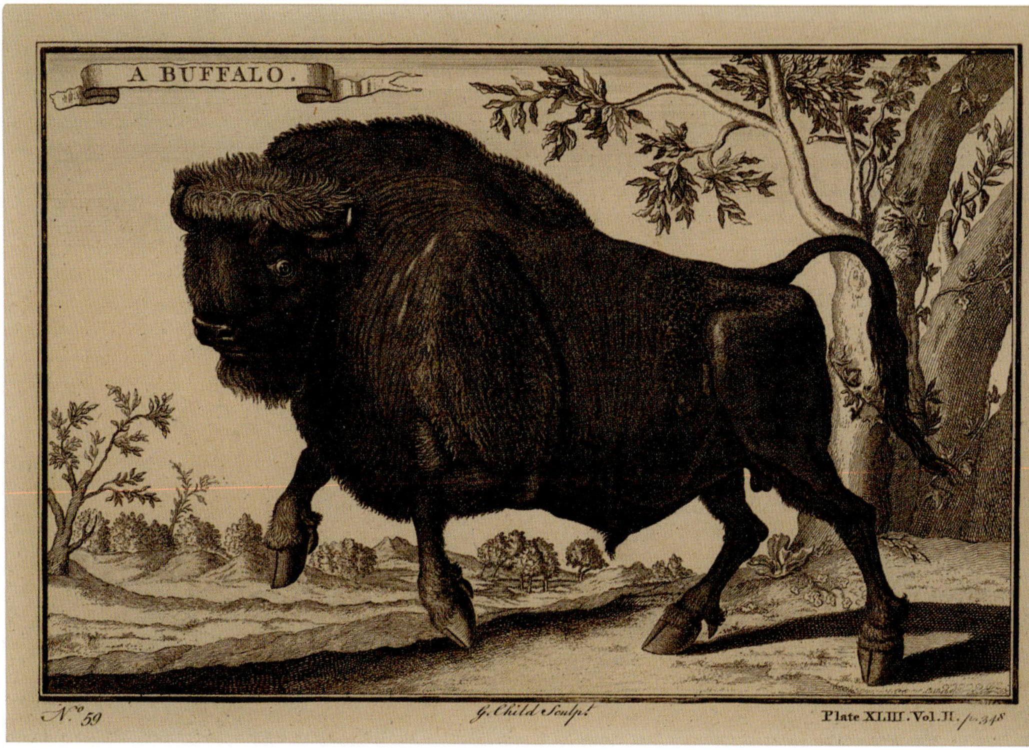

PLATE 83
Cephas G. Childs
A Buffalo, ca. 1820
Copper engraving; ink, paper
7 1/2 × 10 in. (overall)
Museum purchase, 1979 General Obligation Bonds
PC1982.64.1

From the start, New World explorers were fascinated by the American bison, which provided food, clothing, and materials for Ancestral Pueblo and Plains peoples. Through the centuries, the bison—known commonly as buffalo—crossed the land bridge between Asia and North America until millions dotted the countryside. Several million, known as the Texas Herd, ranged into northeastern New Mexico until they were decimated in the 1870s.

In 1598, after an attempt to corral the shaggy animals, Spanish soldier Vicente de Zaldívar Mendoza wrote, "Their shape and appearance are so amazing and amusing, or frightening, that one never tires of looking at them. There is no one so melancholy who if he were to see them a hundred times would not laugh heartily just as often or marvel at the sight of such fierce beasts." Artists could not help but attempt to depict the buffalo. This example by Philadelphia engraver Cephus Childs is a stylized portrayal shown against rococo-style greenery.

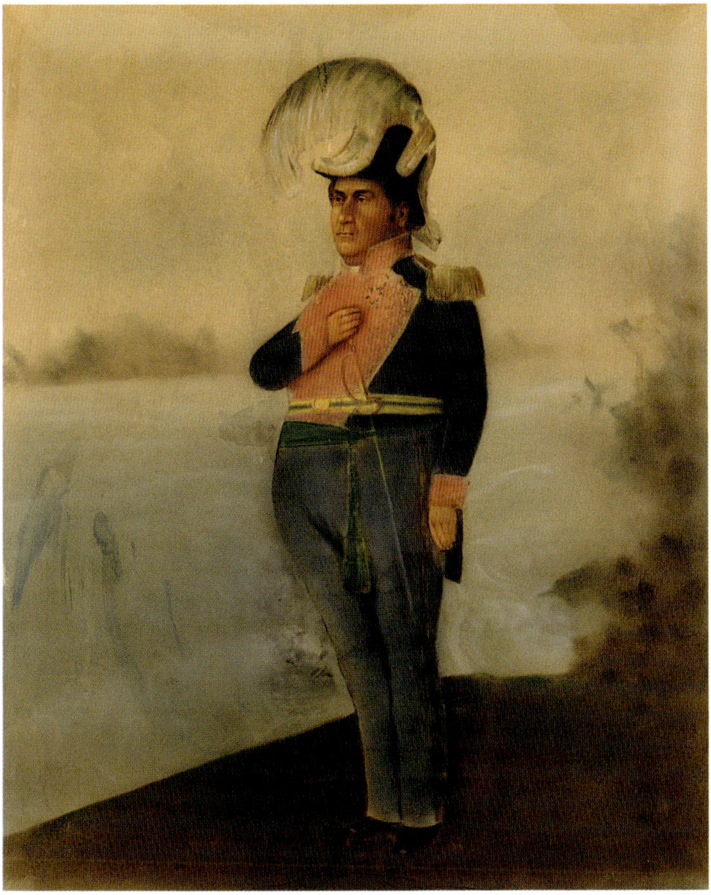

PLATE 84
Alfred S. Waugh, French
Portrait of Governor
Manuel Armijo, ca. 1846
Pastel, paper
28 1/2 × 24 × 1 1/2 in. (overall)
Ward Alan and Shirley Jolly
Minge Collection
Museum purchase, 1995
General Obligation Bonds
PC1998.22.51

Our city has been governed by Spain, Mexico, and the United States. For more than two hundred years Spain aggressively protected her borders but left Alburquerque vulnerable. Mexico acquired Nuevo México after winning independence in 1821. Five years later, the US military under General Stephen Watts Kearney invaded and seized New Mexico, which soon became a territory of the United States. The lives of most residents changed little, though some grew wealthy from improved trade.

General Manuel Armijo (ca. 1793–1853), New Mexico's last Mexican governor, is depicted in full dress. Collector Tony Garcia purchased the portrait from Bill Griffith of Socorro, who bought it in Lemitar, where Armijo lived after the Mexican-American War. From there Garcia sold the painting to historian Ward Alan Minge. Although two were originally made by the artist, this is the only known full-length portrait of the general.

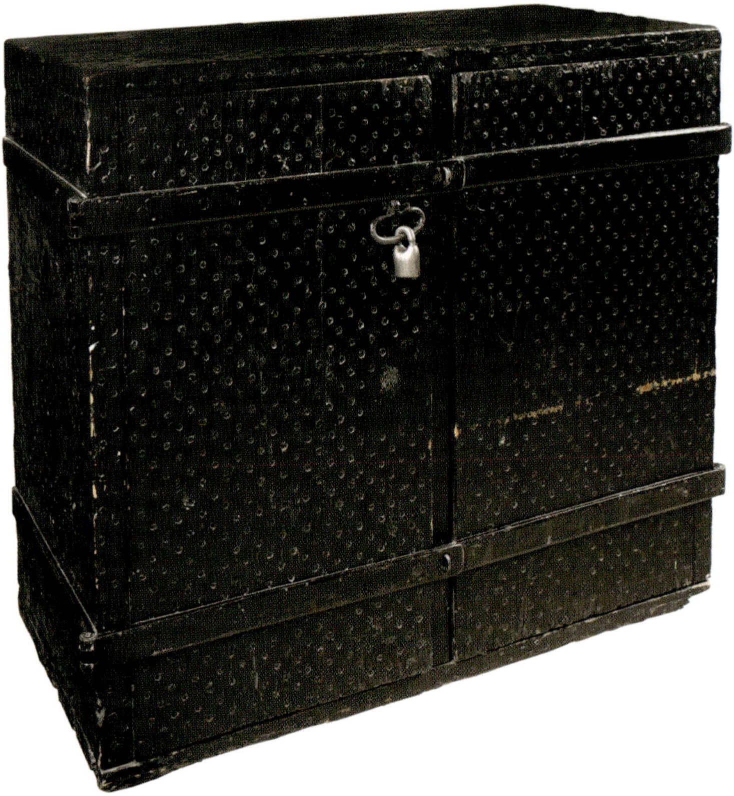

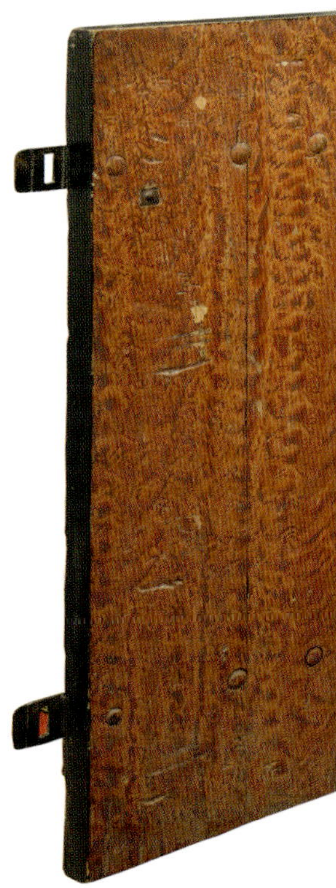

PLATES 85–86
French
Safe owned by Governor Manuel Armijo, 1841–45
41 × 45 × 21 3/4 in. (when closed)
Ward Alan and Shirley Jolly Minge Collection
Museum purchase, 1995 General Obligation Bonds
PC1998.22.35.a

According to his niece, Flora Baca, this safe was made especially for Governor Manuel Armijo, who fled south from Albuquerque to Mexico during the 1846 US invasion of New Mexico. Heavy wooden doors open to reveal eight sizeable drawers marked to hold francs, half dollars, and gold pieces. The safe is encrusted with wrought nails and a substantial iron lock and key, and a lacquer-like black paint covers the entire box.

Armijo eventually returned to live out his days in Lemitar and died in 1853. His descendants lent the safe to the US Army during the Civil War to use at Fort Craig. Ward Alan Minge acquired it and other items belonging to Governor Armijo from Tony Garcia, who purchased the collection from Armijo family heir Cecilia Burton in Socorro.

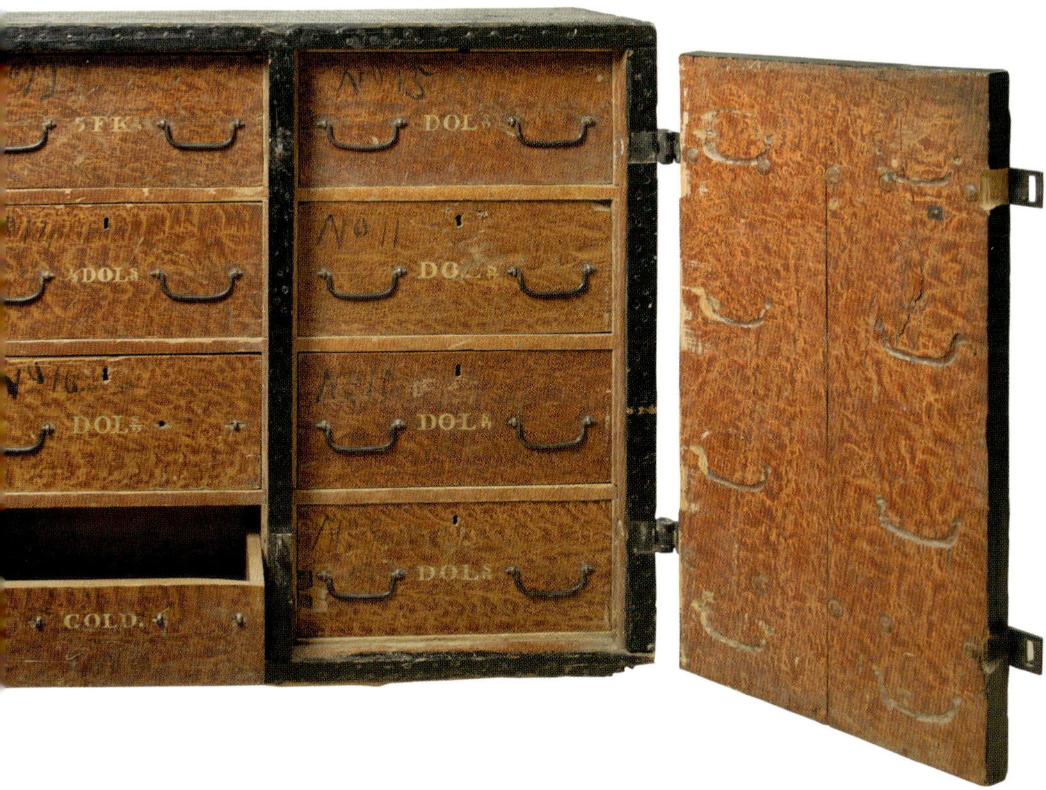

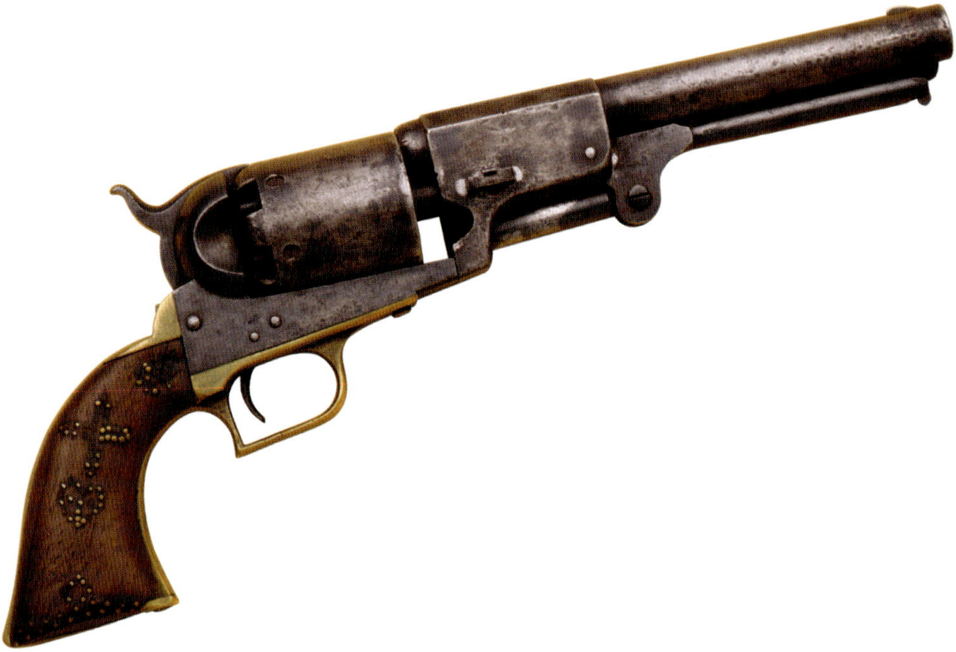

PLATE 87

Samuel Colt, New York City

.44 cal. Colt 1st Model Dragoon Revolver, Serial #6692, ca. 1849

Brass, wood, steel

14 1/2 × 5 1/4 in.

Museum purchase, 1979 General Obligation Bonds

PC1981.218.1

Approximately seven thousand First Model Dragoon pistols were manufactured for use by the US Dragoons, forerunner of the US Cavalry, and by frontiersmen. The heavy six-shot pistols, called "horse pistols" because they were frequently used on horseback, fired a .44 caliber ball packing considerable force. This type of pistol was standard issue among dragoons stationed at the Post of Albuquerque. Brass tacks were added to this pistol in the shape of playing card symbols as decoration or to provide a stronger grip.

Colonel Christopher Houston "Kit" Carson (1809–1868) is one of New Mexico's most well-known citizens. While quartered in Albuquerque's Old Town Plaza, Colonel Carson recruited a militia and commanded the First New Mexico Volunteers in 1862, during the Civil War. Two years later, he led a campaign to remove the Diné (Navajo) to Hwéeldi, or Bosque Redondo, at Fort Sumner. While crossing the Rio Grande on their return to sacred homelands in 1868, the elated but exhausted survivors heard the bells of San Felipe de Neri Church and called our town Bee'eldííldahsinil, or Place Where the Bells Ring.

The year of Carson's death, one of his chairs passed to cousin Sarah Sally Carson, who cared for the colonel's family in Taos. From there it passed down several generations to Minnesotan Dan Bobb, who treasured it for many years. Kit Carson's Shaker slat-back chair retains its original finish and shows wear indicating that he liked to tip back the chair while sitting. The backs of the legs are also worn and the seat has been recaned, suggesting that Colonel Carson could have taken the chair with him on military campaigns.

PLATE 88
Kit Carson's Shaker chair, 1795–1868
New England
Wood (possibly maple), iron
33 1/2 x 16 3/4 x 15 1/4 in.
Gift of the Dan Bobb Family
PC2012.10.1

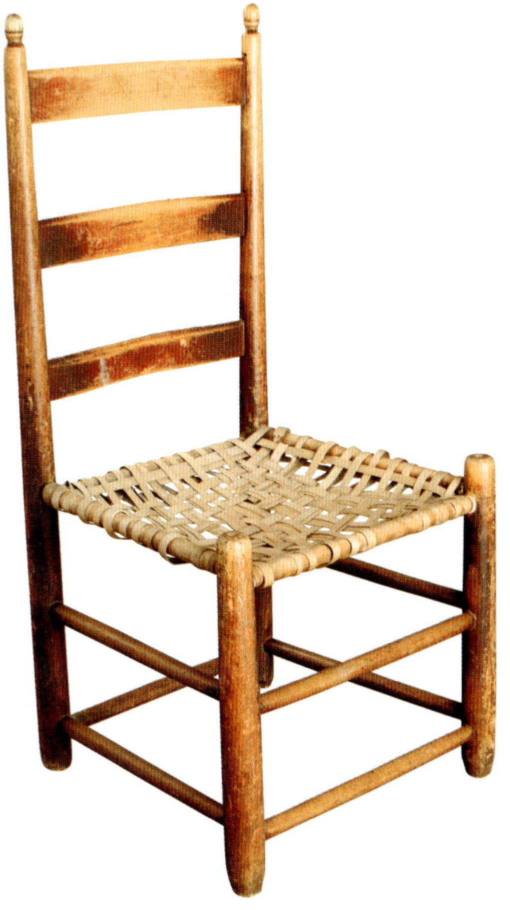

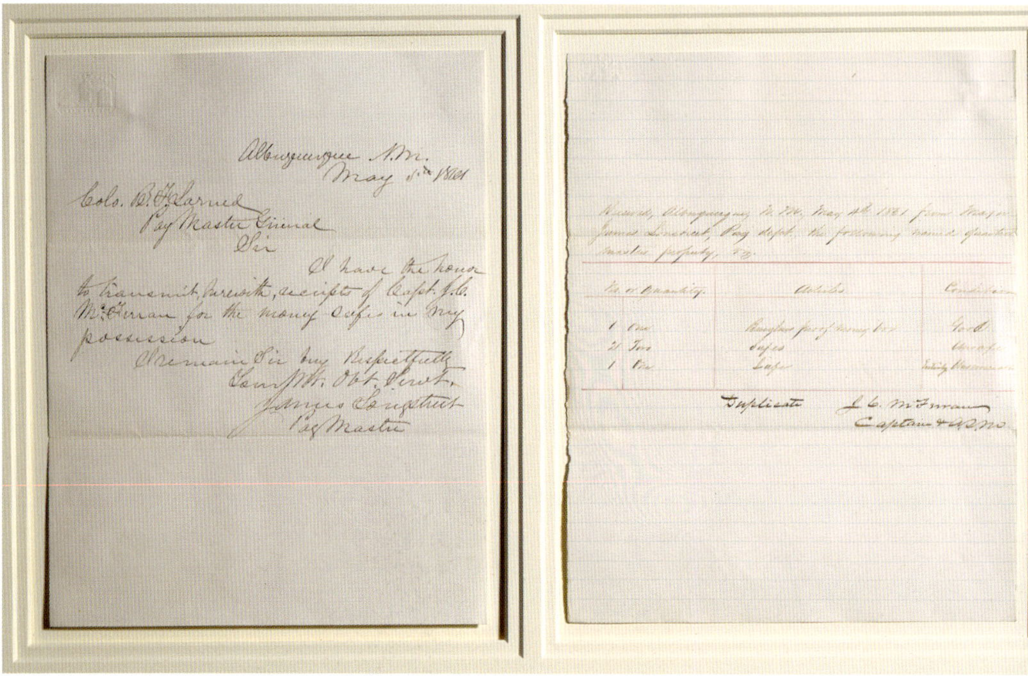

Albuquerque N.M.
May 5th 1861

Colo. B. F. Larned
Pay Master General
Sir
I have the honor to transmit, herewith, receipt of Capt. J. C. McFerran for the money safes in my possession
I remain Sir very Respectfully
Your Mo. Obt. Servt.
James Longstreet
Pay Master

PLATE 89
Letter and inventory of Major James Longstreet
Albuquerque, New Mexico, May 5, 1861
Ink, paper
9 13/16 × 7 3/4 in.
Museum purchase, 1979 General Obligation Bonds
PC1982.105.1a&b

When news of the firing on Fort Sumter reached Albuquerque in May 1861, officers who had delayed making a decision on loyalties were forced to choose sides. One such officer was Paymaster Major James Longstreet, a forty-year-old West Point graduate and veteran of the Mexican-American War. Born in South Carolina, Longstreet had strong Southern sentiments but a loyalty to the Union. He wrote that several officers tried to talk him out of switching to the Confederacy. "It was a sad day when we took leave of lifetime comrades and [gave] up a service of twenty years. Neither Union officers nor their families made efforts to conceal feelings of deepest regret. When we drove out from [Albuquerque], a number of officers rode with us, which only made the last farewell more trying."

In October 1861, Longstreet was made a brigadier general, eventually rising to the rank of lieutenant general in the Confederate Army. He was known as "[Robert E.] Lee's right hand." After the war, he became a Republican, served as US minister to Turkey, and was appointed US commissioner of Pacific railroads.

One of the great ironies of the Civil War is that the tent stove that kept thousands of Union troops warm was invented and patented by the Confederate general who invaded New Mexico. About 1852, Henry Hopkins Sibley (1816–1886), then major of the 2nd Regiment of US Dragoons, designed a field tent patterned after the Comanche tipi. The tents, and a conical stove later added to them, were well received, and the army adopted them as standard issue. Major Sibley received a $5 royalty for each tent manufactured.

At the outbreak of the Civil War, US Army Major Sibley resigned his commission and became Confederate General Sibley, leading the Confederate Army of New Mexico into the Territory, and Albuquerque, in 1862. His tent and stove were manufactured and issued through the Civil War, World War I, and World War II, but Sibley's royalties were suspended before he received the fortune he would have reaped from mass production. This Sibley stove was found near Fort Wingate, New Mexico.

PLATE 90
Unknown US Arsenal
Sibley tent stove, ca. 1860
Iron
29 × 19 in.
Museum purchase, 1979
General Obligation Bonds
PC1981.233.1

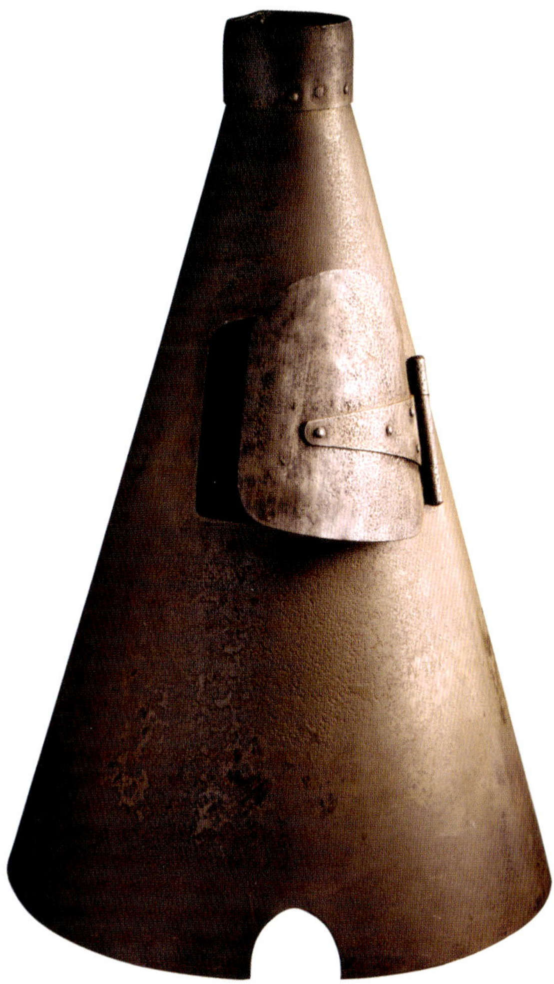

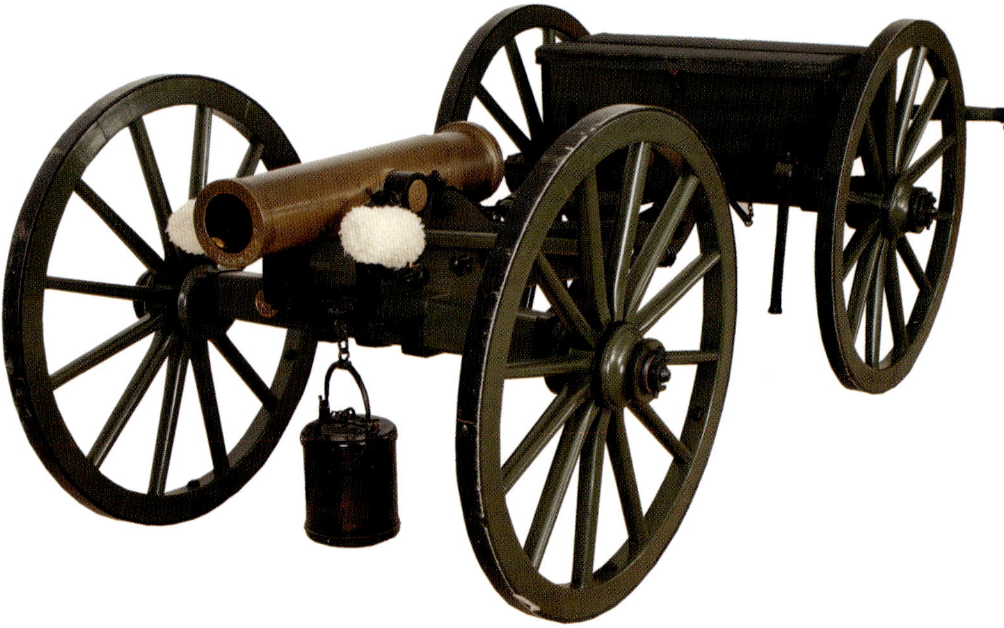

PLATE 91

Cyrus Alger and Company, Boston, Massachusetts
Model 1841 12-pounder mountain howitzer, 1853
Bronze, copper, steel, oilcloth
37 × 8 in.
Transfer, City of Albuquerque Parks and Recreation Department
PC1983.20.2

Replica of prairie carriage, 2008
Marshall Steen Cannon
Oak, iron, paint, oilcloth
43 × 236 × 66 in.
Gift of Dick and Betty Teel
RS2008.8.1

When the Confederate Army invaded New Mexico in 1862, it brought a number of mountain howitzers captured at the Union Arsenal at San Antonio. These were used in the battles of Valverde, Glorieta Pass, Peralta, and Albuquerque and could be packed on horses or mules for fast travel. On the retreat from New Mexico it became obvious that the howitzers would slow the soldiers down, but their carriages could carry supplies and the wounded. To prevent them from falling into Union hands, the army buried eight howitzers in a corral roughly five hundred feet northeast of Old Town Plaza.

Twenty-seven years later, in 1889, ex-Confederate Major Trevanion T. Teel (1824–1899) met Captain Jack Crawford (1847–1917) on a train and discussed the location of the buried howitzer tubes. But the corral was being used as a chile garden and the owner refused to have his crop destroyed. So the excavators filed a mining claim for bronze—a mineral not found in nature—and removed the eight howitzers from a pit about three feet deep. Two were on display in Robinson Park and the Plaza until 1983, when the original tubes were removed, transferred to the Museum, and replaced with replicas.

The Bliss family descendants have worked hard to preserve family memorabilia, including artifacts representing the service of Eleanor Sheldon Bliss's grandfather Captain Zenas H. Bliss (1842–1929) in the Civil War. Bliss served with the Union Army in the 9th Regiment of Vermont Volunteers and then became captain of Company K, 28th Regiment of US Colored Troops (known later as the Buffalo Soldiers). The USCT saw action in Richmond and Petersburg, Virginia, during 1864–65 and was later stationed in Texas.

Captain Bliss kept his company records in this simple but sturdy field desk during the battles for Richmond (Virginia) in 1864 as he witnessed the fall of the Confederacy. His descendants found the desk among household belongings; they donated his Civil War records to the Indiana and Vermont Historical Societies.

After the Civil War, Captain Bliss saw action along the Rio Grande in Texas, where his company fought in the Indian Wars. Bliss moved to Albuquerque in the 1880s, lived at 1212 North Fifth Street, and became a carpenter and a woodworking instructor at the Albuquerque Indian School. He also helped build a log cabin in the Sandias now owned by Presbyterian Healthcare Services. He is buried in Fairview Cemetery.

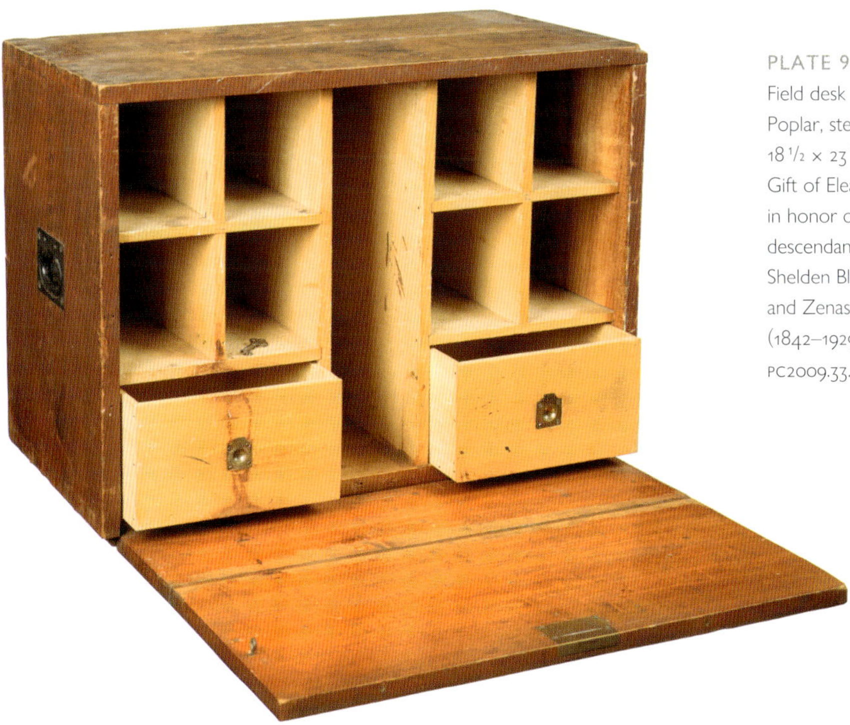

PLATE 92
Field desk
Poplar, steel, brass
18 1/2 × 23 1/2 × 13 in.
Gift of Eleanor Sheldon Bliss in honor of all the proud descendants of Sarah Ann Shelden Bliss (1842–1913) and Zenas Harrison Bliss II (1842–1929)
PC2009.33.1

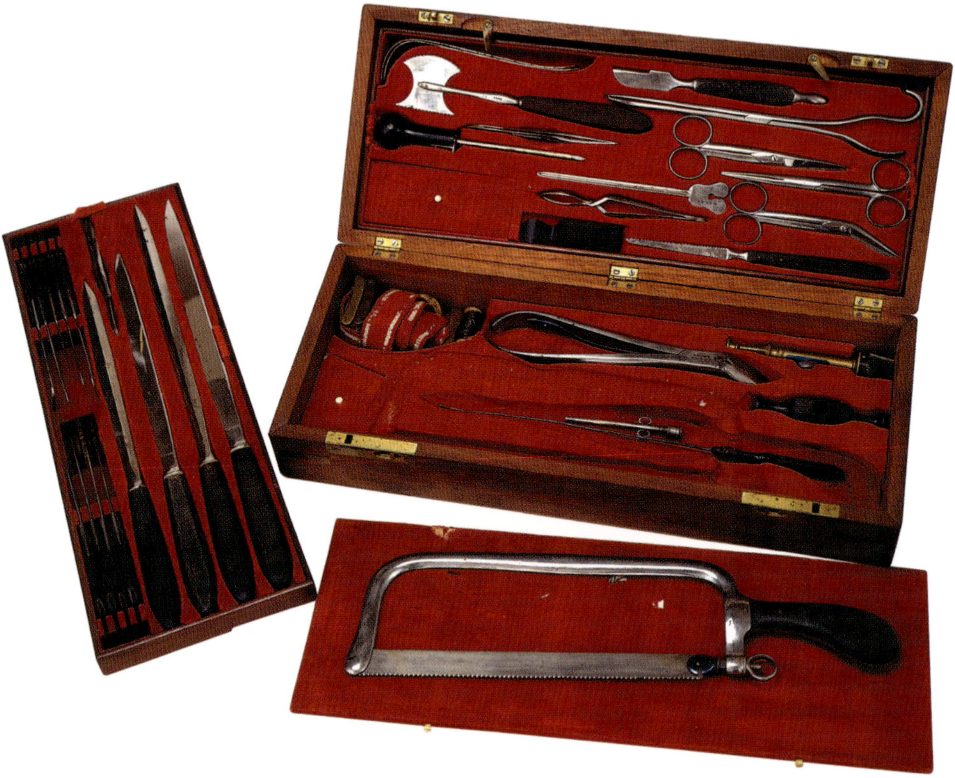

PLATE 93

Dietrich W. Kolbe, Philadelphia, Pennsylvania

Civil War surgeon's kit, ca. 1863–65

Mahogany, brass, velveteen, steel, cotton thread

16 1/2 × 6 1/2 × 4 3/8 in.

Gift of the descendants of John "Jackie" Taylor: Gwyn Fair Ellis, Willett Taylor Fair, James Taylor Rock, and Kenneth Willett Rock

PC2002.26.1

M. L. Amick (1843–1904) was a Union surgeon from Cincinnati who served in the Civil War. Amick received the kit—a type that was used by the US Army during the war—as a gift from a grateful patient.

A nearly complete set, it is one of the largest and most comprehensive Civil War–era kits in a museum collection. Amick's descendant, Gwyn Fair Ellis, is an Albuquerque resident.

PLATE 94

Apache or Comanche

Arrow and lance points, 1750–1850

Iron, possibly brass

$3\ ^1/_4 \times {}^5/_8$ in. (largest)

Gift of William S. Wilson

PC1976.86.290

Apache and Comanche warriors fashioned working projectile points out of just about any available material, including stone, glass, iron, and brass. By the late 1800s, available materials included iron knife blades and the metal from cans of food. While the provenance of these points is unknown, similar examples are often found in the Sandia Mountains.

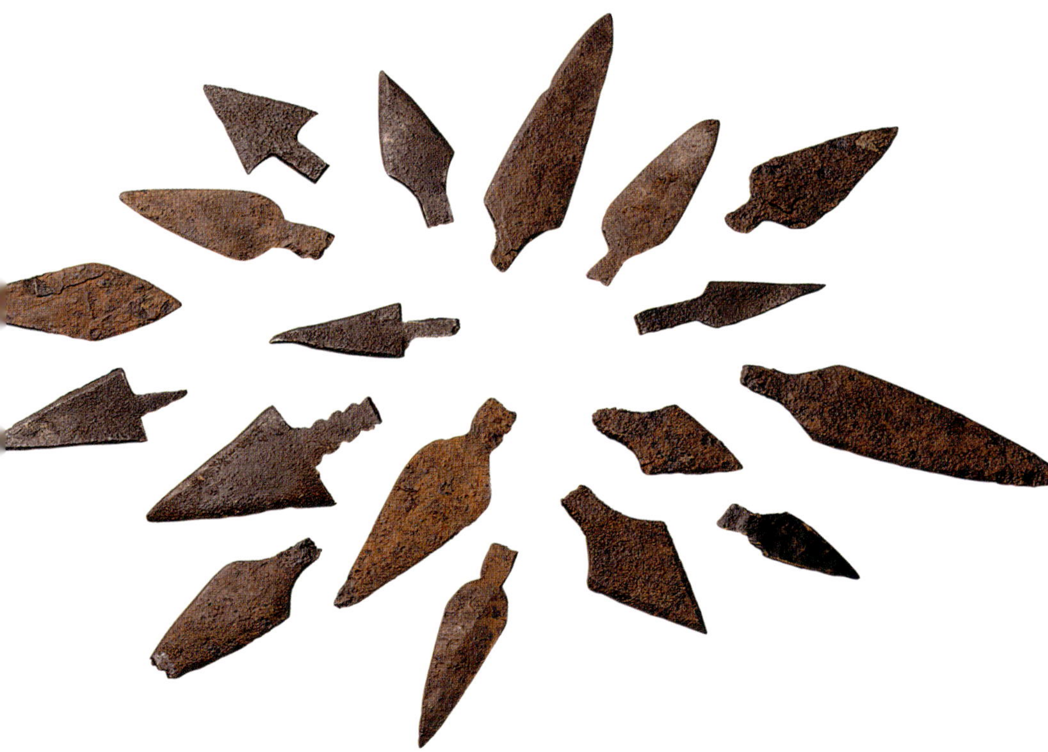

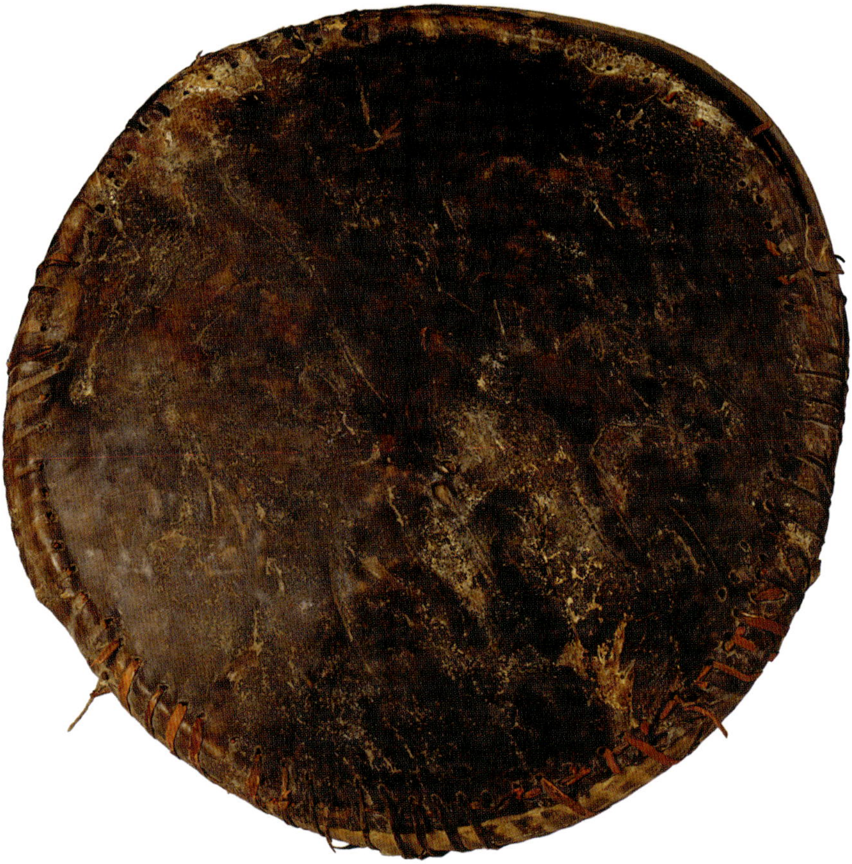

PLATE 95
Comanche
Shield, 1850–60
Hide, straw, pigment
21 × 21 × 3 in.
Museum purchase, 1979 General Obligation Bonds
PC1982.83.1

Comanche warriors' shields were far superior to the thin rawhide shields used by other southwestern Indians; they were also an effective counterpart to Spanish soldiers' hide *adargas* (shield). Warriors stretched hide over a wooden hoop to create a front panel, filled the center with grass or bark, and laced a back panel over the stuffing. The shield could absorb musket and pistol fire and deflect lance thrusts and sword cuts. A faint red outline of human and abstract figures decorates the front panel.

PLATE 96
Comanche
Woman's saddle, ca. 1870
Wood, rawhide, sinew
12 11/16 × 22 1/4 × 9 1/2 in.
Museum purchase, 1979 General Obligation Bonds
PC1982.80.1
Ex-collection Pierre Bovis and Davidson Collection

The Comanche people have always been admired as skilled horse handlers. Only women made and used this type of saddle; they selected tree forks to form the arches and used sinew or hide to sew and shrink wet rawhide over the wooden form. A soft leather strap was suspended between the horns for comfort during travel. Young children were taught to ride by being tied onto a woman's saddle and led around camp.

This saddle was acquired from the Winona Trading Post; its original owner was a cavalry surgeon in the Southwest.

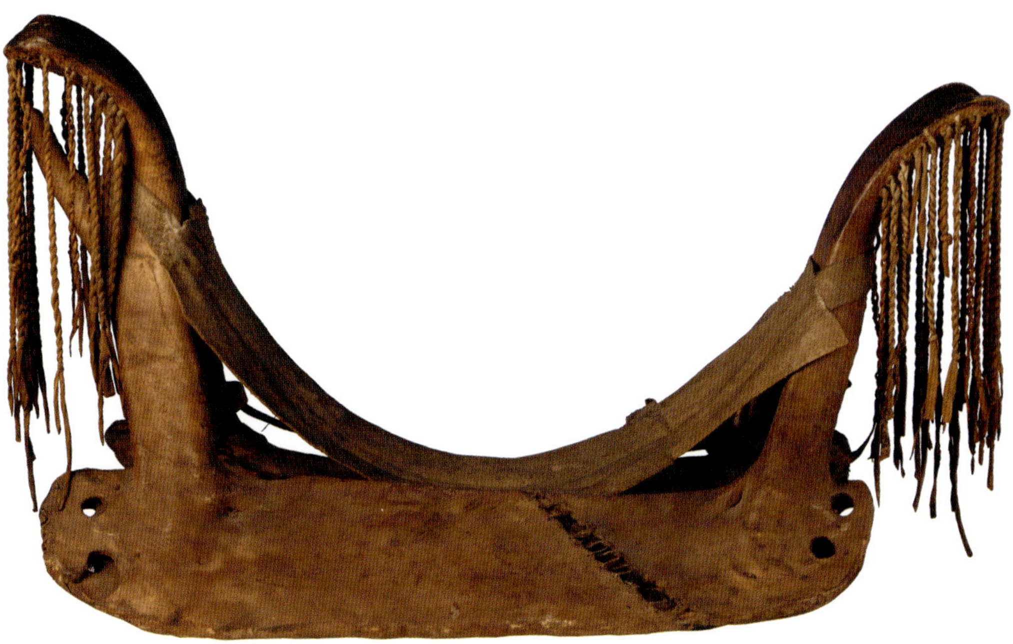

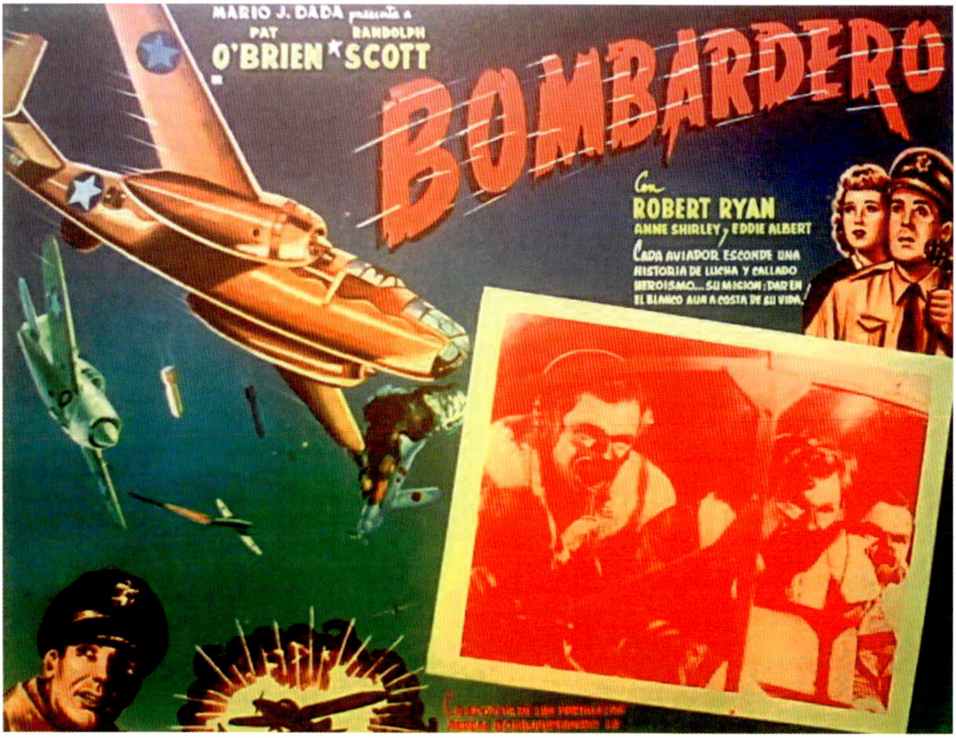
MARIO J. DADA presenta a
PAT O'BRIEN ★ RANDOLPH SCOTT
BOMBARDERO
Con
ROBERT RYAN
ANNE SHIRLEY, EDDIE ALBERT
Cada aviador esconde una historia de lucha y callado heroismo... su mision: dar en el blanco aun a costa de su vida.

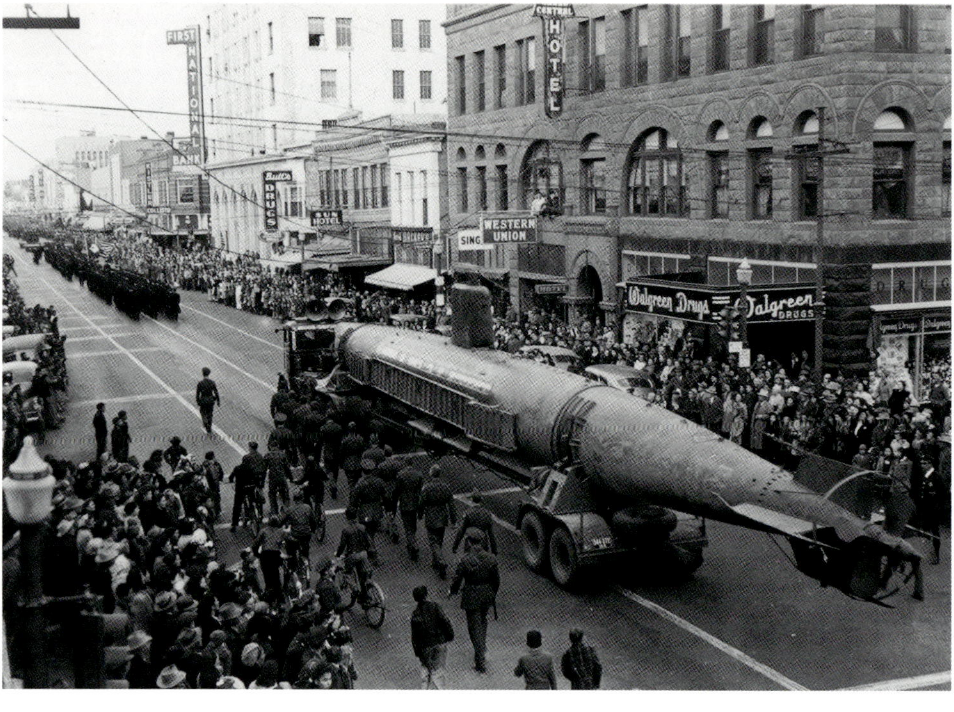
FIRST NATIONAL BANK
CENTRAL HOTEL
Butt's DRUGS
SUN HOTEL
WESTERN UNION
SING
Walgreen Drugs
Walgreen DRUGS

PLATE 97
RKO Pictures
Lobby card, *Bombardero (Bombardier)*, 1943
Offset lithograph; ink, paper
Museum purchase
12 1/2 x 16 1/2 in.
PC2013.23.1

Good weather and access to land made Albuquerque a prime location for the army's 19th Bombardment Group at Kirtland Army Air Base, America's first permanent bombardier training center. Bombardiers learned how to crawl into the nose of a bomber—a vulnerable location during an actual mission—to feed information into one of their most closely guarded secrets, the Norden bombsight. The Norden bombsight linked to the aircraft's autopilot system, enabling the crew to destroy targets at an altitude of twelve thousand feet. Crews were under orders to destroy the sight if necessary and carried hand grenades on board just in case. Eventually, Kirtland graduated more than five thousand bombardiers.

Kirtland's role in training bombardiers during World War II was celebrated in the classic 1943 war drama *Bombardier*, starring Pat O'Brien and Randolph Scott. Kirtland aviation cadets served as extras, while veteran aviators flew B-17s in formation in the end shots. Throughout the film there are glimpses of clear Albuquerque skies, the Sandia Mountains, and the base. Promotional posters and lobby cards were printed in both English and Spanish. Despite scathing reviews, the film won an Academy Award for Best Special Effects in 1944.

PLATE 98
United States Navy parade with Japanese midget submarine, Central Avenue, January 19, 1943
Gift of Arthur Loy
PA1982.118.19

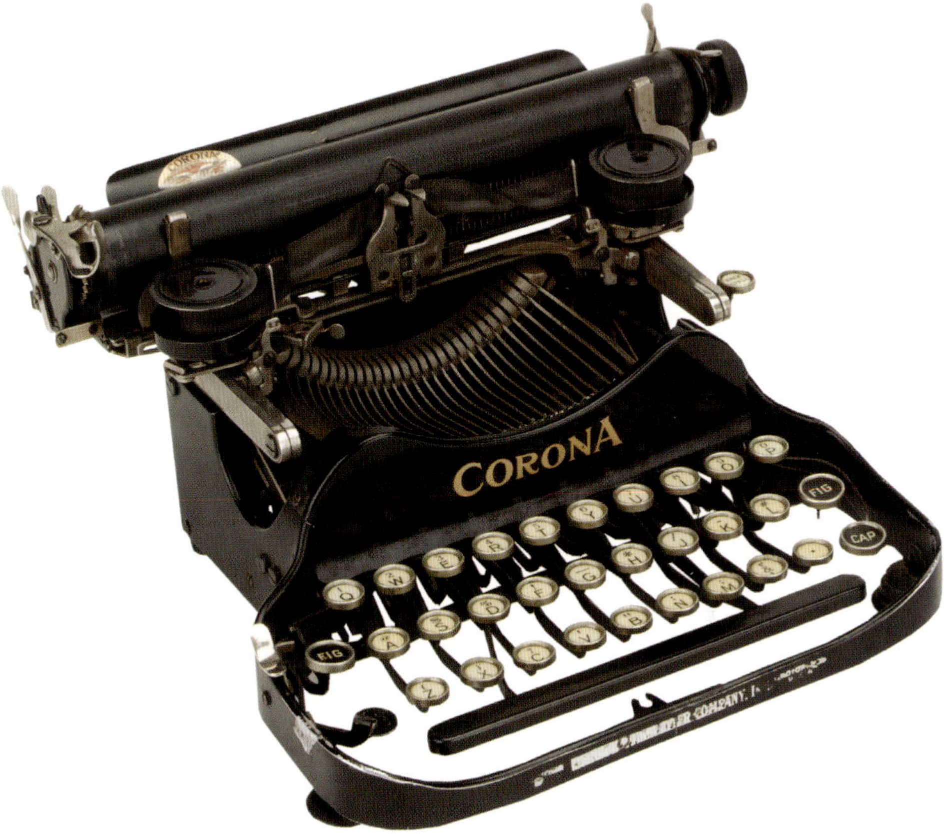

PLATE 99
Smith Corona Typewriter Company
Corona 3 portable typewriter, ca. 1923 (last patent date 1917)
Steel, chrome, paint, plastic, rubber, ribbon, ink
5 3/8 × 12 1/4 × 11 in.
Gift of Harry E. Chrisman and Don Bell in memory of Ernie Pyle
PC1990.80.1

Until killed by a sniper's bullet at Iejima in 1945, war reporter Ernie Pyle (1900–1945), who lived in Albuquerque, wrote about the daily lives of common soldiers. Pyle interviewed Sergeant Don Bell, a rodeo rider, in June or July 1944 outside Saint-Lô, France. Bell recalled that the foxhole they shared caved in during German shelling. Pyle said, "I have my notes, but my little portable typewriter is buried in that hole." They hurriedly abandoned the foxhole, leaving the typewriter behind. Sergeant Bell later salvaged it, kept it through the war, and donated it to the Museum in 1990.

Bell recalled the interview as comforting. He wrote, "Ernie had taken my ma's wisdom and turned it into a soldier's lesson: to find strength in battle you take hold of strength you've known at home . . . and of the faith that underlies it." By the time of his death, Pyle's work was carried in four hundred newspapers. During his lifetime, he received a Pulitzer Prize for journalism and an honorary UNM doctoral degree.

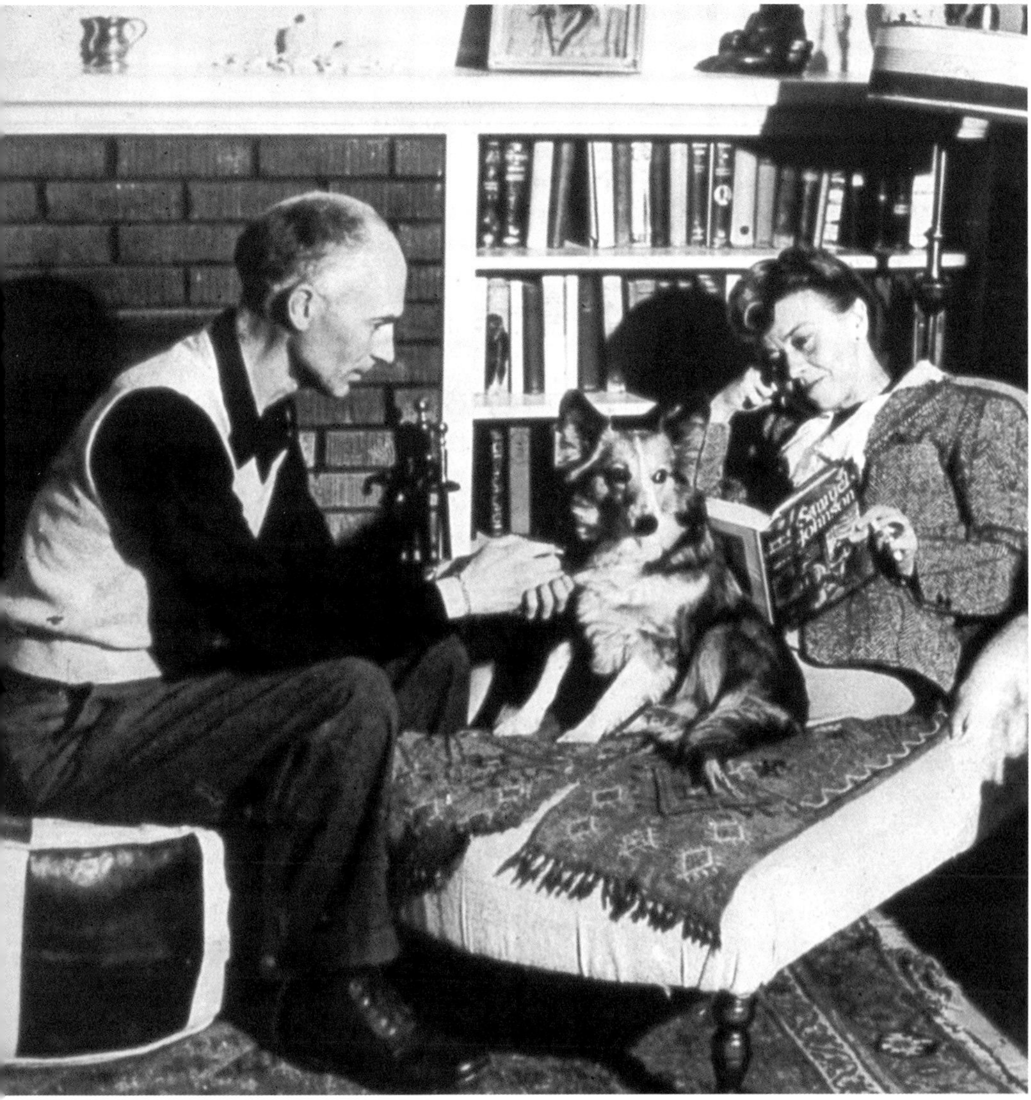

PLATE 100

Ernie Pyle, Cheetah, and Jerry, 1944

Gift of the Albuquerque/Bernalillo County Public Library, Ernie Pyle Branch

PA2003.31.1

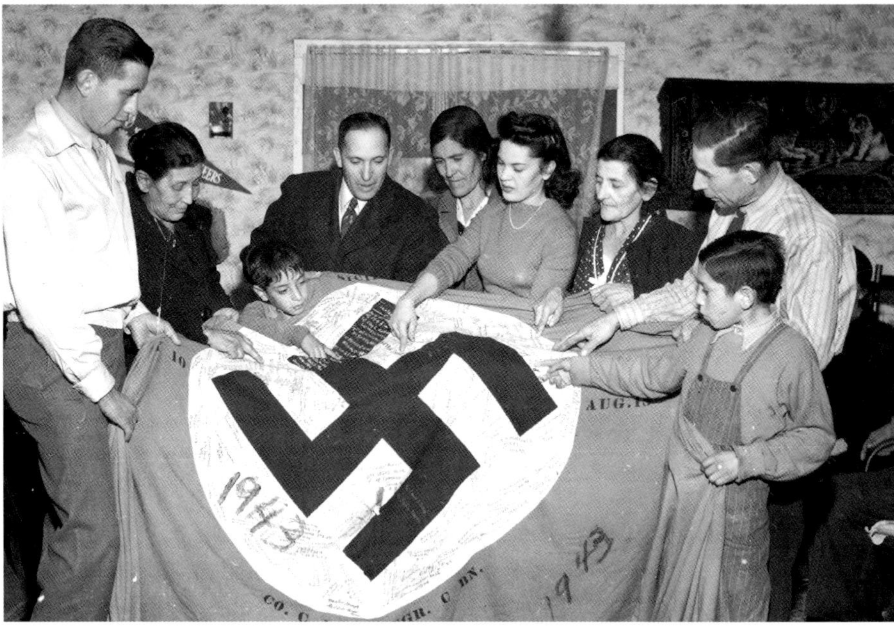

PLATE 101
Nazi banner signed by Company C of the 120th Combat Engineer Battalion, 1943
Linen, ink
57 × 184 in.
Banner: Gift of Kevin Duran
PC2011.12.2
Photograph: Gift of Tony Duran Sr.
PA1984.89.1

In 1920, Adolf Hitler decided that the Nazi Party needed its own insignia for Germany that would convey "a symbol of [its] own struggle," as well as be "highly effective as a poster." On August 7, 1920, at the Salzburg Congress, the insignia became the official emblem for the Nazi Party's flags and banners.

Captured and signed by members of the 120th Engineers of Las Vegas near the end of the war in Europe, this Nazi banner was sent home to the United States by the soldiers and was signed by Sergeant Tony Durán along with Sergeant Eloy L. Gallegos of Las Vegas, Simon Mendosa of Albuquerque, and many others. In the photograph, the captured banner is being inspected by Josie Romero, Manuel "Eloy" Durán, and other family members. Descendant Gilbert Gallegos notes, "This particular flag is special because of the signatures of the soldiers who fought and sacrificed to capture it."

Thanks to the GI Bill, soldiers returned to college after the war and pursued related careers, allowing their descendants—many of whom live in Albuquerque today—to attend the University of New Mexico and cultivate their own careers in engineering and mechanics.

In 1999 Hasbro commemorated the valor of the Navajo Code Talkers, who used their traditional Diné language during World War II to save lives by preserving the security of top-secret communications during the Pacific campaign (1942–45). Words and phrases like *ke-yah-da-na-lhe* (floating island) and *ga-hih* (crow) were code words for "Philippine" and "patrol plane."

Navajo Code Talker GI Joe introduces young people to the beauty and sophistication of the Diné (Navajo) language. With a push of a button, GI Joe repeats seven different phrases in Diné and English, including *jo-kayed-goh nilchi ba-ah-hot-gli* (request air support) and *tse-gah tkin nash-doie-tso nash-doie-tso-a-la-ih hastaa ashdia ye-dzhe-al-tsisi-gi* (hill 165 secured). The recorded voice was provided by one of the original twenty-nine Navajo Code Talkers, Dr. Sam Billison.

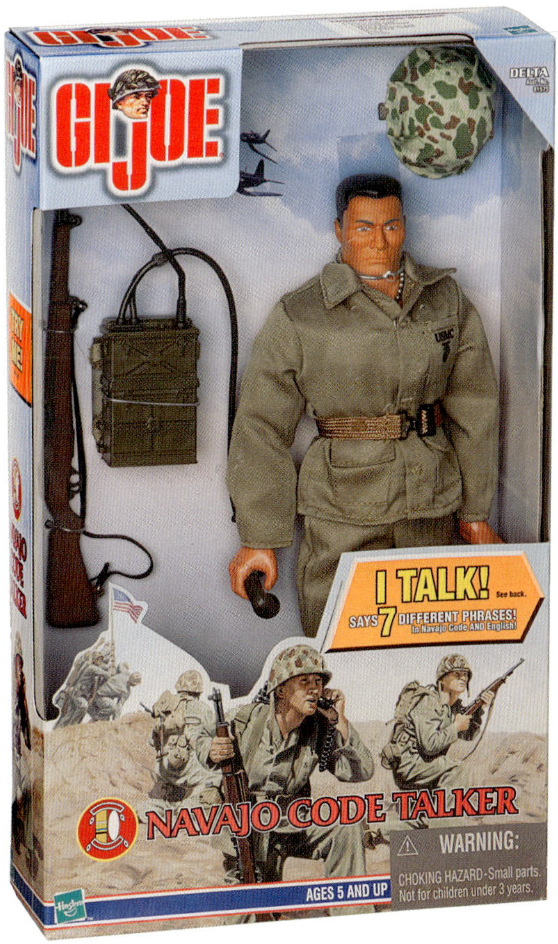

PLATE 102
Hasbro Inc., Pawtucket, Rhode Island
Navajo Code Talker GI Joe, 1999
Plastic, cotton, cardboard, paper
13 1/2 × 8 × 3 in.
Museum purchase, Director's Discretionary Fund
PA2002.88.1

PLATE 103
150th Fighter Wing patch, 2013
Snackostuff.com
Cotton, polyester, Velcro
4 × 4 in.
Museum purchase
PC2013.22.1

Albuquerque's mild climate and land base made it an ideal spot for the nation's first permanent training center for bombardiers of the army's 19th Bombardment Group. Today, Kirtland Air Force Base conducts training, research, development, testing, and munitions maintenance.

The 150th Fighter Wing, stationed at Kirtland, is a unit of the New Mexico Air National Guard. Under different names, members of the unit served during the Korean War (1950–53), stood on alert during the Cuban Missile Crisis (1962), and were deployed in Vietnam (1968–69) and during Operation Desert Storm (1990–91). The 150th also protected the western United States and, later, the Albuquerque International Sunport in the wake of the terrorist attacks of September 11, 2001.

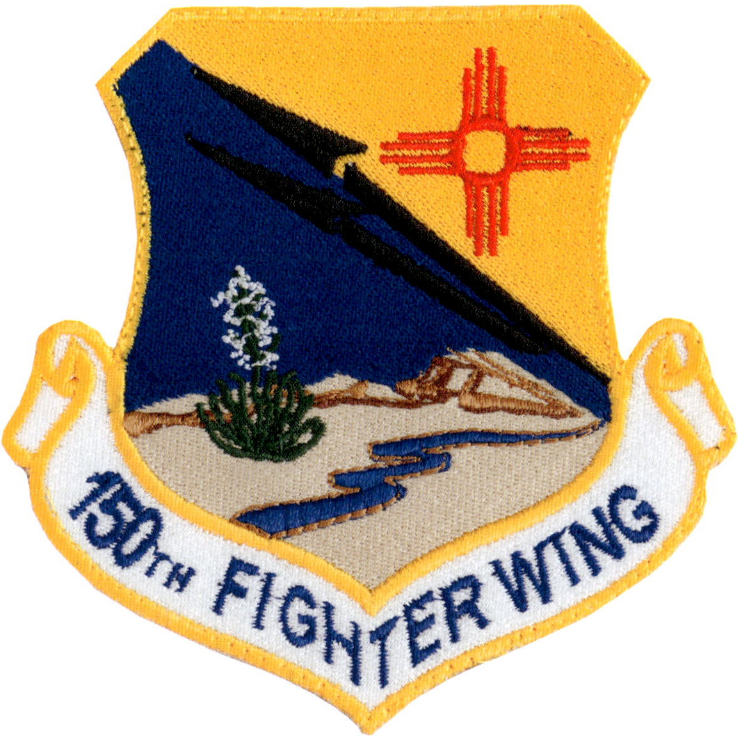
150TH FIGHTER WING

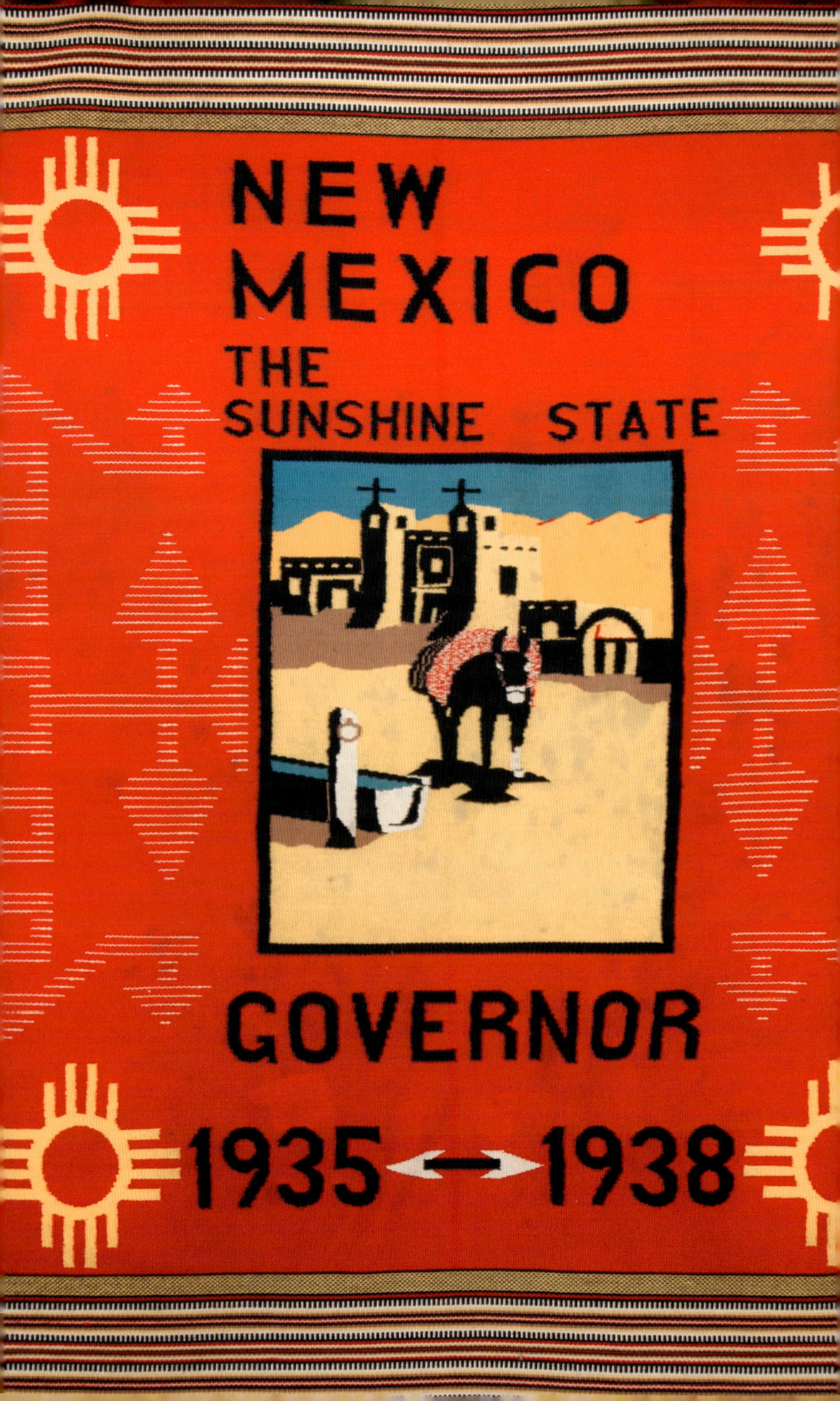
NEW
MEXICO
THE
SUNSHINE STATE
GOVERNOR
1935 1938

Economic Hardship

Despite booms and busts, 15 percent of Albuquerque families still live below the poverty line. Cycles of wool depressions, military pull-outs, bank failures, and bankruptcies aggravate our already fragile local economy.

In response, we are expanding agricultural markets, rebuilding infrastructure, and investing in new technologies. And while back-to-work programs show promise, incomes remain flat. Conditions in Albuquerque sorely test the will to succeed—especially for our poorest residents.

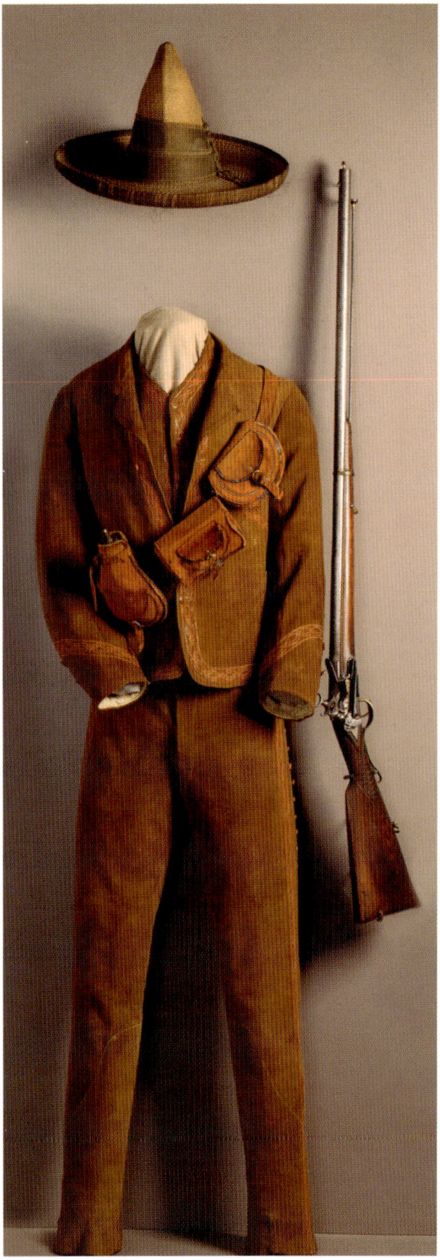

PLATE 104

Northern Mexican or Hispanic New Mexican
Vaquero (cowboy) outfit, ca. 1860–80
Leather, fabric, thread
$54\frac{3}{8} \times 18 \times 5$ in. (overall)
Gift of Mr. and Mrs. William Bates
PC1982.260.1.a–c

This idealized version of a vaquero outfit was probably worn by a *rico* (wealthy landowner) during the period after the Civil War. The combination of a leather jacket, vest, and button-sided pants first appeared in Mexico and California about 1800 and, through time, became the idealized charro (horseman) outfit of modern times.

Just as the American cowboy never dressed in the fashion today associated with "cowboys," the average New Mexican vaquero dressed in a straw sombrero, leather jacket, plain cloth shirt, and leather pants. Ornate decorations found in colonial California, such as silver buttons on pants legs, were beyond the means of most New Mexicans until long after the Santa Fe Trail period.

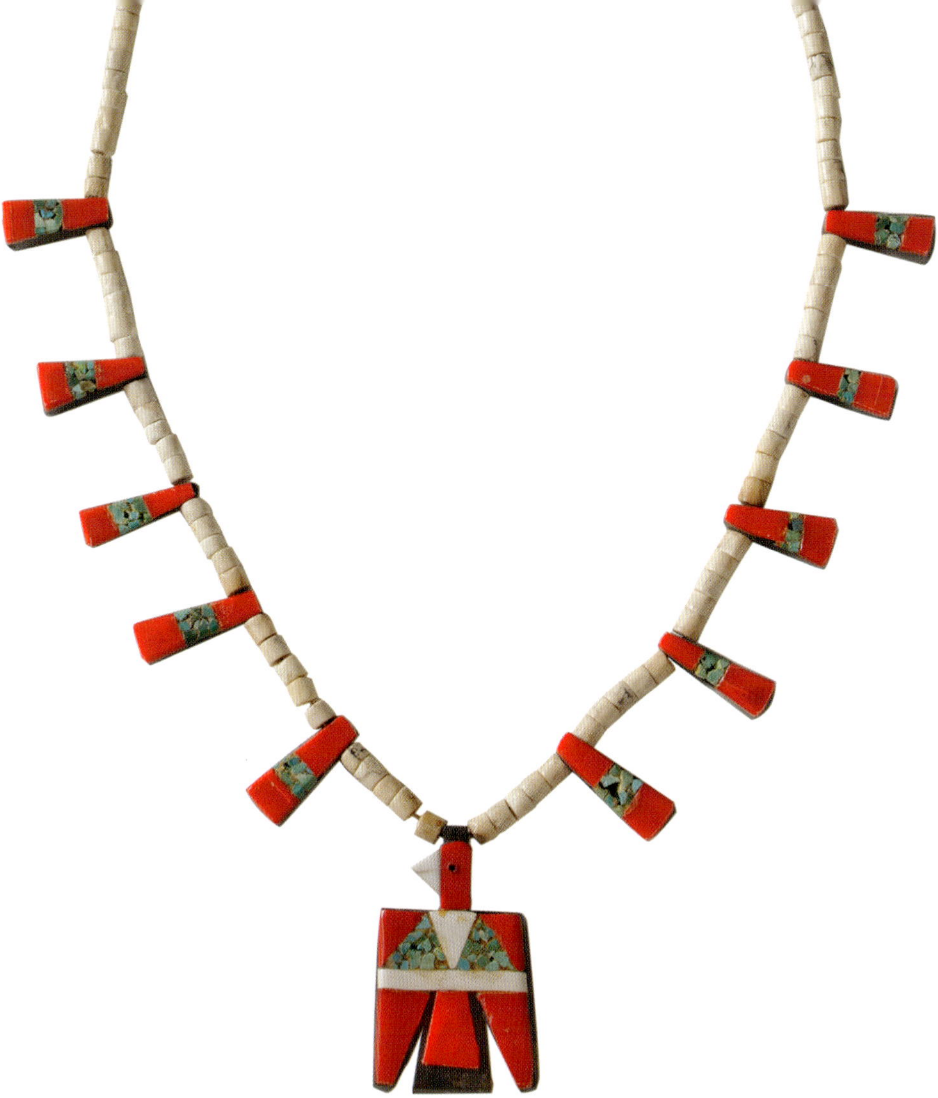

PLATE 105
Kewa (Santo Domingo)
"Thunderbird" necklace, ca. 1930
Battery casing, red plastic, turquoise, adhesive, cordage
Gift of the estate of Dorothy B. Whitten
PC1989.24.10

During the Depression and World War II, silver and turquoise became expensive to buy and even harder to find. Kewa (Santo Domingo) jewelers developed creative strategies to cope with tough economic times by using battery casings, dish drainers, and phonograph records as backing and inlay material.

PLATE 106
Desk belonging to Clyde Tingley, 1930s–60s
Oak, metal
44 × 59 in.
Gift of Jack Stahl
PC1977.69.1

Contemporary Albuquerque took shape during the 1930s and 1940s, thanks to Clyde Tingley (1882–1960). Along with John Milne and Clinton Anderson, Tingley worked with Senator Dennis Chávez and President Franklin Roosevelt to secure funding for an airport, theater, school buildings, and fairgrounds.

Clyde Tingley served as Albuquerque city alderman, commission chairman (now called mayor), and New Mexico governor for two terms. Tingley was a genius at developing partnerships to get federal funding for infrastructure projects. During his political career, Governor Tingley became known for his funny and often awkward phrasing. Referring to construction in Roosevelt Park, he once commented, "I want those auroras [arroyos] all tijerased [terraced] up!"

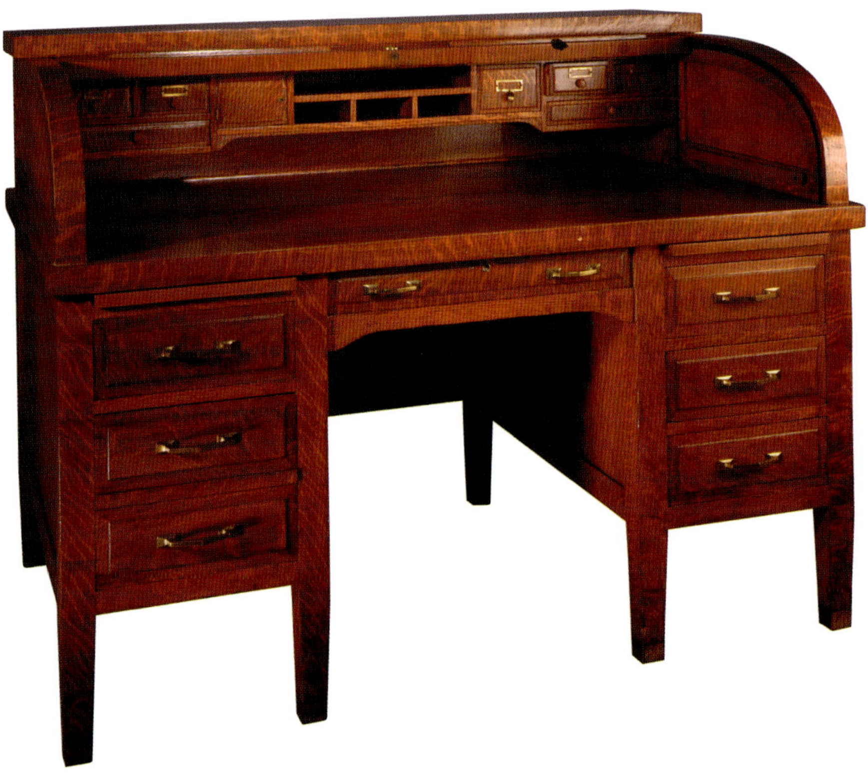

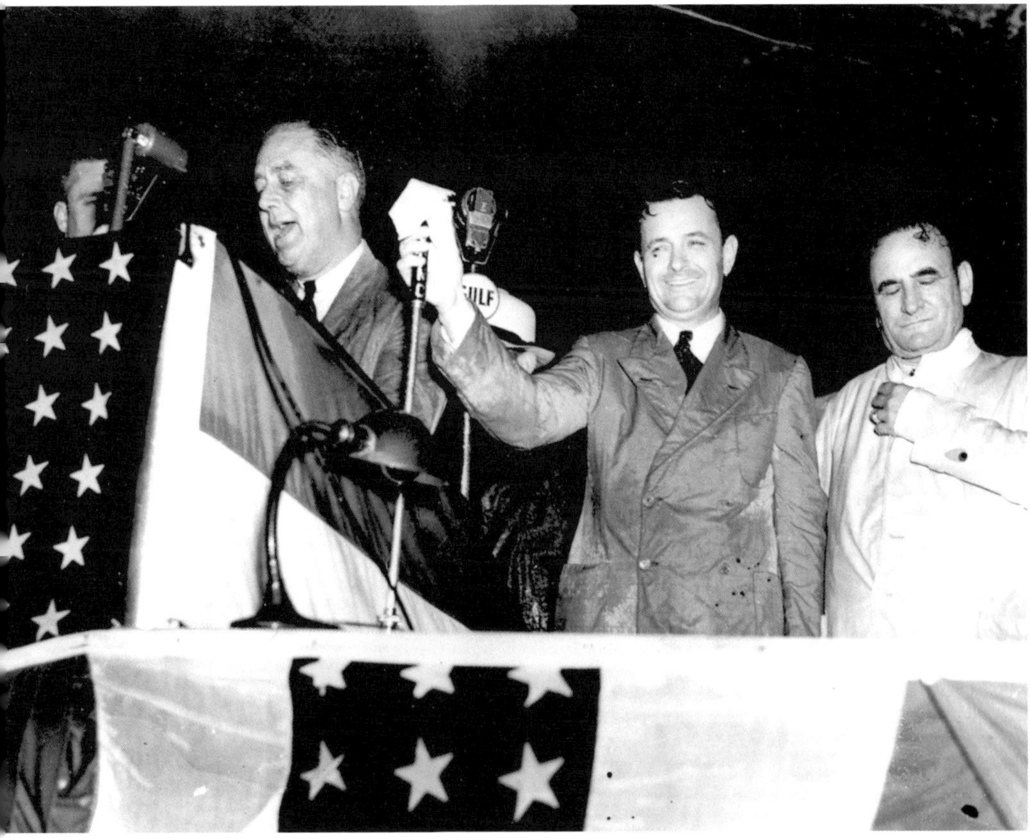

PLATE 107
President Franklin Delano Roosevelt (*2nd from left*) and Governor Clyde Tingley (*far right*), ca. 1935
Gift of Clarence Higgins
PA1976.142.17

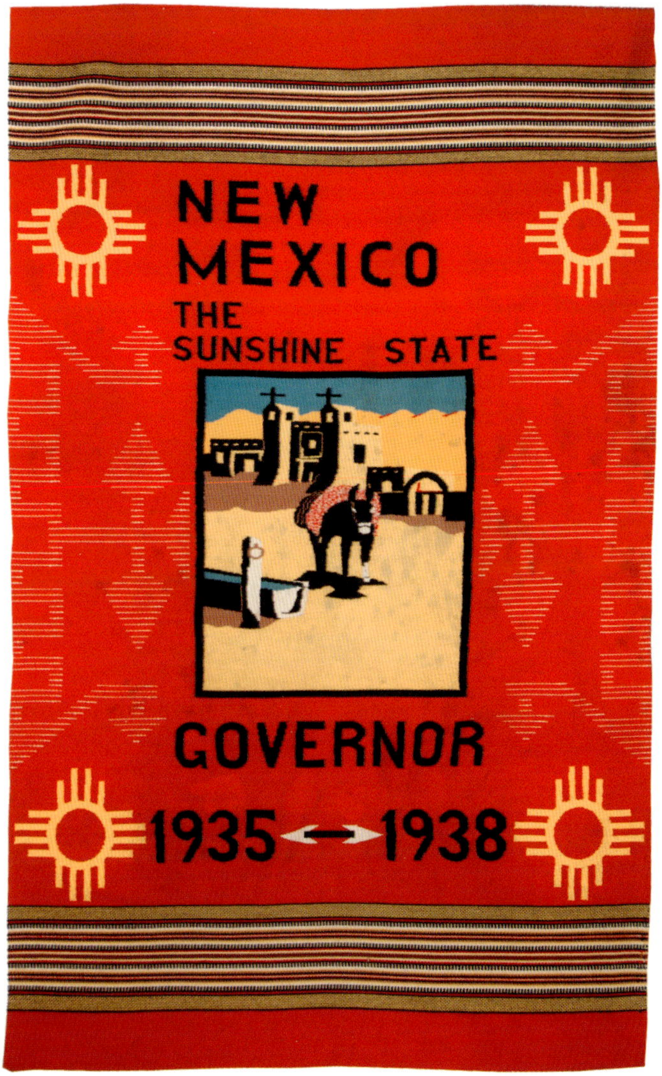

PLATE 108
Chimayó
Commemorative weaving, 1935
Wool, dyes
52 × 34 1/4 in.
Gift of Mrs. Clarence Higgins
PC1984.14.3

This wall hanging, crafted by a traditional weaver from Chimayó, New Mexico, was presented to Clyde Tingley during his service as governor from 1935 to 1938. The donor was a cousin of the governor's wife, philanthropist Carrie Tingley.

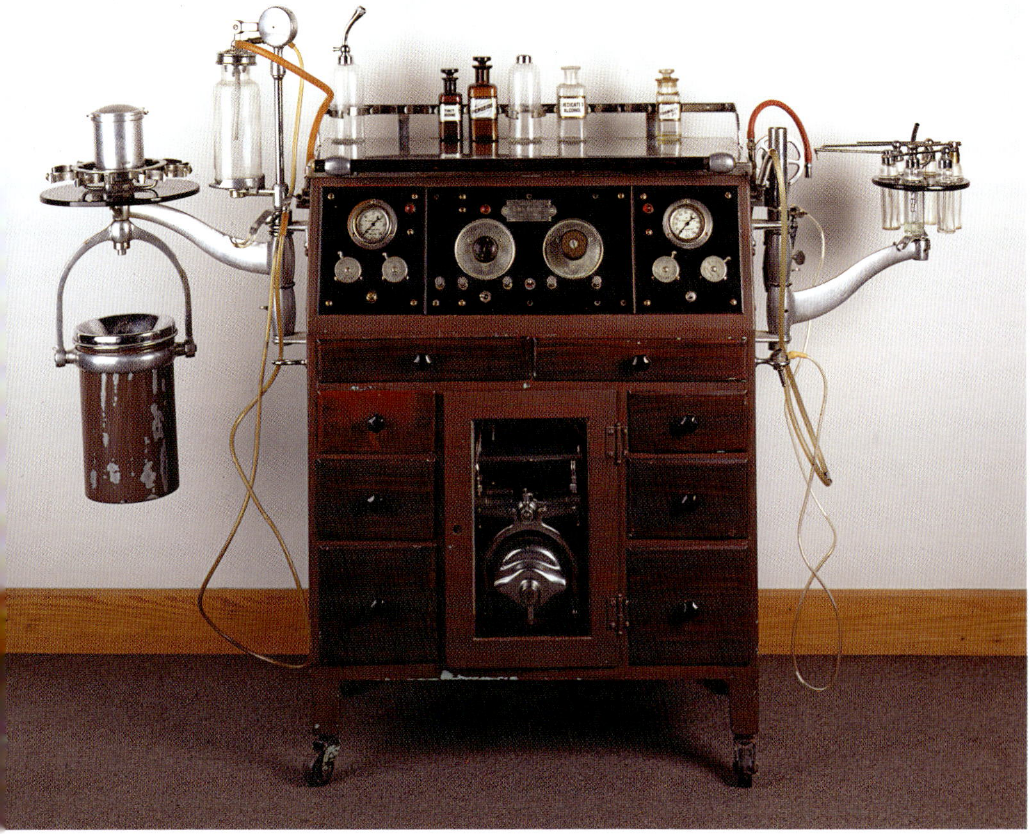

PLATE 109
Sorenson Co., New York
De-luxe Ear, Nose, and Throat Machine
and Treatment Machine, 1930
Wood, steel, chrome, glass
60 × 35 × 26 in.
Gift of Dr. Theodore R. Sadock
PC1987.49.1

As the result of an advertising campaign designed to bring tuberculosis patients to Albuquerque, in part to fuel its economic growth, "lungers"—including Albuquerque's first lady Carrie Tingley and Albuquerque Little Theatre founder Kathryn Kennedy O'Connor—flocked to Albuquerque during the late nineteenth and twentieth centuries.

The Sorenson was considered to be the Rolls Royce of examination equipment for ear, nose, and throat conditions. Its motor provided compressed air and suction, lighting, and power to the instruments. Dr. Sadock purchased the machine from another New Mexico physician when he opened his Albuquerque office in 1954.

PLATE 110
A&P Bar neon sign, late 1930s
Steel, paint, glass, neon, ceramic
85 × 37 1/2 × 12 in.
Transfer, City of Albuquerque Planning Department
PC2015.2.2

The A&P Bar, located south of Central Avenue on Second Street near the back shops, was a favorite hangout for railyard workers and unemployed road rebels. Businessman Arthur Dow owned the establishment for about forty-five years.

After a shooting and other troubles connected to the drive-up bar, along with increasing DUI problems, the A&P was demolished. But the bar's venerable neon sign was salvaged by the City Planning Department in the mid-2000s, then offered to the Museum for preservation.

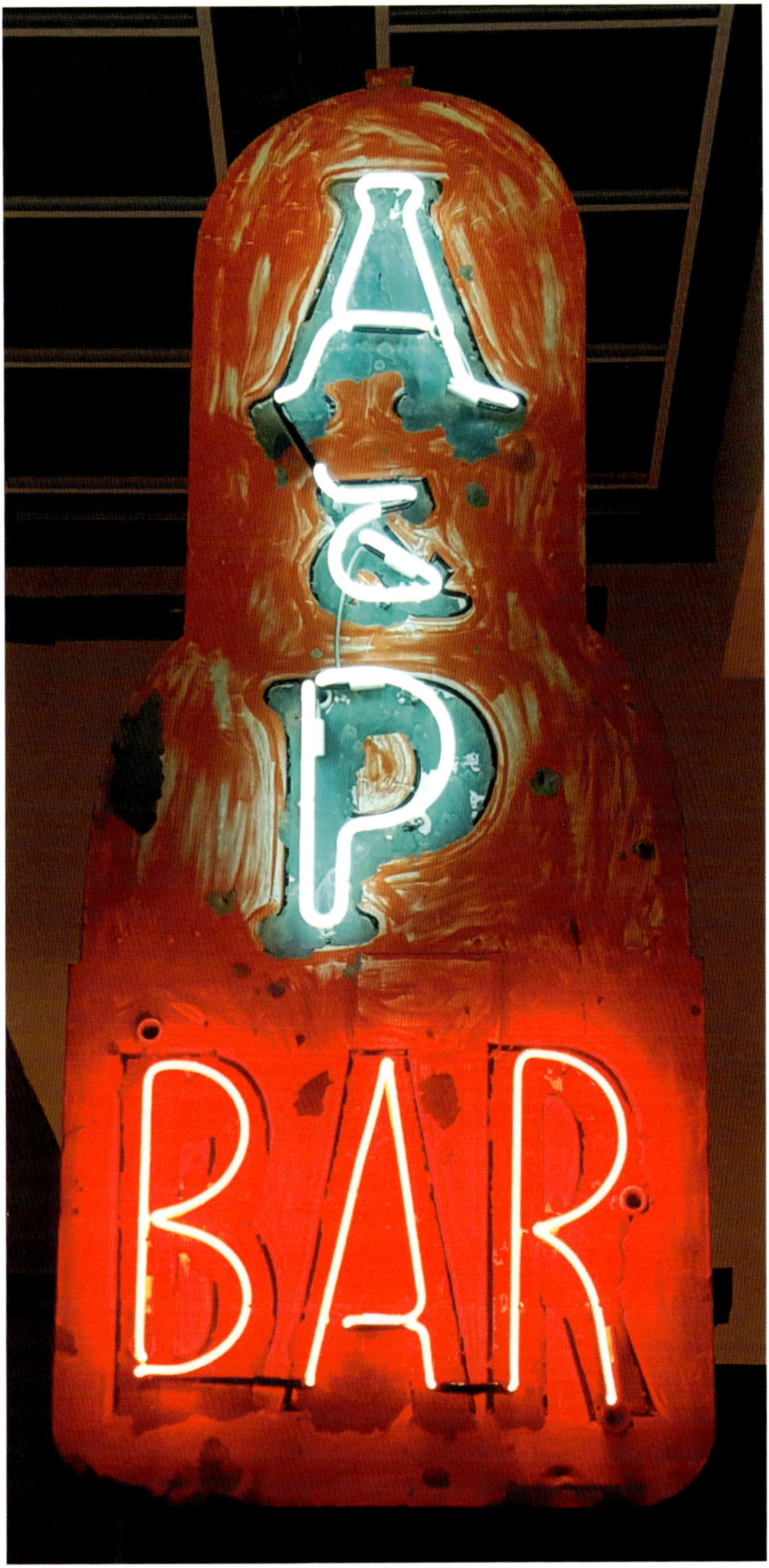
A&P
BAR

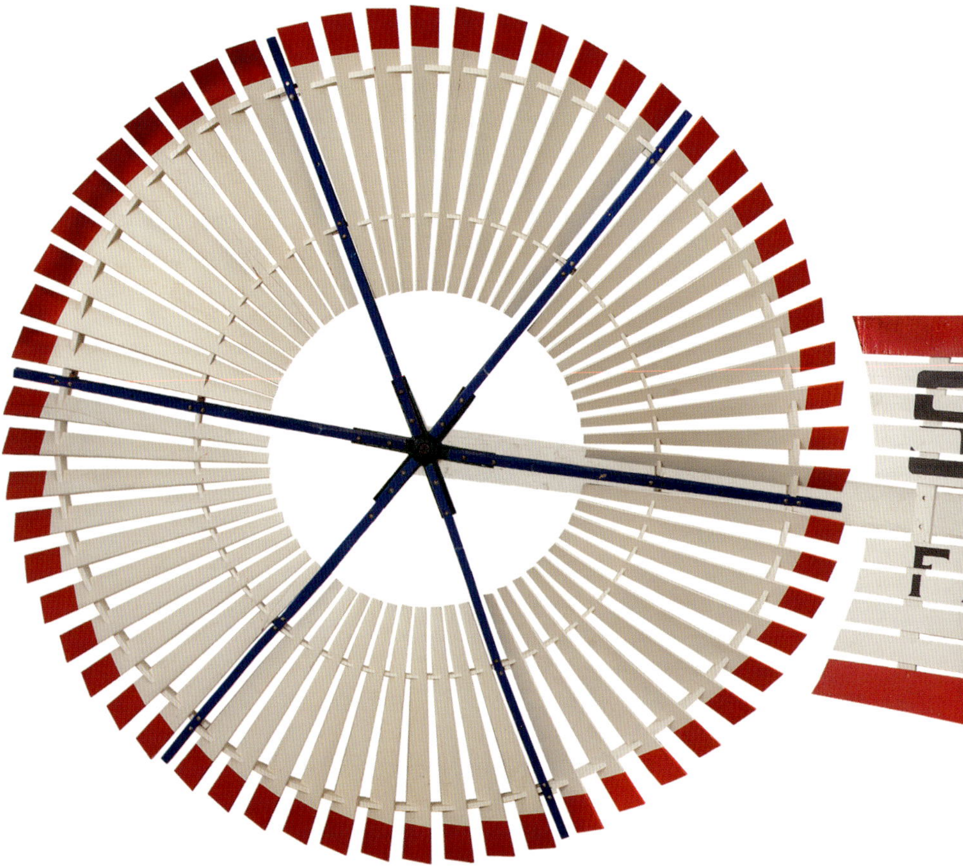

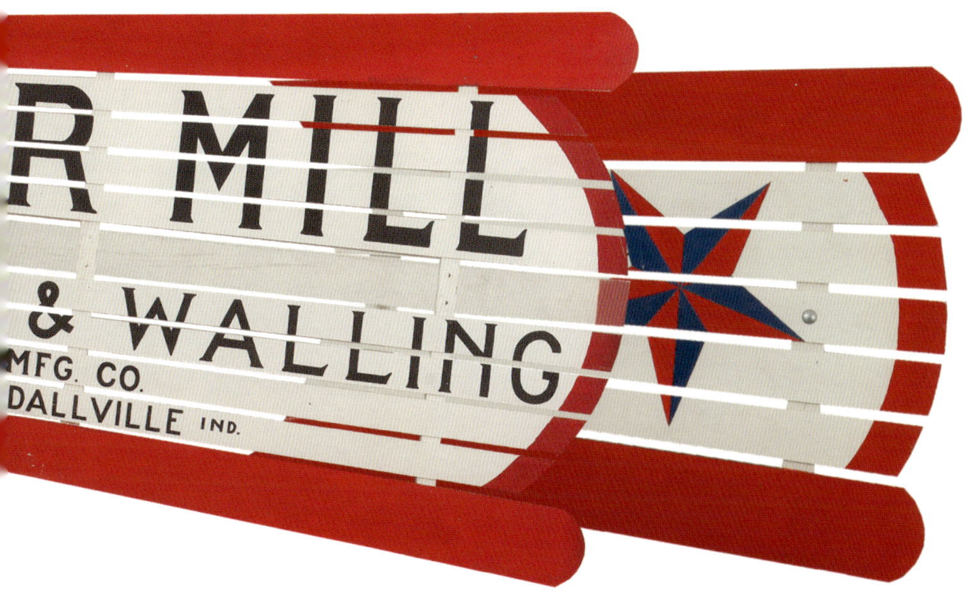

We Are Resourceful

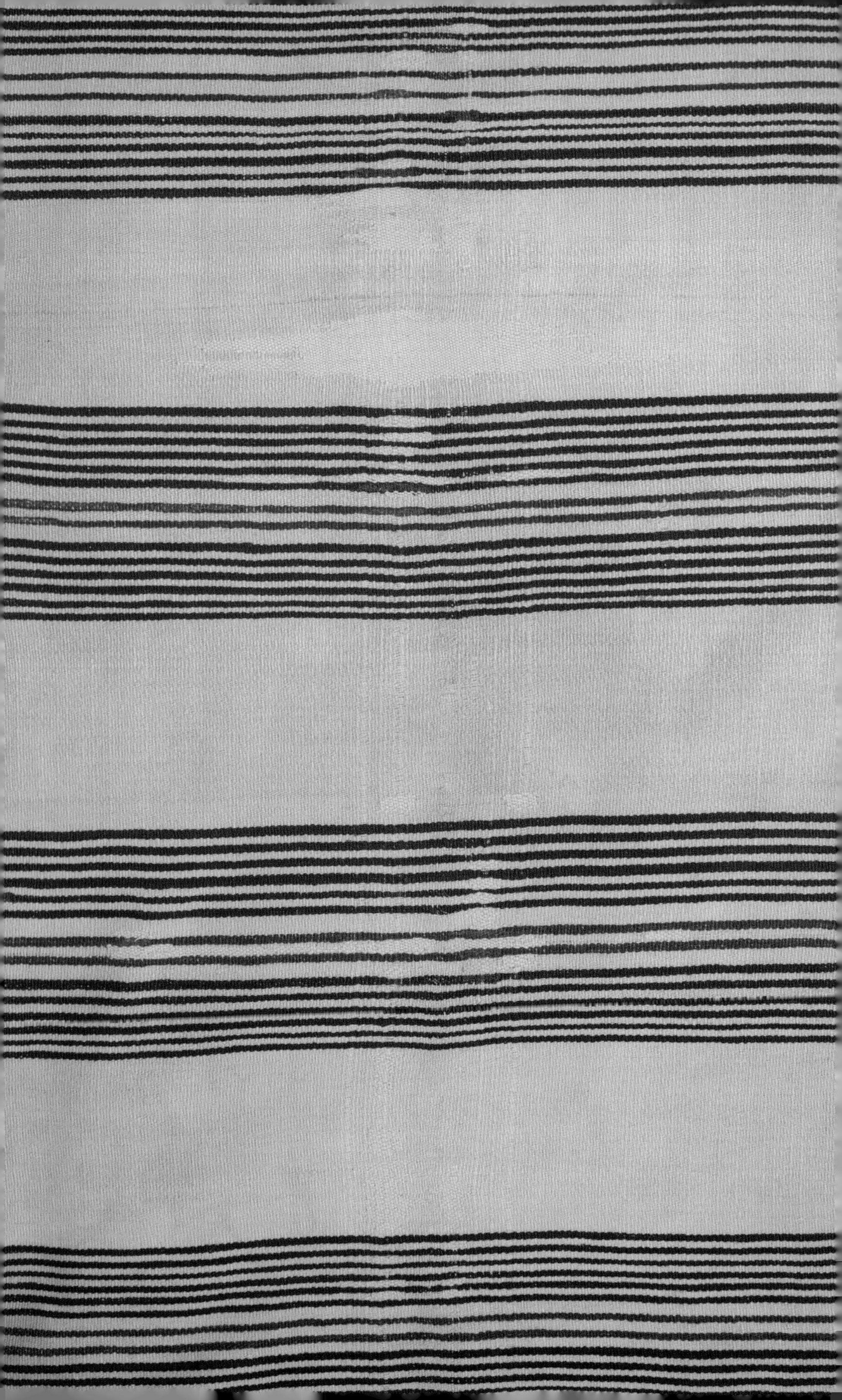

The people of Albuquerque have always been resourceful.

Otherwise, we could not have settled in the valley. Early residents have been frugal and protective of scarce resources, and in difficult times we have fought over them. We find ways of sharing equitably, but growth puts resources at risk. We must conserve resources, or deplete them. Through collaboration, we can find acceptable new uses for our natural resources.

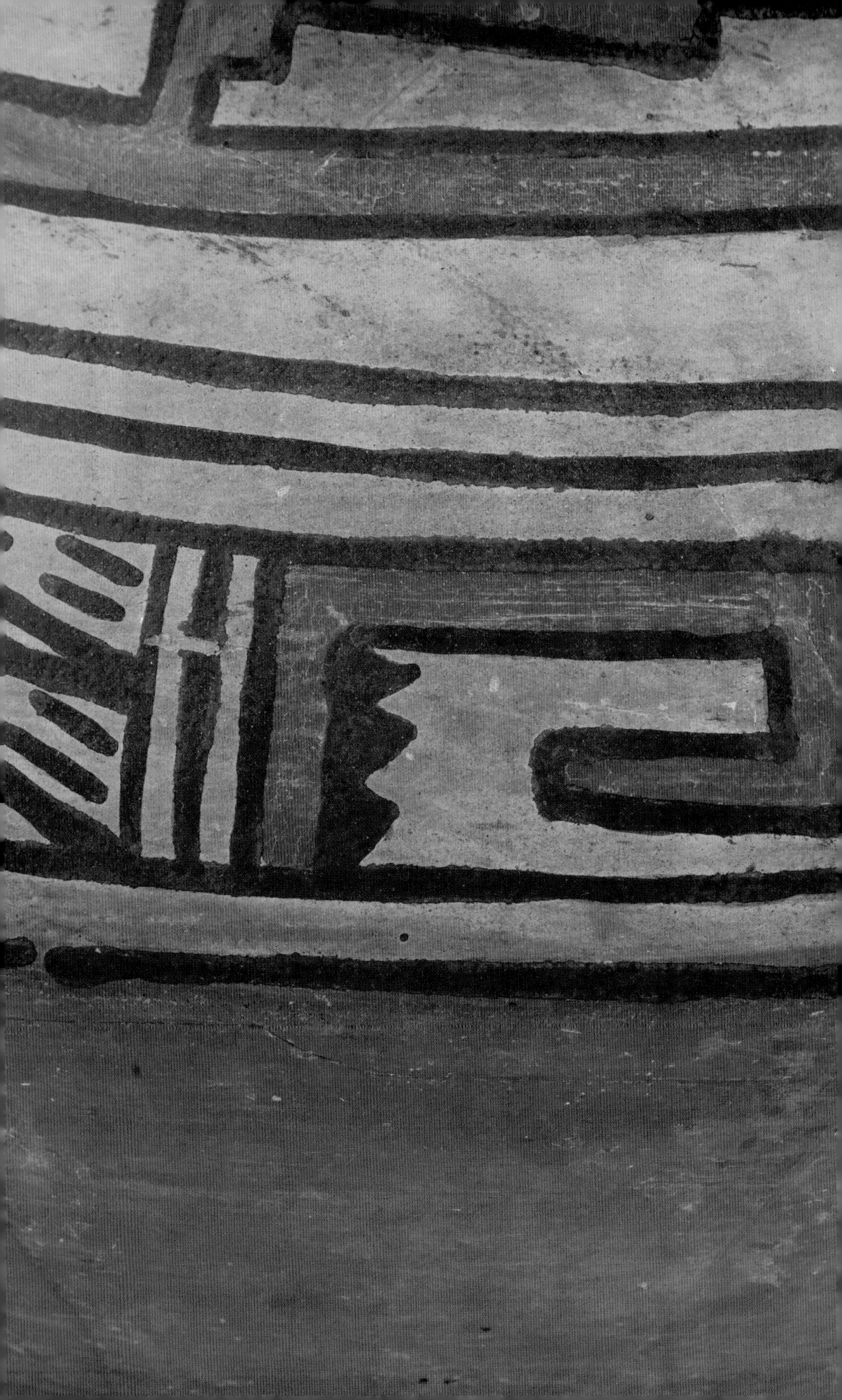

Settlement

Climate shifts, animal extinctions, droughts, and floods challenged early residents of our valley. To survive, they developed new hunting strategies and used everything available—trees, rocks, clay, plants, and animal parts—to create homes, gardens, and irrigation ditches and to make tools and clothing.

Spanish settlers brought additional products, such as domesticated animals, metal technologies, and European and Mesoamerican plants, resulting in a greater variety of available resources.

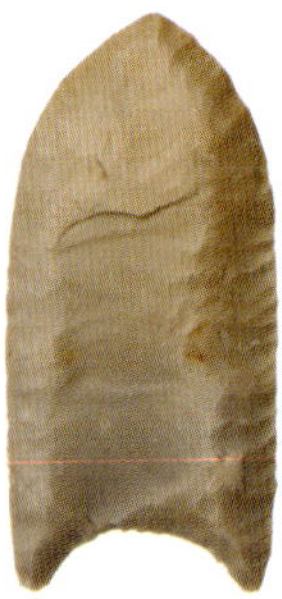

PLATE 111
Folsom point, 8,500 BCE
1 1/2 x 3/4 in.
Gift of William S. Wilson
PC1976.86.281.a

Twelve thousand years ago, mammoths grazed east of the Sandias, and pine trees covered the West Mesa. Clovis and then Folsom people, named after the places where artifacts were found, hunted large game and gathered food in the mountains and near glacial lakes.

Rising temperatures transformed the valley's lush grasslands into a desert. Inhabitants responded by building temporary shelters above the river valley and hunting smaller animals. By 1 CE, Indian communities were domesticating corn and erecting more permanent homes.

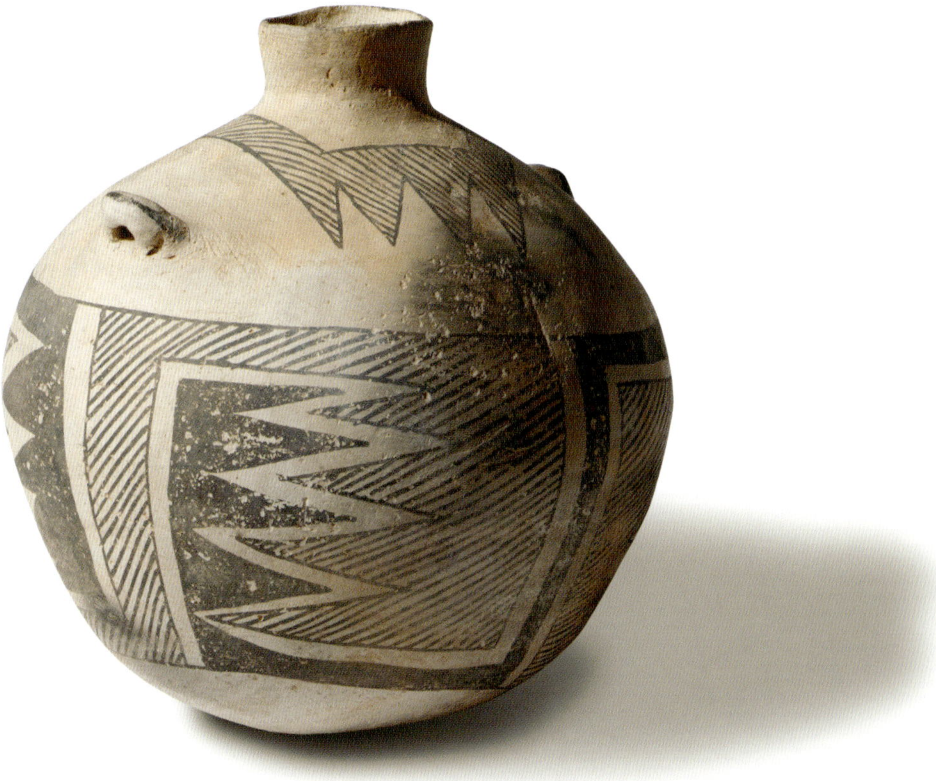

PLATE 112
Ancestral Pueblo
Jar, Socorro Black-on-white, 1050–1300
Clay, slip, mineral paint
7 × 7 in.
Ward Alan and Shirley Jolly Minge Collection
Museum purchase, 1995 General Obligation Bonds
PC1998.22.43

The land, including the materials for pottery, temper, and paint, provided all the resources needed by Ancestral Pueblo potters. Rio Grande White Ware was made along the Rio Grande all the way from San Marcial, south of Albuquerque, north to Taos, New Mexico.

Socorro Black-on-white (1050–1300) was characterized by carefully prepared designs using deep black, finely glazed mineral paint on a thin slip. The designs included combinations of solids and line hatching. This example was acquired through the purchase of Casa San Ysidro from Ward Alan Minge, who often received pottery as thank-you gifts from the pueblos he assisted with land claims.

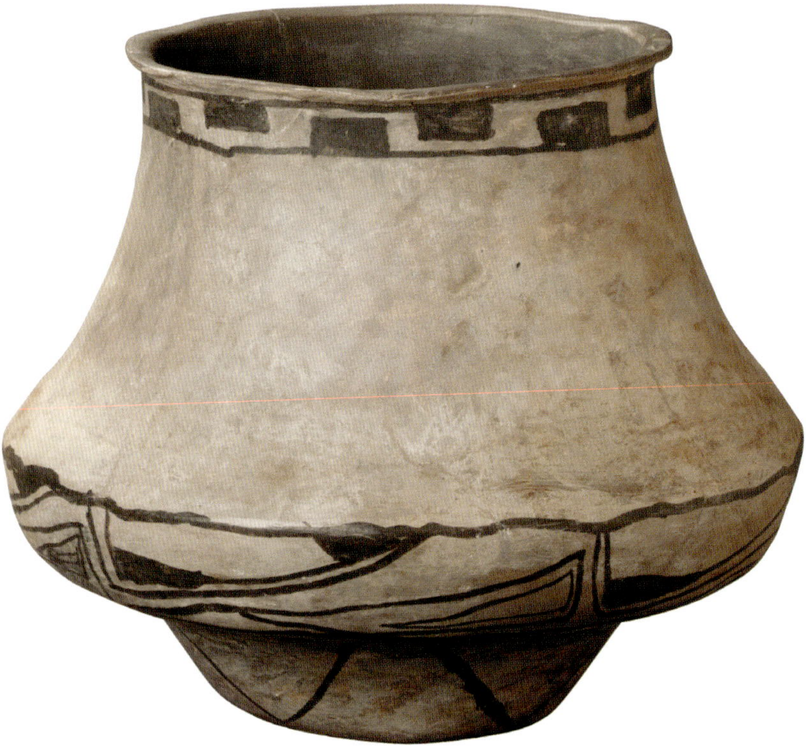

PLATE 113
Tonque Pueblo
Jar, Tsankawi Black-on-white, 1600–80
Clay, slip, paint
10 3/8 × 11 3/16 in.
Gift of Richard A. Bice via the Albuquerque Archaeological Society
PC1974.33.38

Seventeenth-century Pajaritan potters, so named because they moved to Tonque Pueblo from the Pajarito Plateau, created storage jars formed in a *puki*, or pottery mold, with wide mouths and a distinctive "mushroom" shape. The Pajaritans are believed to have lived in a separate community at Tonque Pueblo, sharing resources with the Tonque people.

PLATE 114
Tonque Pueblo
Jar, Rio Grande Glaze Ware, ca. 1450–1600
Clay, slip, glaze paint
7 1/4 × 9 5/8 in.
Gift of Richard A. Bice via the Albuquerque Archaeological Society
PC1974.33.9

Other Tonque Pueblo potters also formed their jars with pukis, but with higher shoulders and in polychrome (multiple paint colors). The motifs on this jar are references to rain—a precious resource in the arid Southwest—and the birds commonly found around water sources. Potters sometimes retained the bases of broken glaze ware jars to make additional pukis.

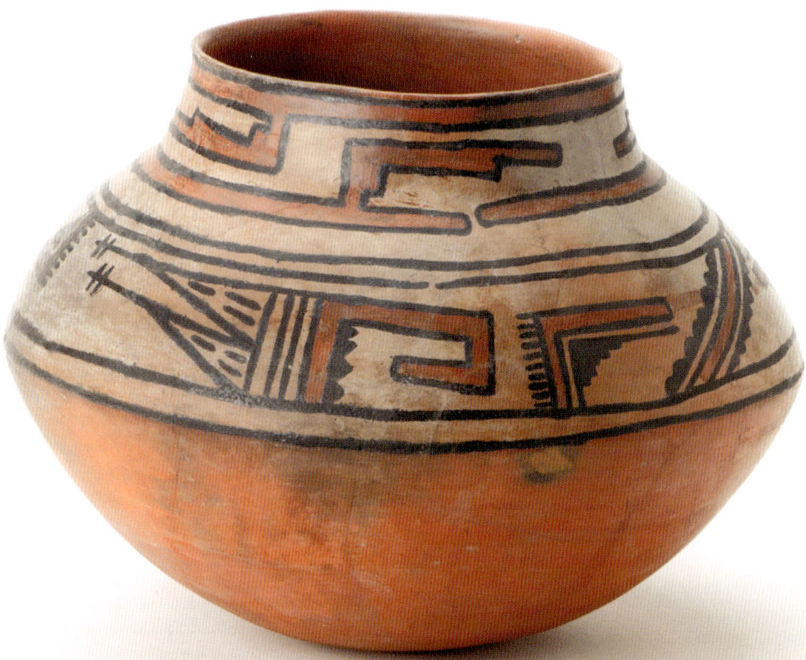

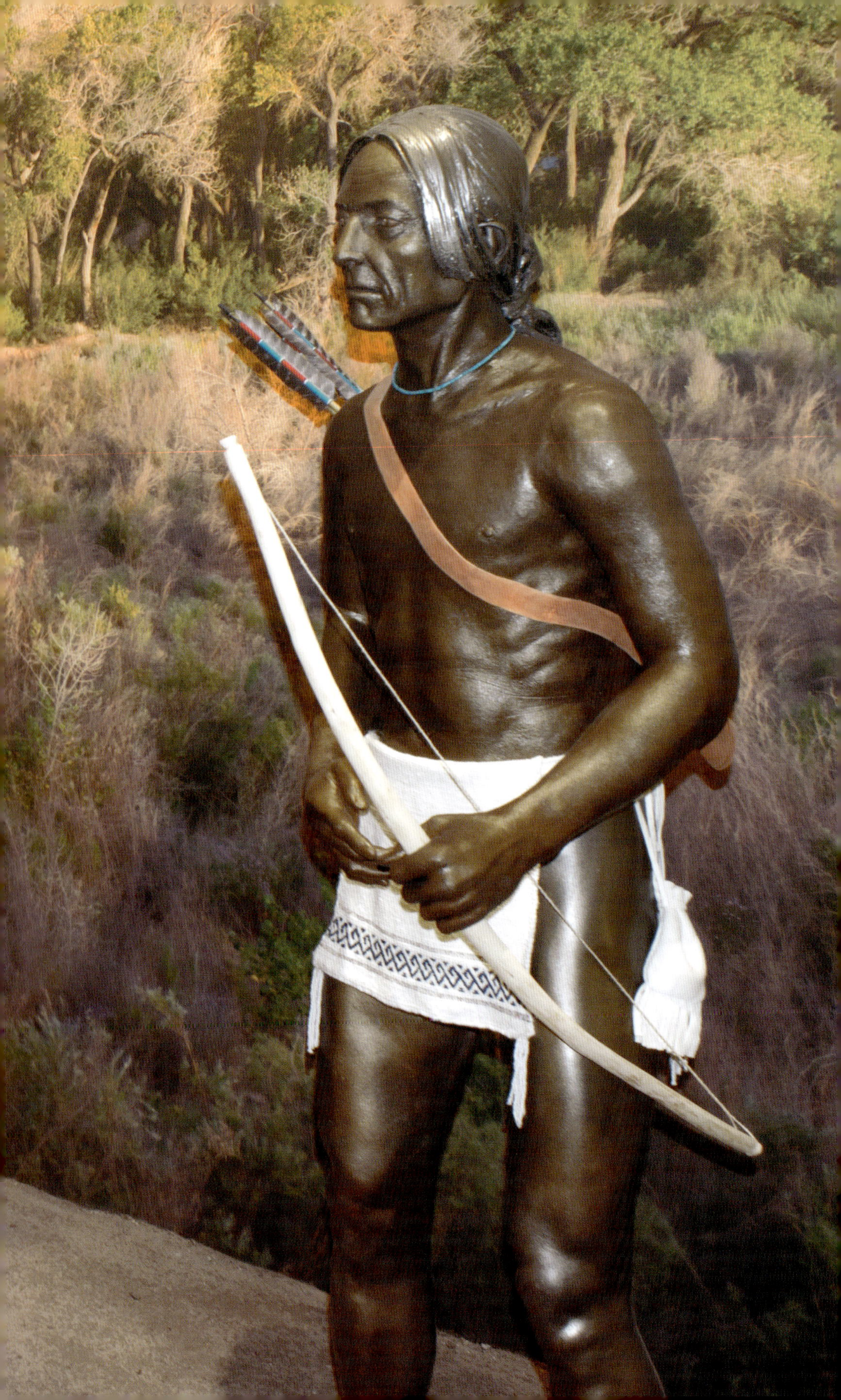

SHARING RESOURCES

Disagreements over water and land are as old as Albuquerque itself. In the seventeenth century, Spain granted water rights and land grants to the Pueblo and Hispano communities. Later infractions resulted in bitter boundary conflicts. Many claims remain unresolved.

We now find ways to share critical resources. Sandia Pueblo, having regained some traditional lands, allows limited public use of the Sandia Mountains, and local residents have united to reduce water consumption after periods of extended drought.

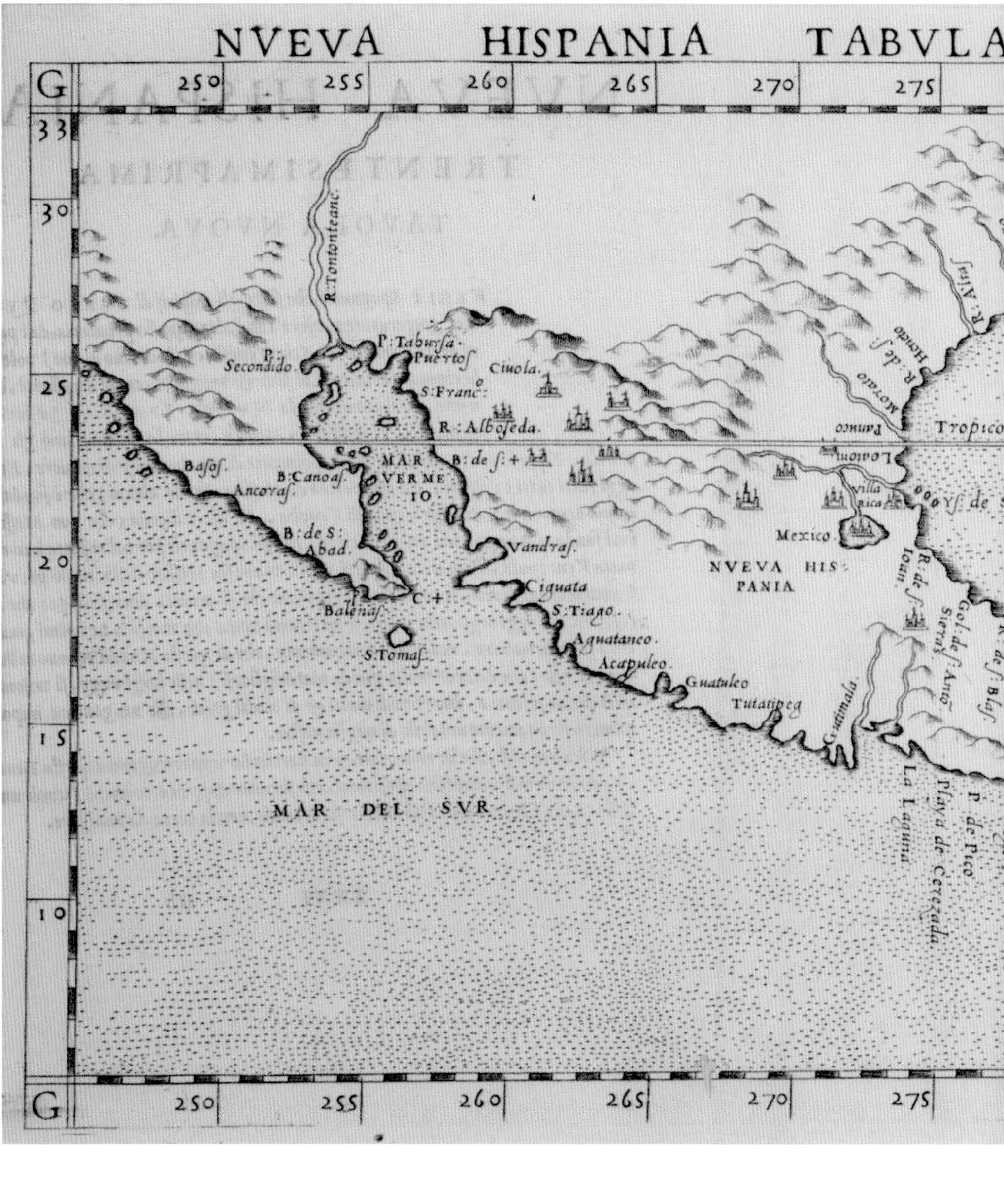
NVEVA HISPANIA TABVLA
MAR DEL SVR
NVEVA HISPANIA
MAR VERMEIO
Mexico
Tropico
Cinola
Acapulco
Ciguata
S:Tiago
Vandras
S:Tomas
Balenas
Guatuleo
Tutatipeg
Aguataneo

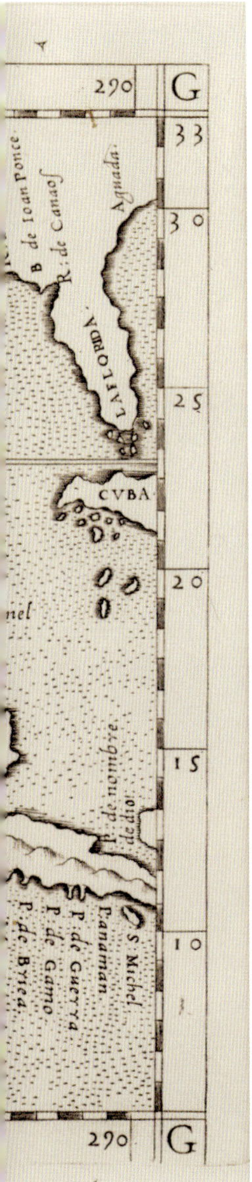

PLATE 115

Girolamo Ruscelli, Italian, 1504–1566

Map, *Nueva Hispania Tabula Nova*, 1561–98

Copper engraving; ink, paper

7 1/2 x 10 1/4 in. (overall)

Museum purchase in honor of Dr. James C. Moore, Four Centuries Bond Fund

PC2005.37.1

Nueva Hispania Tabula Nova was printed more than a century before La Villa de Alburquerque was founded. It is one of the earliest maps reflecting all that was known by other countries about Spain's northern frontier in the sixteenth century. Ruscelli's map mentions places described by explorers Fray Marcos de Niza and Francisco Vásquez de Coronado y Luján, including Civola (the ancestral lands of Zuni Pueblo), west of what is now Albuquerque. Spanish explorers may have carried a similar map on their journeys to Nueva España.

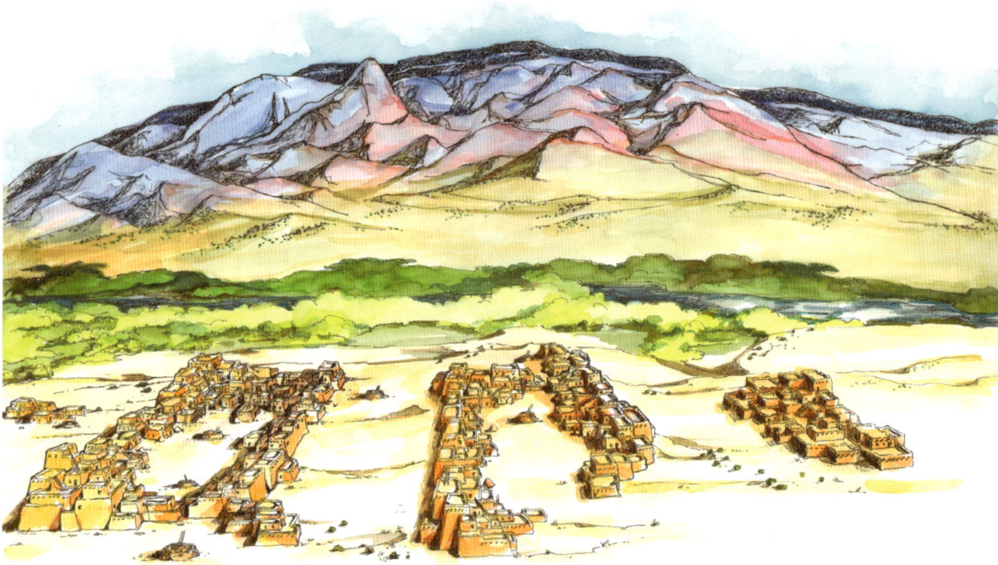

PLATE 116

Charlotte Hill Cobb

Piedras Marcadas, ca. 1540

City of Albuquerque Open Space Division, Open Space Visitor Center

Tiwa-speaking people were probably the first Puebloans in the central valley. They were also great farmers—so successful at stockpiling corn that by 1300, they confidently changed strategies. Building larger homes between Bernalillo and Belén, Tiwas began growing corn on river terraces using gravity-fed irrigation. Their descendants—the Isleta and Sandia people—still farm, working in harmony with the seasons and agricultural cycles.

PLATE 117 ▶

Louie Garcia, Tiwa/Piro

Roberto Valdez, Hispanic New Mexican, Spanish, and Tlaxcalan, German, Italian, Spanish

Tiwa leader, Aztecan warrior, and Spanish horseman, ca. 1540

Steel, iron, brass, leather, fabric, salt, brine, wood, canvas, cotton, indigo, wool, maguey fiber, hide, buckskin, reeds, feathers, dyes

89 × 40 × 100 in. (overall)

Museum purchases, 1979 General Obligation Bonds

PC1981.213.1, 1981.219.1a–i, 1982.20.1.a&b, 1982.19.1.a–k, 1982.35.1.a&b, 1982.13.1, 1982.33.1, 1982.38.1, 2014.9.1–8, and 2014.7.1–8

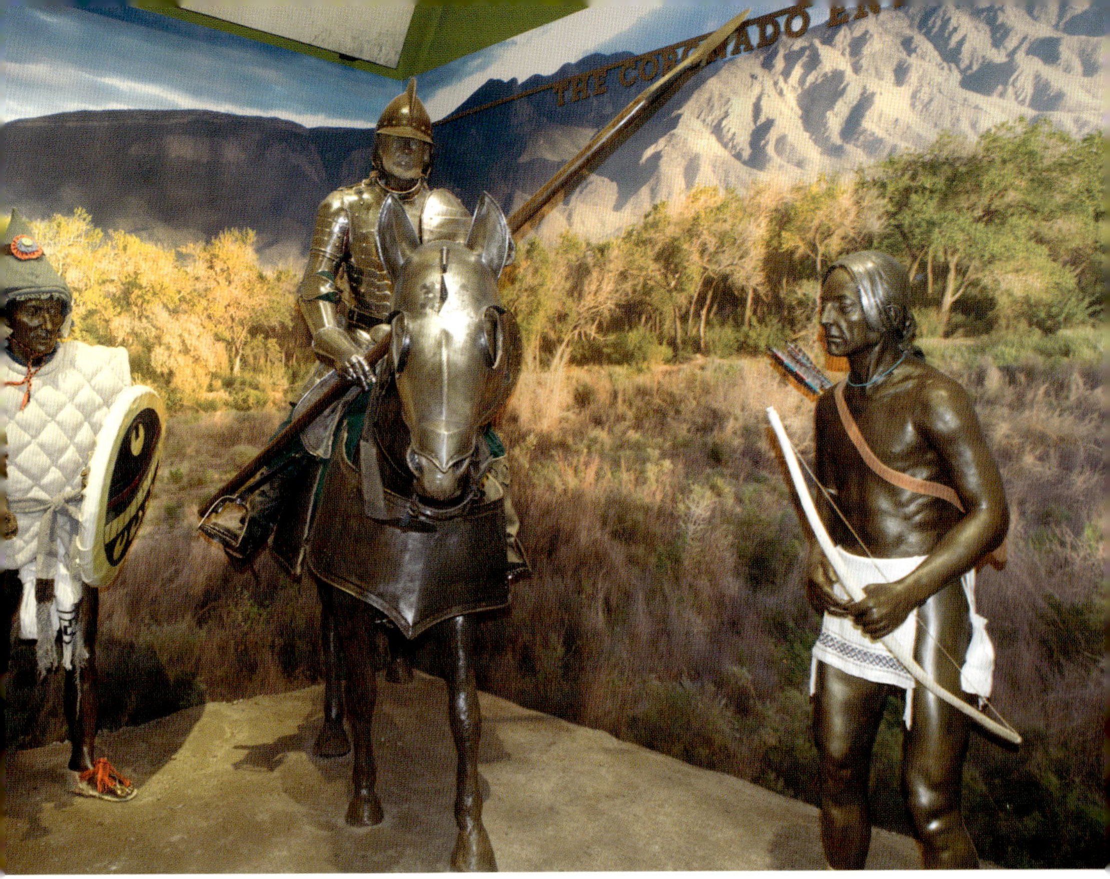

In 1540, Francisco Vásquez de Coronado y Luján led the first entrada (expedition) to New Spain, sparking the first Indian war on American soil. When his artillery captain, Hernando de Alvarado, sent word about the abundance of food in our valley, Coronado chose this area as his winter camp, demanding food, shelter, and clothing. The people of Tiguex fought and never surrendered. Today, their descendants live at the Pueblos of Isleta and Sandia.

The Museum's core history exhibition, *Only in Albuquerque*, depicts the participants of the Coronado Entrada and subsequent Tiwa Rebellion in 1540–41. Tiwa/Piro weaver Louie Garcia created a sixteenth-century Tiwa leader's regalia featuring a woven and dyed breechcloth, a sash with corn pollen pouch, Pueblo moccasins, a turquoise necklace, and a bow and arrows.

Artist-reenactor Roberto Valdez created a uniform in the style of an Aztecan soldier conscripted with the army of Francisco Vásquez de Coronado y Luján, providing warfare support and labor. The Nahuatl-speaking Aztecan soldiers brought their own armor and weapons, including a terrifying *macahuitl* (sword) made from razor-sharp obsidian blades imbedded in wood. The soldier wears a conical hat, a cotton jacket, a shirt, a breechcloth and sash, fiber sandals, and a painted hide shield. The Spanish caballero, wearing a gilded helmet of the Coronado period and Italian half-suit of armor, carries an oval shield and a Spanish boar spur.

PLATE 118
German, Spanish
Caballero (horseman) and Spanish Barb suits of armor, ca. 1540–98
Steel, iron, brass, leather, fabric, wood, canvas, cotton
89 × 40 × 108 in. (overall)
Museum purchases, 1979 General Obligation Bonds
PC1981.213.1, 1981.219.1a–j, 1982.20.1.a&b, 1982.19.1.a–k,
1982.35.1.a&b, 1982.13.1, and 1982.38.1

This Spanish caballero wears a morión (helmet) of the period of conquistador Juan de Oñate y Salazar, as he was presented in *Four Centuries: A History of Albuquerque*. He is depicted riding a Spanish Barb horse *a la brida* (straight-legged) style. The Barbs were prized for their short legs and well-muscled chests, ideal for cavalrymen. They were known for their speed and agility.

This Barb wears a set of German horse armor of the period. Full sets of armor were rare in the Coronado and Oñate campaigns; they were expensive and heated up under the sun, so soldiers often made do with chain mail, leather brigandines, and native gear brought by indigenous Mexican soldiers.

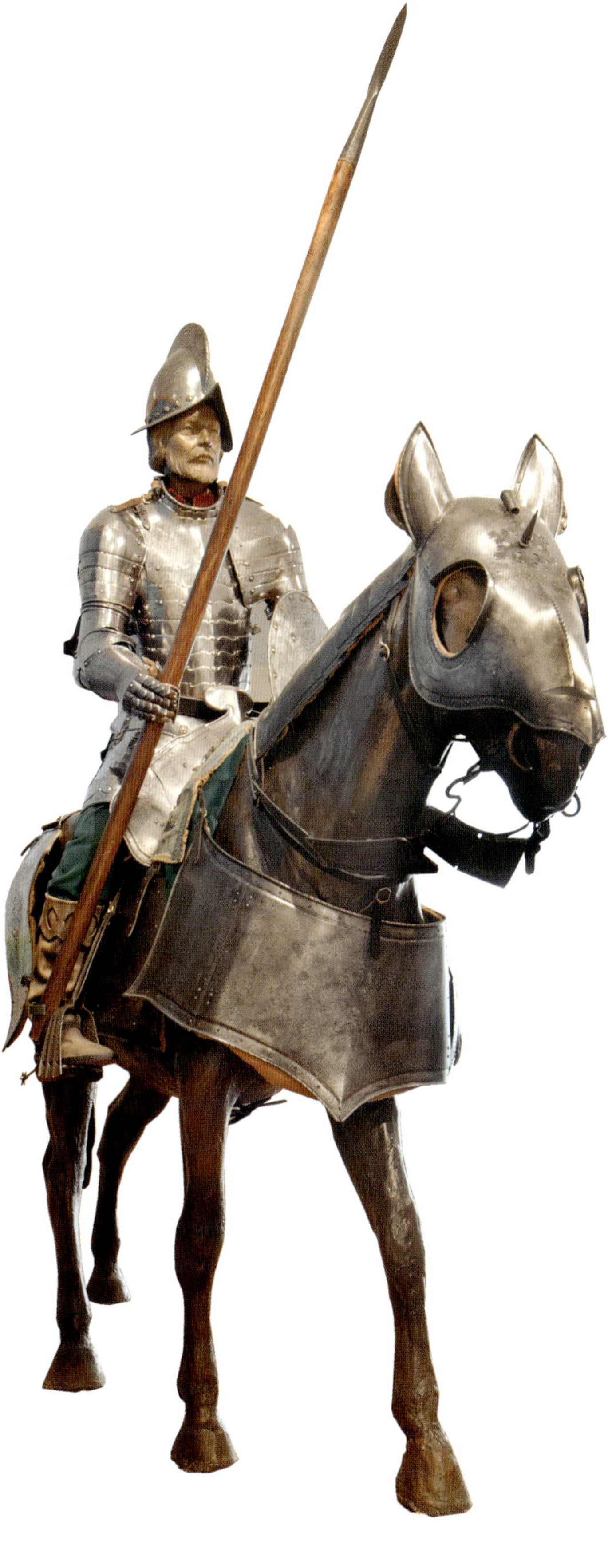

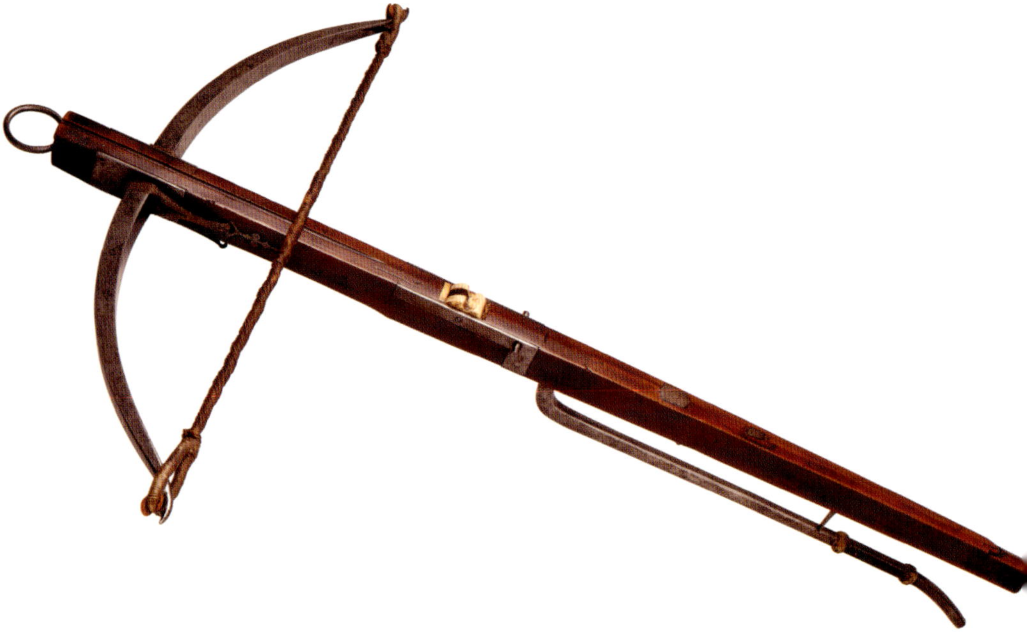

PLATE 119

Spanish; León, Spain

Ballesta/Arbalest, ca. 1550

Wood, steel or iron, fiber, bone

36 5/16 × 25 1/4 × 4 1/8 in.

Museum purchase, 1979 General Obligation Bonds

PC1982.144.1

Crossbows were deadly instruments of war in the hands of conquistadors, but they took a long time to load and the bowstrings frequently broke. They soon fell out of favor and were replaced by noisy, smoke-belching muskets.

Larger than a crossbow, with a mechanism to help draw back the bowstring, arbalests were very powerful but no match for a flurry of well-aimed arrows and rocks. Hammered iron crossbow bolts are important diagnostic artifacts that indicate the presence of a sixteenth-century Spanish exploration party.

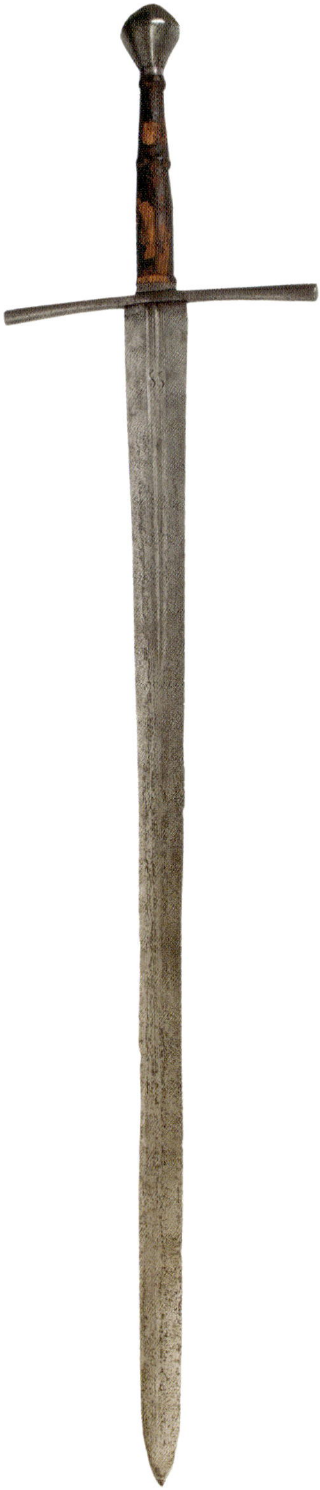

PLATE 120
Italian
Infantry hand-in-a-half sword, ca. 1500
Steel, leather
41 × 7 × 2 in.
Museum purchase, 1985 General Obligation Bonds
PC1986.19.2

Swords were the most common weapon brought by conquistadors, explorers, and militia protecting the settlements of New Spain. Their power inspired awe and fear. The people of the pueblos did not use iron and steel, but news of the brilliantly shiny metal traveled fast, and the people of the Tiwa pueblos were well aware of its pending arrival. Even so, it was hard for a soldier to fight effectively with a sword.

New Spain's earliest settlers and militia were usually poorly equipped, and firearms were usually scarce and inoperable, leaving them to rely upon their lances and swords. Many soldiers eventually became as proficient in the use of the bow and arrow as Pueblo, Apache, and Comanche bowmen, who were sometimes also armed with muskets and pistols.

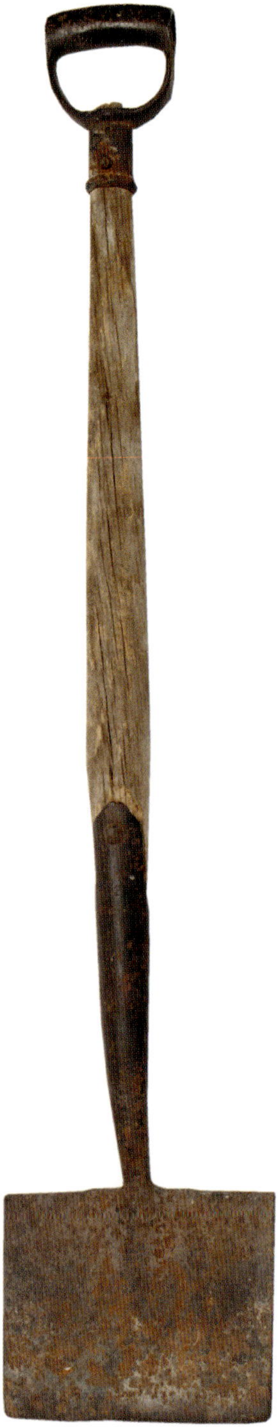

PLATE 121
Terrón cutter, 1930s
Wood, cast and cut iron
37 1/2 × 7 1/2 × 4 in.
Gift of Sidney Ash and Henry Ash
PC2012.34.1

Colonial, Mexican, Territorial, and twentieth-century buildings in Albuquerque and the central Rio Grande valley were usually made from adobe—mud mixed with straw or other temper and pressed into a mold and dried in the sun. Builders also used terrones, or sod bricks cut from the riverbanks that, when dried with root systems intact, also made a perfect building material. Both types of material have been found in the walls of the 1793 San Felipe de Neri Church.

This terrón cutter was used to build structures on the Ash Ranch, north of Albuquerque and west of the Rio Grande, in the early twentieth century.

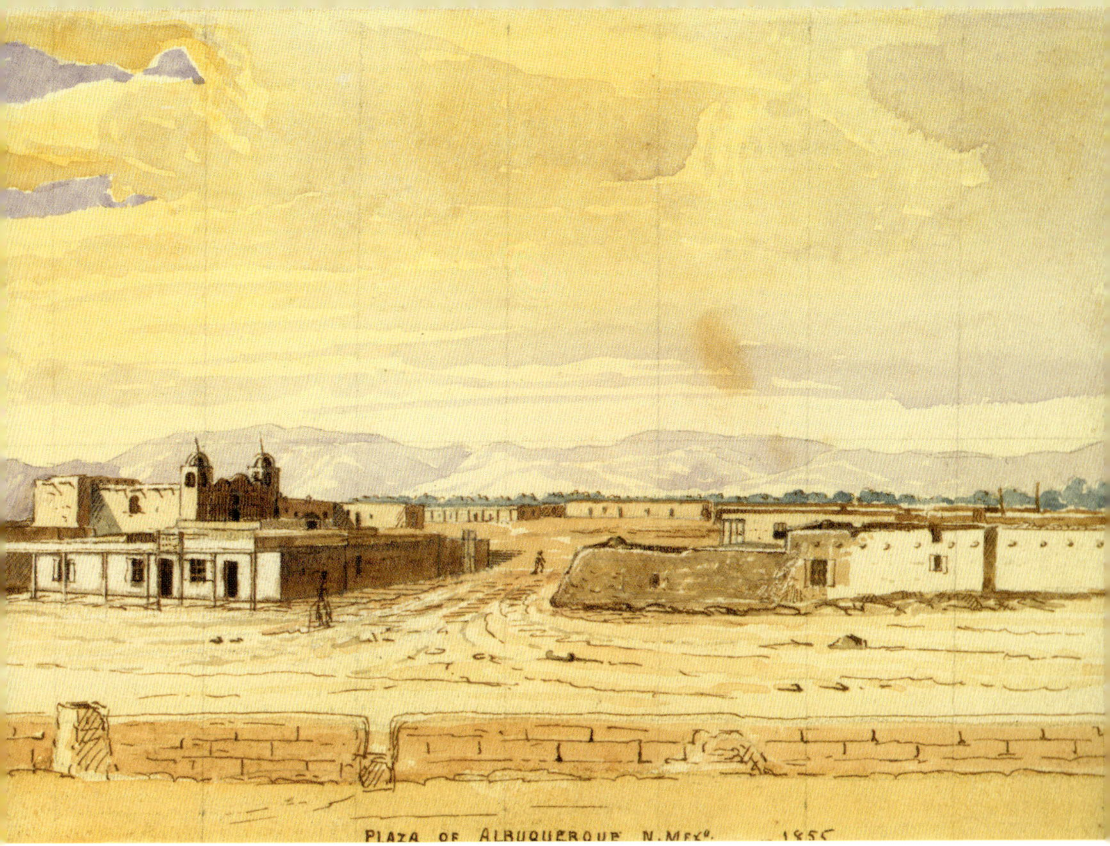

PLATE 122
Joseph Horace Eaton, 1831–1896
Plaza of Albuquerque, 1855
Watercolor, paper
4 7/8 x 7 1/2 in.
Museum purchase, 1983 General Obligation Bonds
PC1985.4.1

Following the Mexican War, Joseph H. Eaton (1815–1896) was stationed on the frontier, where he painted a series of landscapes in New Mexico in the 1850s. Eaton's watercolor, one of the earliest images of Old Town and San Felipe de Neri Church, depicts Albuquerque organized around a central plaza from the perspective of a rooftop parapet looking east. The Moreno Rectory is visible to the right of San Felipe de Neri Church, along with other buildings clearly built with adobe, but featuring shutters and glass window panes of the Territorial style brought to the town over the Santa Fe Trail.

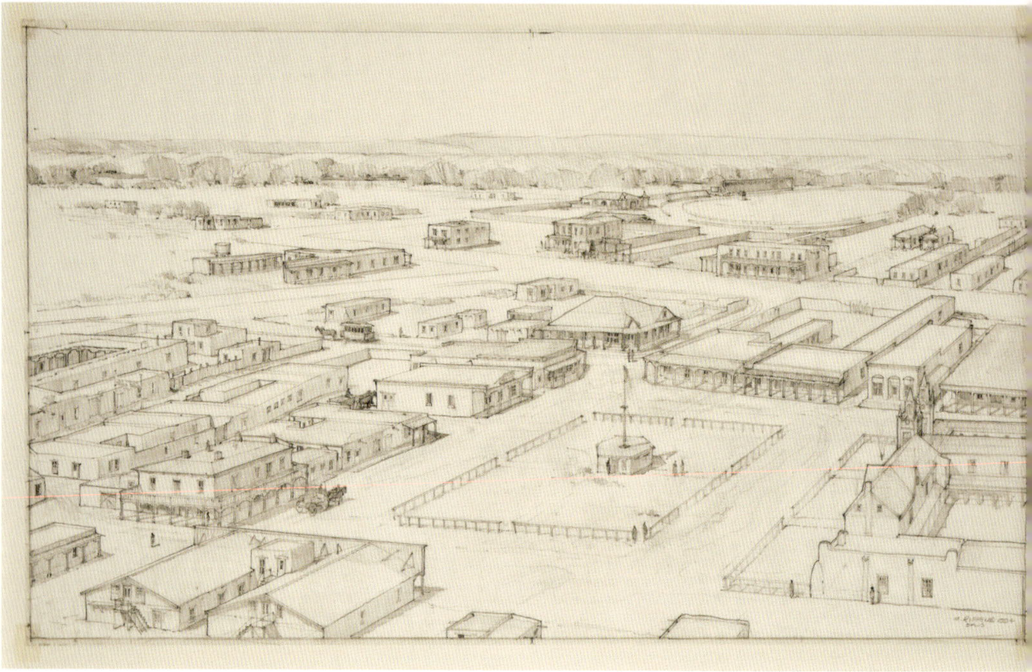

PLATE 123
Morris Rippel
Study for *Old Town a Century Ago*, 1994
Pencil, paper
20 1/4 x 31 3/4 in.
Gift of Morris Rippel
PC2005.2.3

Artist Morris Rippel (1930–2009) used original photographs and Sanborn maps of Old Town to draw the plaza as it looked in 1895, almost two hundred years after its founding, from an angle of view not represented in period photographs. The drawing depicts the plaza looking southwest from the corner of Church and Santiago (now North Plaza and Romero) toward the bosque and West Mesa. By this time, the adobe buildings of the Plaza were embellished with Territorial period triangular door and window pediments and false fronts.

Particularly notable is the false front of the Ambrosio Armijo House and store, a view rarely found in early photographs. Rippel's only intentional discrepancy in the study and resulting painting was the height of the 121-foot flagpole.

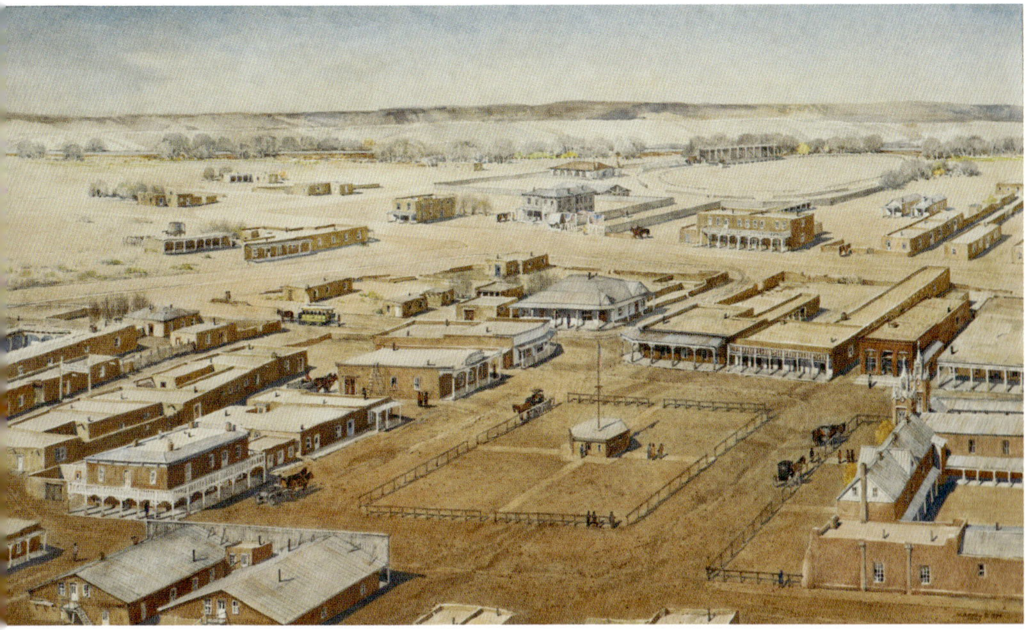

PLATE 124
Morris Rippel
Old Town a Century Ago, 1994
Egg tempera, canvas
18 × 30 in.
Museum purchase, 1993 General Obligation Bonds and donation in memory of Jane Napolitano
PC1994.17.1

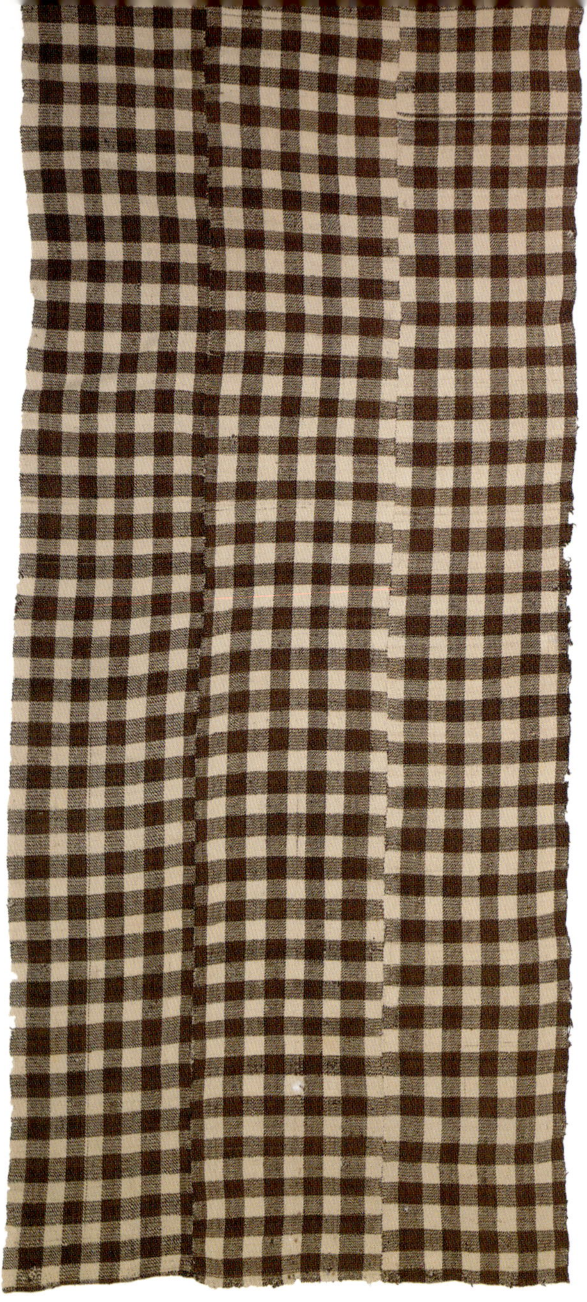

PLATE 125
Hispanic New Mexican
Jerga/Carpet, ca. 1850
Wool
170 × 77 in.
Gift of Ward Alan and
Shirley Jolly Minge
PC2005.4.5

Often described as "black and white" *jerga*, the sack cloth hand woven from the fuzzy kemp or short fibers of the churro sheep was used for everything from sacking material, roof and door coverings, blankets and bedcovers, to carpeting. It sold as yardage, by the vara, a measuring stick about thirty-three inches long used to measure everything from furniture to doorways and buildings. To make carpeting, one had to sew together two or three lengths of the material. Jerga appears in mission inventories as early as 1796. In 1814, a black-and-white jerga similar to this example was listed in a document describing improvements to the cabildo (town hall) in Alburquerque.

PLATE 126
Hispanic New Mexican
Tenamaste/Trivet, ca. 1800–25
Wrought iron, leather
14 × 5 × 7 in.
Gift of Saint John's Thrift Store
PC2010.13.1
Ex-collection Bertha Dutton

In New Spain, iron was as valuable as gold. Soldiers and settlers re-melted everything from wheel rims to swords in order to forge even more crucial supplies such as horseshoes and nails. This tripod was made from a wagon wheel strap.

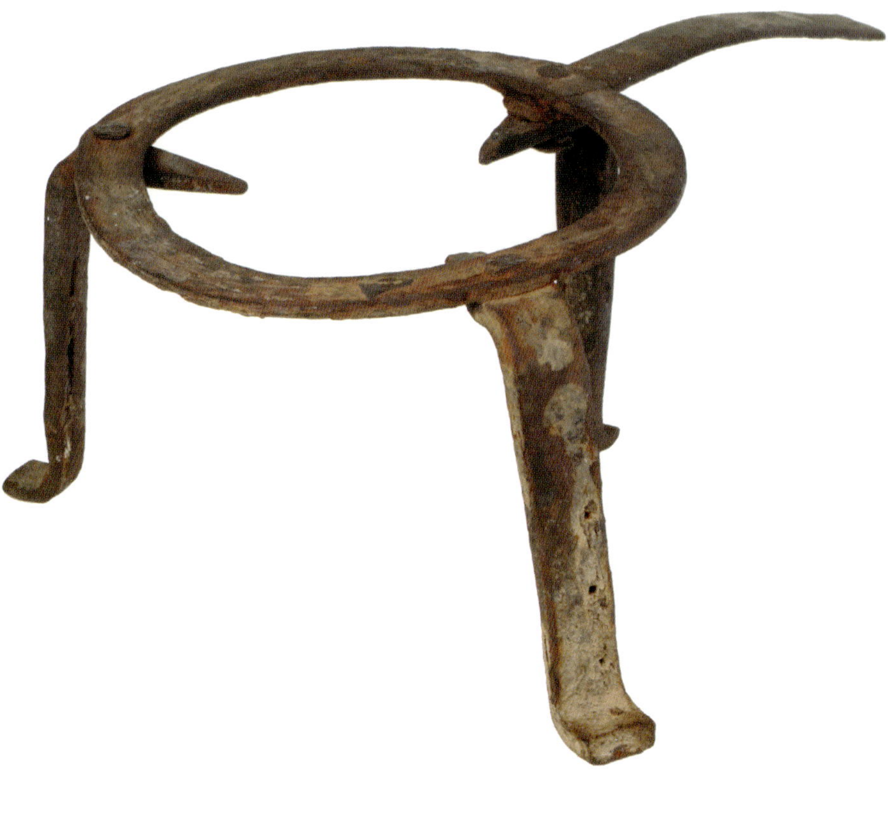

PLATE 127

Mexican

Candado de barra/Padlock and key, eighteenth century

Iron

13 × 7 × 1 1/4 in., 5/8 × 2 1/8 in.

Museum purchase, 1979 General Obligation Bonds

PC1983.103.1.a & b

Competition for scarce resources commonly resulted in thefts. This padlock with its original key was likely used to secure large doors on a church, military structure, warehouse, or government building. Bar locks, such as this example, were mounted on doors with staples called *armellas*. The hasp is detachable, sliding on a shepherd's crook-shaped bar mounted at the top of the lock. In 1776 the original San Felipe de Neri Church at Albuquerque was described as having paneled double doors "with a good lock," probably similar to this example.

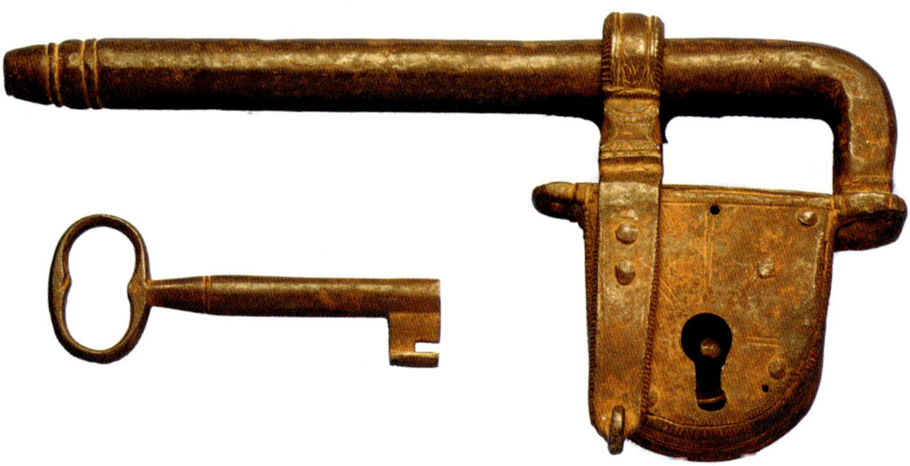

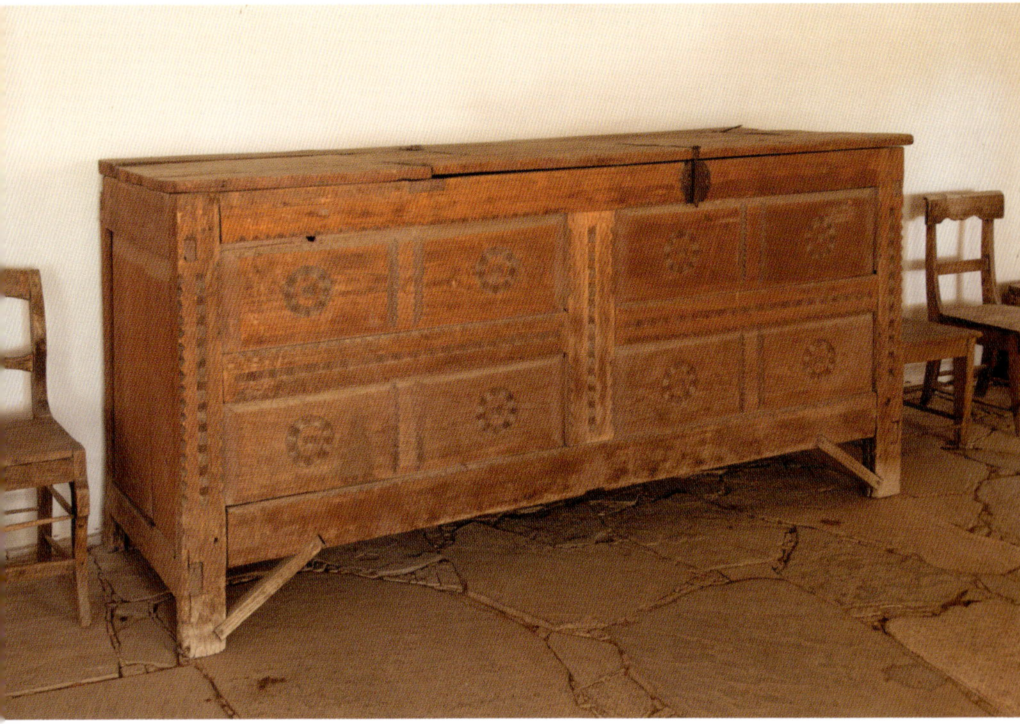

PLATE 128
Valdez family, Velarde, New Mexico
Harinero/Grain chest, early nineteenth century
Pine, iron
49 1/2 × 95 3/4 × 30 in
Gift of Ward Alan and Shirley Jolly Minge
PC1997.51.123

Within the Hispanic New Mexican family, the matriarch of the house held control over use and rationing of the family wheat supply. This chest, one of only about twenty existing examples believed to have been made by the Valdez family, is lidded and could be locked to help keep the stores intact.

Due to the difficulty of finding supplies of iron in the early eighteenth century, grain chests were often made with just a few simple tools—an axe, an adze, a chisel, and a vara. The circular chiseled designs were probably laid out with a compass, and the mortice-and-tenon construction required no nails, only wooden pegs to hold the tenons in place.

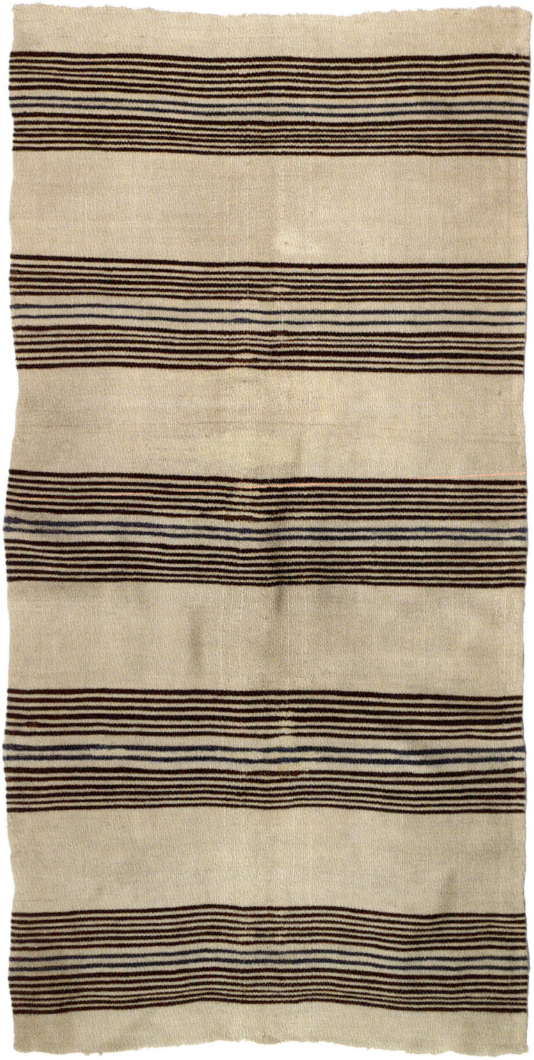

PLATE 129
Hispanic New Mexican
Frazada/Blanket, 1840–50
Churro wool, indigo
83 × 40 3/4 in.
Museum purchase, 1983 General Obligation Bonds
PC1984.25.9
Ex-collection Larry Frank and Michael Caden

New Mexico's chief exports in the sixteenth to eighteenth centuries were *efectos del país* (products of the country), including wool, sheep, and hand-woven blankets, but brisk sales often left local citizens empty-handed and wanting for supplies. By the early nineteenth century, the weaving industry had faltered. After Ignacio and Juan Bazán journeyed from Puebla, Mexico, to New Mexico to teach weaving to the citizens in 1805, the industry again blossomed.

This early blanket has been well worn and loved. The weaver, using mathematical calculations to create a symmetrical five-stripe design, inserted two rows of prized indigo-dye weft yarns within each stripe. The blanket is woven *doble-ancho*, with no center seam, by weaving the piece one-half above the other on the loom—a difficult trick to accomplish.

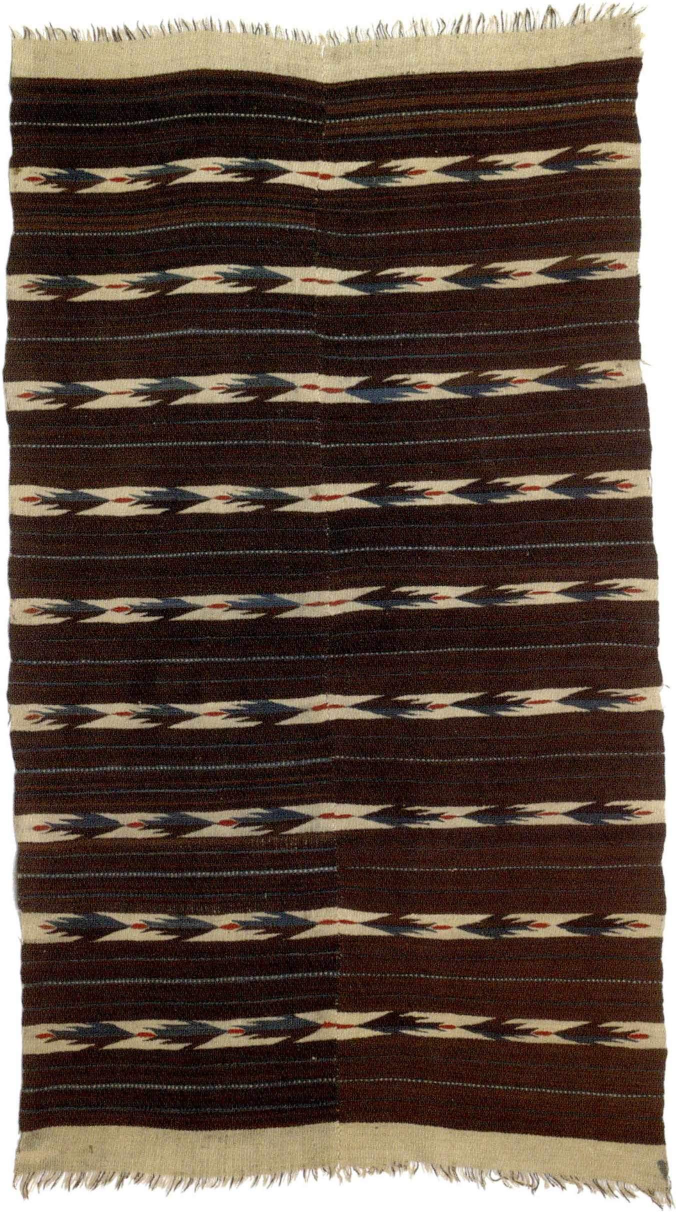

PLATE 130
Hispanic New Mexican
Frazada/Blanket, ca. 1840
Churro, Saxony, and
Germantown wool, indigo,
and cochineal
78 1/2 x 51 in.
Museum purchase, 1983
General Obligation Bonds
PC1984.25.16
Ex-collection Larry Frank
and Mark Winter

Likely because of the scarcity of cochineal dye, which had to be shipped to New Mexico over the Chihuahua or Santa Fe Trails, the weaver of this blanket used short lengths of commercial Saxony yarn to create the red embellishments. The three-colored motifs, called *manitas* (little hands) or palmas (palm leaves), are different colors within each half of the motif and were inspired by Saltillo serape designs. Saltillo weavings were shipped north on the Camino Real/Chihuahua Trail, right through Albuquerque.

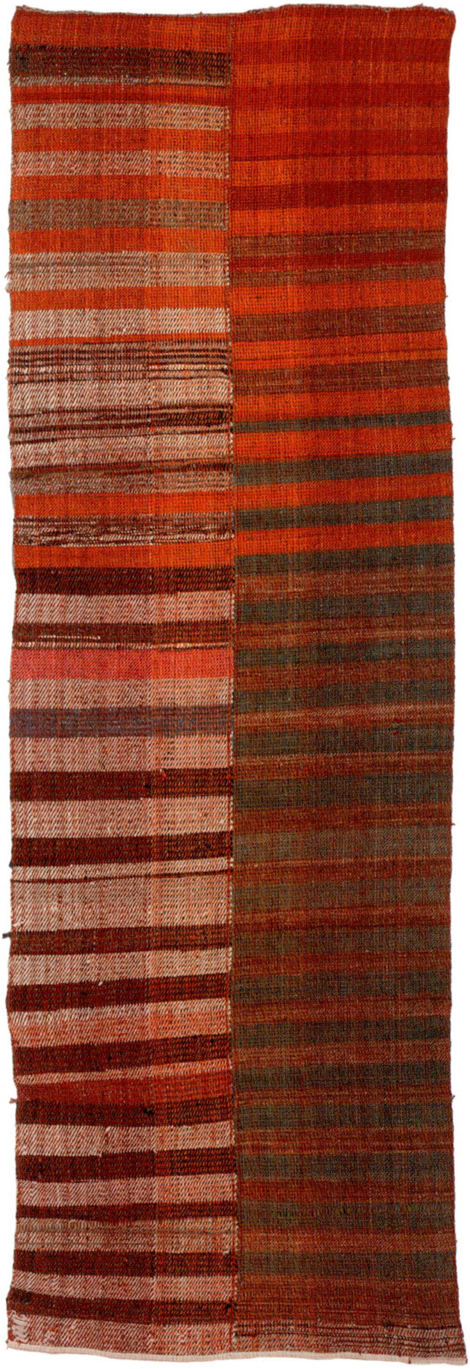

PLATE 131

Hispanic New Mexican

Jerga/Rag rug, after 1880

Merino or Rambouillet wool, cotton rags, synthetic dyes, commercial cotton thread

145 × 50 in.

Gift of Ward Alan Minge

PC2005.45.17

New Mexican weavers and embroiderers saved every scrap of wool, yarn, fabric, and thread for a wide variety of uses. In this very rare jerga, pleated multicolored cotton rags have been woven into the field as the weaver worked the loom. The spacing of the rags gives the rug a striped effect from a distance. Unlike rag rugs from the eastern United States, the side selvages are strengthened by adding paired warps.

The jerga was acquired by Ward Alan Minge from Tony Garcia, who collected it from a family in northern New Mexico in the 1950s–70s.

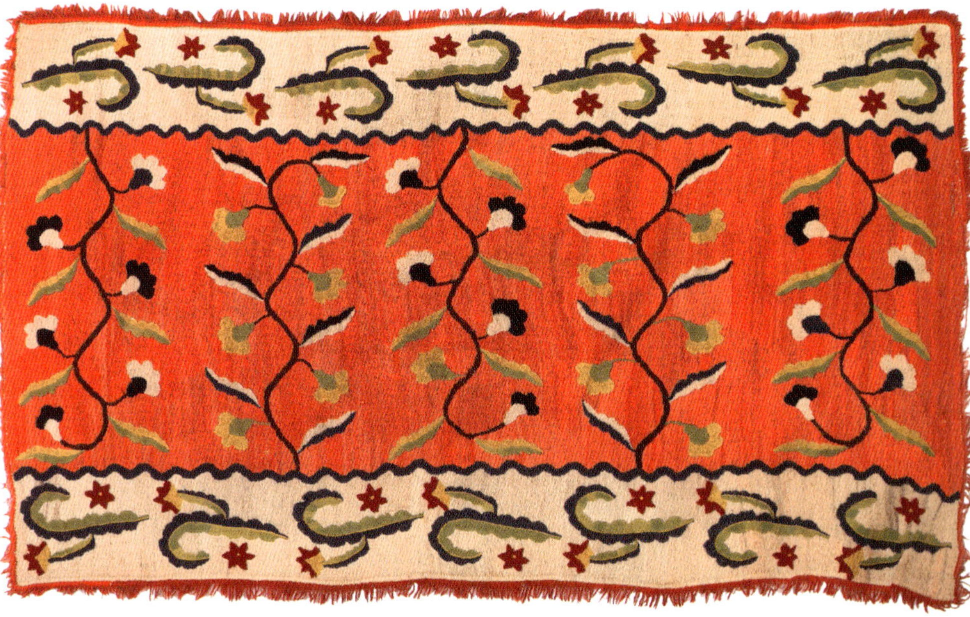

PLATE 132
Hispanic New Mexican
Colcha/Bed or table cover, 1865–75
Wool, indigo, vegetal and/or synthetic dyes, commercial cotton cordage
92 1/2 × 53 in.
Gift of the Albuquerque Museum Foundation, Lucia v.B. Batten Estate
PC2015.26.13

Most colcha embroidery was produced in northern New Mexico but was probably also made in the Río Abajo. The patterns were influenced by local, Spanish, Moorish, Indian, and Asian handcrafts. The earliest designs were geometric; more recent examples are decorated with flowers, vines, religious scenes, and occasionally animals. The stitch is long on top and short underneath, sometimes paired and held in the pair's centers at right angles. By stitching this way, embroiderers could quickly cover the surface of the cloth without wasting precious yarn.

First thought to be a twentieth-century textile, this embroidery is made from natural dyes including cochineal red and vegetal peach, yellow, and green. The fringe may have been added later. The flowers represent morning glories.

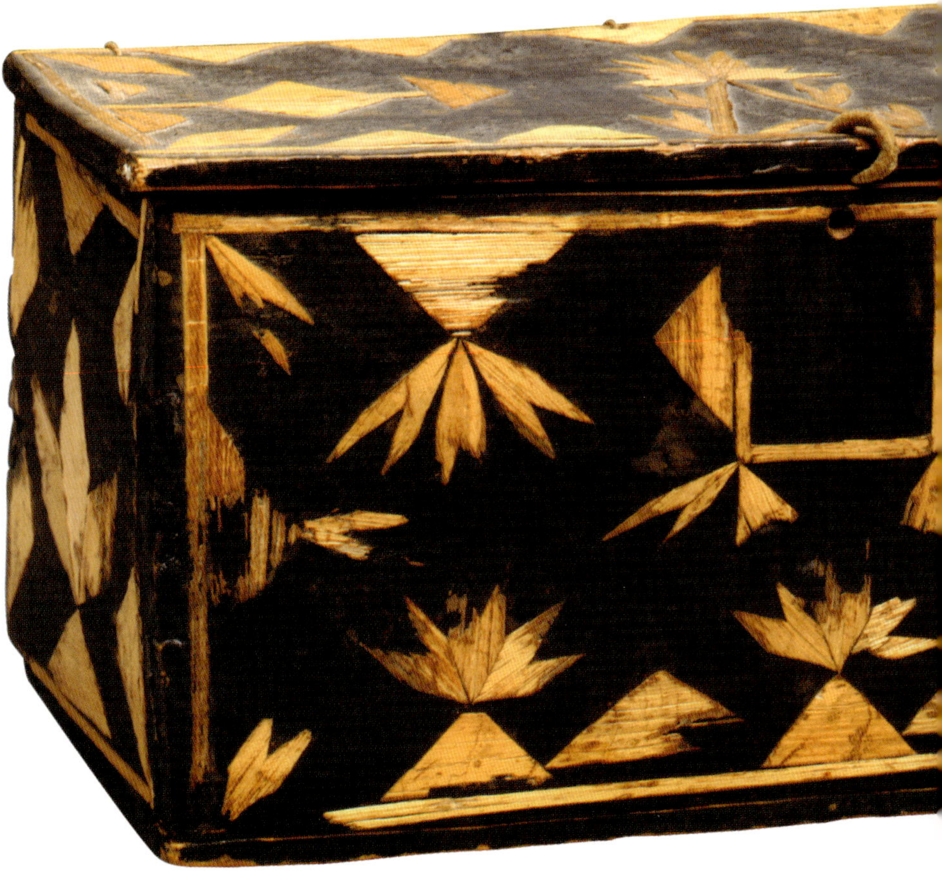

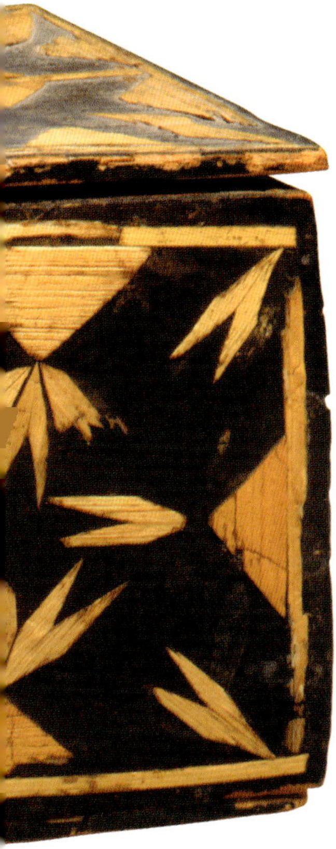

PLATE 133
Hispanic New Mexican
Caja/Straw appliqué box, nineteenth century
Wood, paint, straw, cordage, leather
$4\frac{1}{2} \times 9\frac{1}{2} \times 4$ in.
Gift of Ward Alan and Shirley Jolly Minge
PC1997.51.92

In imitation of gold leaf found in Spain and Mexico, that was rarely available in this region, New Mexican craftsmen appliquéd boxes and crosses with the next best and commonly available golden, shiny material—pressed wheat straw. This box is decorated with arrow and flower motifs. On the front, at the top edge, is a square border designed to look like a lock plate.

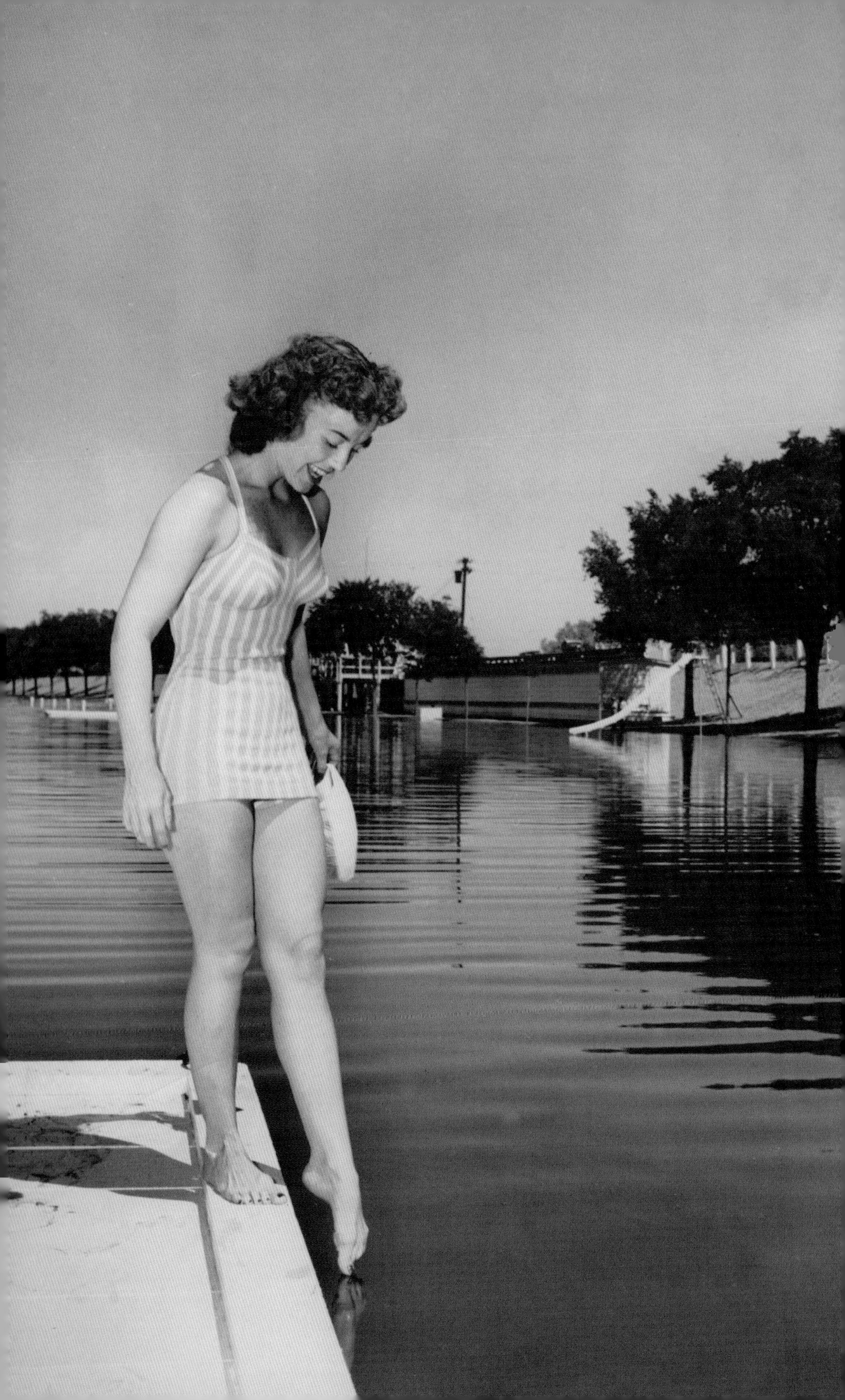

New Uses for Old Resources

We converted a swamp into a zoo, a municipal dump into Tingley Beach, and box-shaped wind patterns into Balloon Fiesta. We made the outdoors our playground—a place to hike, raft, ski, and appreciate. We embrace the life-sustaining qualities of our resources. The river, mountains, sunsets, and open spaces improve our lives, attract visitors, and promote a year-round outdoor lifestyle not possible in other Sunbelt cities.

The way we use land has changed dramatically over time. Until the late 1800s, the river and mountains provided food, firewood, building materials, and places to survive in times of conflict.

In the twentieth century, traditional grazing lands became bombing ranges, office buildings rose from wheat fields, and mountain strongholds turned into residential enclaves. Still, Albuquerque has more open space per capita than any other mid-sized American city.

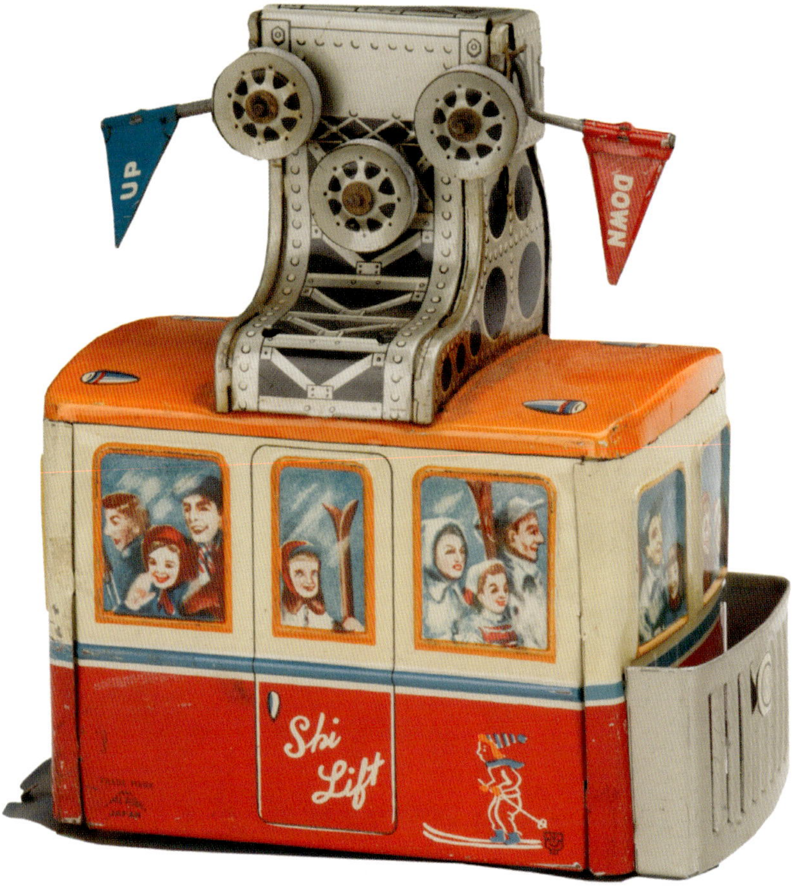

PLATE 134
Alps Ski Lift toy, ca. 1948
ALPS Shoji Company Ltd., Japan
Metal, tin, paint
5 × 5 × 3 in.
Gift of Melissa Smith and Mr. and Mrs. Arthur Ramsey
PC2001.71.2

The ALPS Company was well known after World War II for manufacturing toy vehicles and novelties such as this ski gondola. ALPS produced a range of tinplate/mechanical toy vehicles and space toys, along with numerous animated novelty animals. Many of their early toys had multiple action features, which set Japanese toys apart from their European and American counterparts. Ski toys were popular in the Albuquerque area in the 1940s–60s. Back then, Albuquerque could boast about having the world's longest aerial tram and the nation's longest T-bar ski lift.

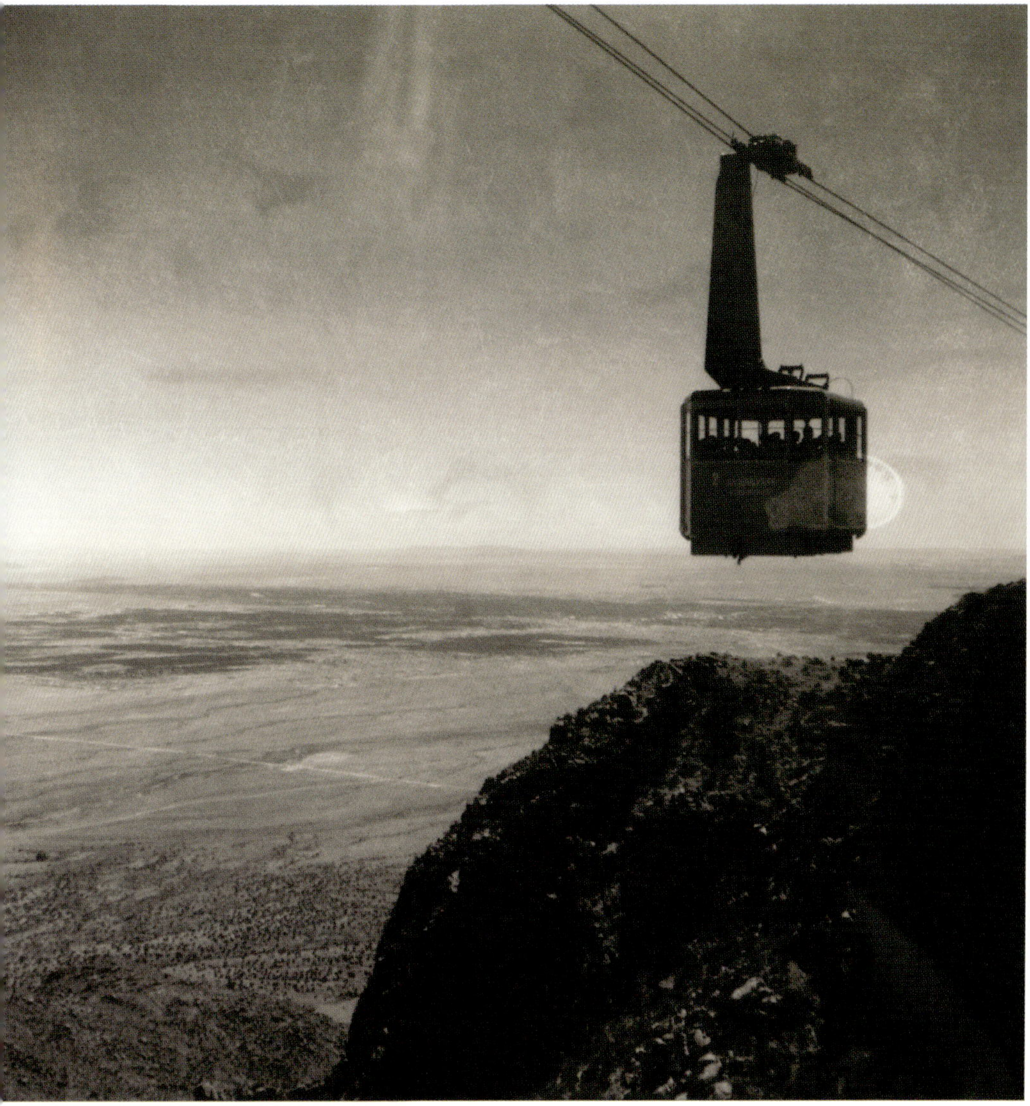

PLATE 135
The Sandia Tram, ca. 1965
Photographer: Andy Gregg
Gift of Andy Gregg
PA1996.37.78

PLATE 136

Double Eagle plaque, 1977
Wood, metal, paint
20 1/8 × 18 × 6 3/8 in.
Gift of Ben Abruzzo
RS1977.1.1

In September 1977, Maxie Anderson and Ben Abruzzo tried to be the first to cross the Atlantic Ocean in the *Double Eagle*, a helium balloon. Delays and bad weather caused them to ditch the *Double Eagle* in twenty-five-foot seas three miles off the coast of Iceland. This plaque, embellished with animated winds and storms, commemorates their harrowing journey. Anderson and Abruzzo, along with Larry Newman, finally crossed the Atlantic in August 1978.

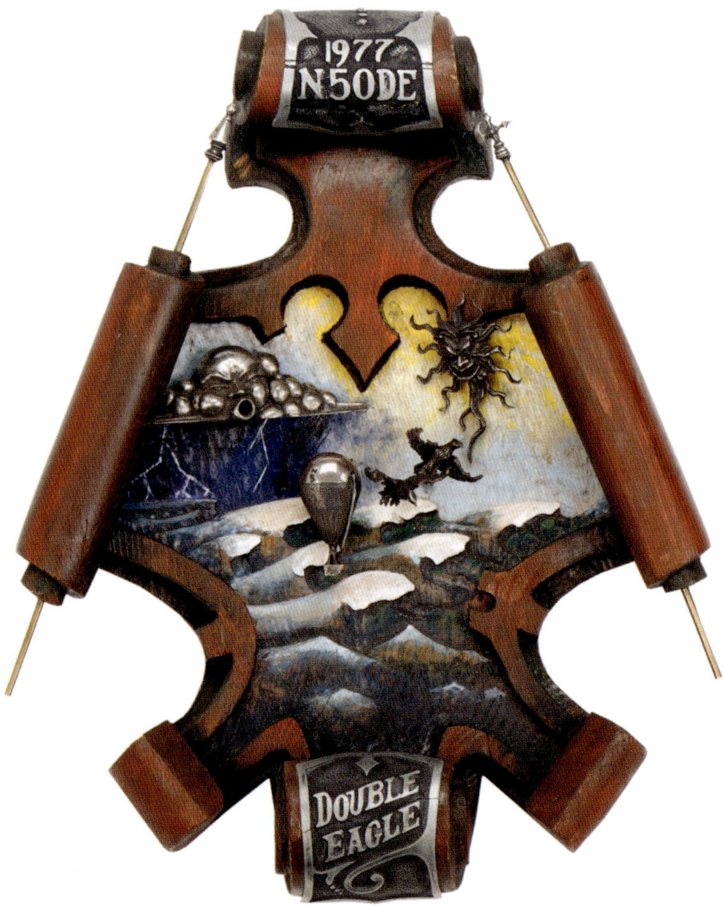

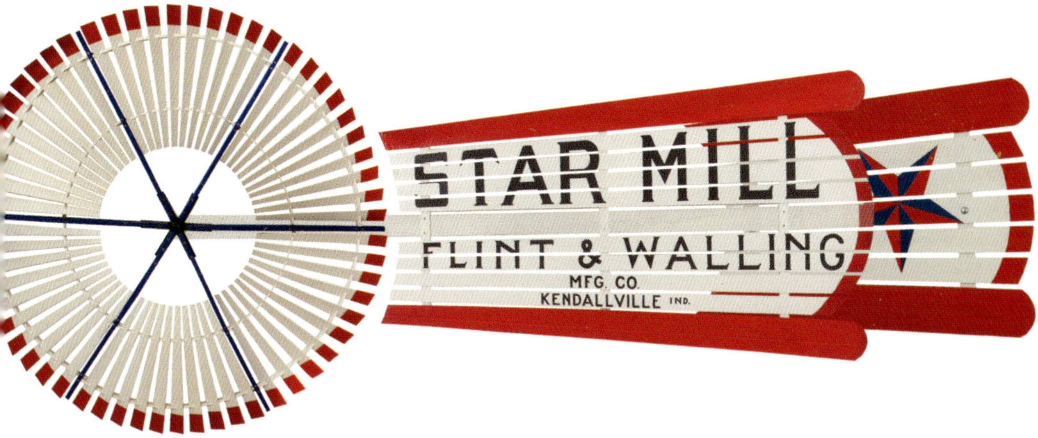

PLATE 137

Star windmill, 1890

Flint and Walling Manufacturing Co., Kendallville, Indiana

Oak, cast iron, steel, paint

124 × 227 × 8 in.

Museum purchase

PC1980.35.1

Driven by Albuquerque's gusty winds, windmills pumped water for thirsty cattle and crops on ranch lands far from the acequia system. Windmills could also mill grain and generate electricity. The Flint and Walling Manufacturing Company's Star windmills were popular with western ranchers.

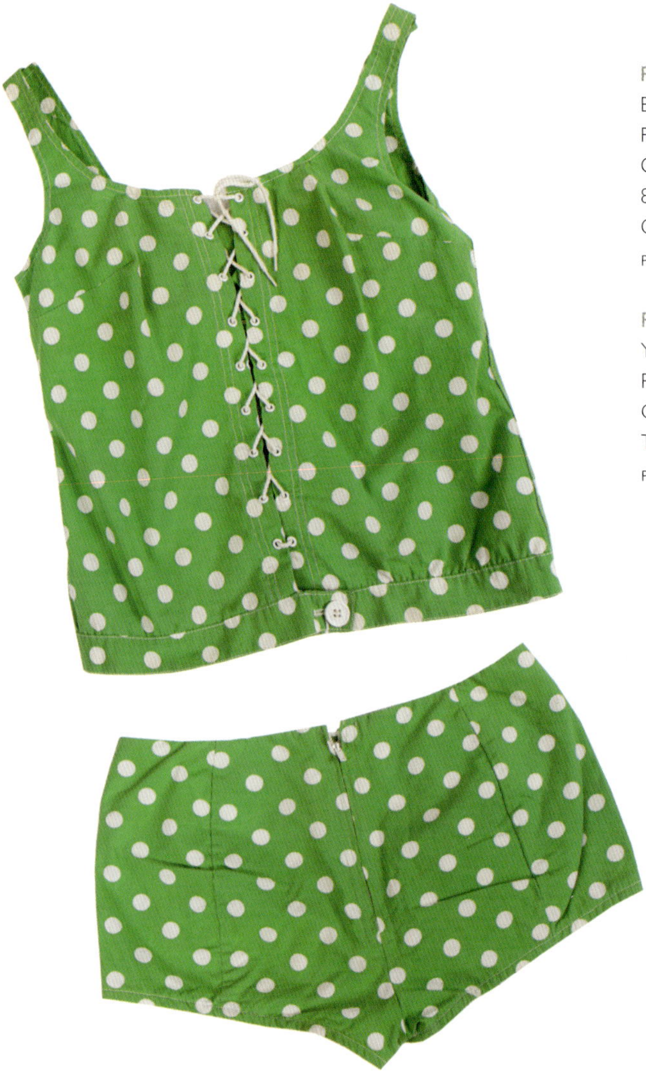

PLATE 138
Bathing suit, 1940s
Petti
Cotton, synthetic dye
8 × 18 in.
Gift of Jo White
PC2009.39.1.1&2

PLATE 139 ▶
Young woman at Tingley Beach, 1949
Photographer: Clarence E. Redman
Gift of Albuquerque National
Trust & Savings Bank
PA1980.185.580

Albuquerque citizens led by Clyde Tingley converted a dump into Tingley Beach—a sunny, sandy mecca for sunbathing and swimming, right in the middle of the city alongside the Rio Grande.

With the development of new fabrics, swimsuits began hugging closer to the body and increasing midriff exposure by the 1930s and 1940s and were considered indecent when worn in public. But during World War II, as the United States War Production Board began restricting the use of natural fibers in clothing, manufacturers increased the production of two-piece swimwear.

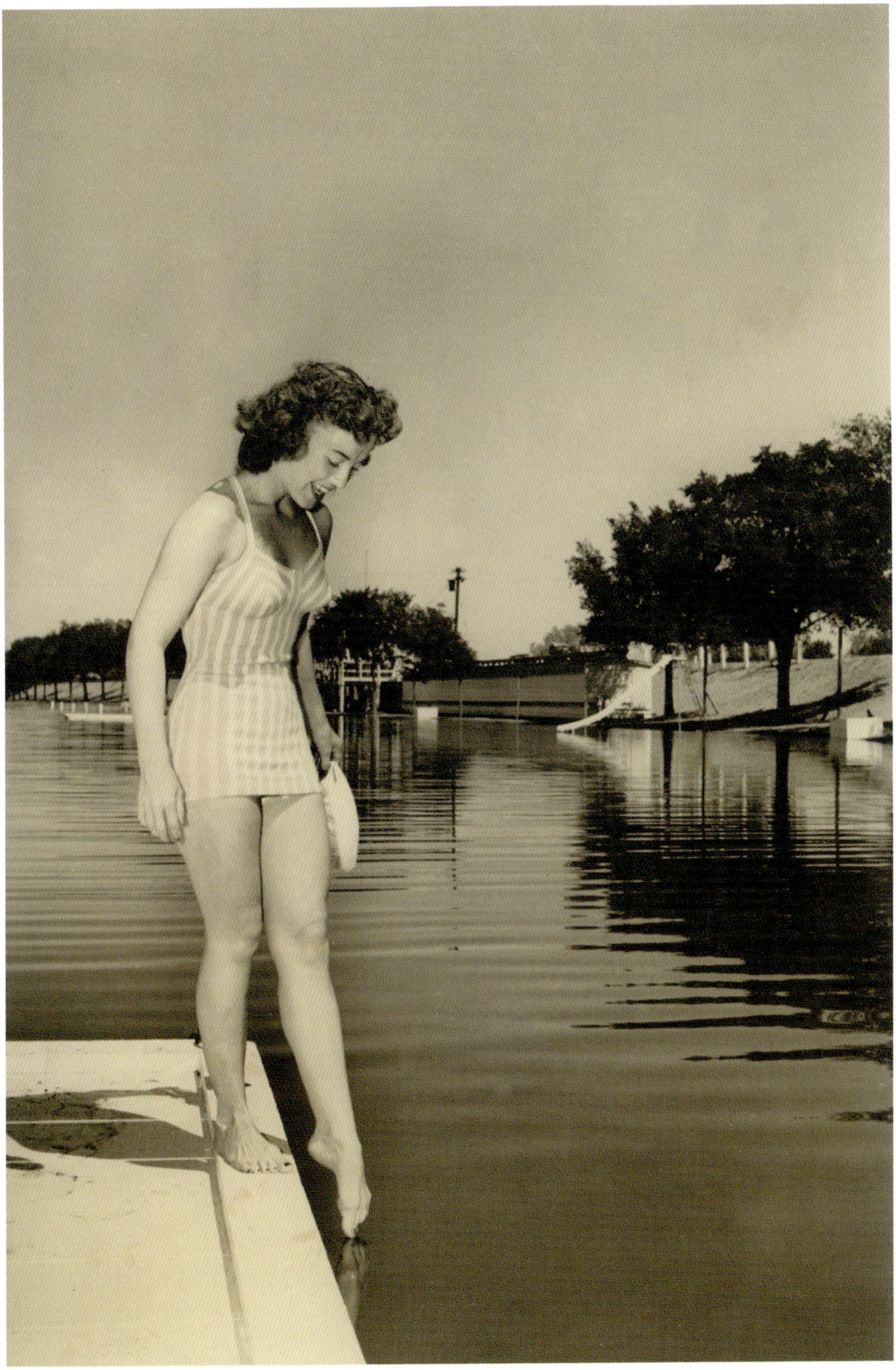

PLATE 140

Desert water bag, 1910–30
Ames Harris Neville Co., San Francisco, California
Canvas, flax, wood, tin, cork, ink
12 1/16 × 14 1/16 in.
Gift of Mr. and Mrs. Joseph Crompton
PC1976.11.14

Before bottled water, water bags kept thirsty travelers cool. The bag hung on a car grill, and the wind did the rest. Drivers had to take care not to run out of water and gasoline between stops.

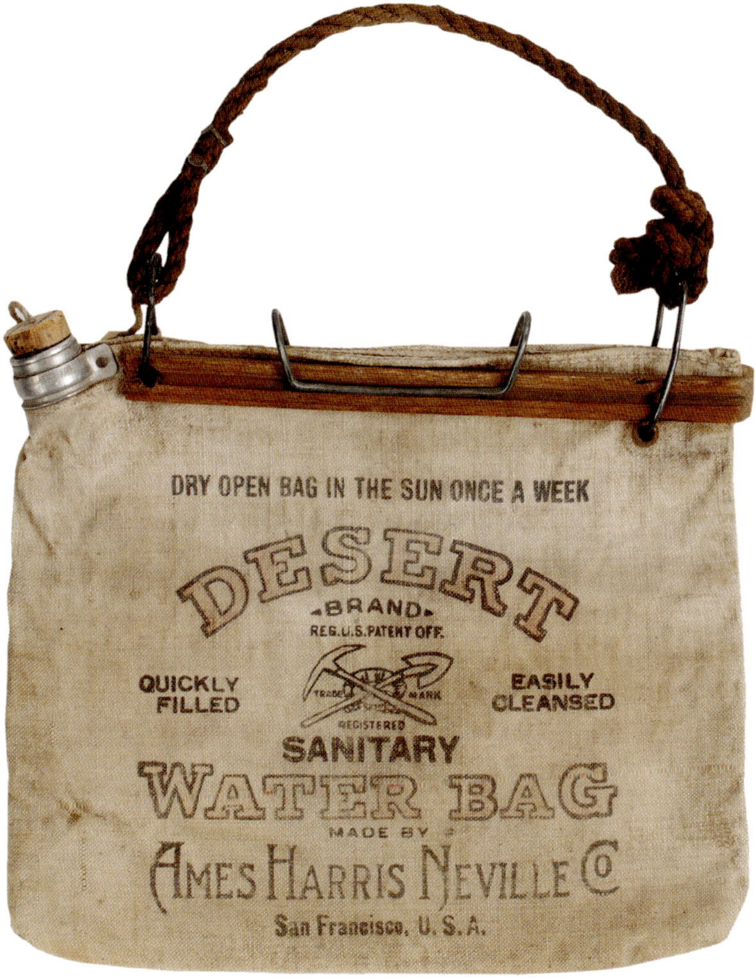

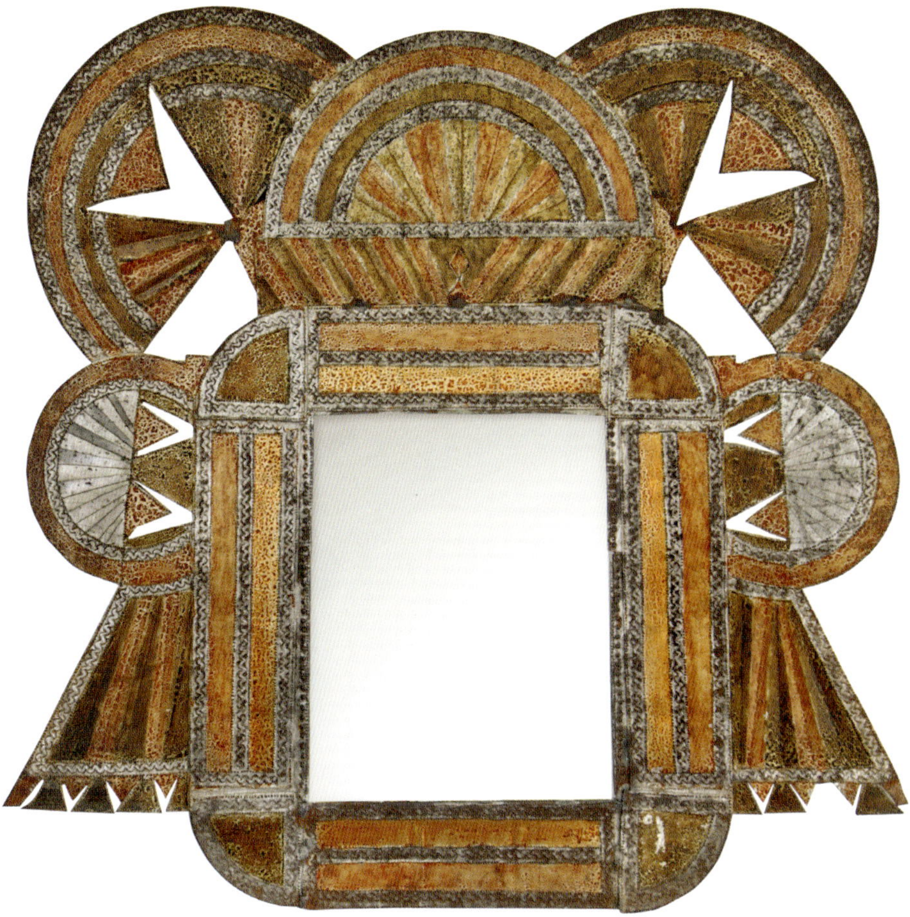

PLATE 141
Higinio V. Gonzales
Marco con espejo/Frame with mirror, 1865–1900
37 × 36 1/2 in.
Gift of Ward Alan and Shirley Jolly Minge
PC1997.51.27

Perhaps the most elaborately conceived of all Higinio Gonzales's creations, this polychrome tin frame probably held a devotional print at one time. As collectors acquired the aging tinwork, some installed silvered glass mirrors—changing their functions from sacred to secular.

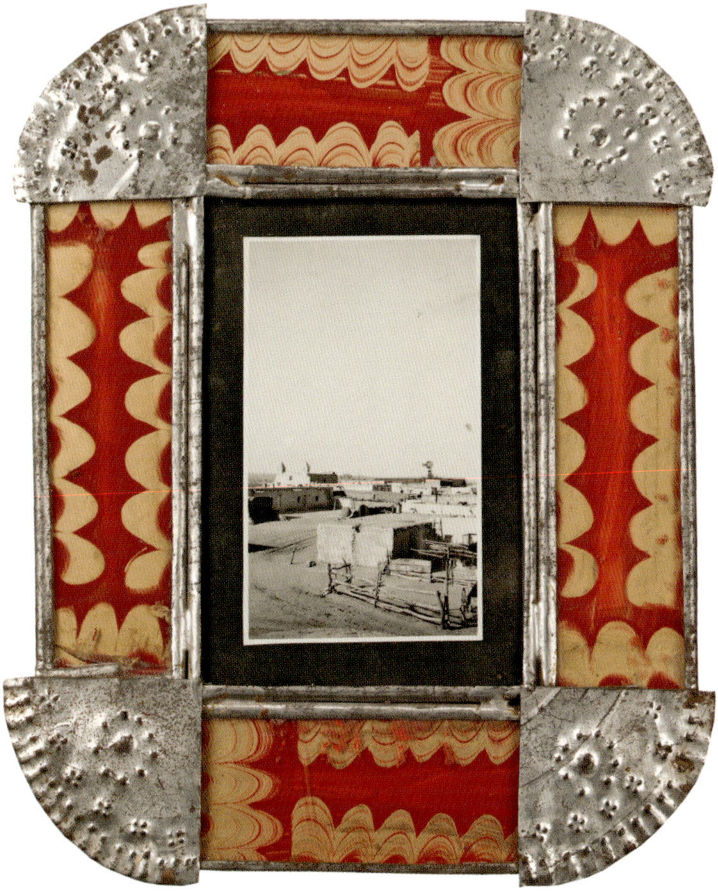

PLATE 142

Isleta Tinsmith, active 1895–1920
Marco con fotografía/Frame with photograph, 1900
Tin, glass, photographic print
12 × 9 7/8 × 3/4 in.
Ward Alan and Shirley Jolly Minge Collection
Museum purchase, 1995 General Obligation Bonds
PC1998.19.5

In the early twentieth century, tin frames once used for devotional prints were made to hold mirrors or secular images. This frame, soldered and painted by a Hispano tinsmith living near the Pueblo of Isleta, holds a turn-of-the-century photograph by one of the Cobb family of photographers, whose studio was located in Albuquerque. The photograph is of Saint Augustine Church at Isleta. The solder used by the tinsmith appears to include pine resin.

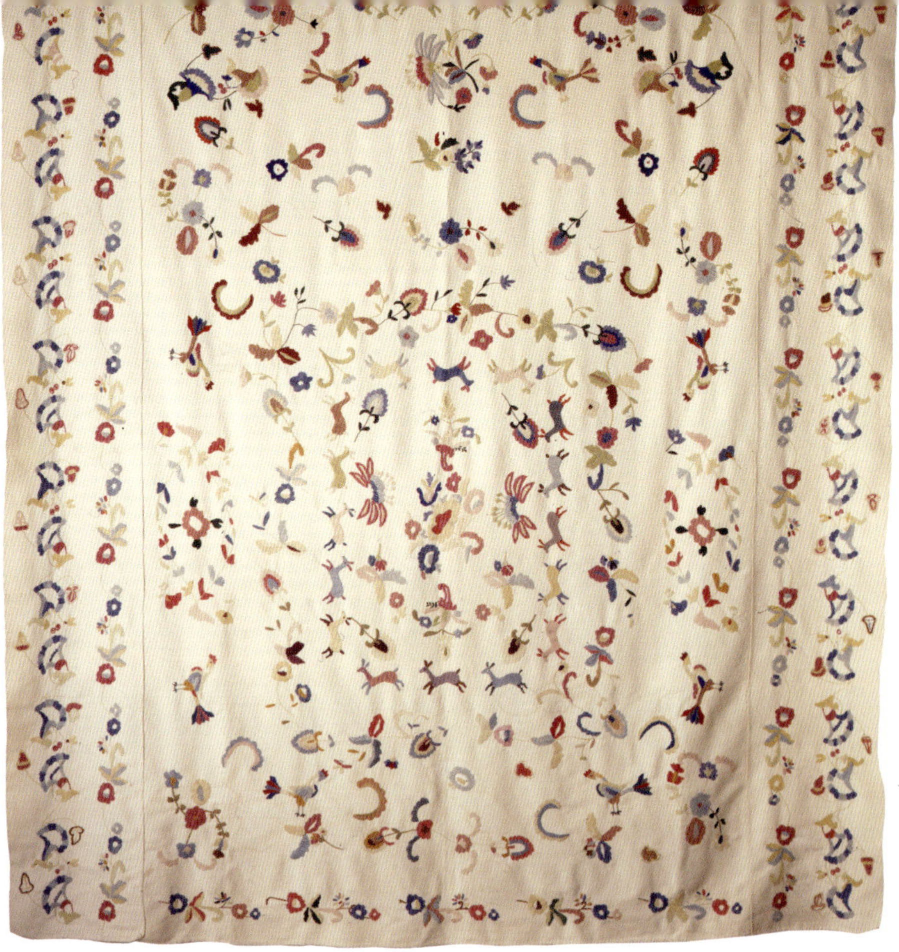

PLATE 143
Frances Delgado Espinosa and Carmen Espinosa
Colcha/Bedspread, 1940–45
Cotton twill, wool, dyes
89 × 83 1/2 in.
Museum purchase, 1985 General Obligation Bonds. Gift of the Albuquerque Historical Society via the Carmen Gertrudis Espinosa Memorial Fund
PC1987.30.1

Frances Espinosa was the mother of Carmen Espinosa (1892–1987, see fig. 1), a founding member of the Albuquerque Historical Society, whose collection was published in the book *New Mexico Colonial Embroidery*. It is believed that this colcha, embroidered in wool on cotton twill with small floral and animal designs scattered across the field, was designed based on Carmen's research on historic colcha embroidery techniques.

Working closely with Brice H. Sewell of the New Mexico State Department of Vocational Education under President Franklin Delano Roosevelt's New Deal administration, Carmen Espinosa wrote and illustrated an instruction manual for tin craft. Her contributions helped to fuel a revival of Hispano arts in the twentieth and twenty-first centuries.

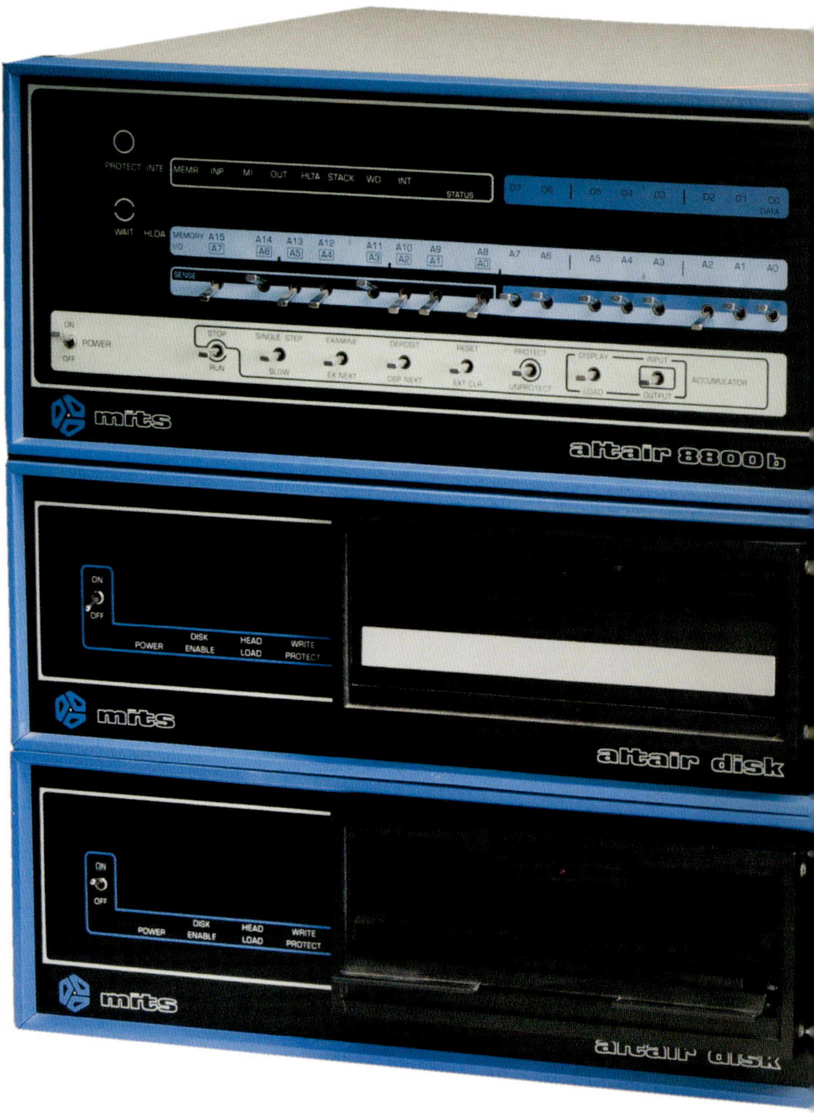
mits
altair 8800b
mits
altair disk
mits
altair disk

We Are Innovative

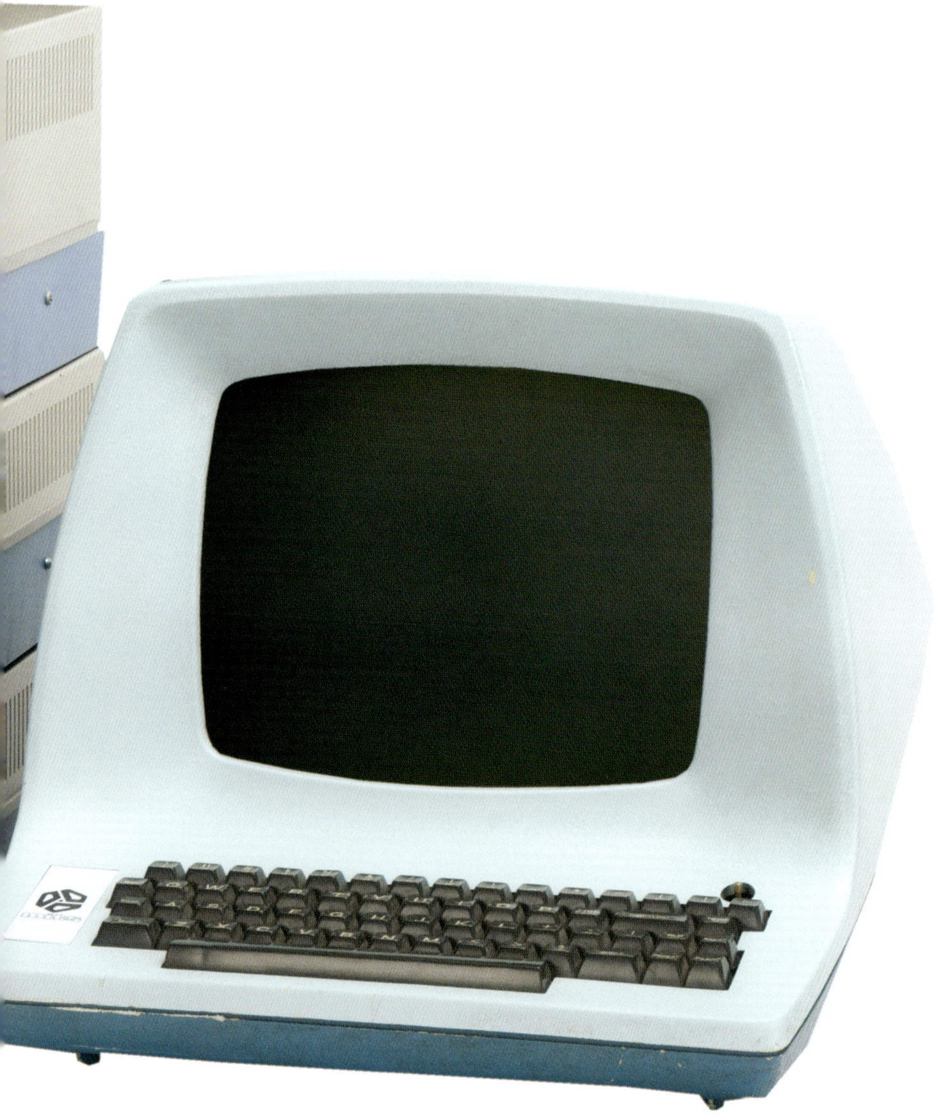

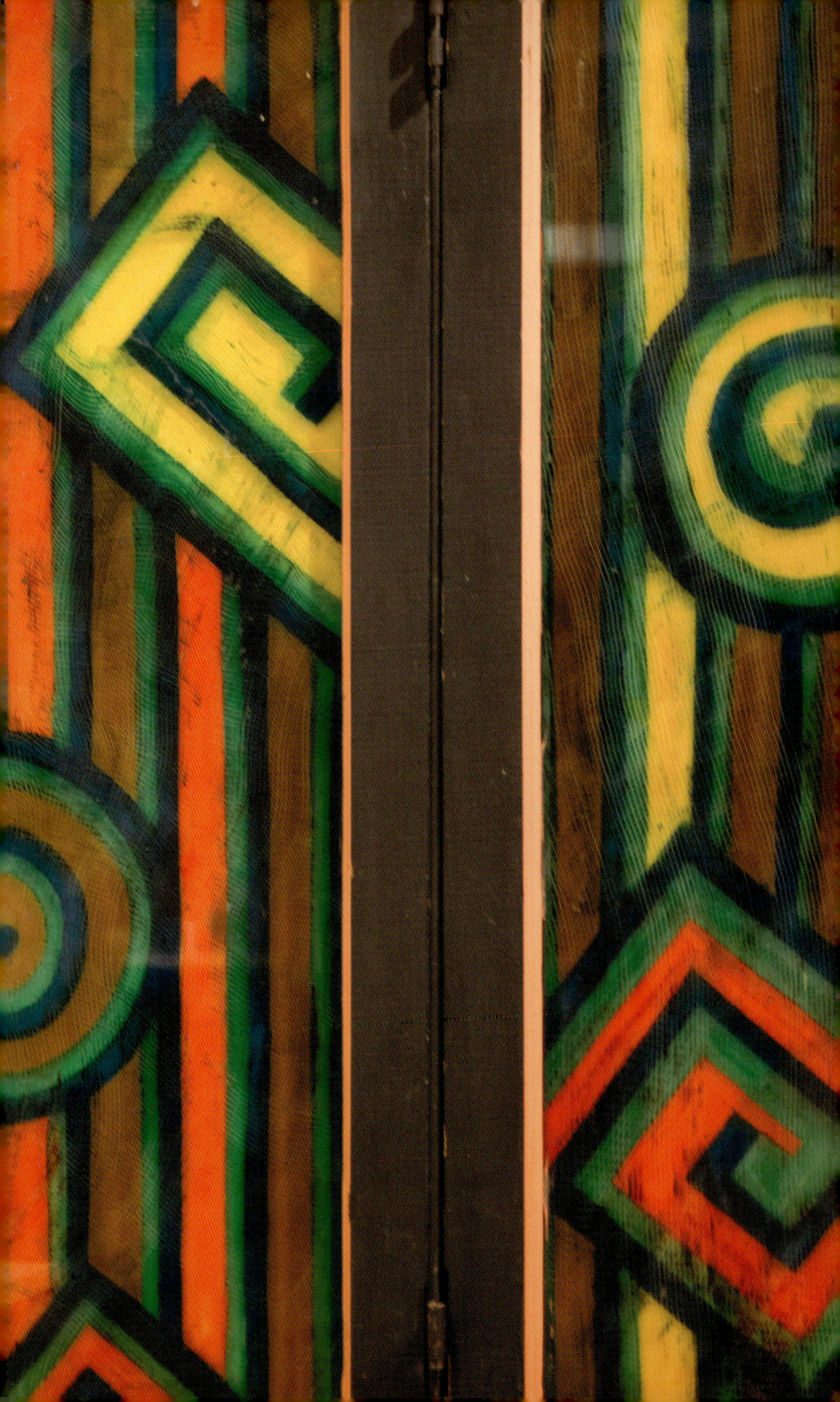

The people of Albuquerque have always been innovative.

As a result, we have become a crossroads for trade and transportation. The railroad, university, and military research and development efforts encourage innovators to make their destination Albuquerque. We are a regional hub.

Our inventions, made in Albuquerque and her environs, have impacted world history. Despite economic challenges, we are facilitators of innovative thinking and creative enterprise.

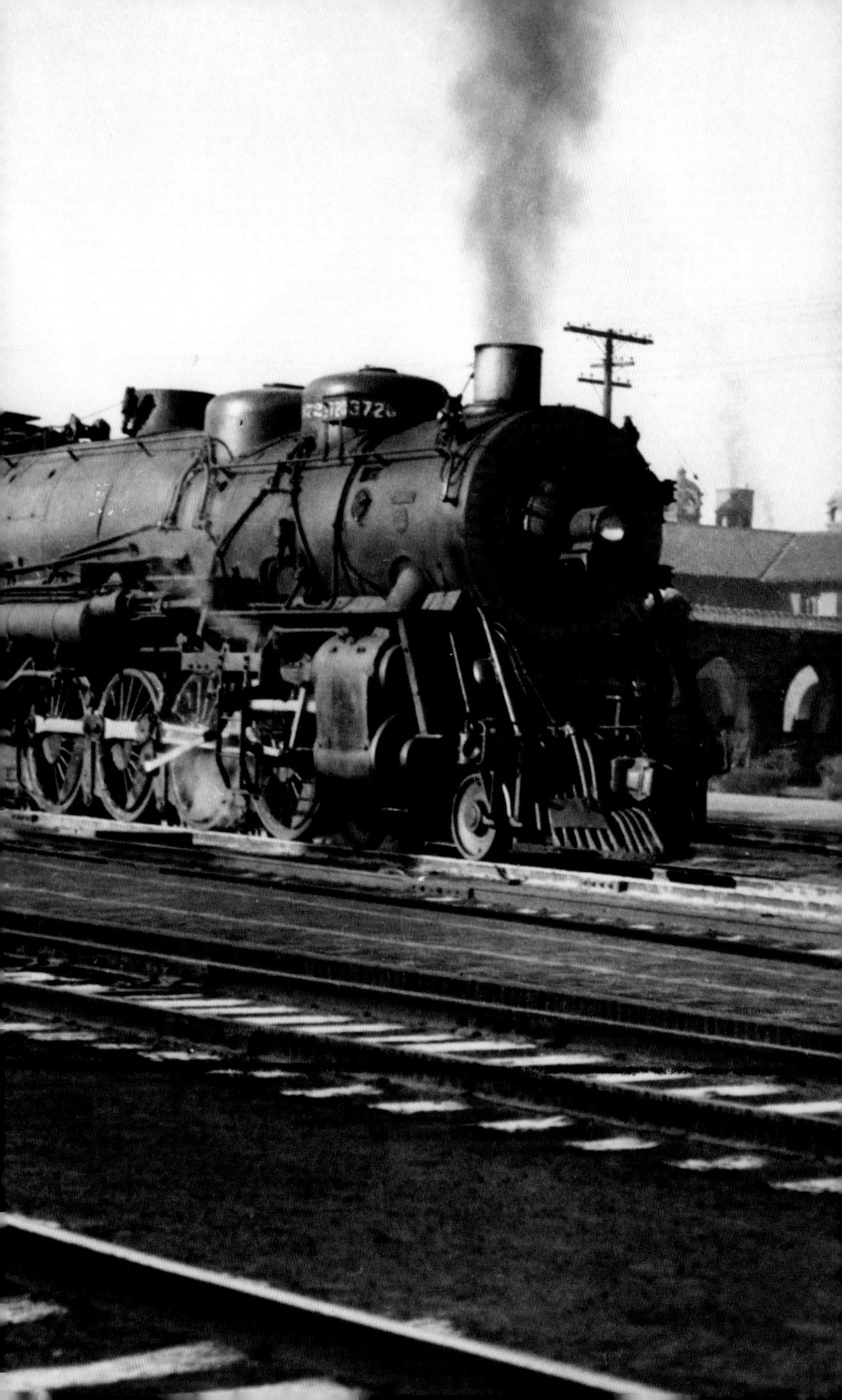

Trade and Transportation

Albuquerque's location along the Rio Grande, near a saddle between the Sandia and Manzano Mountains, made it a natural center for trade and transportation.

Ancestral footpaths became wagon routes, ferry crossings, stage stops, railroad beds, highways, and runways. Isleta Pueblo, Old Town Plaza, and New Town served as their crossing points. The oxcart journey to Mexico City that took six months in 1750 is now a four-hour flight.

PLATE 144
Ancestral Pueblo, possibly Tonque Pueblo
Shell, ca. 1450
Abalone
3 1/8 × 8 11/16 × 6 1/2 in.
PC1976.83.138

Trade in the central valley ran through the Pueblos of Isleta, Sandia, and Tijeras. Into the 1500s and beyond, traders followed ancestral trails to bring cotton and shells from the west, turquoise from the north, macaw feathers from the south, and bison hides from the east. Locally, fast runners brought important news to neighboring pueblos within hours. Centuries before the computer age, well-worn trails brought people, products, and information together.

Traders transported colorful abalone shells from the Pacific coast by foot to the Rio Grande via ancestral trade routes. Turquoise from the Cerrillos Hills area was often used as a medium of trade for nonlocal shell. The abalone shell was used to make pendants, beads, and other ornaments.

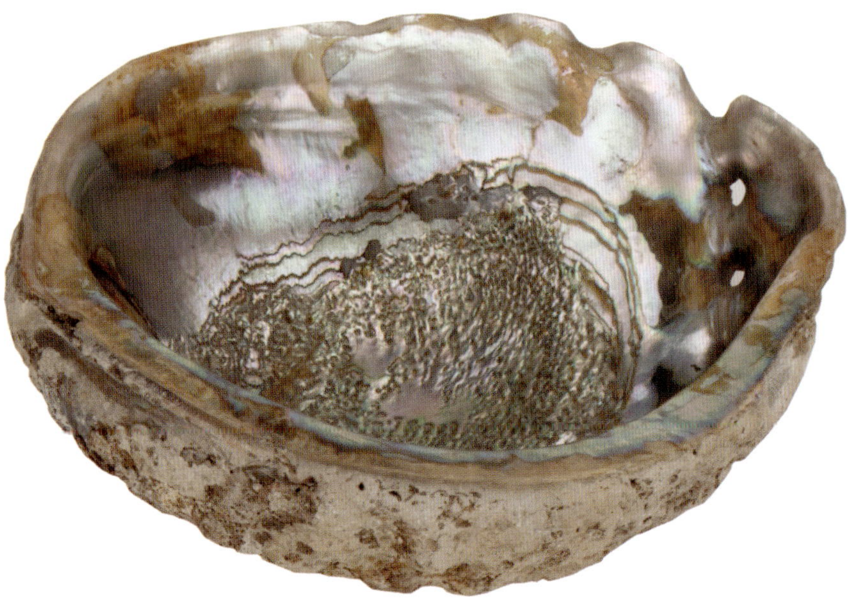

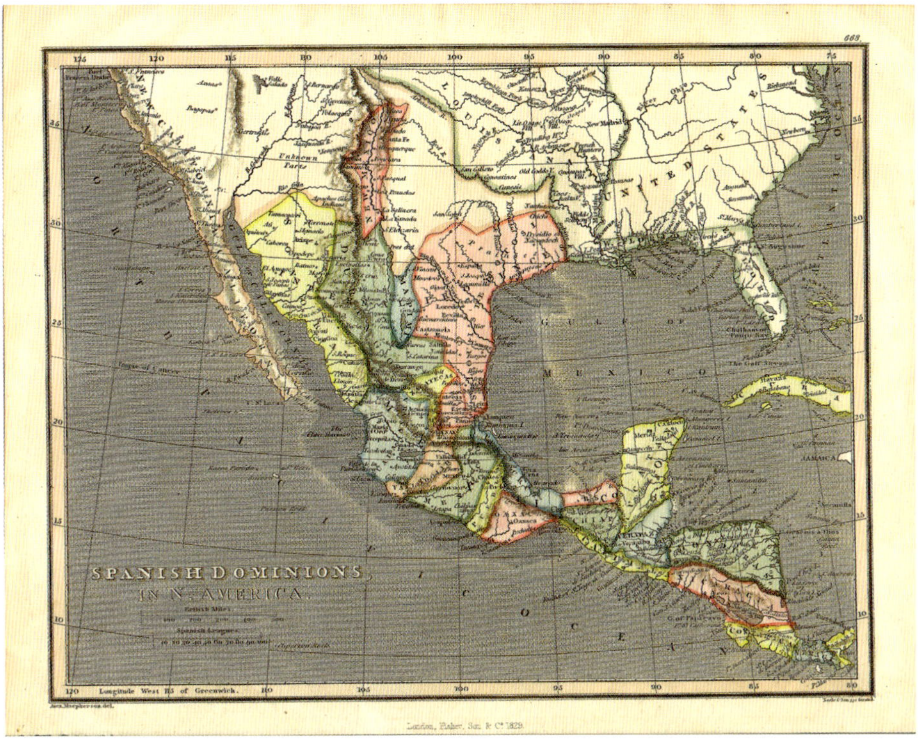

PLATE 145
Fisher and Son Co., London, England
Map, *Spanish Dominions in North America*, 1815
Hand-colored engraving; ink, paper, pigments
8 1/4 x 10 3/4 in.
Gift of Mary V. Franklin in memory of Edith Neuburger
PC1983.95.1

Sheep, weavings, and piñon nuts were exported to Mexico and beyond on galleons via the ports of Acapulco and Veracruz from the 1500s to the early nineteenth century. Vulnerable to storms and pirate attacks, the ships could take years to return. These trade routes also encouraged the export of tools and animal hides obtained from Comanche Indians and the import of exotic goods from countries other than Spain.

As Nuevo México opened its doors to trade with the United States after 1821, wagons on the Santa Fe and Chihuahua Trails transported a wide variety of American and European goods into the valley. Therefore, distances are given in both Spanish leagues and British miles. Both Acapulco and Veracruz are defined on the map, as are Albuquerque—notably spelled with only one "r"—and Santa Fe.

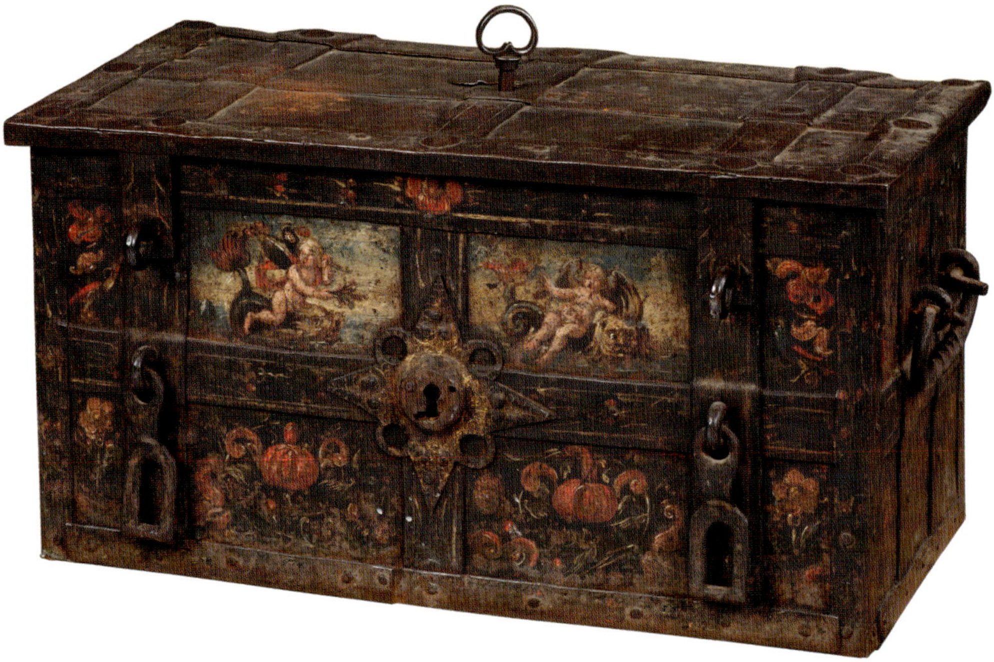

PLATE 146
Cajafuerte/Chest, ca. 1750
Spanish
Iron, steel
16 × 15 × 31 3/4 in.
Gift of Mrs. Betty Hartman
PC1984.31.2

The donor acquired this chest from the estate of Beatrice Ilfeld Meyer (1893–1983), daughter of Louis Ilfeld and niece of Charles Ilfeld. The Ilfelds, Jewish pioneer merchants who immigrated to New Mexico from Germany, played a major role in the economy of nineteenth-century New Mexico. Chests like these were useful for securing coinage and precious metals on the Manila galleon trade and were probably also used in long-distance transport along Colonial period trade trails.

The Ilfelds could have acquired the chest as early as 1867, the year Charles Ilfeld hit pay dirt with his mercantile in Las Vegas, or sometime after 1873, the year his brother Louis arrived in New Mexico. The company eventually moved to Albuquerque, where it operated well into the 1950s.

PLATE 147
Spanish
Writing and document box, ca. 1500
Leather, wood, iron
6 × 14 1/2 × 15 in.
Museum purchase, 1979 General Obligation Bonds
PC1981.224.1

In 1598, Governor Juan de Oñate y Salazar (1550–1626) blazed the inland route commonly known as El Camino Real de tierra adentro (the royal road of the interior land) from Mexico City to Okhay Owingeh (San Juan Pueblo). By 1700, merchants were importing goods into Alburquerque from Mexico, Europe, and Asia, a perilous six-month journey.

Like a briefcase, document boxes held important personal and government papers for short- and long-distance transport. This document box has tooled leather binding with a Hapsburg eagle, pomegranate motifs, and—within the designs of the hinges—the crescent-shaped Moorish naja.

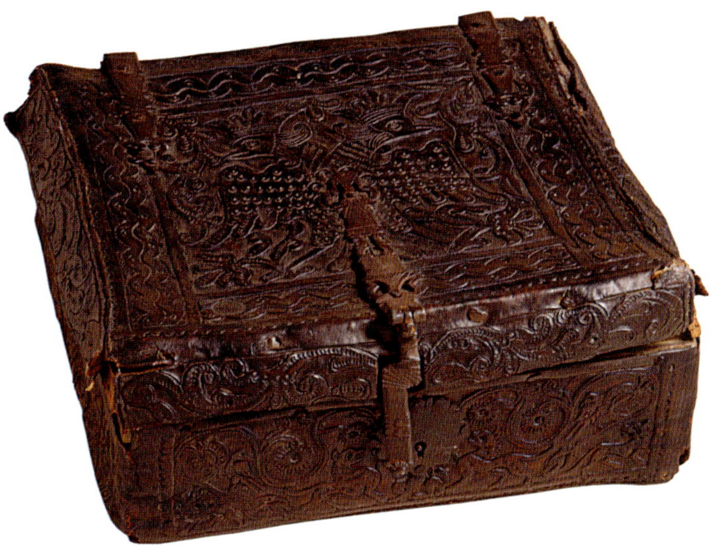

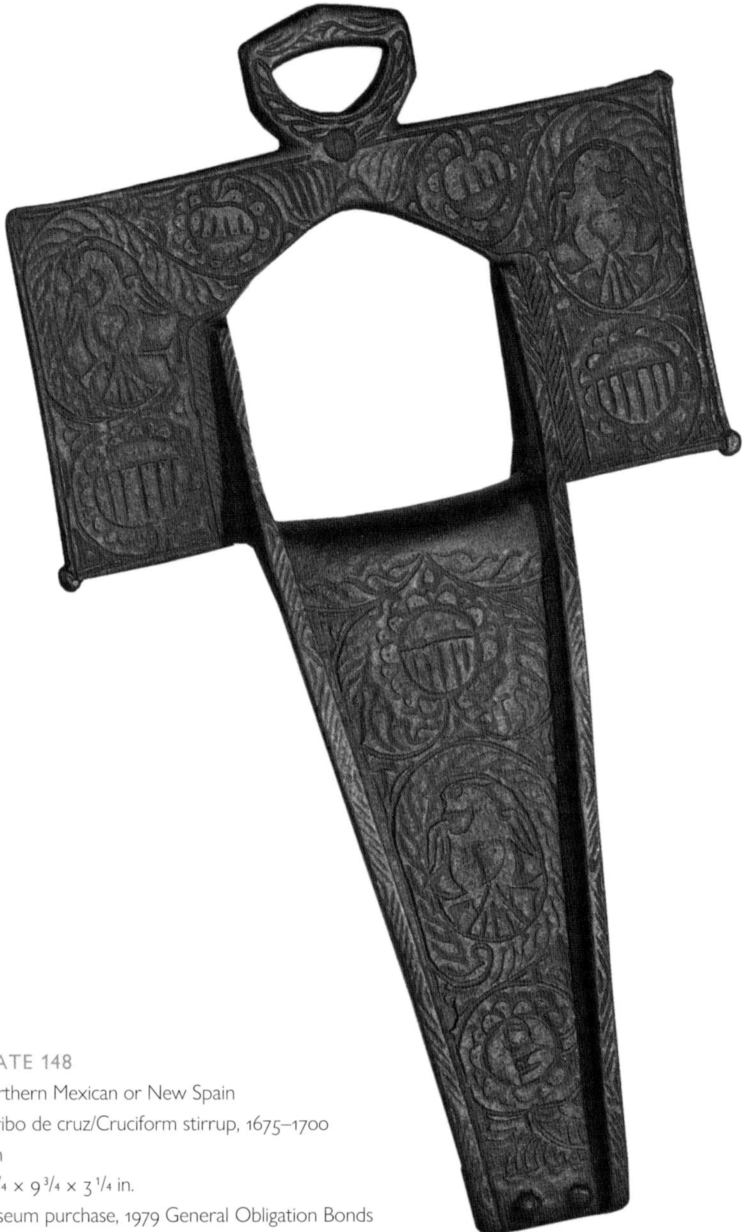

PLATE 148
Northern Mexican or New Spain
Estribo de cruz/Cruciform stirrup, 1675–1700
Iron
15 3/4 × 9 3/4 × 3 1/4 in.
Museum purchase, 1979 General Obligation Bonds
PC1981.117.1

Until prohibited by military regulation in 1772, cruciform stirrups were popular with horsemen. Distributed widely in Mexico, the heavy stirrups eventually made their way into New Spain via El Camino Real, spreading into all the southwestern states, where iron was in great demand. This example resembles a Latin cross and is decorated with incised pomegranates, eagles, hearts, and arabesque shapes.

Albarellos are tall cylindrical jars used to hold apothecary's drugs and ointments, with openings covered by parchment secured with a cord. The jar has a distinctive, slightly concave waist typical of apothecary jars made in Spain, Italy, and even China and shipped to various destinations by the Manila galleons. Eventually, Spain set up formal workshops in New Spain, and maiolica from both Spain and Puebla was transported north on El Camino Real through the Albuquerque area. This albarello is similar in type to maiolica sherds found in archaeological excavations at Santa Fe's Palace of the Governors and may date to as early as the mid-1600s.

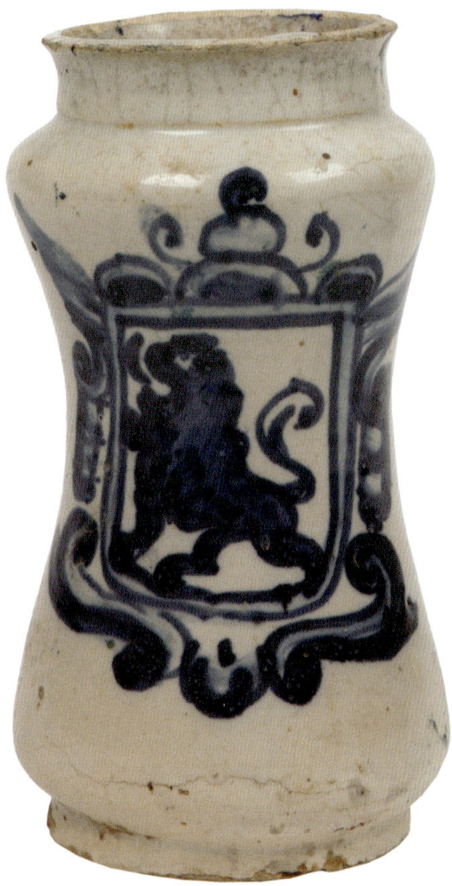

PLATE 149
Puebla, Mexico
Albarello/Apothecary jar, 1650–1750
Maiolica; earthenware, glaze
7 3/4 × 4 3/8 in.
Gift of Eason Eige
PC2014.2.1

PLATE 150
Tlaxcalan, Saltillo area, Mexico
Serape, 1790–1825
Wool, cotton, and vegetal dyes
96 × 48 in.
Museum purchase, 1979 General Obligation Bonds
PC1981.85.1

The origin of the Saltillo weaving tradition has been traced back to Tlaxcalan Indian weavers who settled near Saltillo, New Spain, in the seventeenth century. The classic Saltillo diamond and zigzag patterns are found in early Tlaxcalan art and were probably introduced by them into weavings made on the horizontal loom.

Brought north on El Camino Real, later named the Chihuahua Trail, Saltillo designs were embraced by local weavers, who adapted the designs for use in Rio Grande blankets. After Mexican independence in 1821, Saltillo serapes became a prestige item with the wealthy and fashion-conscious vaqueros (cowboys) of the early nineteenth century and an icon of Mexican cultural heritage and the *charrería* (horseriding) tradition.

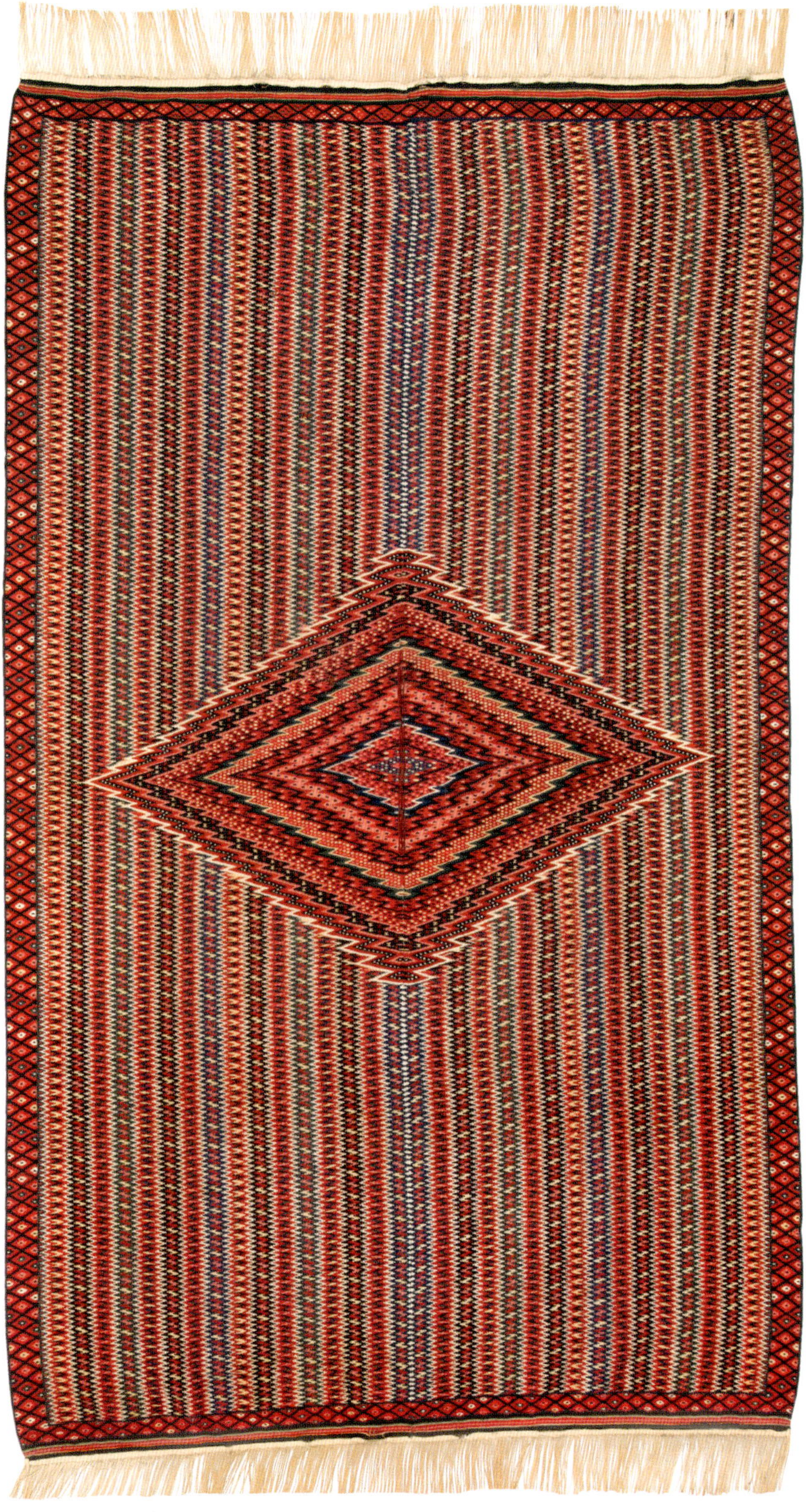

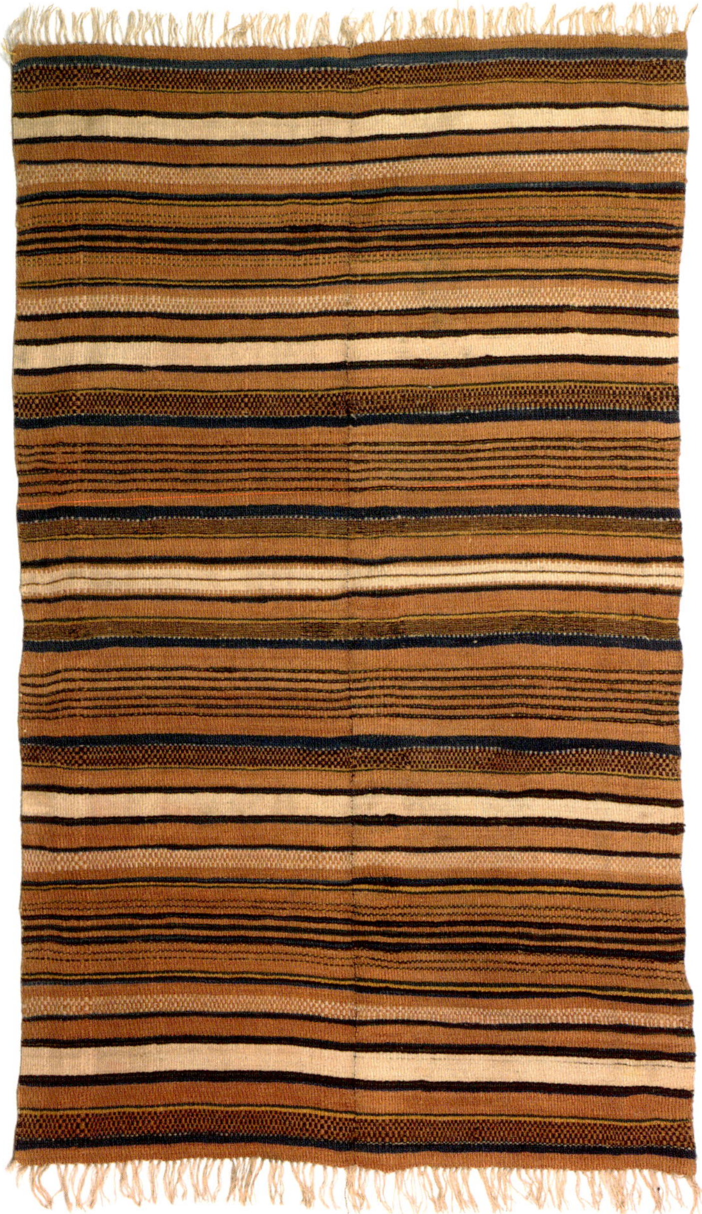

PLATE 151
Hispanic New Mexican
Frazada/Blanket, ca. 1860
Wool; indigo, brazilwood
and vegetal dyes
79 × 50 in.
Museum purchase, 1983
General Obligation Bond
PC1984.25.5

Striped blankets dyed with multicolored bands of reddish gold are often called brazilwood blankets, although the individual dyes could be one of three different species. Brazilwood dyes were carried on the Manila galleons and were so precious that ships carrying them risked pirate attacks.

PLATE 152
Hispanic New Mexican
Trastero/Storage cabinet, ca. 1790
Pine, paint
75 × 28 × 18 in.
Gift of Ward Alan and
Shirley Jolly Minge
PC1997.51.2

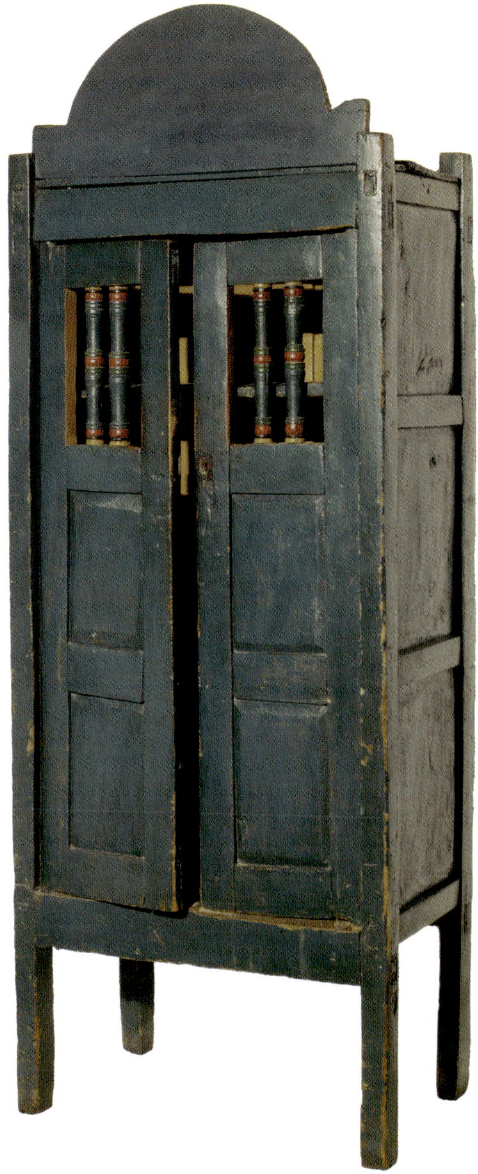

The *carpintero* who made this storage cabinet was very skilled. He incorporated raised panels into the mortice-and-tenon joinery and used pintle hinges instead of metal to swing the doors open. The hand-turned spindles used on the upper third of the door fronts may have been turned on a treadle lathe or acquired from a source outside of New Mexico. The entire piece has been painted with blue house paint, a popular color in the mid-1800s.

The *trastero* was collected north of San Juan Pueblo near Alcalde, New Mexico; Ward Alan Minge believes it could date as far back as the mid-1700s.

PLATE 153
Attributed to Jack Edwards
Carreta/Ox cart (replica), ca. 1983
Cottonwood or pine
95 × 95 × 179 in.
Museum purchase
P174

The carreta (two-wheeled cart) was introduced to New Mexico by the Spanish in the seventeenth century and was adopted by local farmers and merchants and their Pueblo neighbors for agricultural use. The carreta is an ancient design, developed in the Middle East more than three thousand years ago. Pulled by oxen or mules, carretas are still in use in rural areas of Mexico, India, and the Middle East. A four-wheeled version called a *carro* may have been more common for long trips on the Camino Real, but the two-wheeled carreta was more useful for short hauls.

Made without a single nail, carretas can be broken down and reassembled relatively quickly, can carry more, and are easier to load than pack animals. Albuquerque was a center for cart making because of the magnificent stands of cottonwood in the bosque—the cottonwood forest along the Rio Grande. Without grease the wheels squeaked loudly, so carretas were often heard before they were seen.

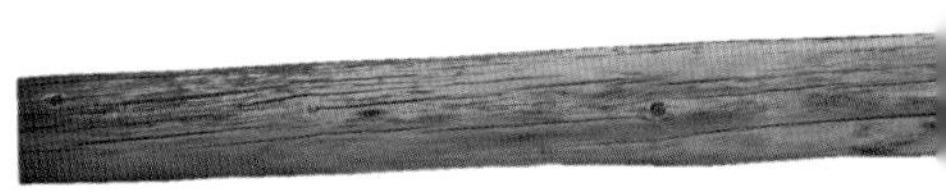

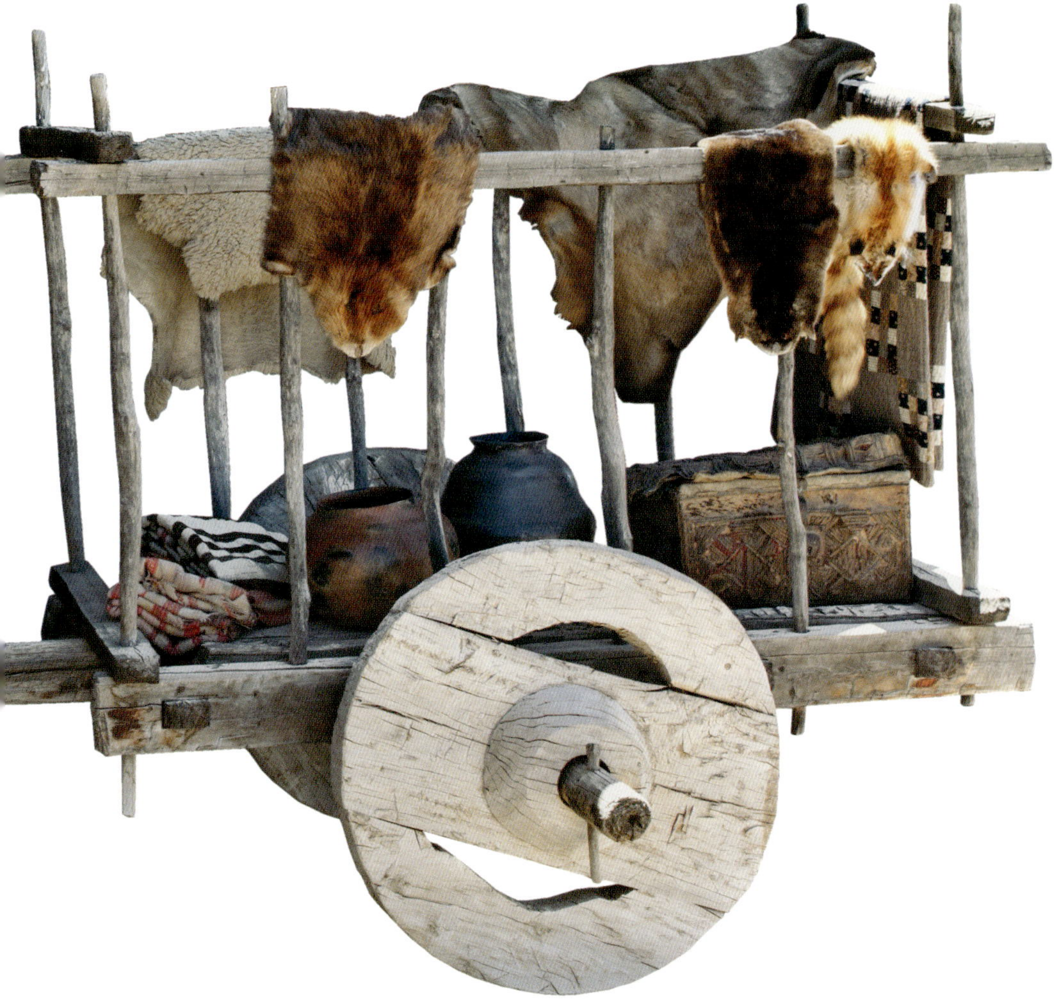

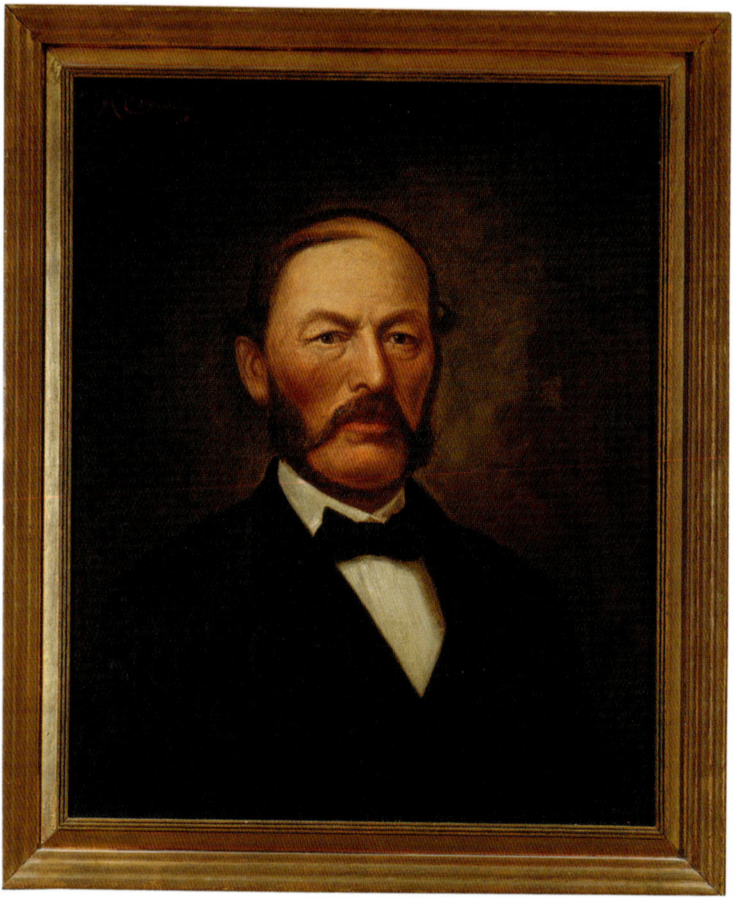

PLATE 154
Joseph M. Collumbin
Portrait of Ambrosio Armijo, ca. 1889
Oil, canvas
31 3/4 x 26 3/4 in.
Gift of the John B. Colligan Family
PC2005.48.1

Ambrosio Armijo (1817–1882) was a prominent merchant and landowner who ran sheep and goods over the Santa Fe and Old Spanish Trails. Armijo built the Armijo House and Store on Old Town Plaza (now La Placita Restaurant) around 1879; his wife Candelaria Griego de Armijo and their children lived just behind the store in the old Casa Armijo (now Patio Market, owned by the Albuquerque Museum Foundation). Joseph Collombin's portrait of Ambrosio Armijo, made not long before Armijo passed away, was painted from a carte de visite (visiting card) taken a few years earlier.

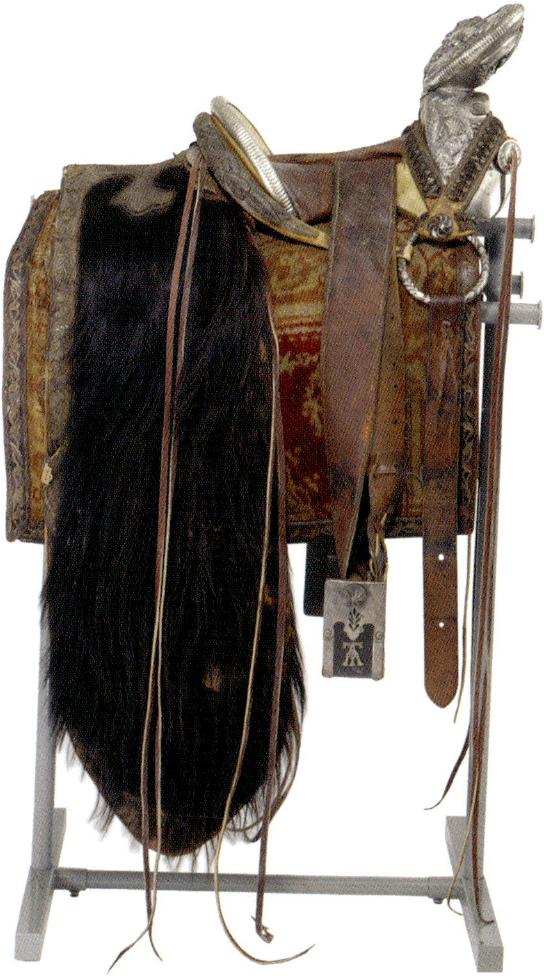

PLATE 155
Mexican
Silla de montar/Ambrosio Armijo's gentleman's saddle, 1860–70
Silver, wood, leather, cloth, wool
39 × 21 1/2 × 28 in.
Gift of John B. Colligan
PC1984.29.1

Don Ambrosio Armijo was born about 1817 in a farming community on Los Poblanos Ranch north of Old Town. Armijo was the nephew of Mexican governor Manuel Armijo and a well-known merchant, politician, and public servant. A noted trader on the Santa Fe and Chihuahua Trails, Armijo probably purchased the saddle on one of his trading ventures to Mexico. It is a remarkable example of the richly adorned saddles used by affluent Mexican gentlemen after 1850.

This saddle is noted for its large "dinner plate" horn decorated with two silver medallions—one depicting the Eagle and Snake emblem of Mexico, the other the biblical Lion of Judah. This saddle remained in the Armijo family from the 1860s until John B. Colligan's donation to the Albuquerque Museum in 1984. George Washington Armijo rode it in 1911, when he was selected to act the part of Don Diego de Vargas Zapata y Luján Ponce de León y Contreras in the Santa Fe Fiesta.

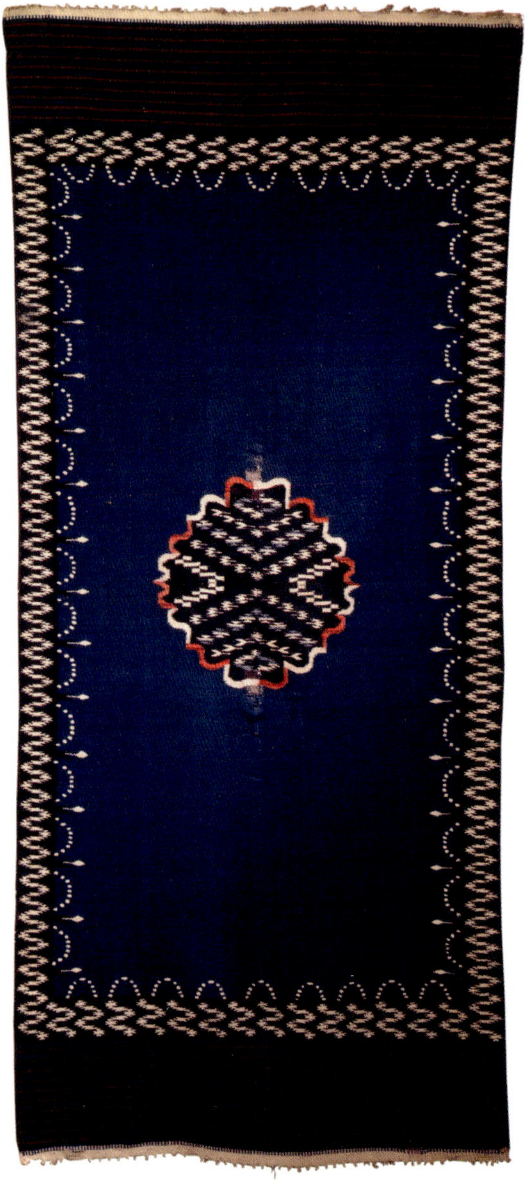

PLATE 156
Tlaxcalan
Saltillo serape, ca. 1840
Wool, indigo dye
73 × 37 in.
Gift of John B. Colligan
PC1997.42.1

After Mexican independence in 1821, El Camino Real became the Chihuahua Trail, linking Albuquerque to the Santa Fe and Old Spanish Trails. Franz Huning, Ambrosio Armijo, and other ambitious merchants soon began importing products from other countries and exporting local products to the Midwest and West.

Albuquerque merchant Ambrosio Armijo brought this blanket, an antique at the time, to Albuquerque from Chihuahua, Mexico, via the Chihuahua Trail. Its central medallion is inspired by Chinese designs that spread via the Manila galleon trade.

PLATE 157
Eastlake chair, 1870s–80s
Wood, metal, fabric
$42\frac{1}{2} \times 31 \times 24$ in.
Gift of Dolores Swanson
PC2009.4.2

Ambrosio Armijo very likely had an Eastlake parlor set, including this chair, shipped to Albuquerque over the Santa Fe and Chihuahua Trails. It was part of the Armijo household and was eventually passed down through the Armijo and Colligan families. After more than a century, the parlor set—composed of two chairs and a couch—was reunited at the Albuquerque Museum in 2009. The Museum is proud to serve as the Armijo, Borradaile, and Colligan "family museum."

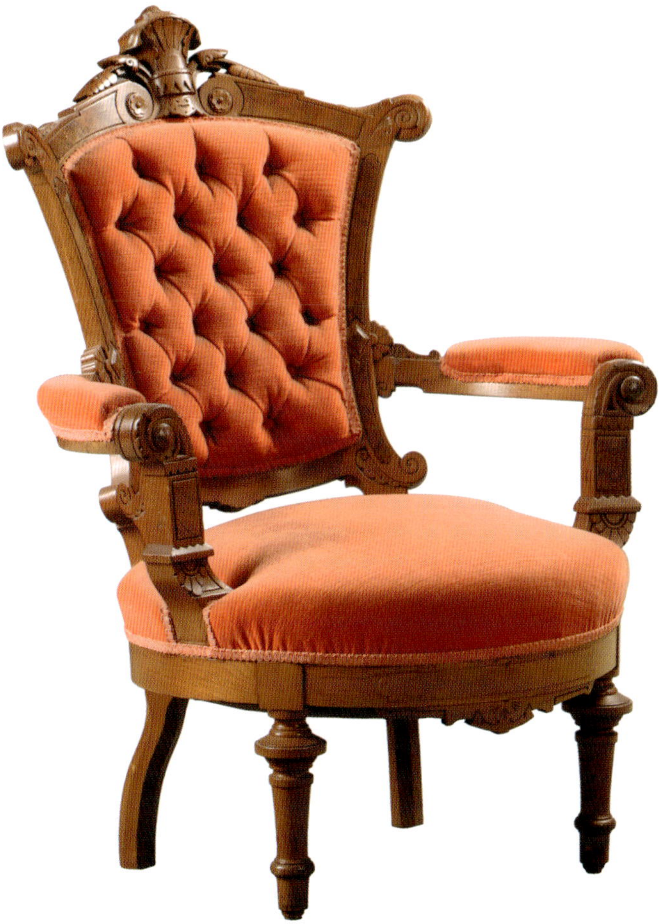

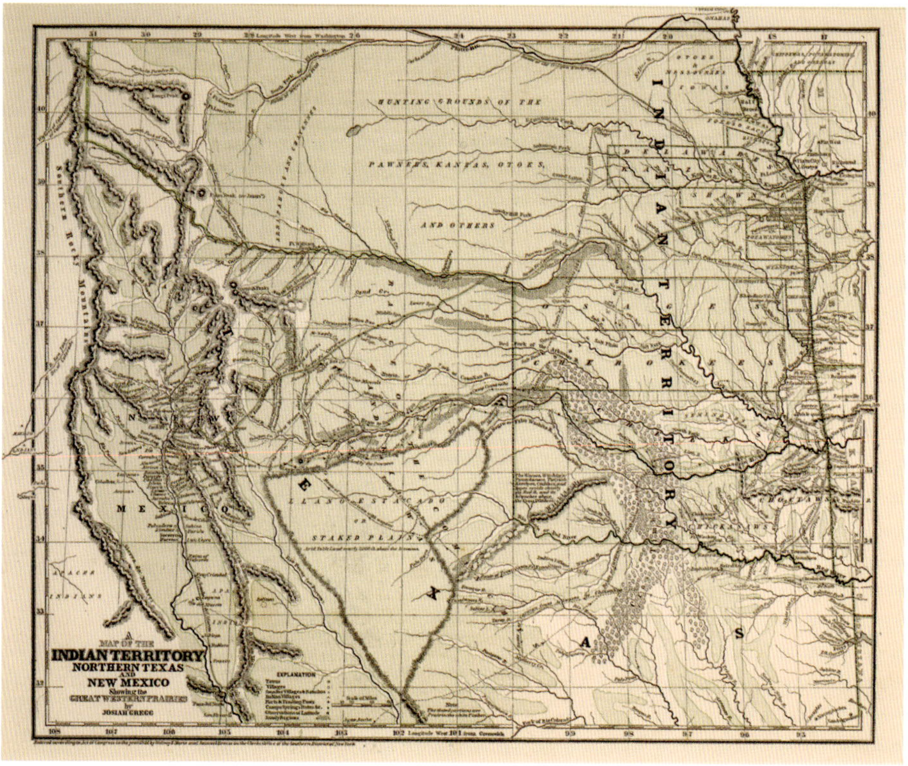

PLATE 158
Josiah Gregg, 1806–1850
Map, *A Map of the Indian Territory, Northern Texas, and New Mexico Showing the Great Western Prairies*, 1844
Publisher: Sidney E. Morse and Samuel Breese, New York
13 3/4 × 17 in.
Museum purchase, 1979 General Obligation Bonds
PC1981.155.4

This map originally accompanied the first edition of Josiah Gregg's classic book on the Santa Fe Trail trade, *Commerce of the Prairies*. New Mexico is in the lower left quadrant. The Santa Fe Trail is marked "Regular Route of the Santa Fe Caravans" and runs through the center of the map.

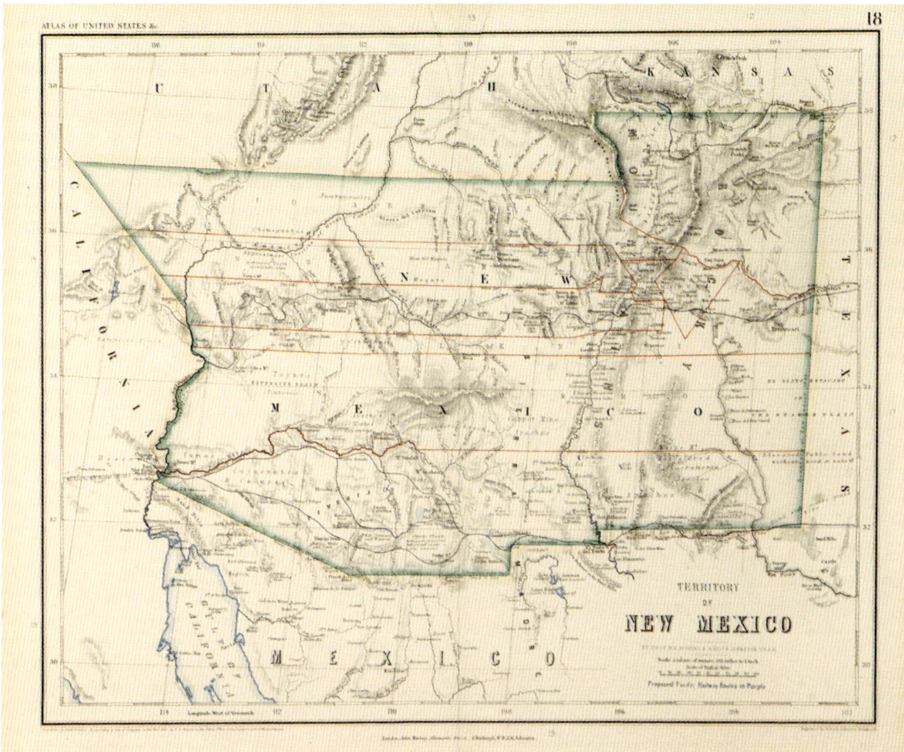

PLATE 159

Artists: H. D. Rogers and A. Keith Johnson

Engravers: W. and A. K. Johnson

Printer: John Murray

Map, *Territory of New Mexico*, 1857

Engraving; ink, paper

14 × 17 1/2 in.

Museum purchase, 1979 General Obligation Bonds

PC1982.130.1

Less than a decade after New Mexico became a US territory and five years before the Civil War reached Albuquerque, plans were in place to connect America's eastern and western towns with a railway system.

In 1857, the territories of Arizona and Colorado had not been created by the US Congress. Utah and Kansas territories occupied what would become Colorado, and New Mexico stretched from Texas to California. This map was created to illustrate the proposed route of a Pacific Railway line—the line is marked in purple. New Mexico's borders are outlined in green shading, water bodies are in blue, proposed routes in purple (later addition), and regions are in red.

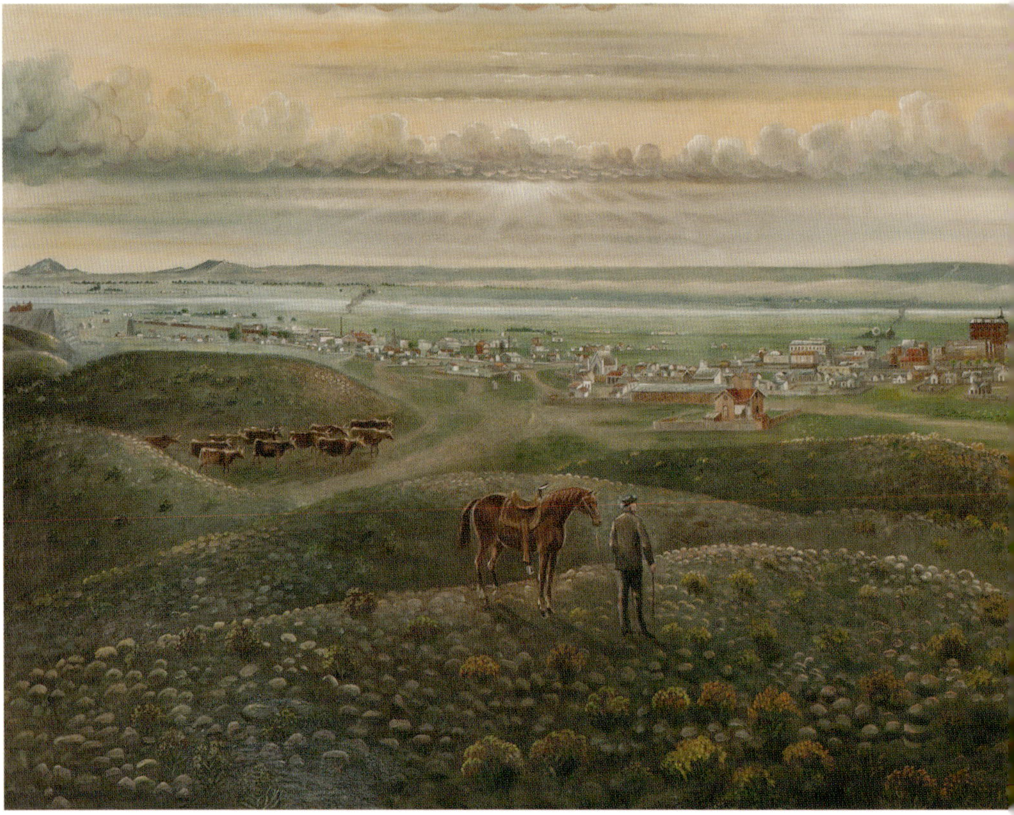

PLATE 160
Leon Trousset, French
Painting, *New Town, Albuquerque*, 1885
Oil, canvas
32 × 74 in.
Gift of Jim McCanna
PC1994.26.1

Itinerant painter Leon Trousset (1838–1917) painted New Albuquerque from the East Mesa sand hills facing west, overlooking the New Town district, railroad tracks, and Old Town to the Rio Grande and bosque. He traveled from city to city painting familiar scenes, then selling copies to make a living.

Trousset's depiction of the railroad boomtown emphasizes the north–south orientation of the central Rio Grande valley and the trails running parallel to the river, including the Camino Real, the Chihuahua Trail, the early Route 66, and today's Interstate 25.

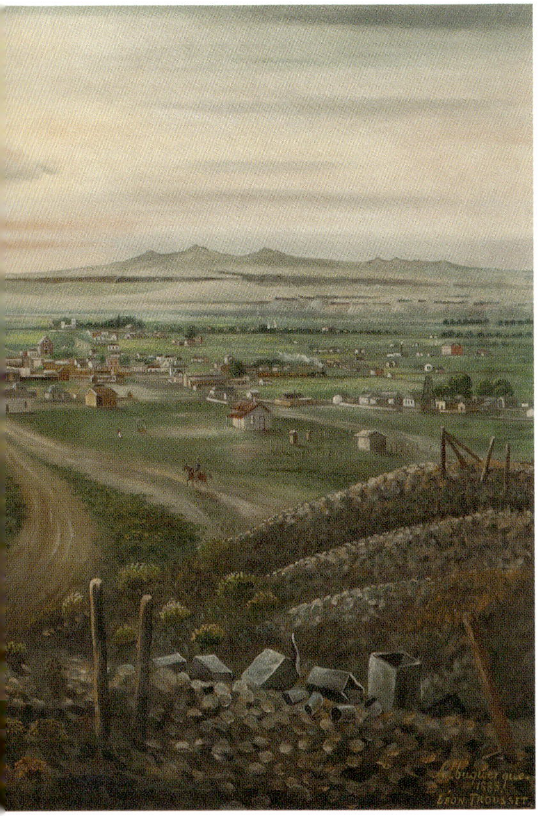

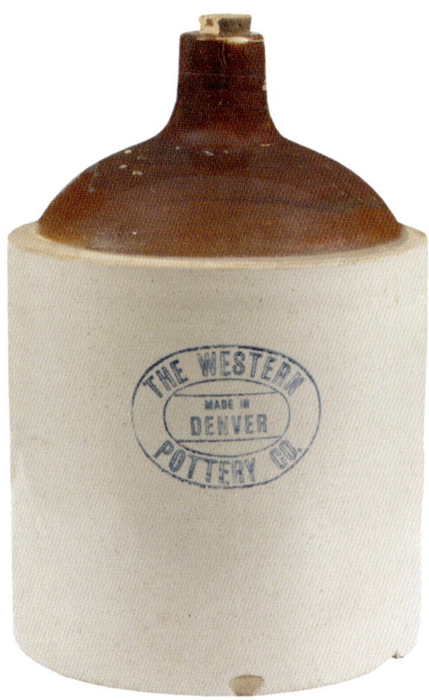

PLATE 161
Western Pottery Co., Denver, Colorado
Wine jug, ca. 1880
Ironstone, cork
12 7/8 × 9 in.
Gift of Mrs. Joseph Tondre
PC1972.2.6

With the railroad, supplies that would have taken weeks or months over the Santa Fe Trail could now arrive here in days. The Tondre family of French wine makers used this ironstone wine storage jug obtained from a company in Denver.

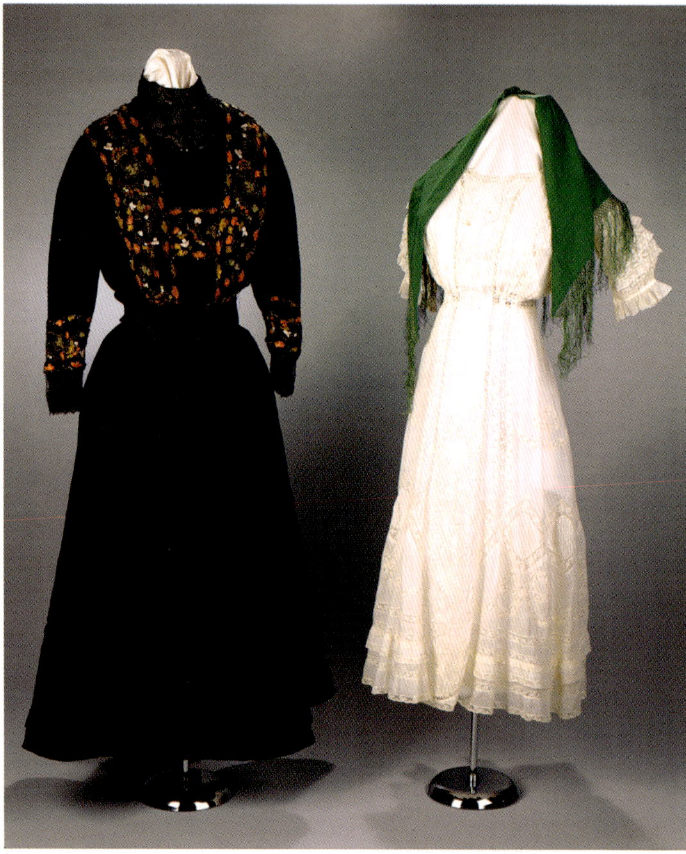

PLATE 162
Blouse (*left*) and dress (*right*), 1908 and 1910
Silk, embroidery thread, beads, sequins, netting, metal wire
15 5/8 × 22 5/8 in. (blouse)
15 5/8 × 47 9/16 in. (dress)
Gift of Grace Borradaile Buchanan, Don Ambrosio Armijo Family, via the Albuquerque Historical Society
PC1967.2.23 & 26

By the time the railroad arrived, Old Town homes looked very different from just twenty years earlier. Victorian furnishings, decorative arts, and clothing shipped in from the Midwest and Europe were all the rage, and locally made clothing, blankets, and rugs were passed over for more colorful and highly decorative versions.

The black embroidered silk blouse belonged to Ambrosio Armijo's daughter Teresa Armijo de Symington. The white lace dress belonged to Armijo's granddaughter Grace Borradaile. Originally the dress was created for her mother in 1908 in Saint Louis, was floor length, five yards in circumference, and featured 180 yards of lace and a handmade French embroidery panel. Grace refashioned the dress for her graduation.

PLATE 163

Atchison, Topeka and Santa Fe Railway

Locomotive bell, 1920s

Brass, steel, paint

26 × 21 1/2 × 16 1/4 in.

Gift of the Atchison, Topeka and Santa Fe Railway Company via Pat Hill

PC1975.21.1

In January 1880, after unsuccessfully negotiating for land in Bernalillo, the Atchison, Topeka and Santa Fe Railroad (AT&SF) announced that the company would build rail yards about one and a half miles east of Old Town Plaza. Sharing a division point with the Atlantic and Pacific Railroad, they eventually built a depot and back shops. In 1902, the depot and Fred Harvey Eating House were replaced by the two-and-a-half-block-long, Mission-style Alvarado Hotel.

The arrival of the railroad changed everything. Shipments that once took months now arrived in days. A wooden depot and freight office arose, seemingly overnight, near the tracks at Railroad Avenue and Front Street. Nervous local freighters moved their businesses to New Albuquerque, already filling up with fortune-seeking entrepreneurs. By 1882, gross receipts for the AT&SF and the Atlantic & Pacific Railroad totaled $27 million (in today's equivalent).

Pat Hill, a local public relations employee of the AT&SF, arranged for the Museum to receive this bell as a gift from the company to the people of Albuquerque.

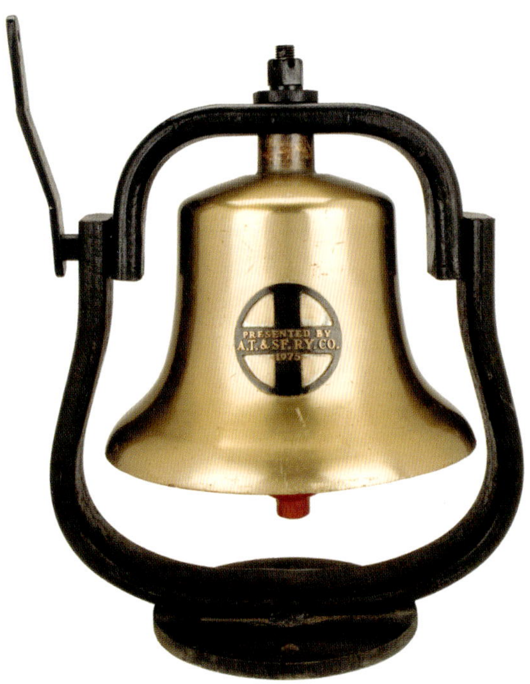

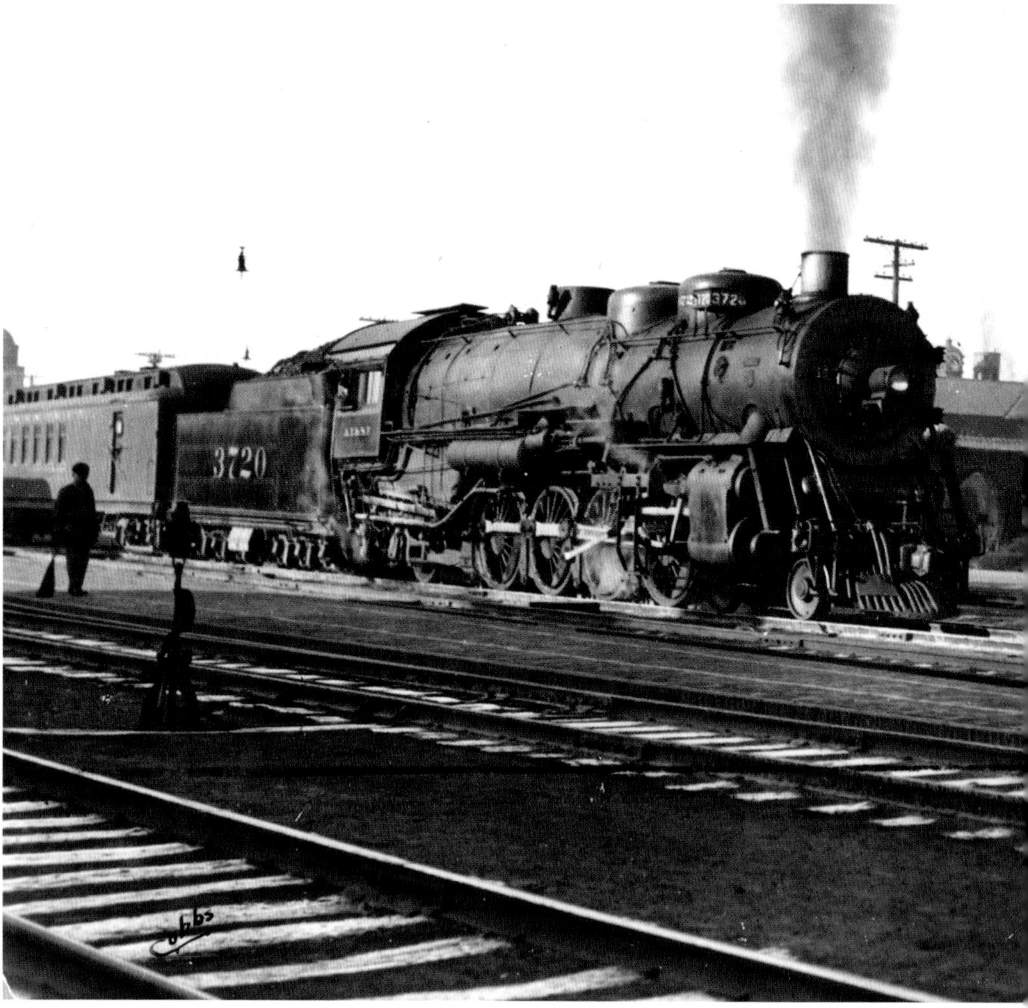

PLATE 164
Locomotive at the Alvarado Hotel, 1925
Photographer: Daphne Cobb
Ward Hicks Collection, Gift of John Airy
PA1982.181.96

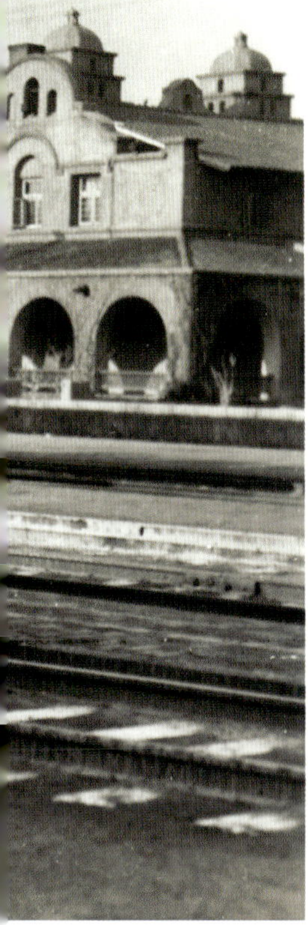

PLATE 165
Railroad lantern, 1920s–30s
Dietz and Company, New York
Metal, glass
12 ¾ × 6 ¾ × 6 ½ in.
Gift of the John Keleher Family
PC2012.13.1

Robert and Edwin Dietz of Dietz and Company manufactured this red-globed railroad lantern in the early 1900s. The Dietzes' company was eventually sold and they moved to Albuquerque, where they purchased land in the North Valley that became known as Dietz Farms.

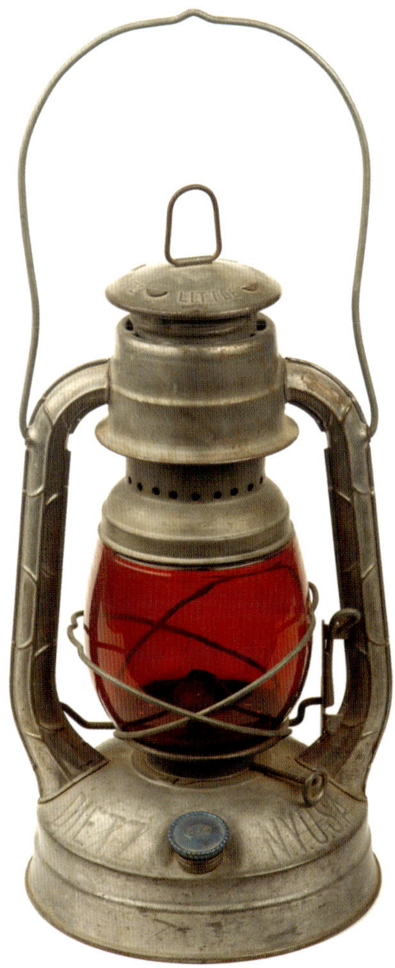

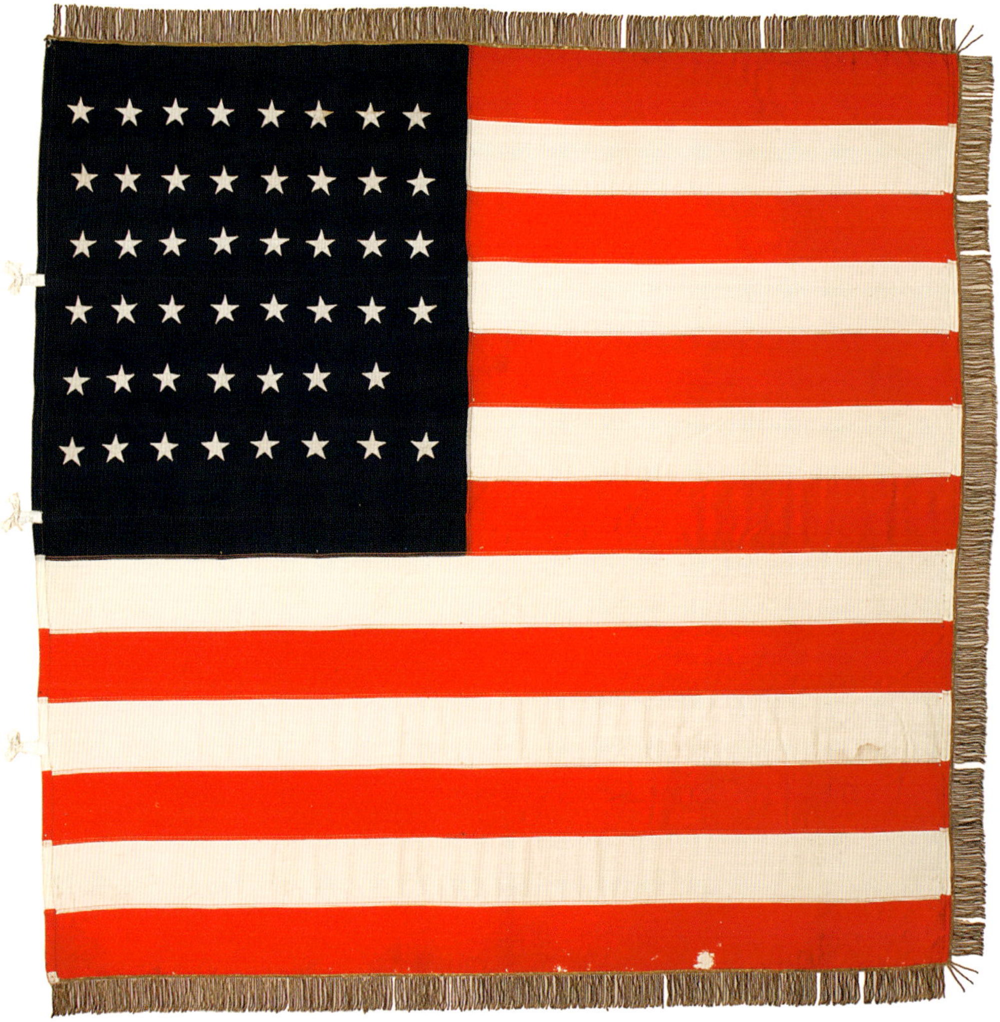

PLATE 166

Forty-seven-star flag, 1912

Linen, metallic thread

78 × 64 × 1/2 in.

Museum purchase, Four Centuries Bond Fund

PC2008.19.1

On January 6, 1912, partly as a result of a constitutional convention held at the Alvarado Hotel, New Mexico became the forty-seventh state to join the United States. Five weeks later, Arizona became the forty-eighth. As a result, the flag that debuted on July 4, 1912, was a forty-eight-star flag, so only four or five forty-seven-star flags exist today.

This flag was found in an attic in Atlanta, Nebraska, inside its original oilcloth case along with a two-piece flagpole with gold tassels.

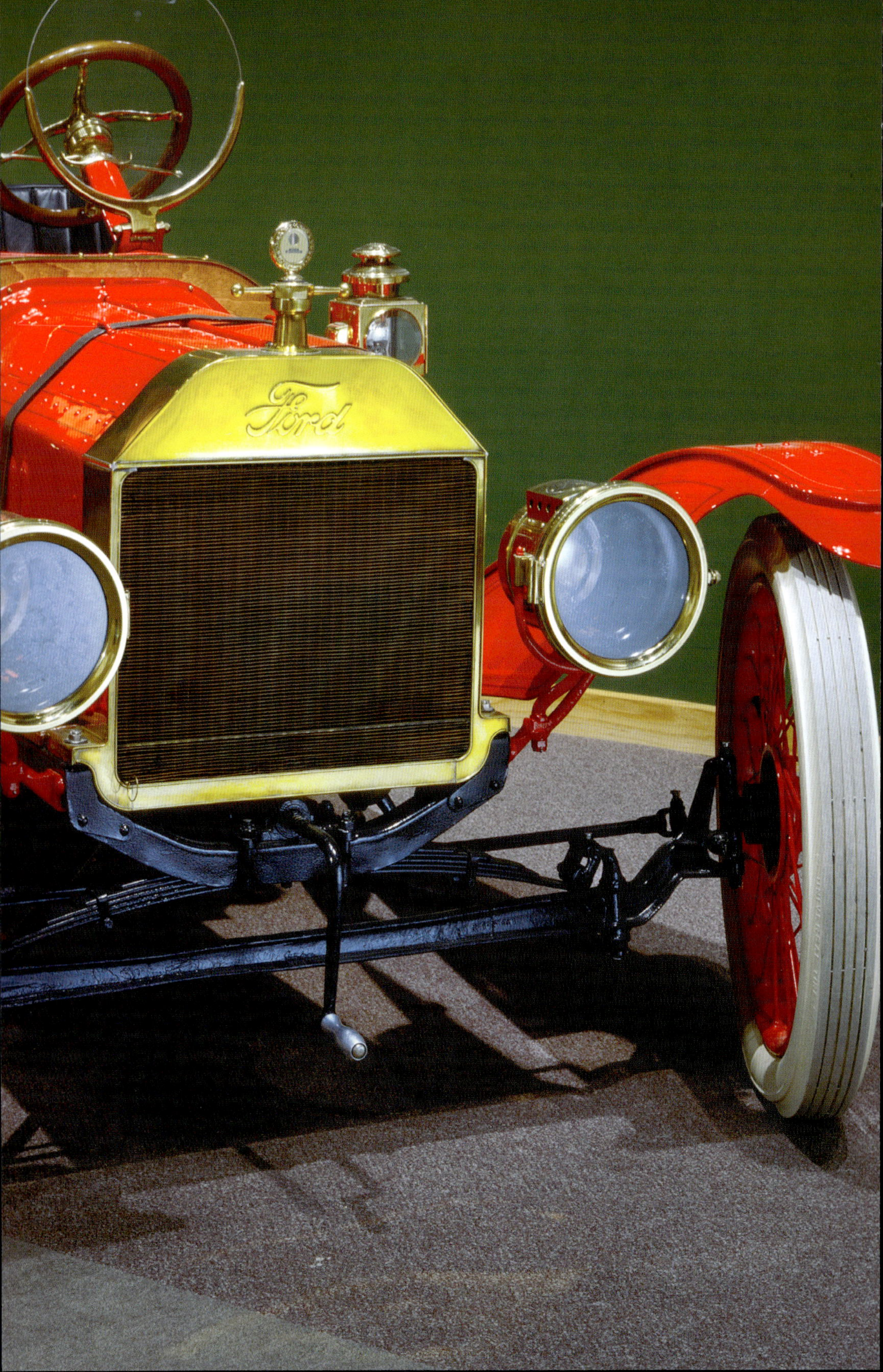
Ford

Destination Albuquerque

By the twentieth century, town founders were marketing Albuquerque as a destination. The Commercial Club's fairground spectacles drew national attention. Tuberculosis patients flocked here for sunshine and clear air. Fred Harvey and the AT&SF promoted Albuquerque through railroad excursions to the "exotic Southwest."

Later, Dust Bowl refugees, war veterans, and tourists motored along Route 66 through Barelas, Albuquerque, and Los Ranchos. Many decided to stay.

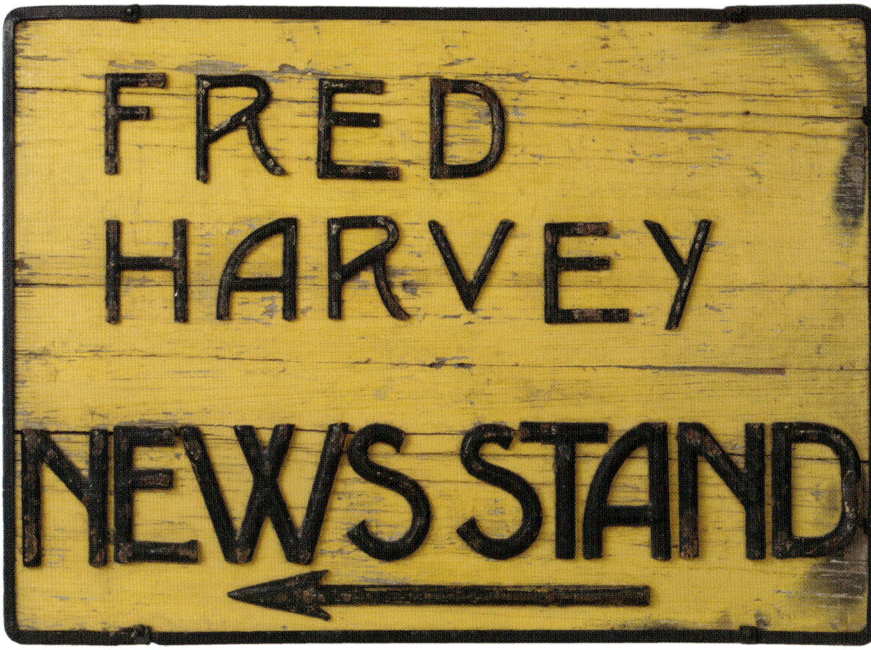

PLATE 167
Sign from the Alvarado Hotel newsstand, 1930s–40s
Wood, metal, paint
24 × 34 × 1 7/8 in.
Museum purchase
PC2014.8.1

The Alvarado Hotel lodged train travelers from all across the country, introducing them to the Southwest through first-rate Fred Harvey lodging and service. Tourists and locals enjoyed the hotel's gardens, veranda, dining hall, lunchroom, and brick walk. Guests encountered musicians in the lobby and, stepping outside, watched celebrities pose for photographs.

This Fred Harvey sign guided train travelers and motorists to an outdoor newsstand near the brick walk. An additional stand was located inside the Alvarado. The donor's father, Dale Richard Lusk, collected the sign in the 1970s after the venerable hotel was demolished.

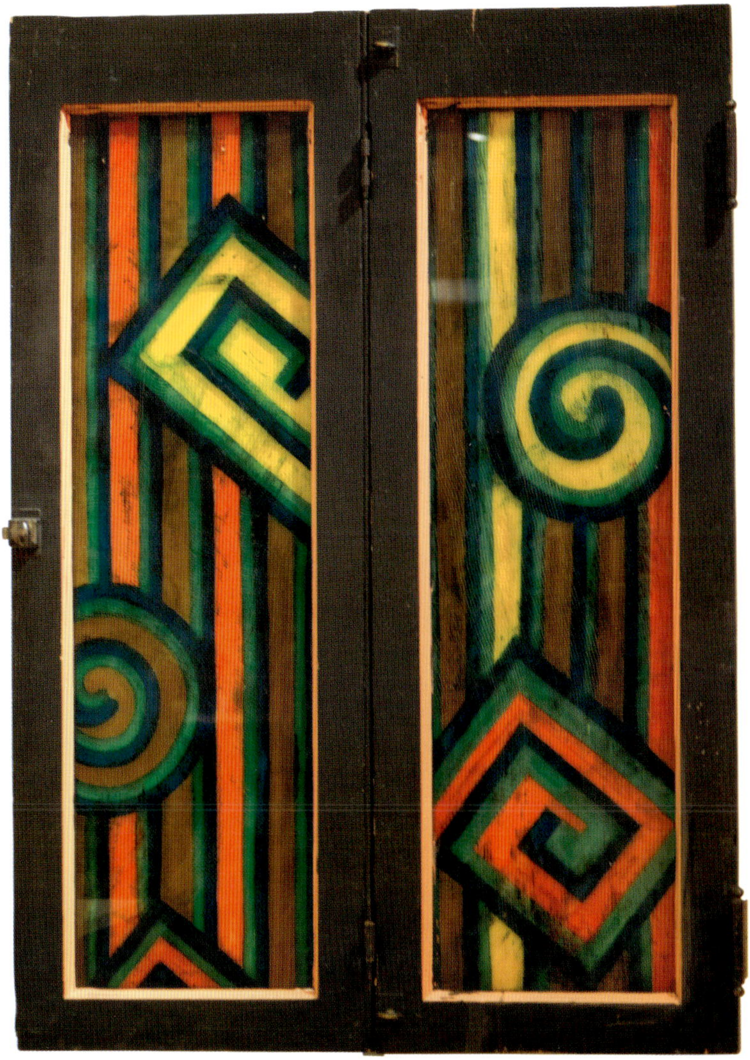

PLATE 168
Fred Geary
Windows from the Alvarado Hotel, ca. 1944
Wood, metal, paint
44 1/2 × 34 × 2 in. (overall)
Gift of the family of Irwin and Barbara Roberts
PC2014.29.1.a&b

Santa Fe Railway architect Mary Elizabeth Jane Colter (1869–1958) brought artist Fred Geary (1894–1955) to Albuquerque around 1944 to paint the windows of the Alvarado Hotel's Cocina Cantina lounge. Geary used a colorless glaze scraped with a comb to create wavy effects between the double-paned glass.

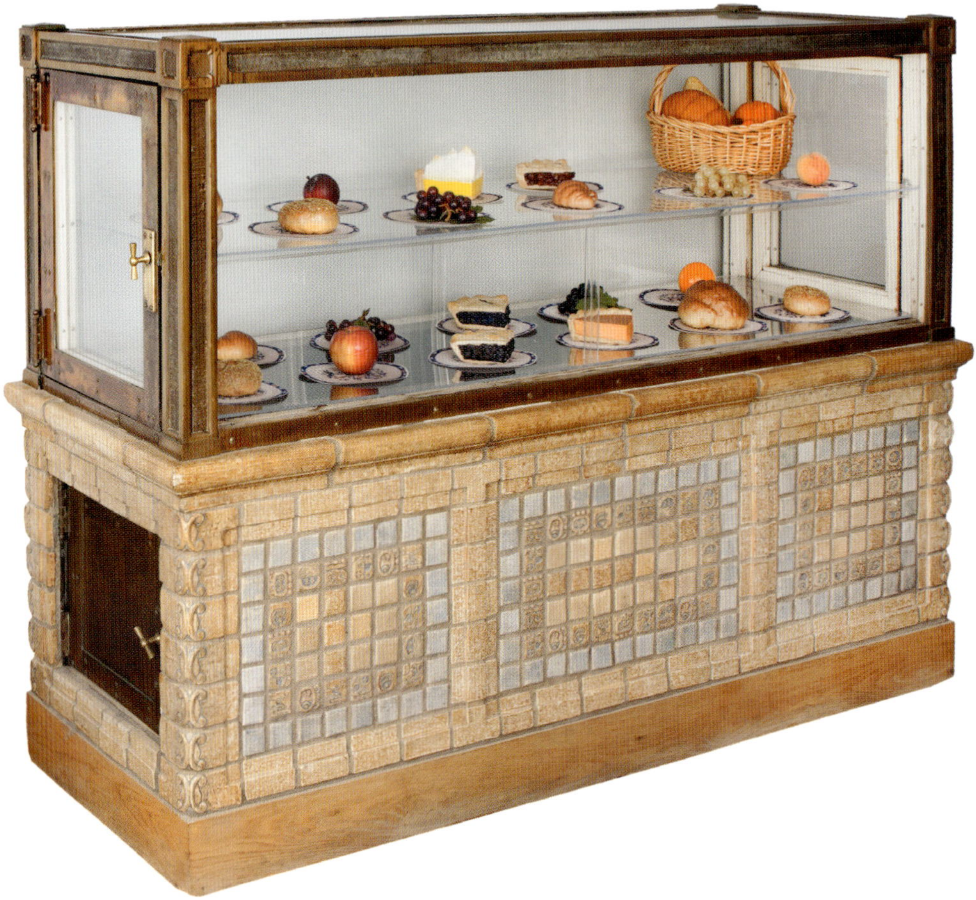

PLATE 169

Mary Elizabeth Jane Colter, 1869–1958
Pie case, 1922
Jewett Refrigerator Co., Buffalo, New York
Batchelder Tile Co., Los Angeles, California
Wood, clay, copper alloy, iron, glass, wood
54 × 73 1/4 × 27 1/2 in.
Museum purchase, Four Centuries Bond Fund
PC2006.49.1

Noted architect Mary Elizabeth Jane Colter renovated the Alvarado Hotel's lunchroom in 1922, decorating its interior with Batchelder tile and copper-clad furnishings. Having practiced coppersmithing in the 1890s, Mary Colter was fond of metals and designed them into her renovation. She had refrigerator cases made by the Jewett Refrigerator Company tiled with "La Maya" tile from the Batchelder Tile Company. The case design >

demonstrates Colter's ability to infuse projects with her own creative touches and to use the materials of other artisans to their best advantage.

The cases contained fruit, rolls, cake, and pie. Unlike today's portions, Fred Harvey's serving was one-fifth of a pie. Albuquerque resident Helen Horwitz recalls, "I remember the pies, especially the cherry pie. It was solid cherries and wonderfully sweet, with a flaky crust. . . . There were cantaloupes in the pie cases, but who wants cantaloupe when you can have cherry pie?"

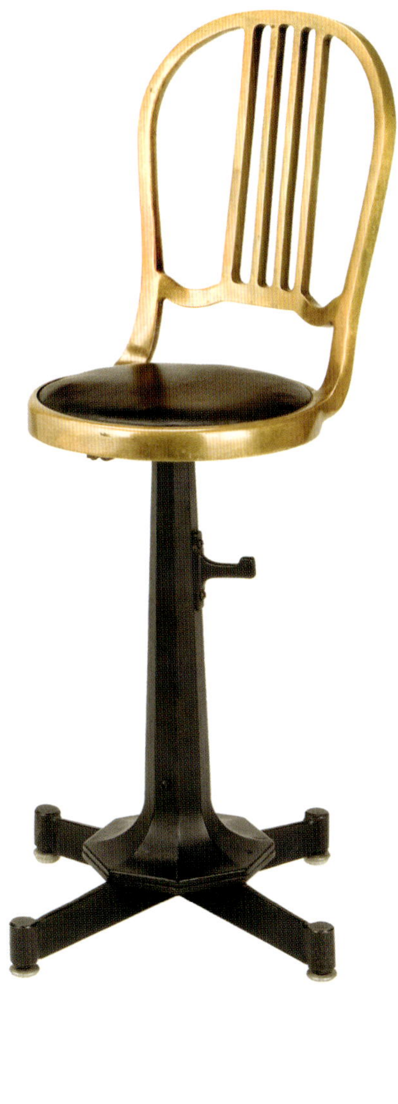

PLATE 170
Pie stool, 1922
Brass, iron, leather or fabric
36 × 13 × 17 in.
Museum purchase, Director's Discretionary Fund
PC2003.78.1

Harvey Girls in crisply starched black-and-white uniforms served railroaders, passengers, traveling servicemen, and locals. Menu staples included the Monte Cristo sandwich and Fred Harvey's famous coffee.

Patrons of the lunchroom sat along a black Belgian glass counter on "pie stools" (because that is what one ate when sitting on them). They also recall twirling around in the swiveling stools. Similar stools were purchased for Fred Harvey establishments in the Midwest.

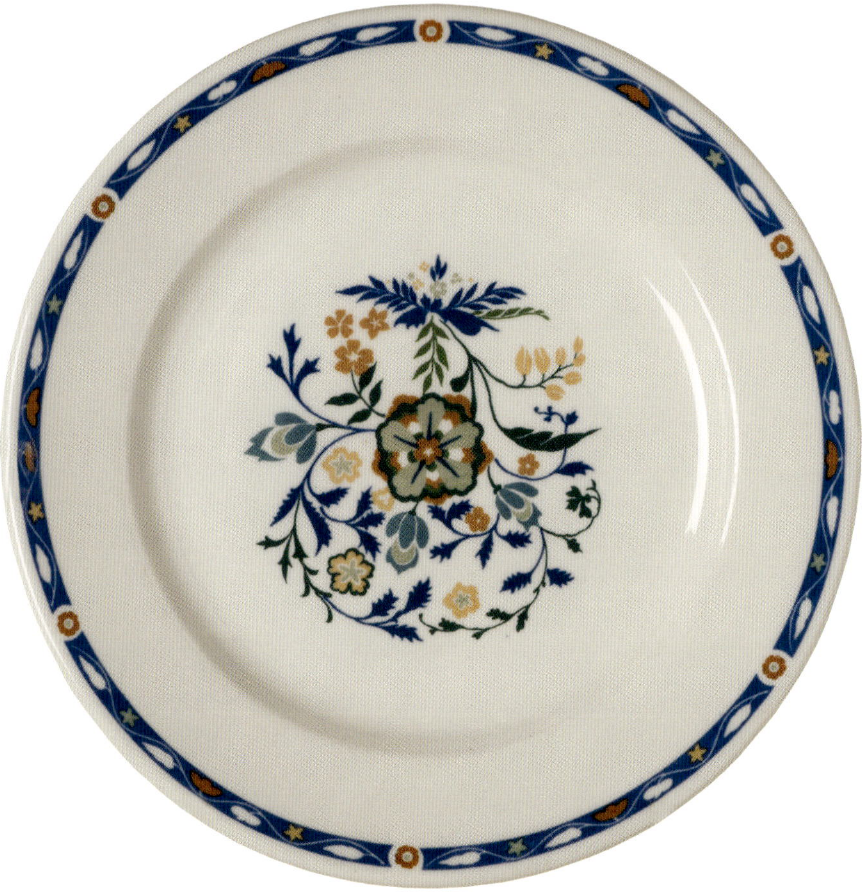

PLATE 171
Encanto dinner plate, 1959
Syracuse China Co., Syracuse, New York
Vitreous china
1 5/8 × 9 in.
Museum purchase, Four Centuries Bond Fund,
Alvarado Hotel exhibit budget
PC2008.56.1

When Mary Elizabeth Jane Colter redesigned the Alvarado lunchroom in 1922, she ordered this distinctive dishware by the Onondaga Pottery Company. The Encanto plate pattern was white with an underglaze blue band of red and green flowers and vines, a buff-colored edge line (later eliminated), and a central medallion of flowers and leaves. She began ordering the same pattern for La Fonda in Santa Fe sometime after 1926.

Encanto could be custom ordered with various decorative units. The Alvarado used the version with the central medallion early on; later, just the edge band. The last order for Syracuse Encanto was placed in 1965.

PLATE 172

Gong and beater, after 1902

Brass, oak, hide, buckskin, cordage

3 × 14 1/4 in. and 2 1/2 × 21 in.

Gift of Arthur G. Hays Jr., Louis D. Hays, and Dorothy Hays Hendron

PC2014.36.1.a&b

Hotel resident and tuberculosis survivor A.W. Hays and his wife, Grace, acquired this iconic dinner gong just before the Atchison, Topeka and Santa Fe Railway demolished the Alvarado Hotel in January 1970. The gong's ring was so loud that passengers could hear it inside the train.

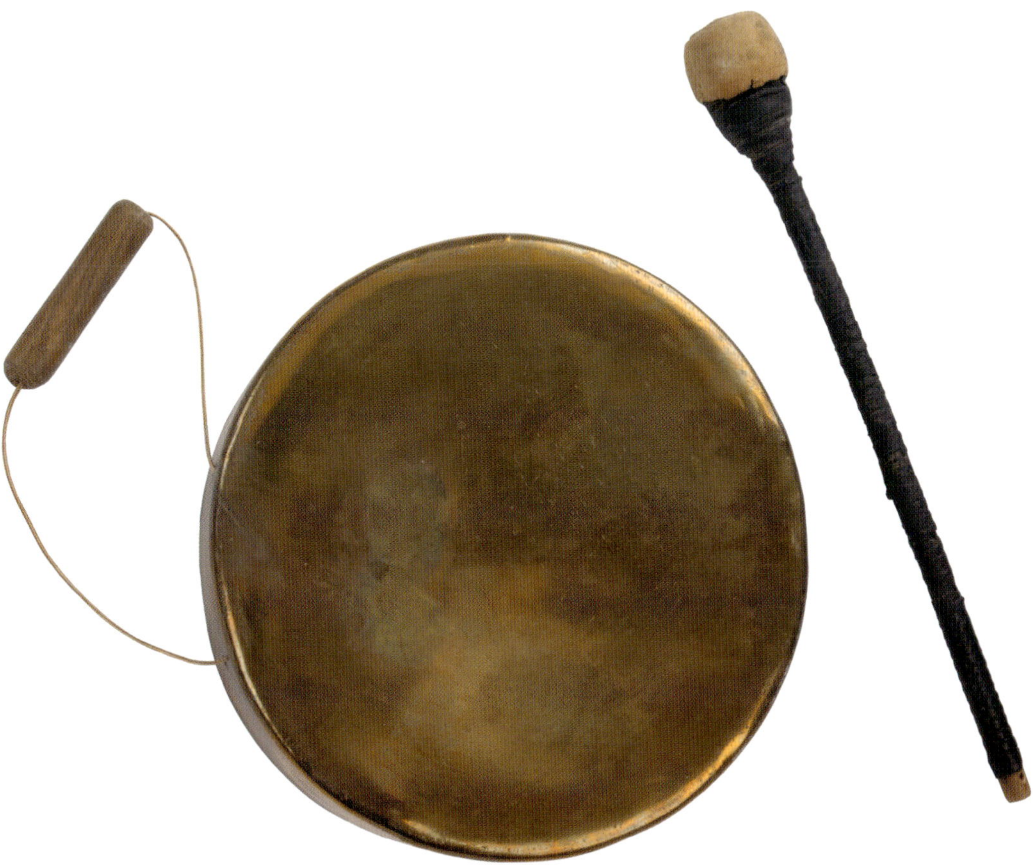

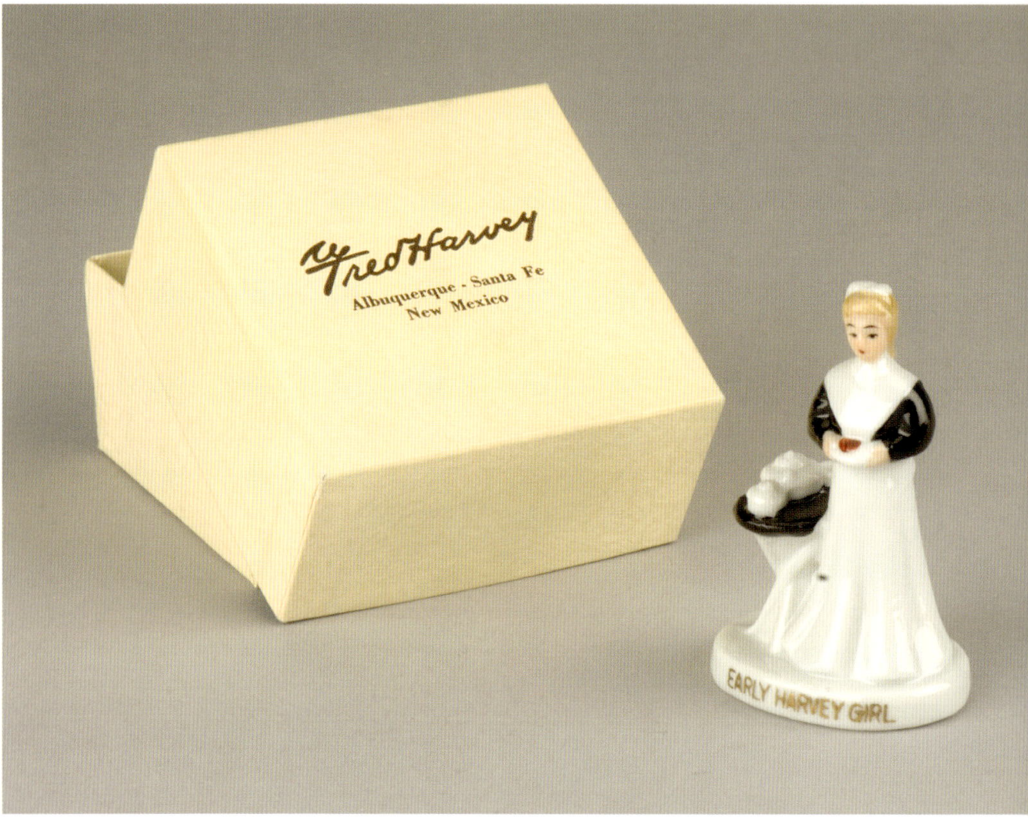

PLATE 173
Harvey Girl figurine and gift box, after 1952
Japan
Porcelain, cardboard, ink
2 3/4 × 1 in. (figure)
Gift of Betty-Mae Hartman
PC1984.31.11.a–c

The Alvarado Hotel lunchroom was open day and night and could serve a thousand patrons per day, thanks to Harvey Girls like Neva Davis, Opal Hill, Effie Jenks, Grace Jones, Genevieve Livingston, and June McCrary. Harvey Girls wore regulation black-and-white uniforms; at the Alvarado, they switched to white in the summer. Harvey Girls from the Alvarado were allowed to attend classes at the University of New Mexico but had to return to the hotel before curfew or be locked out. This souvenir figurine was a popular item for sale to visitors.

PLATE 174
Hispanic New Mexican or Anglo
Coffered chest, 1915
Pine, iron
33 1/2 × 15 1/2 × 31 in.
Gift of Clarence Dickinson
PC1986.60.1.a

Purchased at the Alvarado Hotel Indian Building, this chip-carved coffered chest was inspired by furniture made by the Valdez family of Velarde, New Mexico.

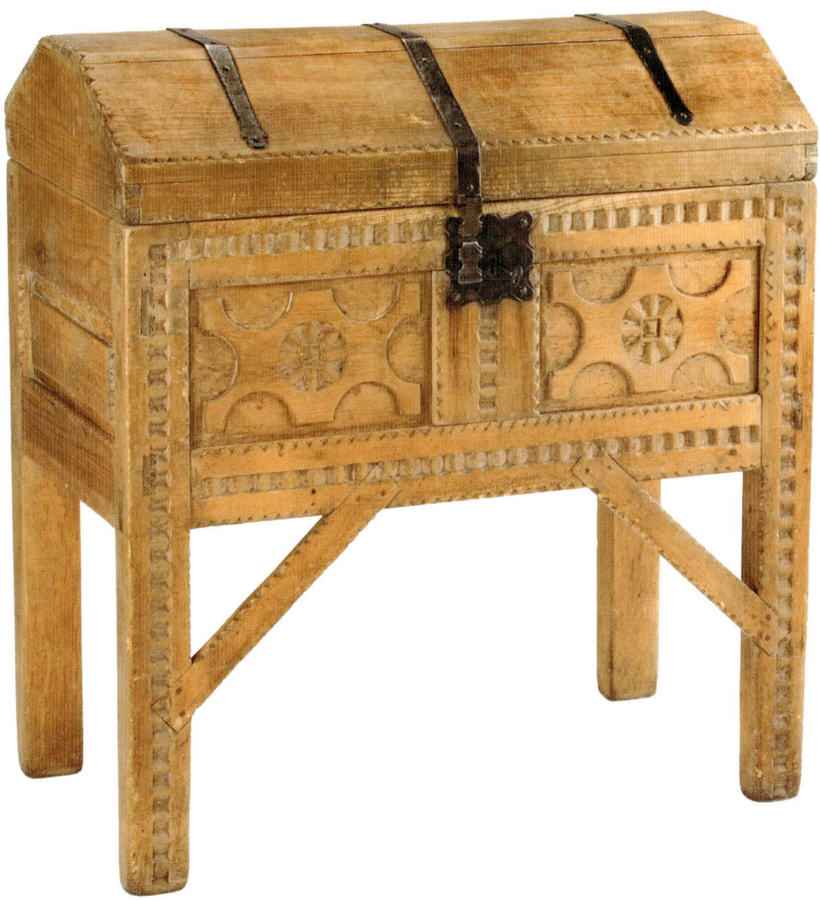

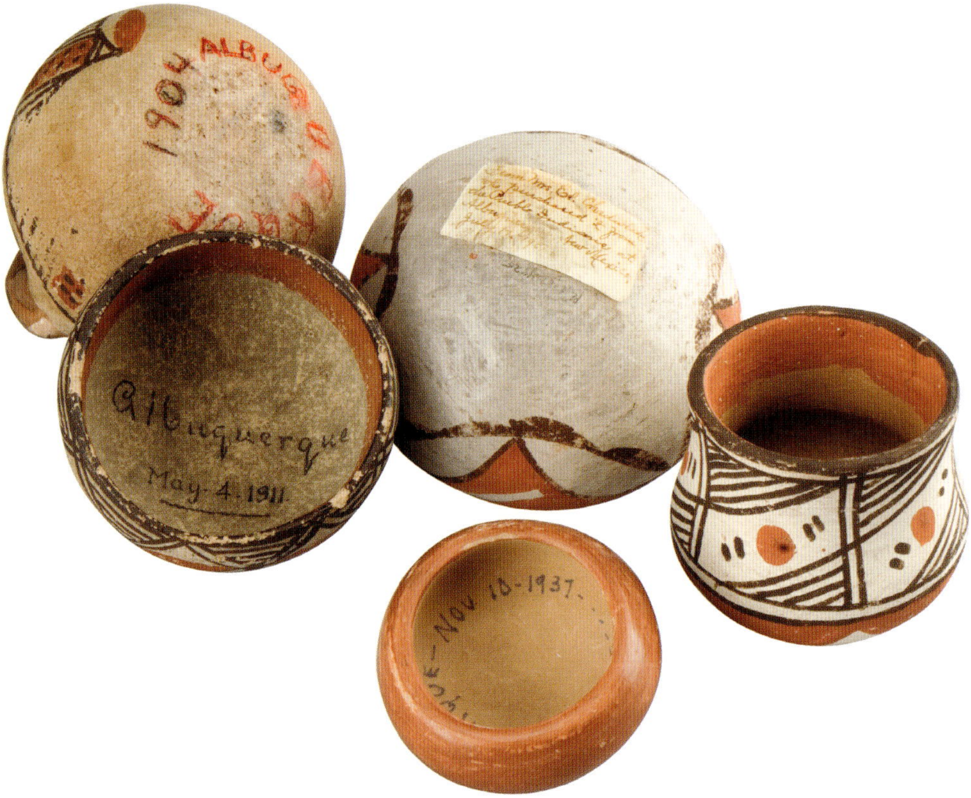

PLATE 175
Isleta
Miniature pottery, Isleta Polychrome and Isleta Red Ware, 1904–37
Natural clay, paint
4 × 4 in. (maximum)
Gift of Nancy Tucker
PC2007.48.25–29

When miniaturized, pottery could also be sold by Pueblo potters to tourists directly through the train's windows.

PLATE 176

Plate, ca. 1950; vase, 1912; and creamer, ca. 1910

Wheelock, Vienna, Austria

Porcelain, gold

$\frac{1}{2}$ × 7 in., 5 × 3 $\frac{1}{2}$ in., and 2 × 3 × 1 $\frac{1}{2}$ in.

Gift of Phyllis S. Anderson, Charles Nuanes, and Nancy Tucker

PC1991.14.1, PC1981.14.1, and PC2007.48.33

Souvenirs of the Alvarado Hotel could be found all over town. The bottom of the plate is stamped "for Borradaile and Co., Albuquerque."

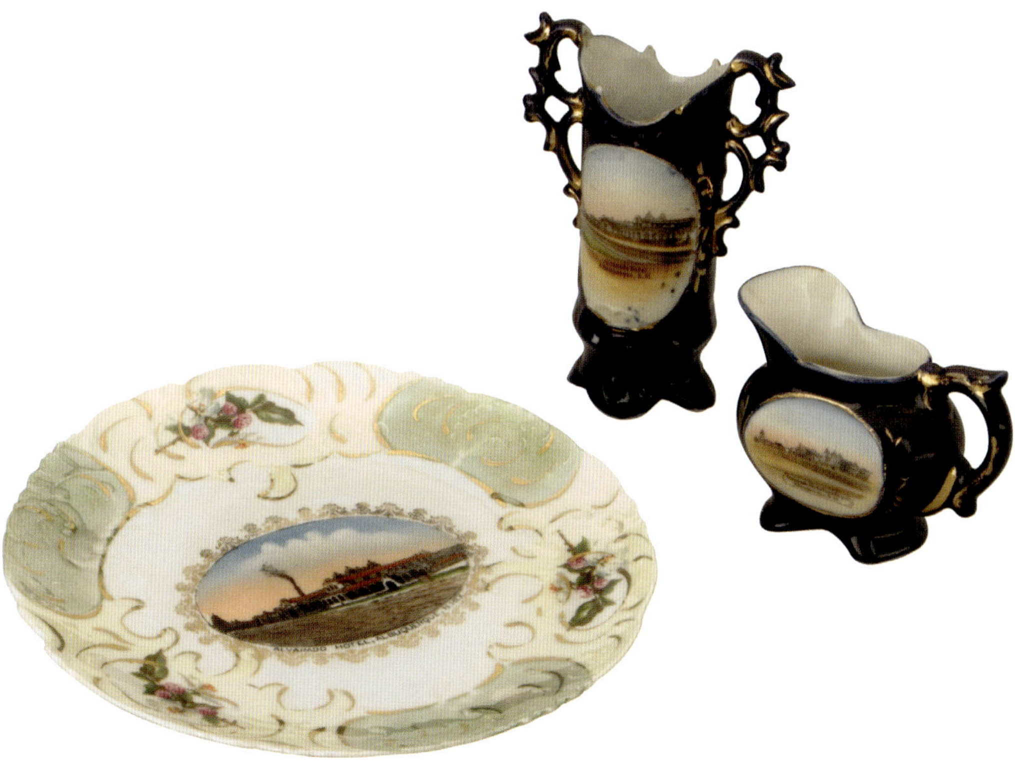

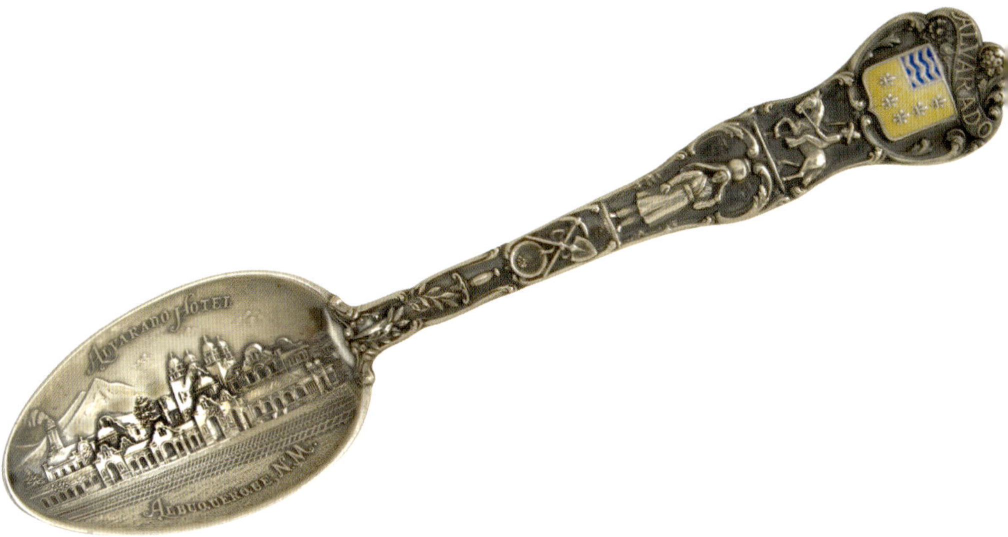

PLATE 177
Souvenir spoon, ca. 1905
Sterling silver, enamel
1/4 × 5 3/4 × 1 in.
Gift of Nancy Tucker
PC2006.17.2

The spoon is decorated with typical local scenery including the Alvarado coat of arms, an Indian maiden carrying an olla, and a trackside view of the Alvarado Hotel. Set against the massive, Alps-like Sandia Mountains, the hotel's towers appear to be multiple stories high.

PLATE 178
Trunk, 1920s
Leather, metal, cloth
25 × 29 1/2 × 15 7/8 in.
Gift of Rudy and Fran García
PC1984.93.1

In 1926, the Fred Harvey enterprise and R. Hunter Clarkson developed automobile excursions called Indian Detours. They provided sightseeing trips to living pueblos, archaeological sites, and geographic wonders. This studded leather trunk may have been used in the Indian Detours vehicles as a lunch box for parties of four or more.

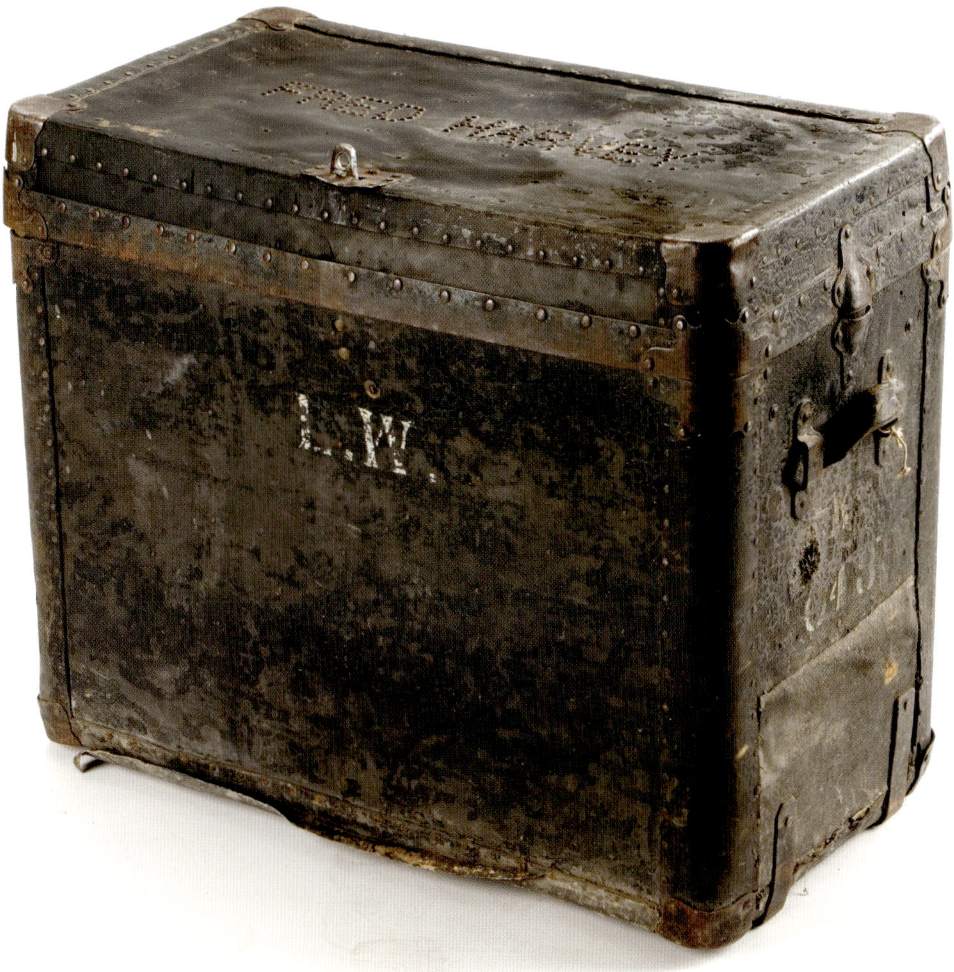

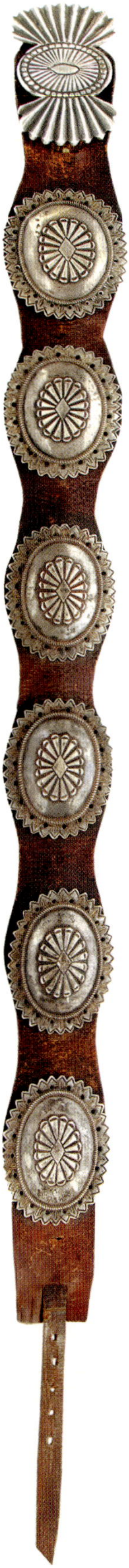

PLATE 179
Navajo
Concha belt, 1875–80
Silver, leather, copper
3 1/2 × 45 × 1 in.
Gift of Eason Eige
PC2010.5.1

The Fred Harvey Indian Department, supervised by J. F. Huckel and managed by Herman Schweizer, purchased some of the earliest examples of weaving, pottery, and silverwork in the region from traders such as J. L. Hubbell in Ganado, Arizona. This concha belt, collected by Eason Eige at Kewa Pueblo, is a superb example of heavy, hand-forged, punched, and chiseled silverwork made by Navajo silversmiths in the late nineteenth century.

PLATE 180 ▶
Navajo
Beeldléí/Weaving, 1890–1900
Germantown yarn, aniline dyes
62 3/8 × 47 9/16 in.
Gift of Irwin Moise
PC1977.115.1

This tapestry weaving, known as a Hubbell Revival weaving, is made from four-ply Germantown yarn. The yarn, colors, and design were all favorites of influential trader John Lorenzo Hubbell. Hubbell opened his trading post in 1876 at Ganado, Arizona. He was a man who respected traditional Navajo culture and encouraged weavers to create specific Navajo blanket patterns. The thin red and white stripes ("beading") are inspired by an Ancestral Pueblo technique. Hubbell also encouraged the use of pictorial elements, such as the bow, arrows, and knives woven into the field.

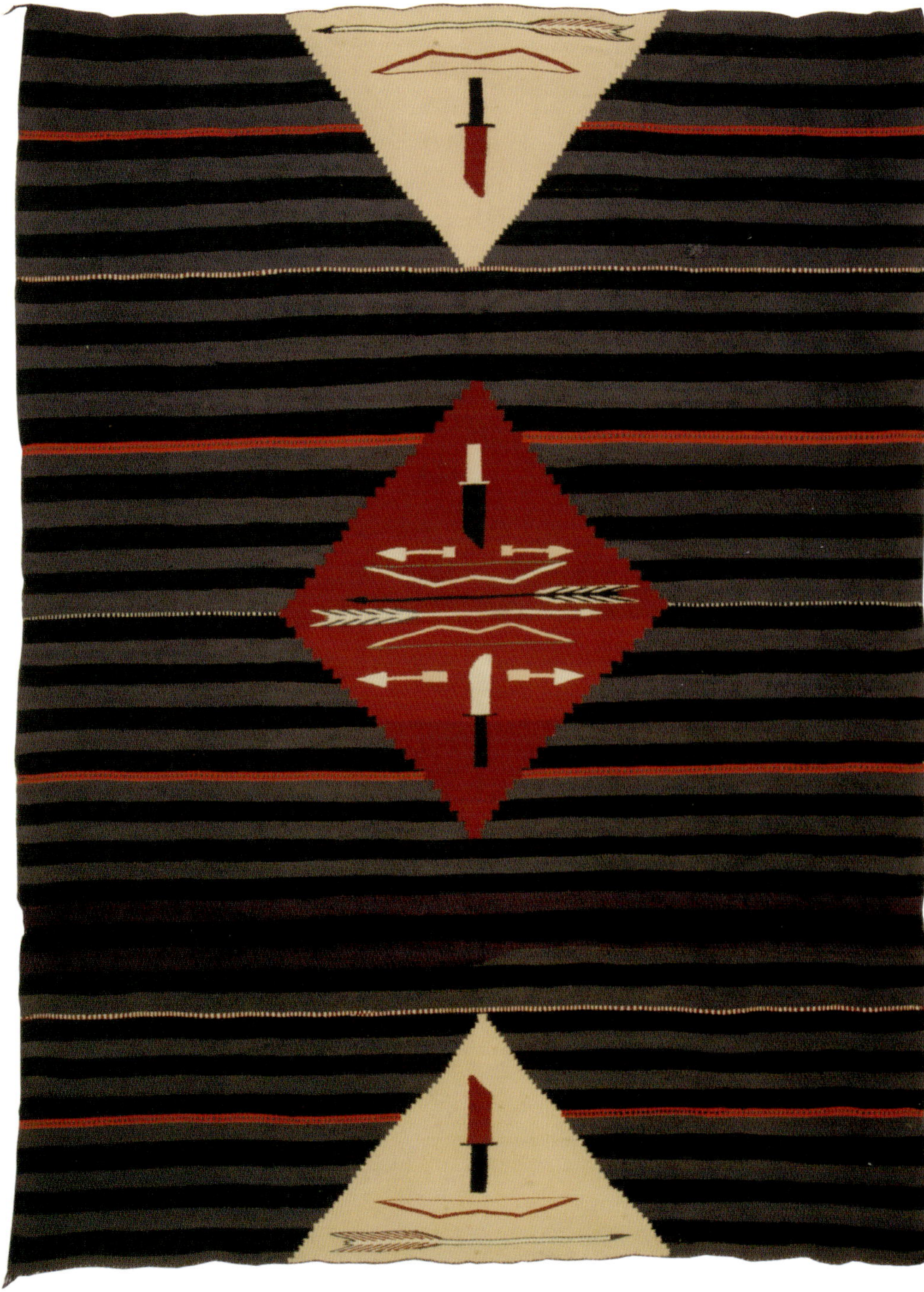

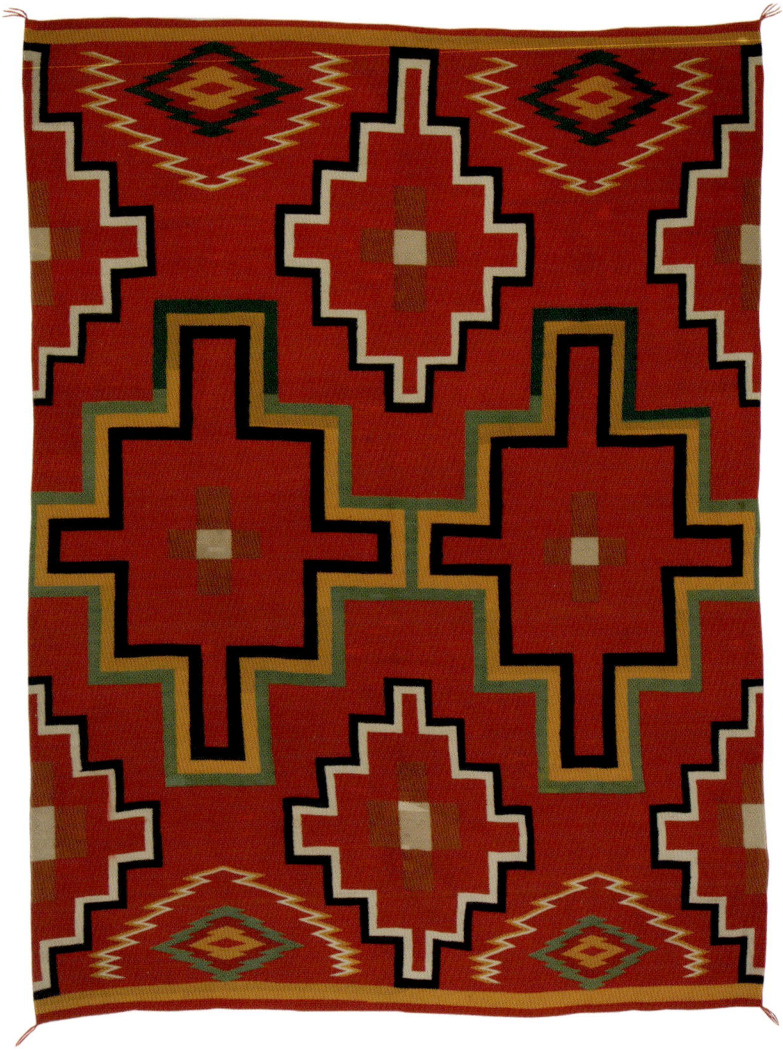

PLATE 181
Navajo
Beeldléí/Blanket, 1875–85
Germantown yarn, aniline dyes
87 1/2 × 68 1/4 in.
Gift of Louis Monti in loving memory of Harry G. Lienau
PC2016.26.1

This tapestry was woven with Germantown yarn. The US government distributed over sixty thousand pounds of the yarn to the Diné between 1868 and 1875; more than half of it was dyed red. During this time, Germantown yarn was made from three strands (plies) twisted together. After 1875, Germantown weavings used yarn manufactured with four plies. The weaver used four-ply yarn on this Germantown blanket.

PLATE 182
Nampeyo, Hopi-Tewa
Bowl, 1905–07
Natural clay and paint
$3\,^{3}/_{16} \times 9\,^{5}/_{16}$ in.
Museum purchase, Four Centuries Bond Fund
PC2009.18.1

Famed potter Nampeyo (ca. 1860–1942) made this beautiful bowl while working as an artist-demonstrator at Hopi House, Grand Canyon, Arizona, for the Fred Harvey Company in 1905 and 1907. The interior features the Nampeyo family's famous Quartered Eagle design. The bowl retains its original Fred Harvey tag, which was only applied to pottery made during Nampeyo's visits. M. G. Brock, an Albuquerque entrepreneur, purchased the Nampeyo bowl from the Indian Building at the January 1970 Alvarado Hotel auction, along with carnival glass from the dining room.

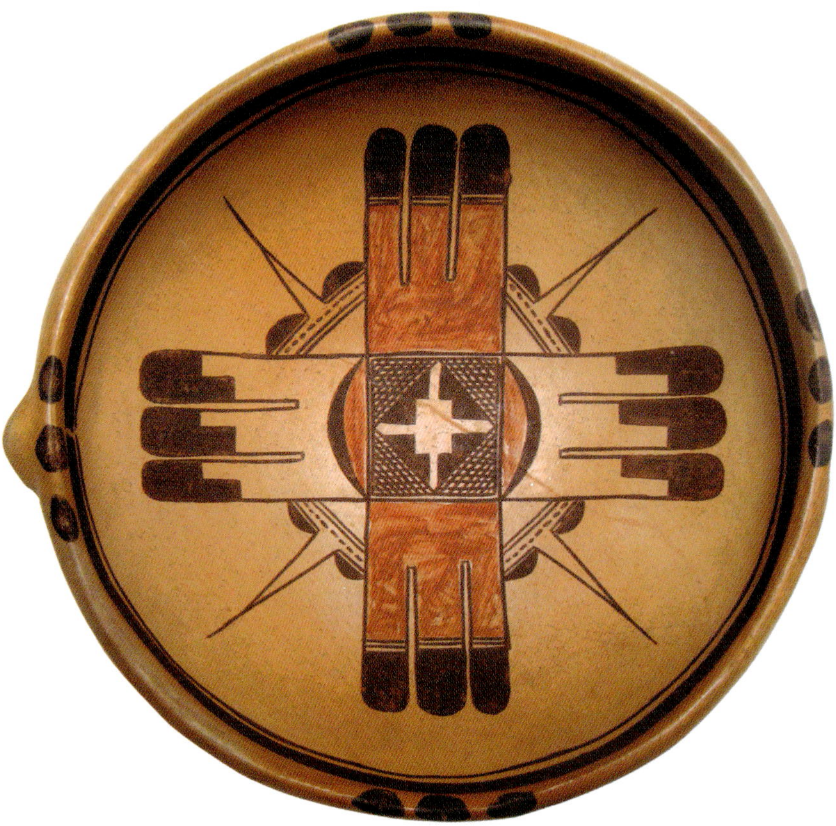

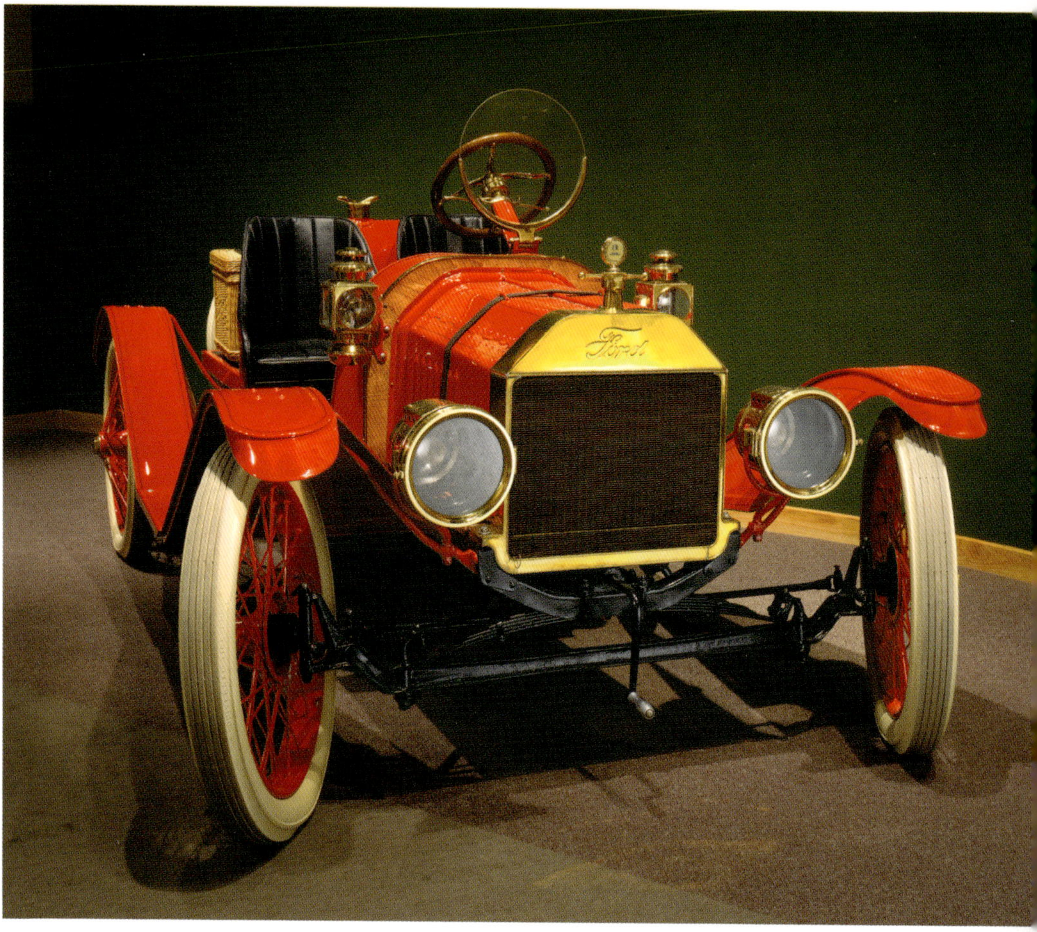

From the beginning, America fell in love with the automobile. This Ford Model T Speedster began its life as a Roadster, which originally included a top but no doors. The first owner converted it to a Speedster around 1919. Even though the Speedster has only two gears—forward and reverse—it can reach speeds up to 60 miles an hour. Designer Henry Ford boldly moved the steering wheel to the left side so that passengers could get out onto a clean curb.

The ornamental cap on the radiator doubles as a temperature gauge. For night driving, the front headlamps are lit with carbide and the side lamps with kerosene. This Model T represents an early example of how the utilitarian automobile was modified for higher performance and the fun of open-air motoring.

◀ PLATE 183

Model T Speedster, 1912, with 1920s modifications
Ford Motor Company, Detroit, Michigan
Metal, leather, rubber, vinyl, plastic, glass, wood
60 x 63 x 142 in.
Gift of Robert Jacobs
PC1997.35.1

PLATE 184

R. L. Dodson, Mr. Trotter, Booth Bell, and Ken Worth in Dodson's 1899 Locomobile, ca. 1910
Museum purchase, 1989 General Obligation Bonds
PA1990.13.240

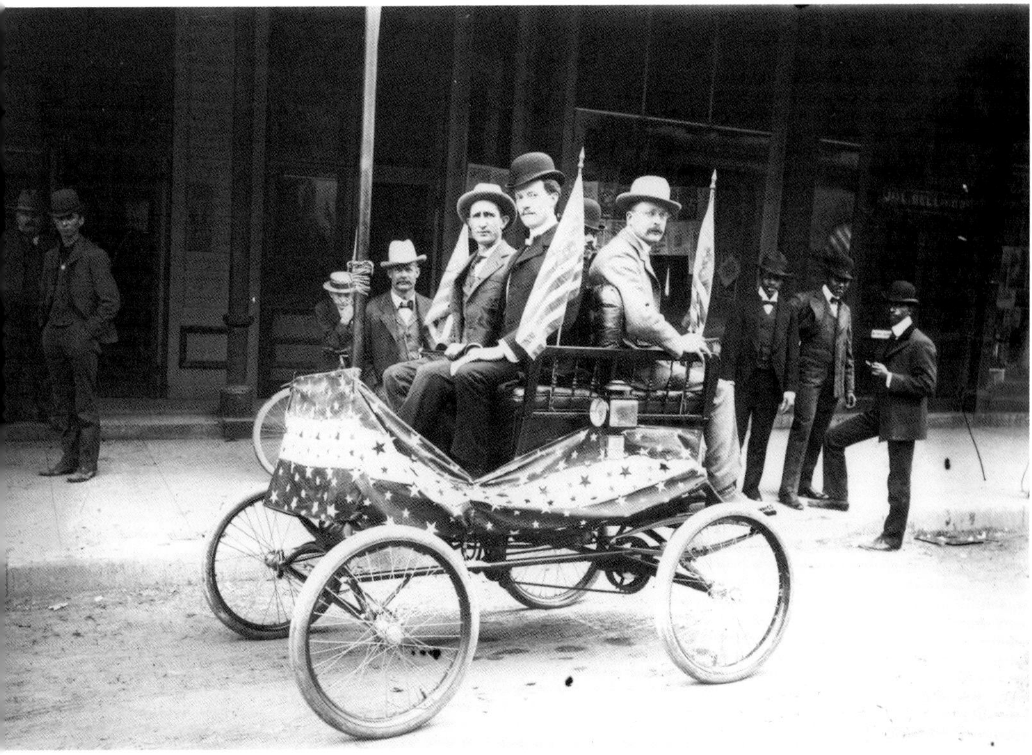

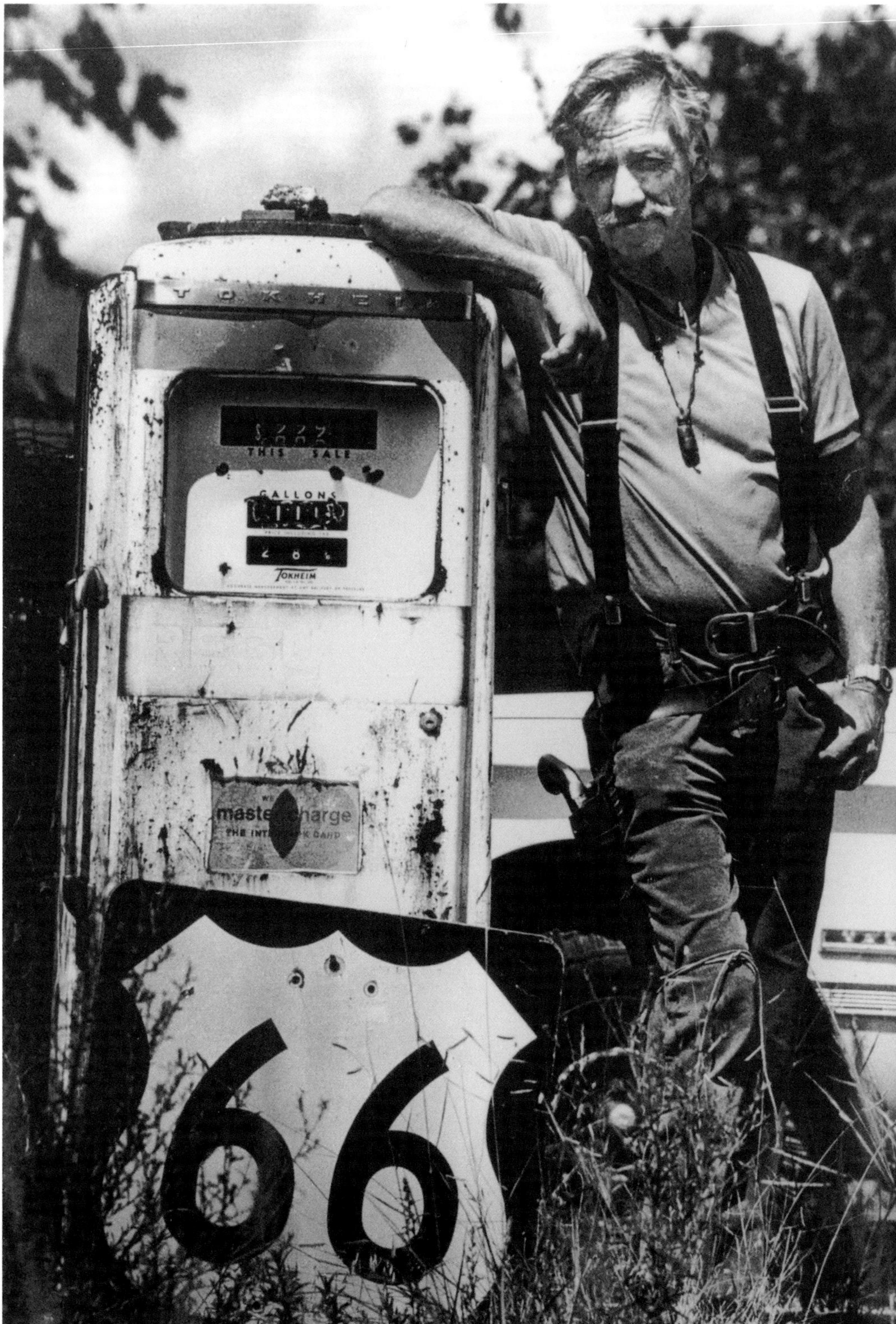
THIS SALE
GALLONS
TOKHEIM
66

◀ PLATE 185
Bob Audette, ca. 1988
Gift of Bob Audette
PA2000.20.3

PLATE 186
Route 66 highway sign, 1940–50
Steel, paint, reflective coating
16 × 17 × 3/8 in.
Museum purchase, Special Revenue Fund
PC2013.8.1

In 1925, the federal highway system assigned even numbers to east–west routes, and north–south routes received odd numbers. Because Kentucky governor William J. Fields wanted the number 60 passing through his state, the number 66 was assigned to the Chicago–Los Angeles route.

Each state was responsible for the production and maintenance of US route shields; several variants have existed over the years. This sign, looking very close to the 1948 version, was posted somewhere between Glenrio and Manuelito, New Mexico.

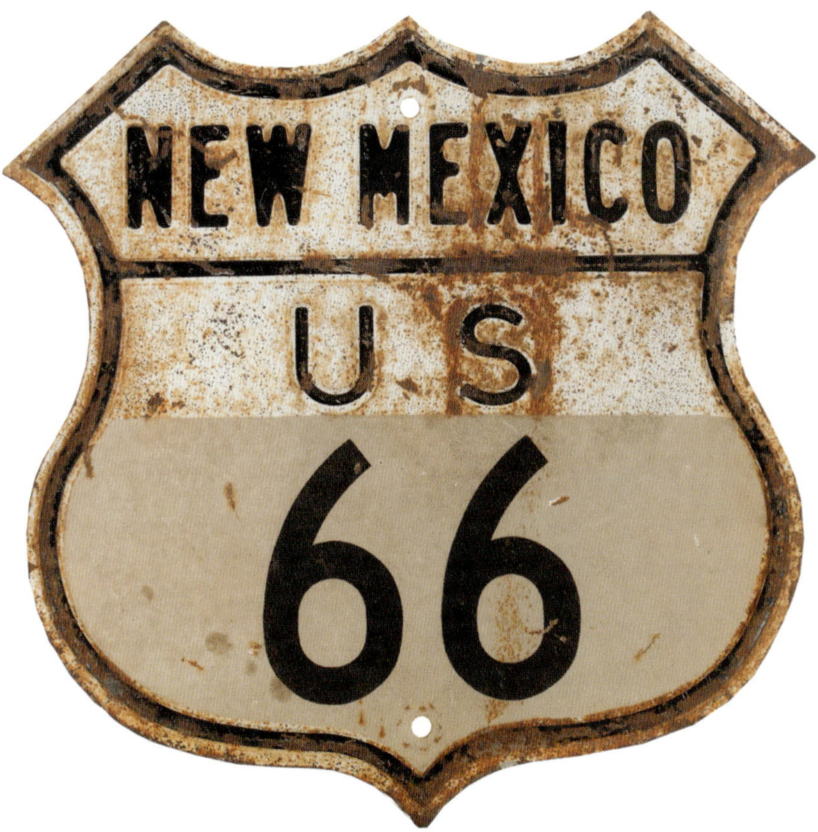

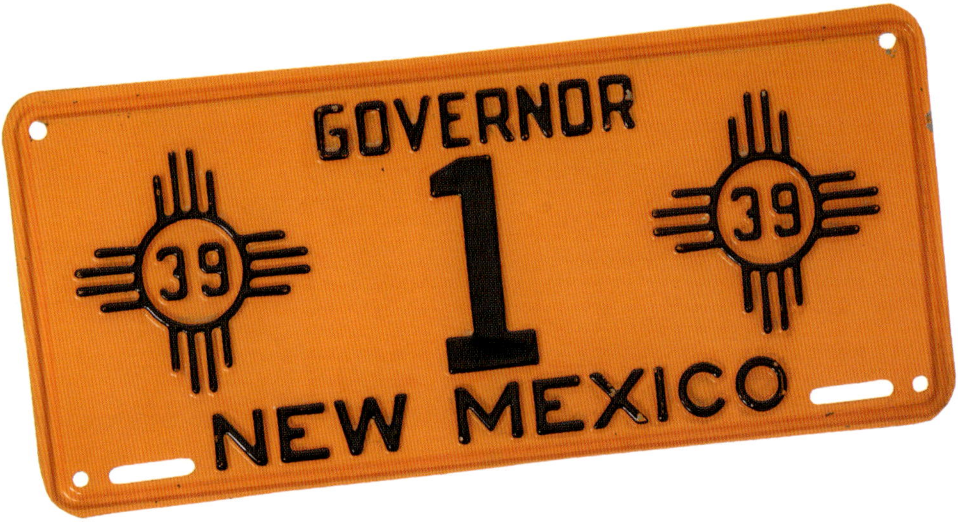

PLATE 187
State of New Mexico
Governor Clyde Tingley's license plate, 1939
Steel, paint
5 × 13 × 3/8 in.
Gift of Mrs. Clarence (Catherine) Higgins
PC1986.6.16

Within two generations, automobiles began replacing wagons on the dusty streets of Albuquerque. A national love affair had begun. Route 66 was commissioned in 1926 as a national highway from Los Angeles to Chicago. Originally running along Fourth Street through Barelas, Albuquerque, and Los Ranchos, it was realigned in 1937 along Central Avenue through Atrisco and Tijeras. For tourists and migrants, the "Mother Road" became synonymous with hot meals, warm beds, and souvenirs.

Governor Tingley's license plate is from 1939, the last year he held the office. After returning to Albuquerque, he served in various administrative capacities until his death in 1960. In addition to his accomplishments as governor, Tingley is noted for building major infrastructure in Albuquerque during the New Deal era, which eventually allowed a realignment of Route 66 along the entire east–west axis of urban Albuquerque—fifteen-plus miles of potential revenue from hungry, tired travelers.

PLATE 188
Zia
Jar, Zia Polychrome, 1900–25
Clay, slip, paint
20 × 19 1/2 in.
Gift of the Albuquerque Museum Foundation, Lucia v.B. Batten Estate
PC2015.26.21

Train and automobile travelers purchased handmade traditional pottery at various stops along the tracks and roadsides of New Mexico. Indian pottery was very popular as home decor and mementos of adventures through the Southwest. The surface of this large polychrome jar is decorated with geometric designs, berry-laden plants, and curvy chicken-like birds—motifs that likely originated from Euro-American folk arts.

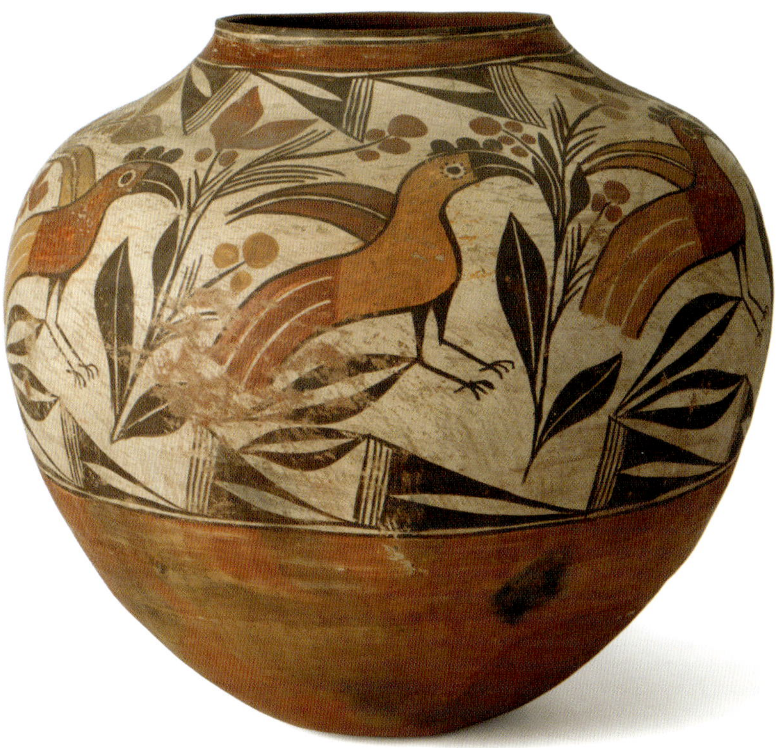

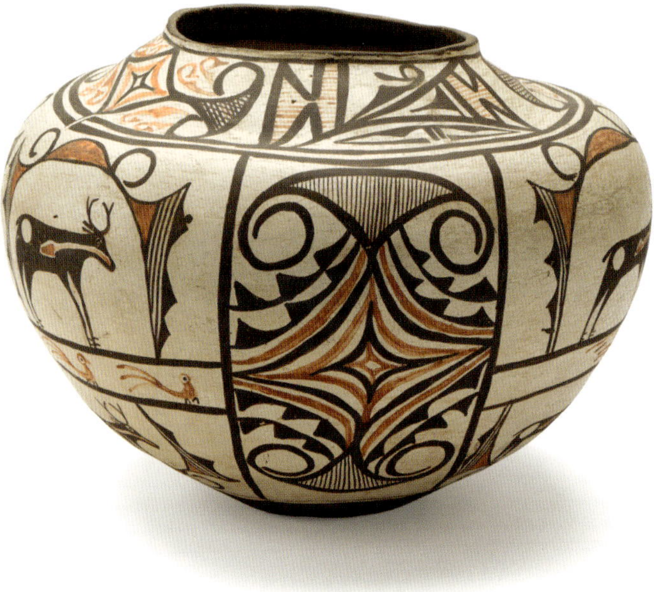

PLATE 189
Zuni
Jar, Zuni Polychrome, 1900–20
Clay, slip, paint
10 1/2 × 14 in.
Gift of Drs. Bette K. and John R. Graham in memory of Dr. Bette Kaufman Graham
PC2008.21.12

Zuni potters began incorporating animals into their vessels, often with heart-line motifs, around 1860–70. This example from circa 1920 features deer with heart lines representing the life and breath of the animal. But by then Zuni pottery sales were in decline, and other arts were beginning to take hold, including silversmithing and beadwork.

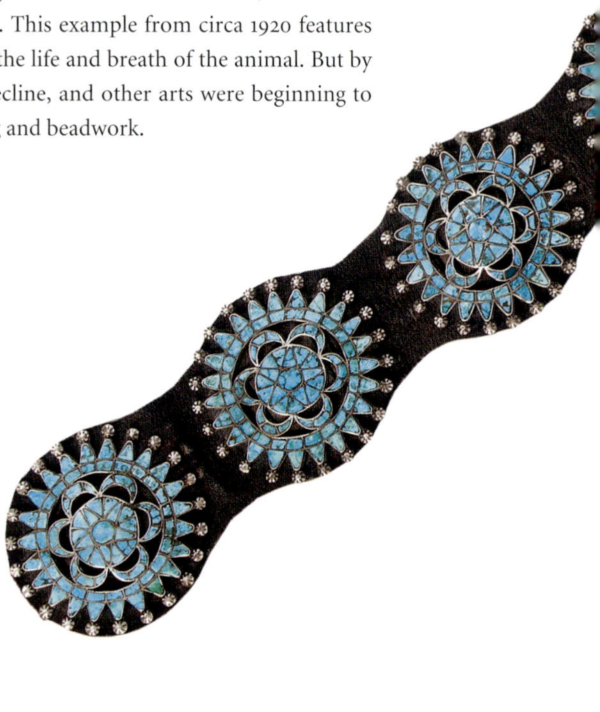

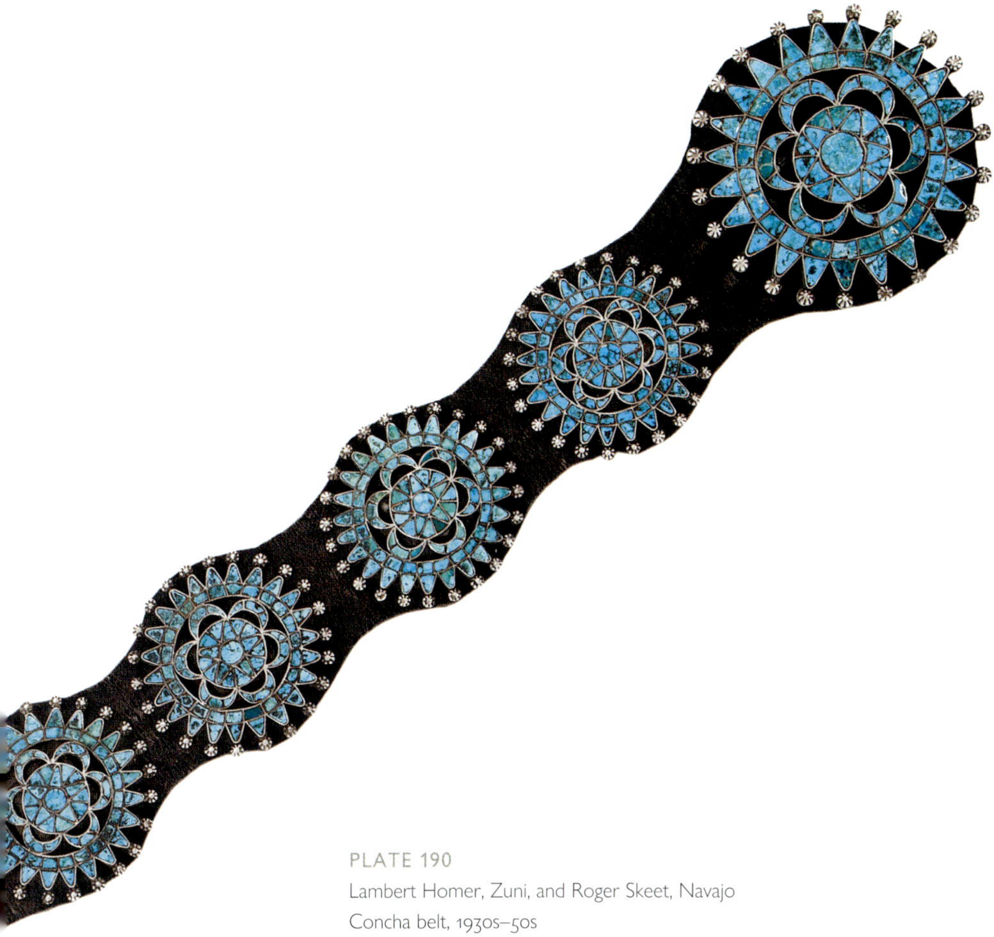

PLATE 190

Lambert Homer, Zuni, and Roger Skeet, Navajo

Concha belt, 1930s–50s

Silver, Villa Grove turquoise, leather

4 × 48 × 5/8 in.

Gift of Kenneth Alan Wallace and his children, Andrew, Aaron, Susanna, Megan, and Glen

PC2010.34.1

Two artists collaborated to create this concha belt for Zuni trader C. G. Wallace, who offered high-quality turquoise for sale at his C. G. Wallace Trading Post. Lambert Homer (1917–1972) cut the stones, and Roger Skeet (1900–1969 or 1970) completed the silverwork. The Navajo Nation borrowed this belt from C. G. Wallace for the 1973 Nixon Inaugural Parade in Washington, DC.

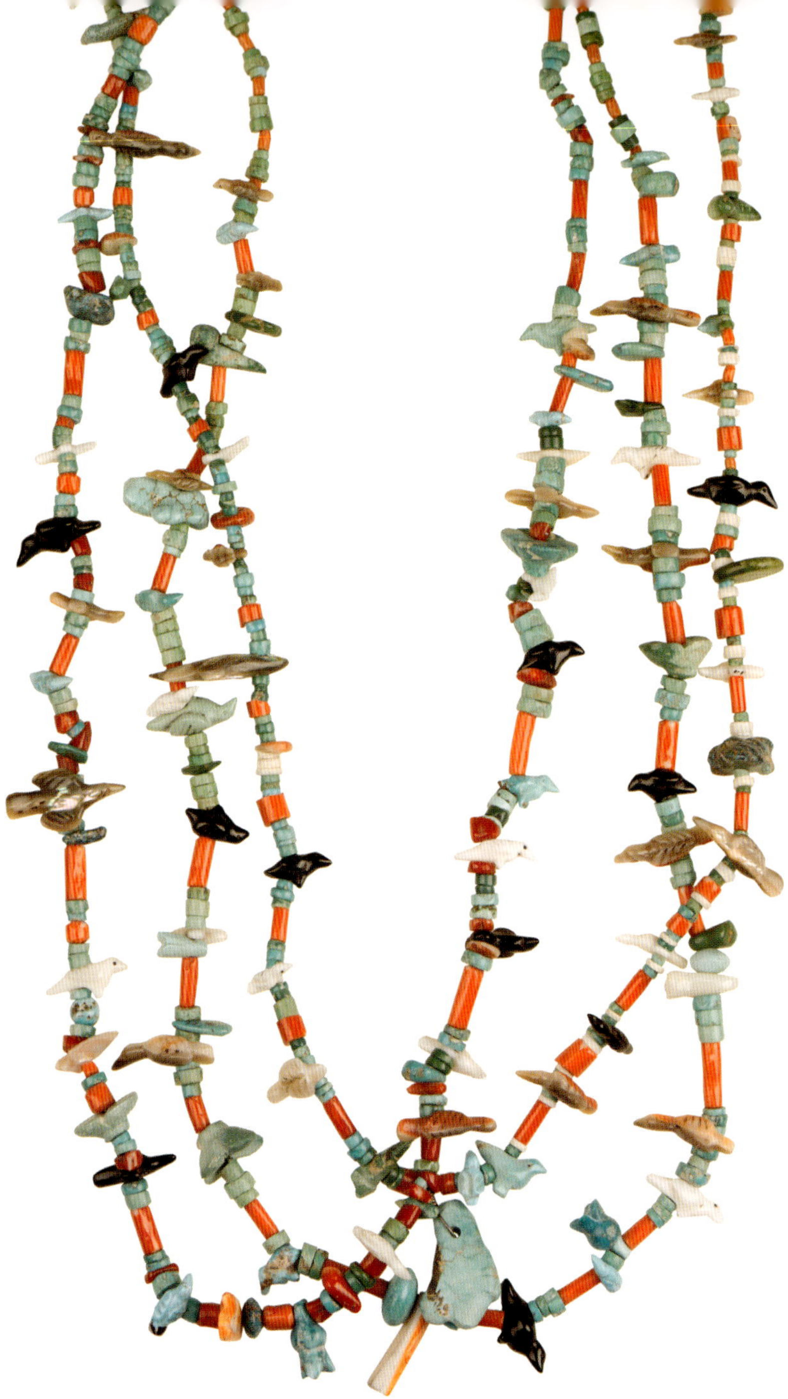

Leekya (1889–1966) was the most famous Zuni carver of his time. By the 1950s his coral, turquoise nugget, and fetish necklaces were popular with tourists visiting Zuni Pueblo and trading posts dotting Route 66. This necklace is adorned with disk and tab beads, bird and bear carvings, and a squash blossom or pomegranate.

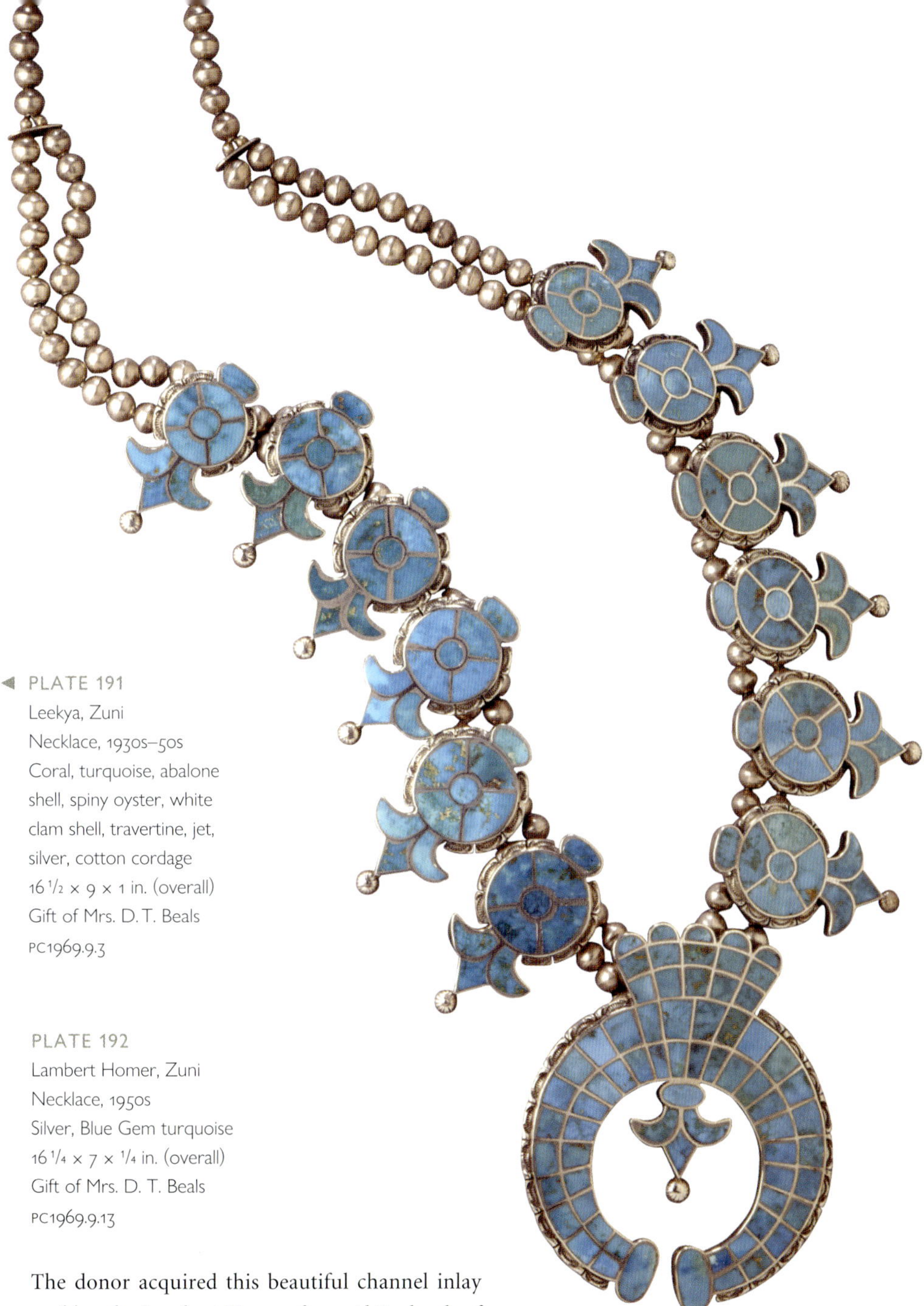

◀ PLATE 191
Leekya, Zuni
Necklace, 1930s–50s
Coral, turquoise, abalone shell, spiny oyster, white clam shell, travertine, jet, silver, cotton cordage
16 1/2 × 9 × 1 in. (overall)
Gift of Mrs. D. T. Beals
PC1969.9.3

PLATE 192
Lambert Homer, Zuni
Necklace, 1950s
Silver, Blue Gem turquoise
16 1/4 × 7 × 1/4 in. (overall)
Gift of Mrs. D. T. Beals
PC1969.9.13

The donor acquired this beautiful channel inlay necklace by Lambert Homer from Al Packard, of Packard's on the Santa Fe Plaza. Based on the trader's code, KTIH scratched into the back, he probably acquired it from C. G. Wallace at his trading post in Zuni, his shipping point in Gallup, or the De Anza Motor Lodge in Albuquerque.

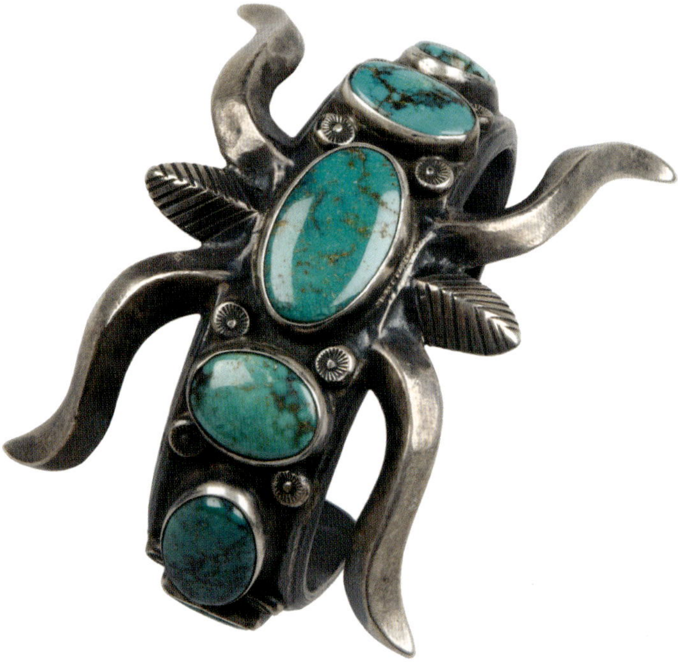

PLATE 193
Navajo
Bracelet, 1950s
Silver, Red Mountain turquoise
2 1/2 × 3 × 2 1/4 in.
Gift of Eason Eige
PC2010.5.107

The 1950s were a heyday for beautifully designed Navajo cast silverwork. This cast bracelet features embellished chiseled designs and stamped drops; its design may represent a water bug.

PLATE 194
Zuni
Brooch, early 1960s
Silver, Kingman turquoise
$3\ ^3/_4 \times 3\ ^1/_2$ in.
Gift of Eason Eige
PC2010.5.131

This brooch belonged to Anne Goodman of the Covered Wagon Trading Post, who noted on the back what the dire consequences would be if her husband, Manny, sold it. Manny Goodman opened the Covered Wagon on Route 66 in Tijeras in 1949 but moved the trading post to Old Town after construction of I-40 threatened his livelihood.

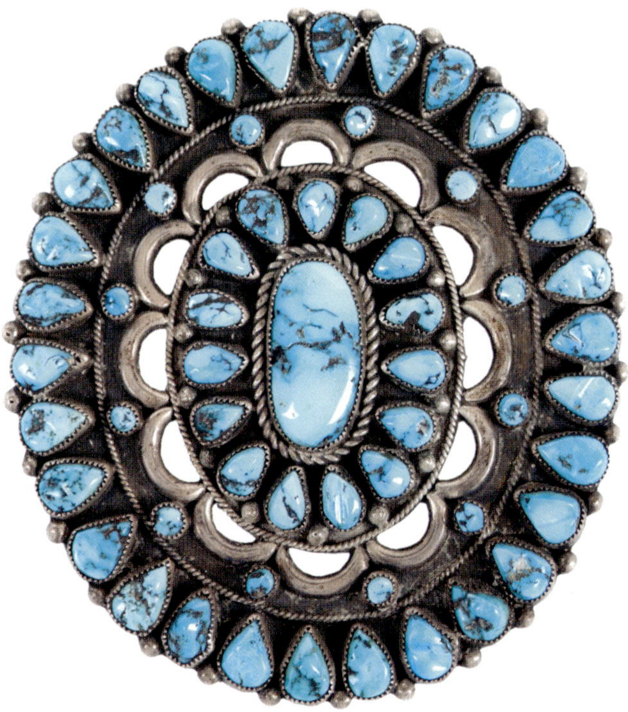

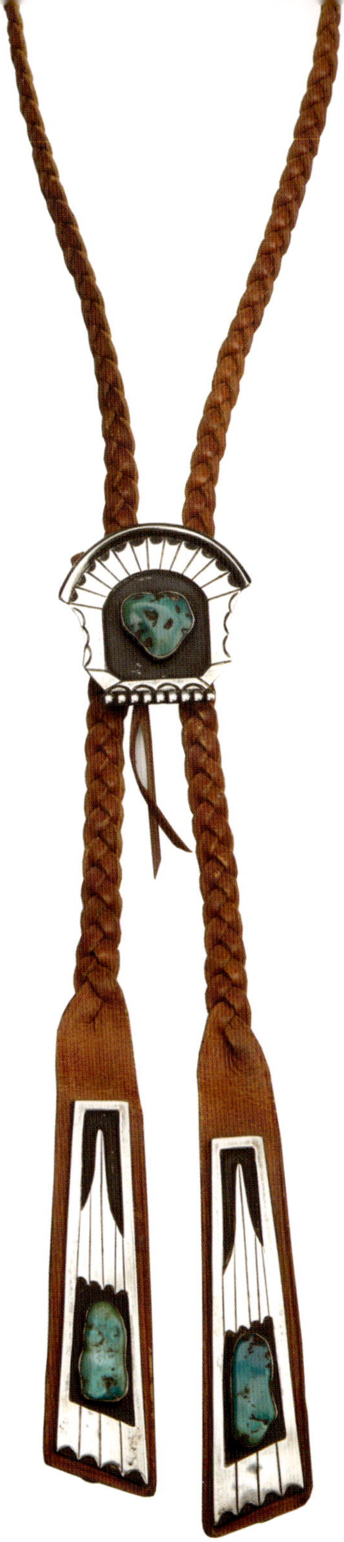

PLATE 195
Bolo tie, ca. 1964
Commercial silver, turquoise, leather
18 × 1 5/8 in.
Gift of Norman L. Sandfield
PC2014.38.28

Maisel's Indian Trading Post sold southwestern and Mexican curios for over sixty-five years in downtown Albuquerque. By the 1940s, the trading post had become the largest of its kind on Route 66. The store closed after Maurice Maisel died in the 1960s.

In that decade, the Maisel's catalog featured a bolo similar to this one, with a commercially mass-produced, stamped headdress design, embellished by a nugget-cut stone most likely handcrafted by one of the hundreds of Native American jewelers once employed there.

In the 1980s Maisel's grandson Skip reopened the shop. Family and friends have donated numerous examples of Maisel's early inventory, as well as the store's original John Gaw Meem–designed counter and cash register, and family photographs to the Museum.

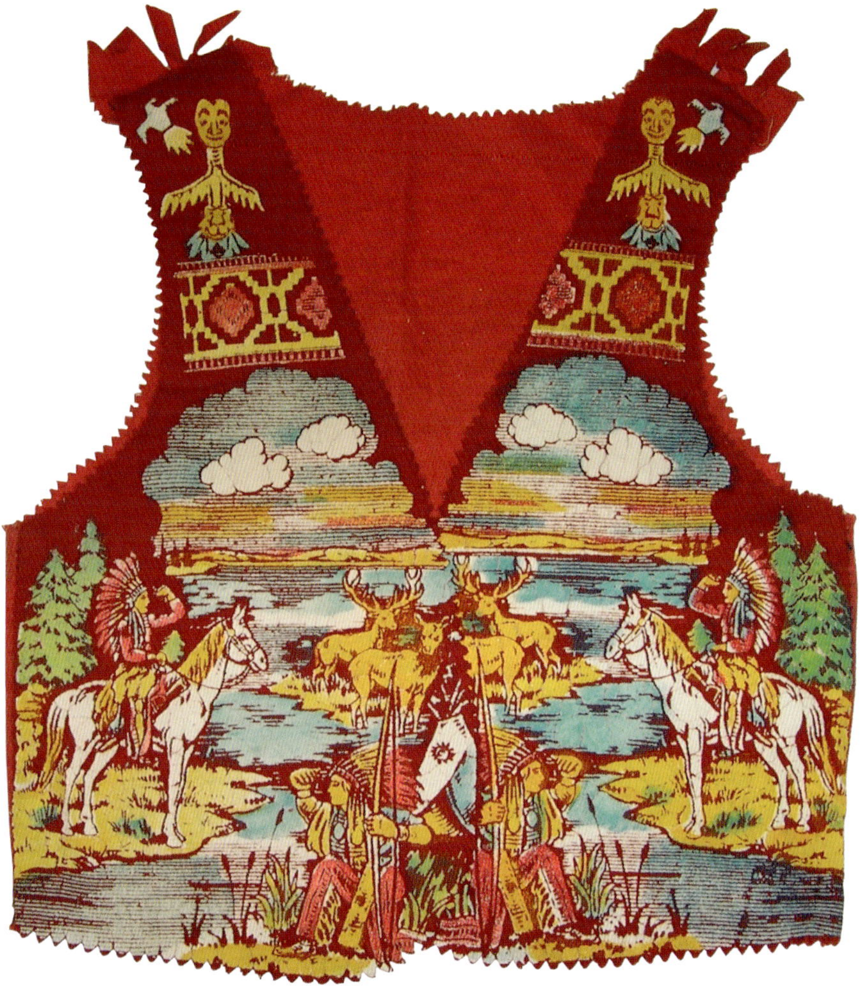

PLATE 196
Vest, 1940s–50s
Cotton flannel, ink
12 × 14 1/2 in.
Gift of Nancy Tucker
PC2007.68.5

Albuquerque's fifteen-mile urban strip of Route 66 was a favorite source for souvenirs; everything from moccasins, western wear, cowboy boots, Indian jewelry, tarantula paperweights, and rattlesnake mugs could be purchased here—and still can be. This vest features the trendiest themes of the 1940s–50s, including knife-wing birds, cowboys, and tipis.

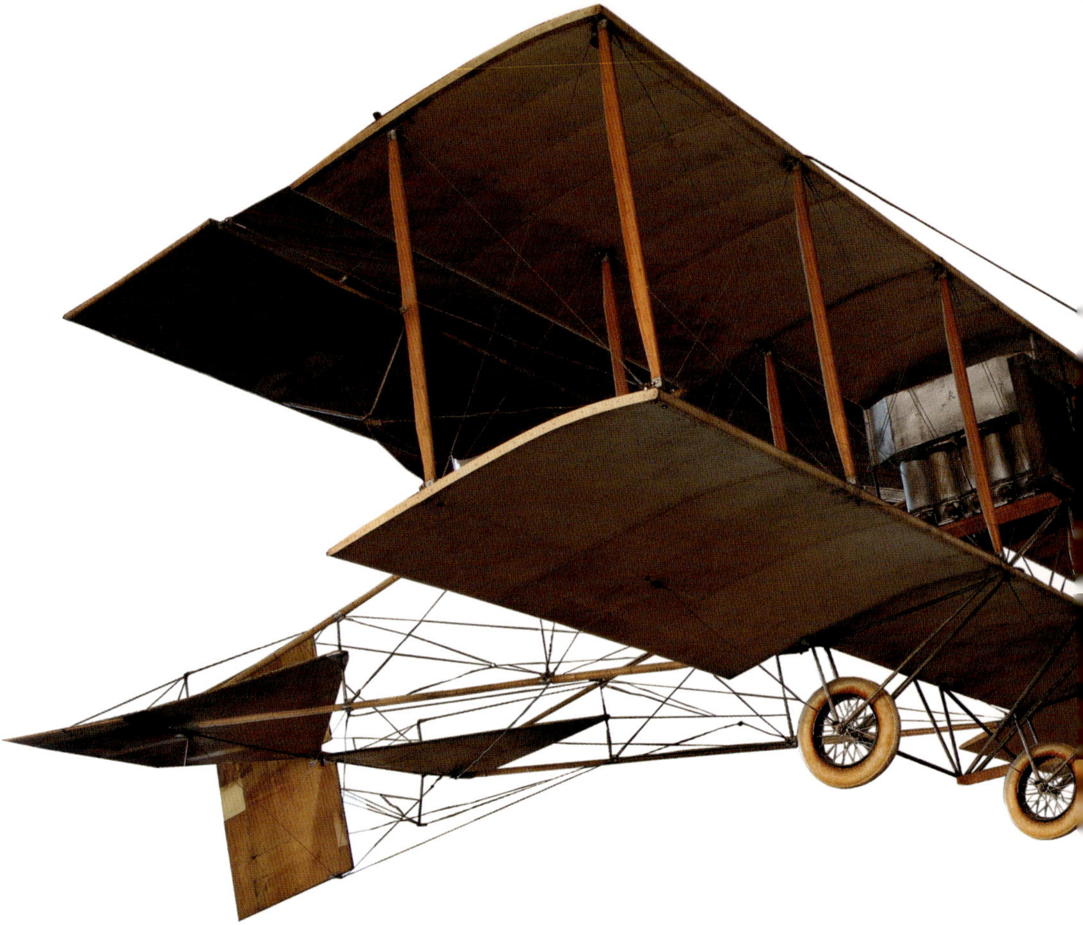

Jay Ingram and Charles Foster of the Pioneer Aeroplane Exhibition Company, based in Decatur, Texas, built five biplanes designed after the Curtiss Pusher. Between 1914 and 1916 they contracted with county fairs in the Midwest, staging exhibition flights similar to those held at Old Town's Territorial Fairgrounds.

This biplane may be the only unrestored example of an original Curtiss-design pusher. It was designed after the first biplanes flown in New Mexico by Charles Walsh in 1911 and Lincoln Beachey in 1912. The Albuquerque Museum and the Albuquerque International Sunport jointly purchased the biplane for the people of Albuquerque; it is currently on display at the Sunport.

The biplane was custom built from raw lumber, bamboo, wire, and fabric painted with varnish. The six-cylinder Roberts engine was fueled by a 20:1 ratio of gasoline and castor oil. Located in the back of the biplane, the propeller pushed rather than pulled the craft through the air. The aircraft's original blue-painted shipping crates are the only ones known to exist.

◀ PLATE 197
Curtiss-style "pusher" biplane, ca. 1914
Pioneer Aeroplane Exhibition Company
Wood, bamboo, dope, linen, iron or steel, rubber
96 × 396 × 324 in.
Joint purchase: Albuquerque Museum and City of Albuquerque Aviation Department
PC1987.41.1

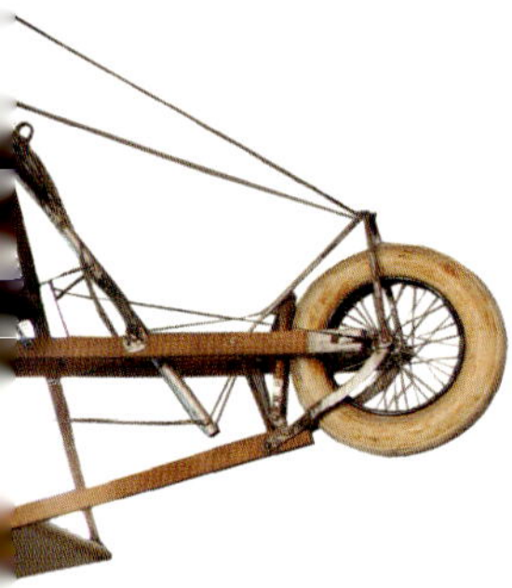

PLATE 198
Aerial view of Albuquerque, 1913
Photographer: Roy Stamm
Gift of Holly Hening Junker and Gordon Stamm Reiter
PA2001.32.48

The Territorial Fair Committee engaged aviators Charles Walsh, Lincoln Beachey, and Roy Francis to thrill local crowds with aircraft aerobatics. In 1911, businessman Roy Stamm became Walsh's first brave passenger. Two years later, Roy Stamm strapped himself into the passenger seat of Francis's Wright Biplane to shoot New Mexico's earliest aerial photographs.

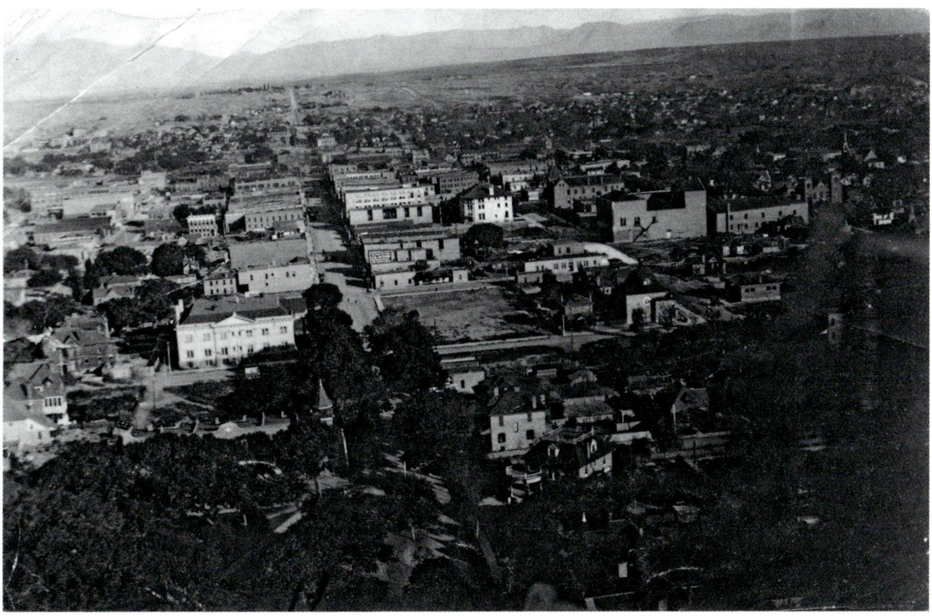

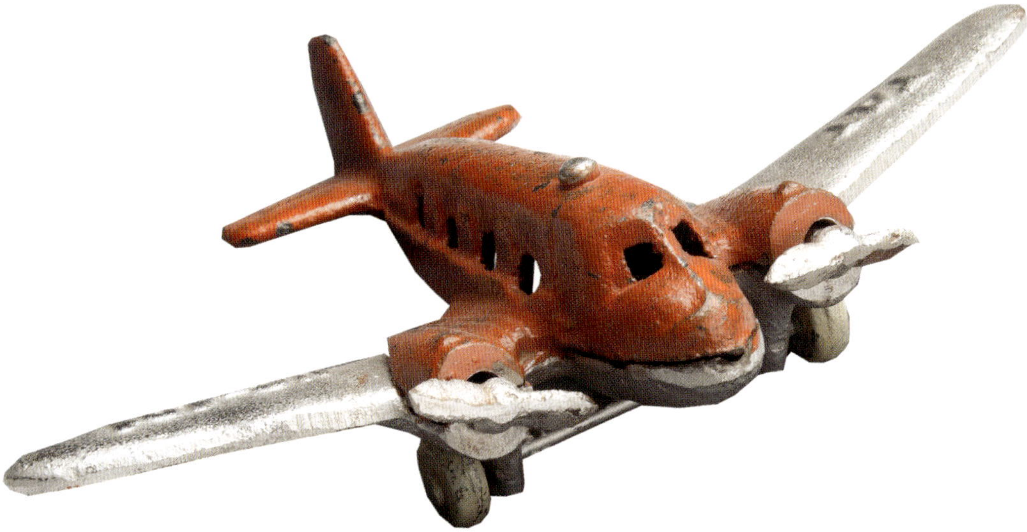

PLATE 199
Toy airplane, ca. 1930
Hubley Toys, Lancaster, Pennsylvania
Die-cast metal, paint
2 × 6 1/4 × 5 3/4 in.
Gift of Marilee Schmit Nason
PC2012.1.1

Frank Speakman and William Franklin built Albuquerque's first airport—complete with an adobe hangar—in 1928. One year later, Transcontinental Air Transport (TAT) selected Albuquerque as its western region headquarters due to its location and flying conditions.

TAT offered coast-to-coast service by air and train. It merged with rival Western Air Express in 1930, eventually becoming Trans World Airlines. This miniature represents a TAT DC-1 or DC-2, which replaced the Ford Trimotors used by the company until the early 1930s.

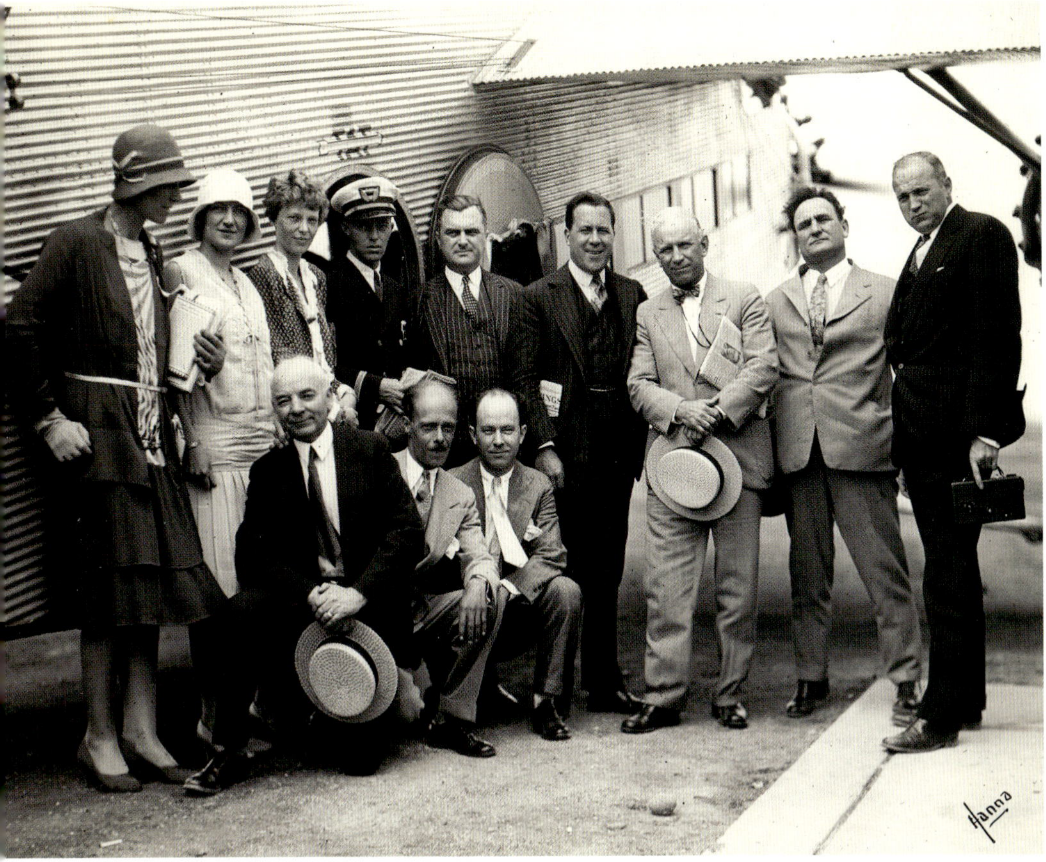

PLATE 200

Amelia Earhart (*third from left*), Clyde Tingley (*second from right*), and others in front of a TAT Ford Trimotor, July 14, 1929

Photographer: Hanna and Hanna

Gelatin silver print

8 × 10 in.

Gift of the Albuquerque/Bernalillo County Public Library

PA1978.141.268

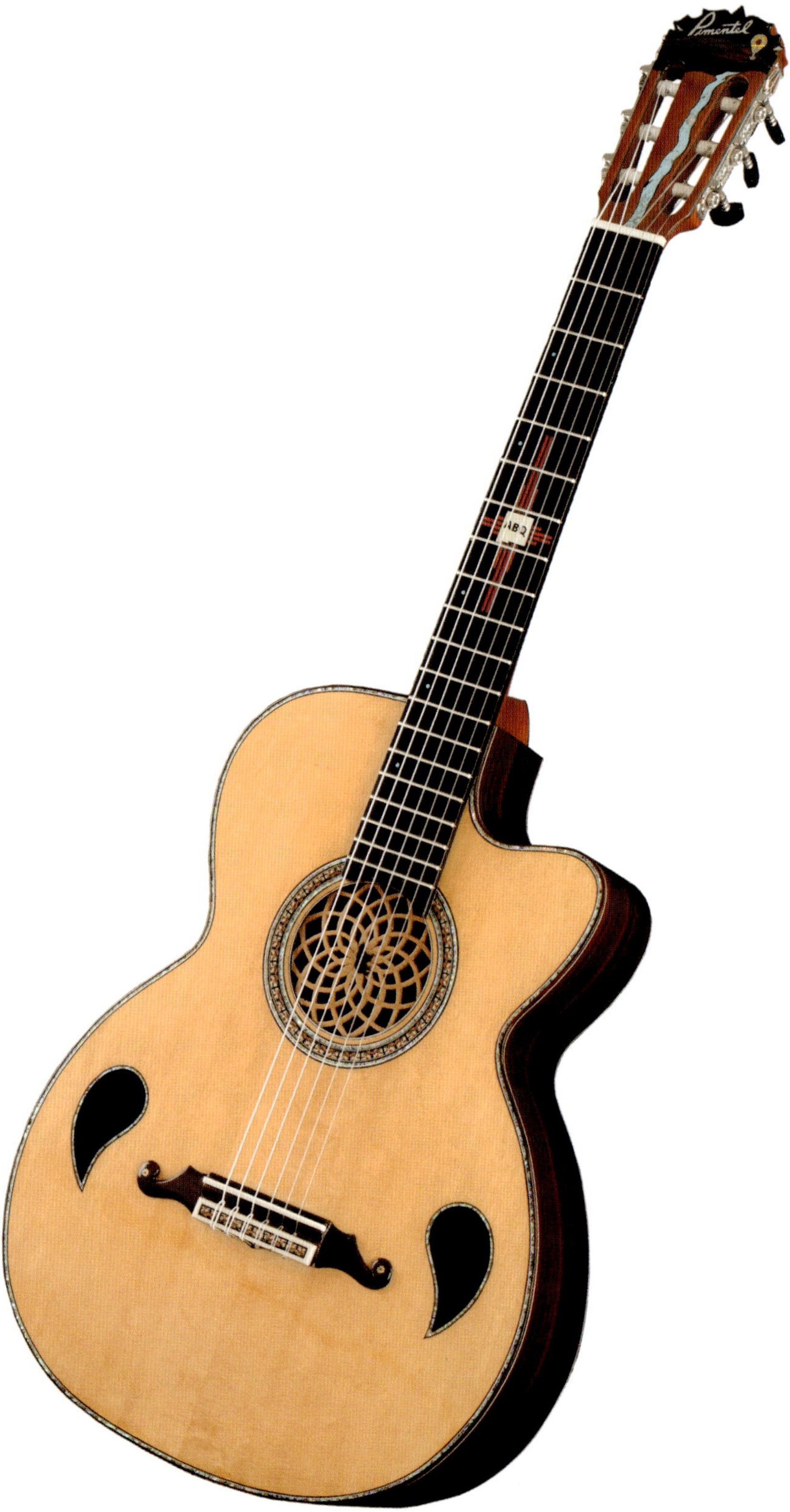
Pimentel
ABQ

Made in Albuquerque

The central Rio Grande valley has produced unique forms of lead-glazed pottery and blankets, clothing and musical instruments, and locomotive repair parts. Since the Cold War, our citizens have improved nuclear technology, invented personal home computers, and have even flown into space.

PLATE 201
Ancestral Pueblo
Jar, Agua Fria Glaze-on-red, 1350–1450
Clay, slip, glaze paint
11 × 14 1/2 in.
Ward Alan and Shirley Jolly Minge Collection
Museum purchase, 1995 General Obligation Bonds
PC1998.22.17

Around 1300, pueblos near the Rio Grande and Galisteo Basin invented pottery decorated with a black glaze paint made with galena, an iron ore found near Placitas and Cerrillos. The earliest glaze ware pottery comes from the Albuquerque area. It was used in ceremonies and communal feasts and was traded throughout the region. Unlike other cultures that used glaze paint for waterproofing, Rio Grande potters used it to paint distinctive designs incorporating imagery of birds, weather, and people. After firing, the glaze turned a shiny, silvery black color.

The jar was received by the Museum via the acquisition of Casa San Ysidro and had been given to Ward Alan Minge by a rancher with land in the Malpais (badlands). The three birds painted on the body of the jar appear to be male Gambel's quail with rare double plumes.

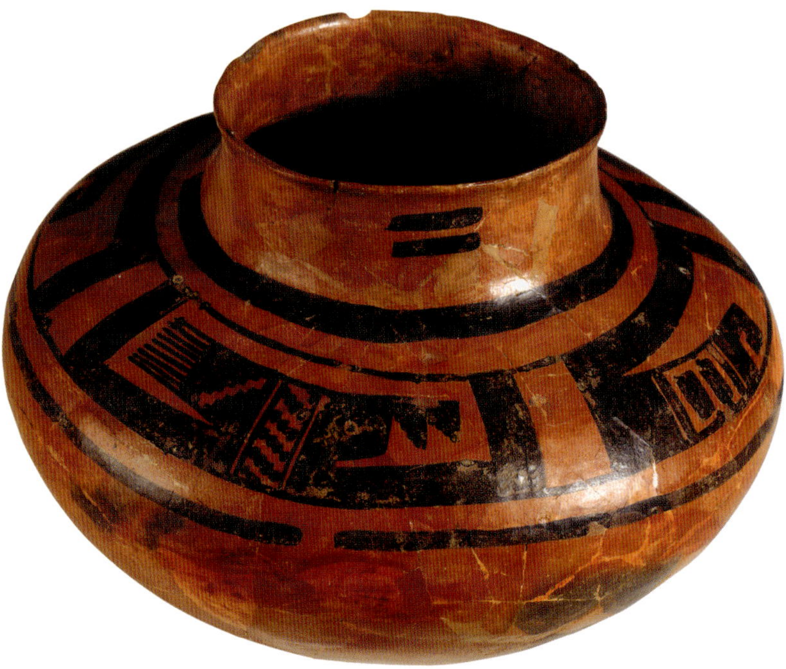

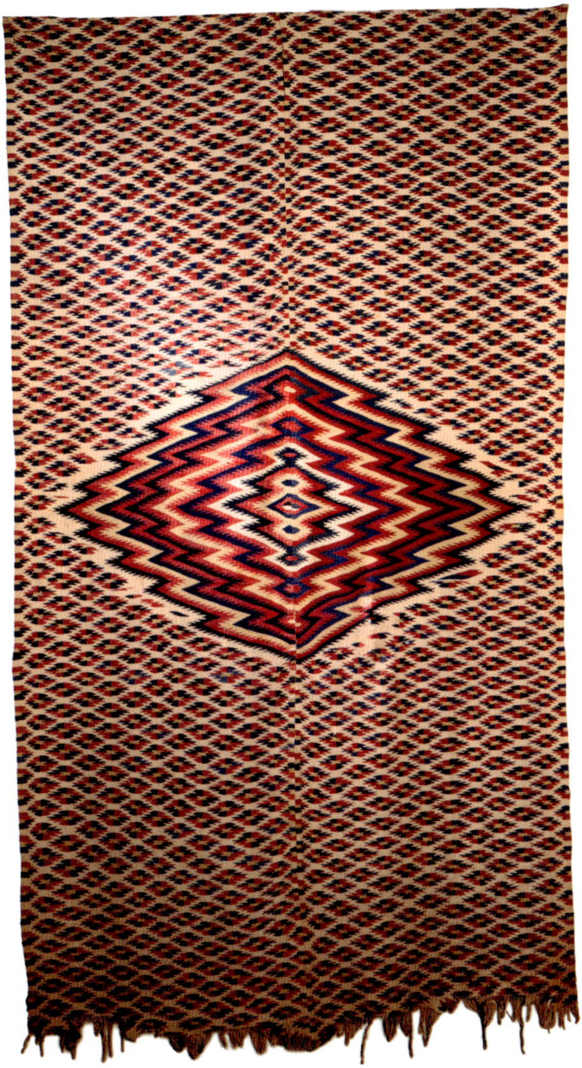

PLATE 202
Hispanic New Mexican
Frazada/Blanket, 1840–65
Wool; cotton; indigo, brazilwood, and cochineal dyes
91 × 49 in.
Museum purchase
PC1982.137.1
Ex-collection Harvey Mudd and Joseph Carr

By the 1800s, wool *frazadas* were a valuable export item. Merchants coveted these handmade local products for their bright designs and waterproof qualities. Families worked together to shear the churros, spin and dye the yarn using local and exported dyes, and weave the fabric on horizontal looms. The designs were influenced by Spanish, Tlaxcalan, and Pueblo weavings shipped along El Camino Real.

After Saltillo serapes became popular, weavers in New Mexico began to copy the design system of the Mexican weavings. A central diamond is surrounded by a field of small diamonds, but the border common to Saltillo serapes is not present. A border of fringe was chopped off the top and bottom at some time in the past, perhaps to use for the repairs near the center seam that suggest this blanket was well loved. Ex-collection of Harvey Mudd and Joseph Carr.

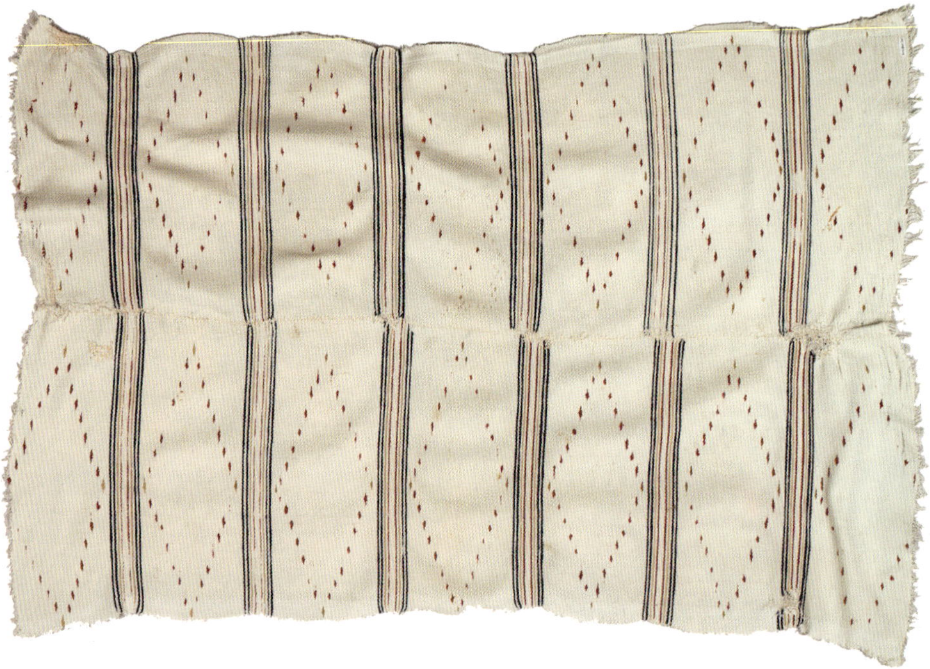

PLATE 203
Hispanic New Mexican, Chávez family
Frazada de algodón/Cotton blanket, 1820–50
Cotton; wool; wool bayeta; indigo, cochineal, and sappanwood dyes
81 × 45 in.
Ward Alan and Shirley Jolly Minge Collection
Museum purchase, 1995 General Obligation Bonds
PC1998.20.9

Land along the Rio Grande between Algodones and Belén was ideal for growing cotton. Weavers living just north and south of Albuquerque responded by making lightweight blankets from handspun cotton. They were used as summertime bedcovers and lap robes.

Rio Abajo (Lower River) cotton blankets are rare; only about nine have been found in museum collections. Woven by the great-great-grandfather of Luz Chávez of Lemitar, New Mexico, this is the earliest Rio Grande weaving in the History Collection. Tony Garcia collected the blanket for Ward Alan Minge, along with the loom from which it was woven and several additional weavings. The field is cotton, but the stripes are woven with wool, causing age-related shrinkage that, along with the bright white field, helps curators to recognize these rare textiles.

The reddish gold stripes are dyed with sappanwood, a thorny tree that grows in Sri Lanka, Malaysia, and India, so the dye must have arrived here via ship and overland trade and was precious enough to use in small amounts—as was the raveled, cochineal-dyed *bayeta* cloth, used with the sappanwood-dyed wool to create the diamonds between the stripes.

PLATE 204
Hispanic New Mexican
Frazada/Blanket, before 1850
Wool, indigo dye
78 × 47 in.
Museum purchase, 1983 General Obligation Bonds
PC1984.25.21
Ex-collection Larry Frank, Mark Winter, and Michael Caden

At sixty wefts per inch, this blanket represents the height of Saltillo-style weaving along the Rio Grande. It features an elaborate modified Saltillo-style diamond center, a border, zigzags, and two shades of indigo blue. The weaver added blue in the center to adjust minor imperfections.

Accomplished weaver Irvin Trujillo notes that the weaver was working through a learning curve. "The center design looks like a beginning attempt at a Saltillo center diamond. The weaver reached the edge of the piece early and had to take the design inward, until half the length desired was reached."

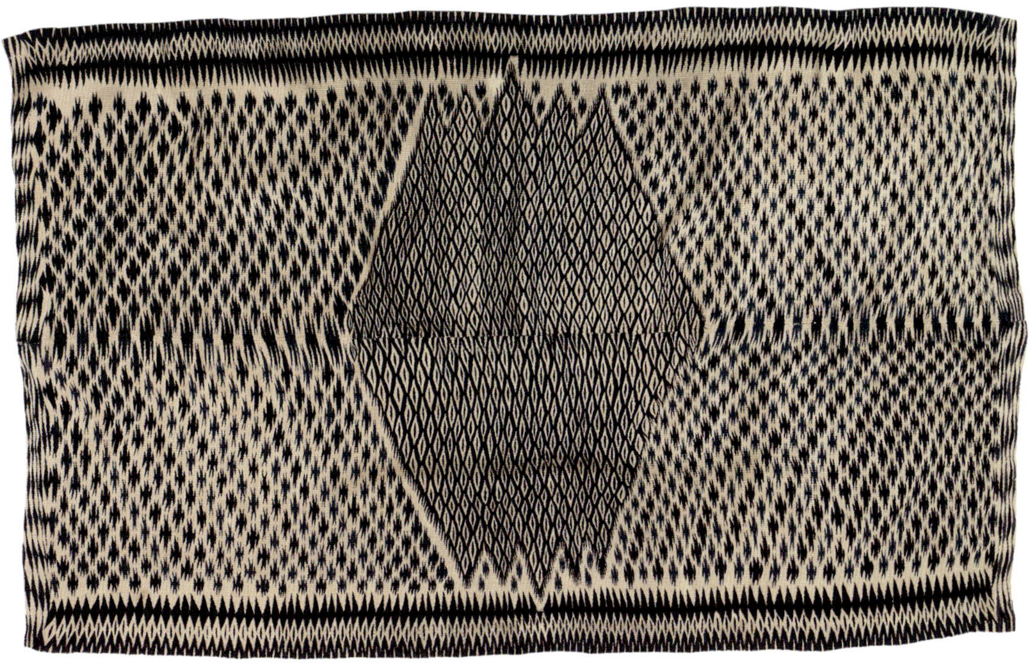

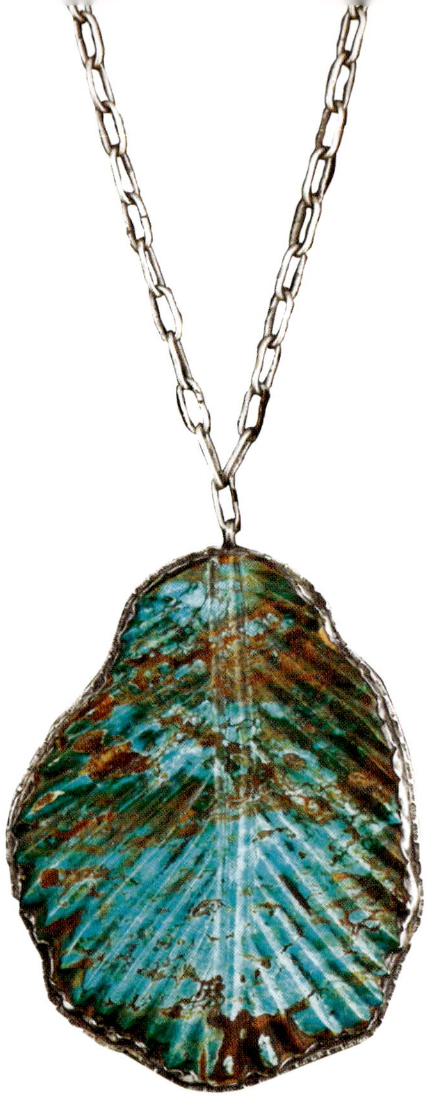

PLATE 205
Dan Simplicio, Zuni
Necklace, 1950s
Silver, turquoise
14 1/4 × 5/8 × 1/4 in.
Gift of the Dazzo Family
PC2003.74.2

World War II veteran Dan Simplicio (1917–1969) was the only Zuni silversmith working in Albuquerque in the mid-twentieth century, which likely influenced his unique jewelry style. Simplicio was known for massive, carved coral jewelry, turquoise leaves, and carved nuggets with elaborate jagged, scalloped, or foliate silver bezels.

This leaf necklace with handmade chain was acquired by the donor's father, attorney Samuel Dazzo, in the 1940s or 1950s. Initials scratched into the reverse indicate that it was originally in the private collection of trader C. G. Wallace, who could have given it to Dazzo in return for legal services.

PLATE 206
Deana McGuffin
Cowgirl boots, *Dia de los Muertos*, 2013
Pearlized lamb leather, calfskin, nylon thread, sterling silver conchas by Michael Turano
Leather, sterling silver, nylon thread
17 1/2 × 5 3/8 × 10 3/4 in. (each)
Museum purchase
PC2014.6.1.a&b

Albuquerque is proud to include McGuffin Boots as New Mexico's only woman-owned boot business. Owner/artist Deana McGuffin hails from a long line of boot makers, including her grandfather C.C. McGuffin of Carrizozo and Roswell and her father, L.W. McGuffin of Portales.

Deana remembers, "I used to watch my dad and told him I wanted to learn the family business. But it was that old thing . . . he didn't think girls could do that kind of stuff. . . . I finally convinced him to let me learn, and I'm glad I did. I've stuck with this for more than twenty-five years now."

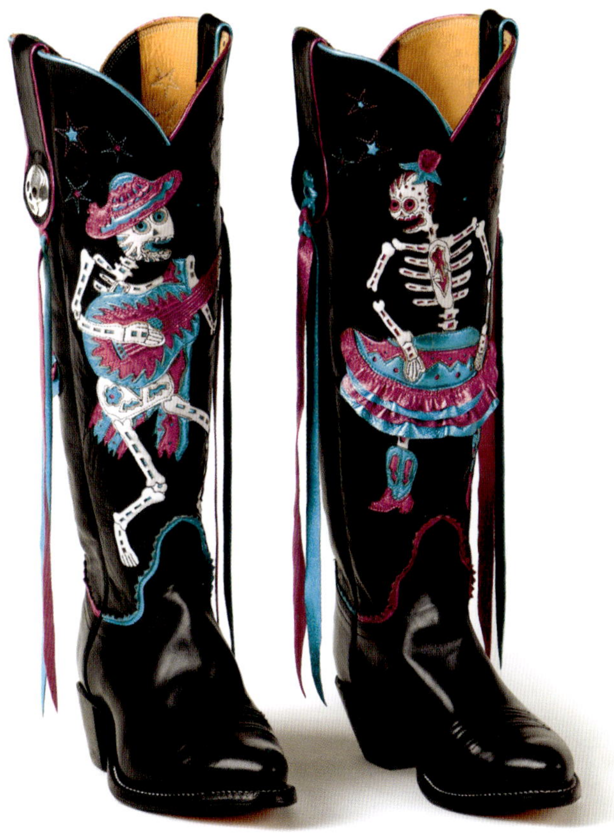

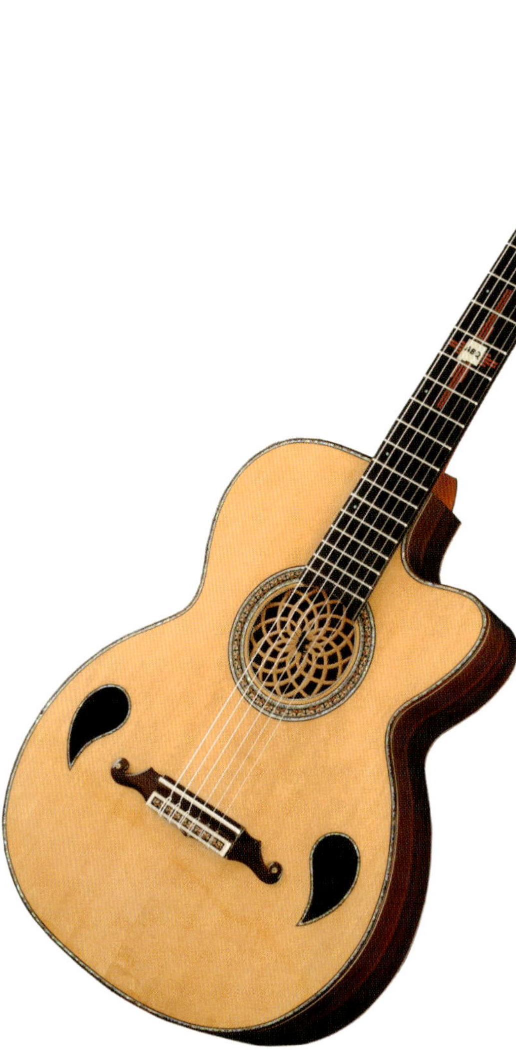

PLATE 207
Rick, Robert, and Victor Pimentel,
Pimentel and Sons
Guitar, *Classical Grand Concert Renaissance Museum Dreamcatcher*, 2014
East Indian rosewood, spruce, ebony, coral, silver, abalone, mother-of-pearl, turquoise, dyes, bronze, steel, nylon, glue, wood
39 1/2 × 15 × 5 in.
Gift of Pimentel and Sons in memory of Lorenzo and Agustín Pimentel and in honor of their mother, Josefina Pimentel
Museum purchase, Trust and Agency Fund
PC2014.10.1

Through a gift/purchase arrangement, Ricardo, Roberto, and Victor Pimentel spent almost a year creating this classical guitar for the Museum's history exhibition *Only in Albuquerque*. The Pimentel brothers learned luthier skills from their father, Lorenzo, who learned the trade in Mexico. The family's philosophy is simple: The soul of a guitar cannot be made; it must be born.

Unlike most contemporary luthiers, Pimentel crafts each instrument by hand. The interior "honeycomb" bracing system enhances the guitar's sound projection and tonal qualities. The sound hole features Lorenzo Pimentel's famous Santuario design. A sun symbol on the fret board is customized with coral and mother-of-pearl inlay, inscribed with *ABQ* in honor of the city.

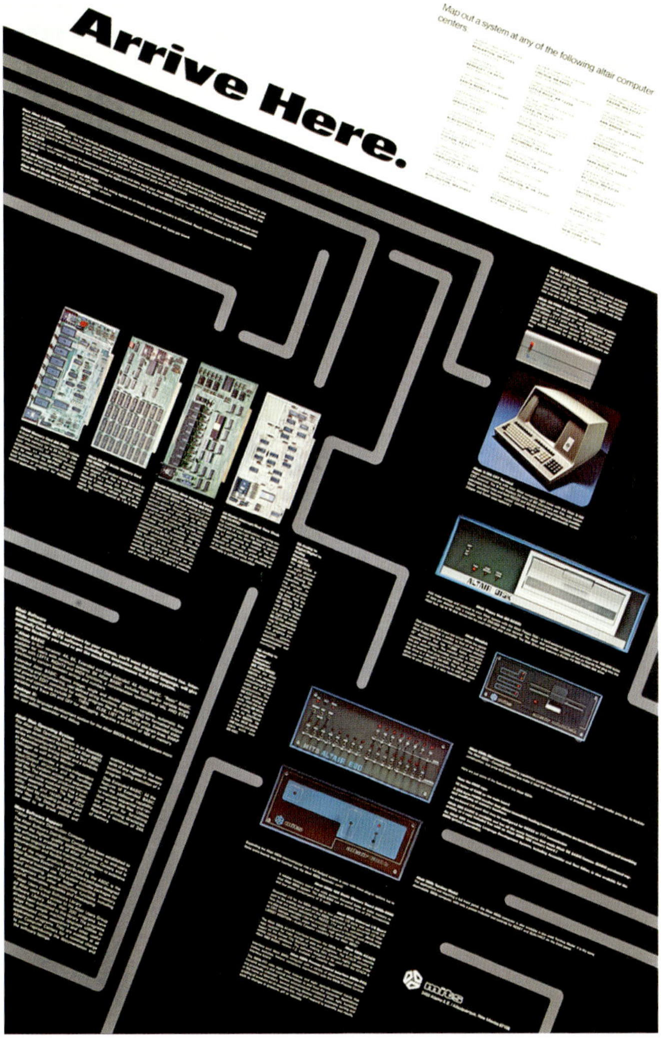

PLATE 208
Tom Antreasian, MITS
Promotional poster, 1975–76
Ink, paper
35 1/2 × 25 in. (sight)
Gift of Tom Antreasian
PC2013.5.3

In 1969 Ed Roberts and Forrest Mims founded MITS (Micro Instrumentation and Telemetry Systems) to begin manufacturing electronic calculators and, eventually, personal computers. As a result of their innovations, the world's first trade show for personal computer users—the Altair World Trade Show—was held in March 1976 at the Albuquerque Airport Marina Hotel.

Attendees from eight countries tested out the Altair 8800, perused promotional literature, and toured the MITS factory on Alamo Avenue SE near the airport. This showcase for H. Edward Roberts's creation helped spark a worldwide computer revolution.

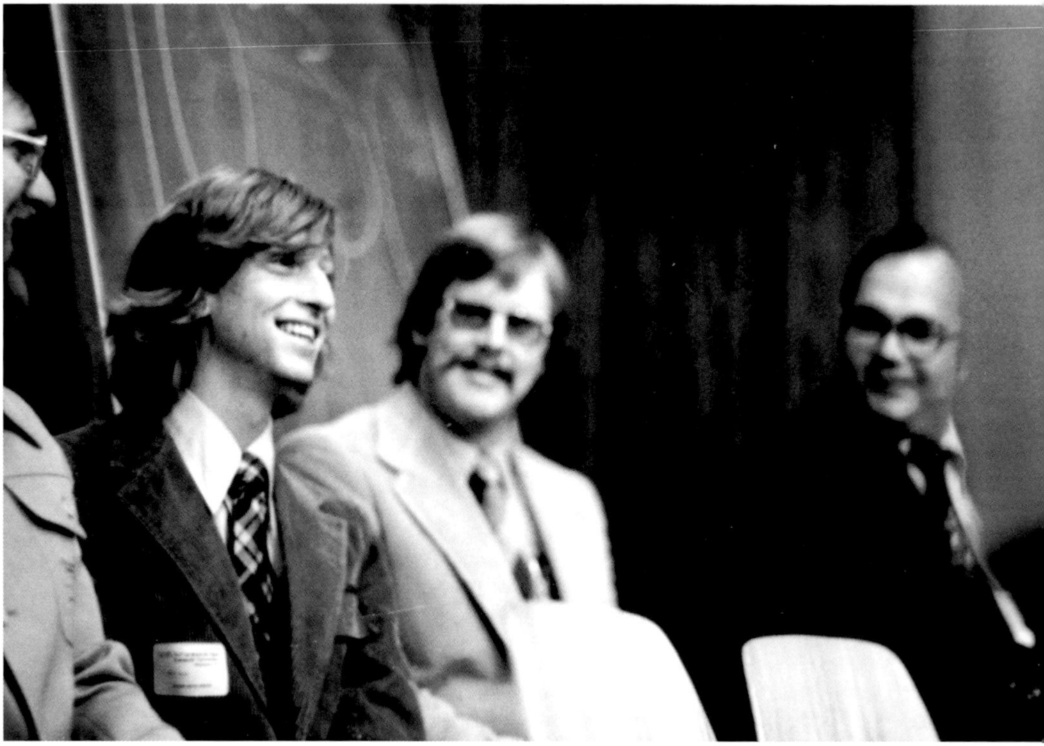

PLATE 209
Left to right: Unidentified, Bill Gates, Paul Allen, and Ed Roberts speaking at the Altair World Trade Show, March 1976
Photographer: Tom Antreasian
Gift of Tom Antreasian
PA2013.1.10

PLATE 210

MITS, Albuquerque

CRT monitor, computer, and floppy disk drives for the Altair 8800b, ca. 1975–77

21 × 17 × 17 in. and 15 × 17 × 22 in.

Gift of Stephen Lambert, George Moran, and Explora Science Center and Children's Museum

Metal, plastic, glass

PC1986.3.1.a–c and RS2013.21.1

It all began in Albuquerque. H. Edward Roberts yearned to invent an affordable personal computer. *Popular Electronics* agreed to feature his creation—if he could meet their Fall 1974 publication deadline.

Although the prototype was lost in shipment, Roberts succeeded, and his Altair (named after the brightest star in the constellation Aquila) made the magazine's cover. Sales skyrocketed, catapulting Roberts's company, Micro Instrumentation Telemetry Systems, from near-bankruptcy to $3 million in sales within three years.

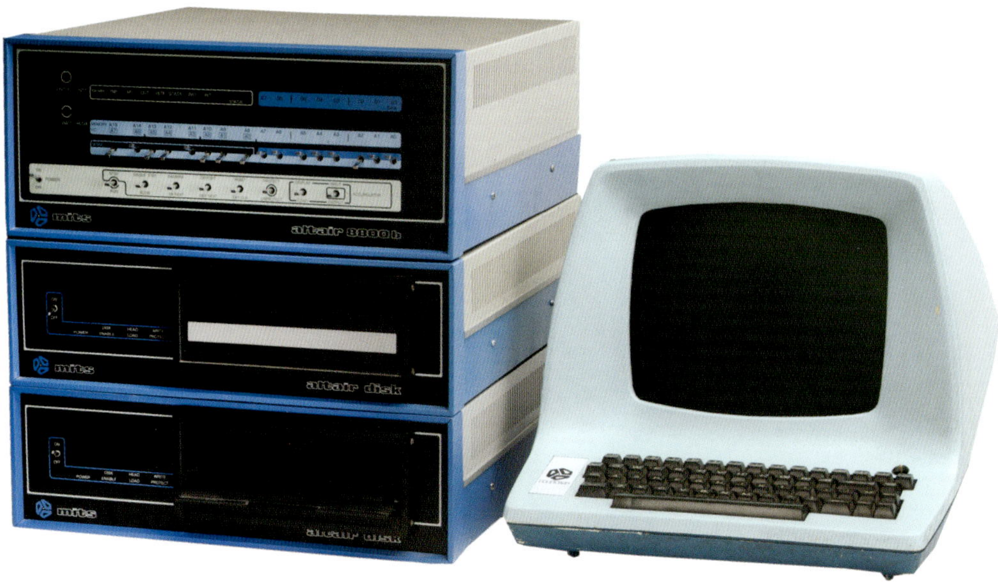

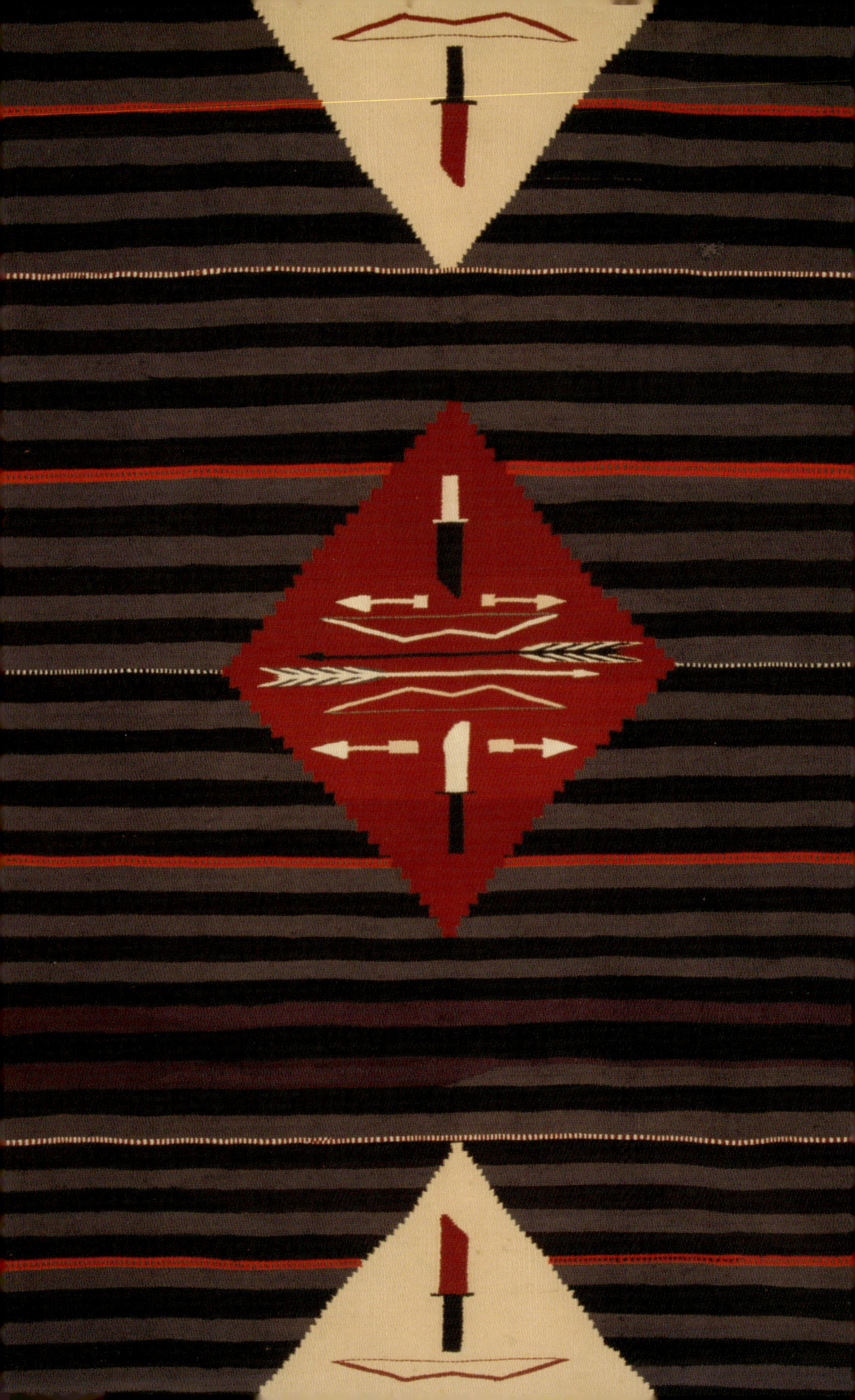

Bibliography

Alberts, Don E. *Balloons to Bombers: Aviation in Albuquerque, 1882–1945*. Albuquerque: Albuquerque Museum, 1987.

Batkin, Johnathan. *Pottery of the Pueblos of New Mexico, 1700–1940*. Colorado Springs, CO: Taylor Museum of the Colorado Springs Fine Arts Center, 1987.

Benson, Nancy. *New Mexico Colcha Club: Spanish Colonial Embroidery and the Women Who Saved It*. Santa Fe: Museum of New Mexico Press, 2008.

Coulter, Lane, and Maurice Dixon Jr. *New Mexican Tinwork, 1840–1940*. Albuquerque: University of New Mexico Press, 1990.

Dixon, Maurice M., Jr. *The Artistic Odyssey of Higinio V. Gonzales: A Tinsmith and Poet in Territorial New Mexico*. Norman: University of Oklahoma Press, 2015.

Espinosa, Carmen G. *New Mexico Colonial Embroidery*. Santa Fe: NM Dept. of Vocational Rehabilitation, 1935.

Fisher, Nora, comp. and ed. *Spanish Textile Tradition of New Mexico and Colorado*. Santa Fe: Museum of New Mexico Press, 1994.

Garcia, Tony. *The Beginning of the Casa San Ysidro in Corrales, New Mexico, and the Provenance of Its Spanish Colonial Artifacts*. Albuquerque: self-published, n.d.

Hammett, Kingsley H. *Early New Mexican Furniture: A Handbook of Plans and Building Techniques*. Santa Fe: Fleetwood Press, 1999.

Hedlund, Ann Lane, ed. *Blanket Weaving in the Southwest*. By Joe Ben Wheat. Tucson: University of Arizona Press, 2003.

Howard, Kathleen L., and Diana F. Pardue. *Inventing the Southwest: The Fred Harvey Collection of Native American Art*. Flagstaff, AZ: Northland Publishing, 1996.

Johnson, Byron. *Old Town, Albuquerque, New Mexico: A Guide to Its History and Architecture*. Albuquerque: Albuquerque Museum, 1980.

McKay, Mary Terence, and Lisa Trujillo. *The Centinela Weavers of Chimayo: Unfolding Tradition*. Chimayo: Centinela Traditional Arts, 1999.

Mera, H. P. *Spanish-American Blanketry*. Introduction by Kate Peck Kent. Santa Fe: School of American Research Press, 1987.

Minge, Ward Alan. *Casa San Ysidro: The Gutiérrez/Minge House, Corrales, New Mexico*. Santa Fe: Museum of New Mexico Press, 2017.

Moore, James. "The Albuquerque Museum of Art and History." In *Albuquerque, Portrait of a Western City*, edited by Mary Kay Cline, 35–38. Albuquerque: Clear Light Publishing, 2006.

Pardue, Diana F. *Shared Images: The Innovative Jewelry of Yazzie Johnson and Gail Bird.* Santa Fe: Museum of New Mexico Press, 2007.

Pierce, Donna, and Marta Weigle. *Spanish New Mexico: The Spanish Colonial Arts Society Collection.* 2 vols. Santa Fe: Museum of New Mexico Press, 1996.

Simmons, Marc. *Albuquerque: A Narrative History.* Albuquerque: University of New Mexico Press, 1982.

Simmons, Marc, and Frank Turley. *Southwestern Colonial Ironwork: The Spanish Blacksmithing Tradition from Texas to California.* Santa Fe: Museum of New Mexico Press, 1980.

Slaney, Deborah C. *Blue Gem, White Metal: Carvings and Jewelry from the C. G. Wallace Collection.* Phoenix: Heard Museum, 1998.

______. "Frazadas de algodón: The Rio Grande Cotton Blanket Tradition." *Tradición Revista* (Summer 2008).

______. "Introducing Easterners: The Indian Detours." In *Jewel of the Railroad Era: Albuquerque's Alvarado Hotel,* 83–87. Albuquerque: Albuquerque Museum, 2007.

______. *Wonders of the Weavers/Maravillas de los tejedores: Nineteenth-Century Río Grande Weavings from the Collection of the Albuquerque Museum.* Albuquerque: Albuquerque Museum, 2005.

Steele, J. Thomas, *Works and Days: A History of San Felipe Neri Church, 1868–1895.* Albuquerque: Albuquerque Museum, 1983.

Taylor, Lonn, and Dessa Bokides. *New Mexico Furniture, 1600–1940.* Santa Fe: Museum of New Mexico Press, 1987.

Time-Life Books, eds. *The Spanish West.* Alexandria, VA: Time-Life Books, 1976.

Van Ness, John R. and Christine M., eds. *Spanish and Mexican Land Grants in New Mexico and Colorado.* Manhattan, KS: Sunflower University Press, 1980.

Wheat, Joe Ben. *Blanket Weaving in the Southwest.* Edited by Ann Lane Hedlund. Tucson: University of Arizona Press, 2003.

Zaldívar Mendoza, Vicente de. "Expedition to the Buffalo Plains, 1598." In *Don Juan de Oñate, Colonizer of New Mexico, 1595–1628.* Coronado Cuarto Centennial Publications, 1540–1940, Volume V. Edited by George P. Hammond and Agapito Rey, 398–405. Albuquerque: University of New Mexico Press, 1953.

About the Author

Deborah Slaney received her bachelor of arts degree in southwestern anthropology at the University of Arizona in 1979 and her master of liberal studies/museum emphasis at the University of Oklahoma in 1992. She has been the Albuquerque Museum's curator of history since 2001. Her publications include *Blue Gem, White Metal: Carvings and Jewelry from the C. G. Wallace Collection*; *Wonders of the Weavers/Maravillas de los tejedores: Nineteenth-Century Río Grande Weavings from the Collection of the Albuquerque Museum*; and *Jewel of the Railroad Era: Albuquerque's Alvarado Hotel*. She was the consulting curator for the Museum's *Only in Albuquerque* exhibition; she curated the exhibitions *Fabulous: The New Look of Albuquerque in the Fifties*; *Jewel of the Railroad Era: Albuquerque's Alvarado Hotel*; *Route 66: Radiance, Rust, and Revival on the Mother Road;* and *The Leekya Family: Master Carvers of Zuni Pueblo* and served as project director for *Dreamscape Desperado: Billy the Kid and the Outlaw in America* and *Hollywood Southwest: New Mexico in Film and Television*.

Photo Credits

Damian Andrus: plate 152

Heugh Edmondson: plate 46

David Nufer: figures 3, 13, 14, 16, 17, 18, 19; plates 1, 4, 5, 6, 8, 10, 14, 16, 18, 19, 20, 21, 22, 23, 26, 27, 29, 31, 32, 33, 34, 35, 36, 37, 38, 39, 40, 43, 44, 50, 54, 55, 56, 57, 58, 59, 60, 62, 63, 64, 68, 70, 71, 72, 77, 78, 79, 84, 85, 86, 88, 91, 92, 94, 95, 97, 99, 102, 103, 104, 105, 106, 108, 110, 111, 112, 113, 114, 115, 117, 118, 119, 120, 122, 123, 124, 125, 126, 127, 128, 129, 130, 131, 132, 133, 134, 136, 137, 138, 140, 141, 142, 143, 144, 149, 151, 153, 158, 159, 161, 163, 165, 166, 167, 168, 169, 170, 171, 172, 173, 174, 175, 176, 177, 178, 179, 180, 181, 182, 183, 185, 186, 188, 189, 190, 191, 192, 194, 195, 196, 197, 199, 203, 204, 205, 206, 207, 208, 210

Robert Reck: figure 11

Dick Ruddy: figures 9, 15; plates 3, 9, 12, 13, 17, 28, 42, 45, 47, 48, 49, 51, 52, 53, 61, 66, 67, 73, 74, 75, 76, 80, 81, 82, 83, 87, 89, 90, 93, 96, 109, 121, 145, 146, 147, 148, 150, 154, 155, 156, 157, 160, 162, 193, 201, 202

Leslie Venzuela: figure 12

Index

Page numbers in *italics* refer to illustrations.